T0241811

Lecture Notes in Artificial Intelligence (LNAI)

Vol. 345: R.T. Nossum (Ed.), Advanced Topics in Artificial Intelligence. VII, 233 pages. 1988.

Vol. 346: M. Reinfrank, J. de Kleer, M.L. Ginsberg, E. Sandewall (Eds.), Non-Monotonic Reasoning. Proceedings, 1988. XIV, 237 pages. 1989.

Vol. 347: K. Morik (Ed.), Knowledge Representation and Organization in Machine Learning. XV, 319 pages. 1989.

Other volumes of the Lecture Notes in Computer Science relevant to Artificial Intelligence:

Vol. 203: B. Buchberger (Ed.), EUROCAL '85. Proceedings Vol. 1, 1985. V, 233 pages. 1985.

Vol. 204: B.F. Caviness (Ed.), EUROCAL '85. Proceedings Vol. 2, 1985. XVI, 650 pages. 1985.

Vol. 221: E. Wada (Ed.), Logic Programming '85. Proceedings, 1985. IX, 311 pages. 1986.

Vol. 225: E. Shapiro (Ed.), Third International Conference on Logic Programming. Proceedings, 1986. IX, 720 pages. 1986.

Vol. 230: J.H. Siekmann (Ed.), 8th International Conference on Automated Deduction. Proceedings, 1986. X, 708 pages. 1986.

Vol. 231: R. Hausser, NEWCAT: Parsing Natural Language Using Left-Associative Grammar. II, 540 pages. 1986.

Vol. 238: L. Naish, Negation and Control in Prolog. IX, 119 pages. 1986.

Vol. 256: P. Lescanne (Ed.), Rewriting Techniques and Applications. Proceedings, 1987. VI, 285 pages. 1987.

Vol. 264: E. Wada (Ed.), Logic Programming '86. Proceedings, 1986. VI, 179 pages. 1987.

Vol. 271: D. Snyers, A. Thayse, From Logic Design to Logic Programming. IV, 125 pages. 1987.

Vol. 286: B. Bouchon, R.R. Yager (Eds.), Uncertainty in Knowledge-Based Systems. Proceedings, 1986. VII, 405 pages. 1987.

Vol. 301: J. Kittler (Ed.), Pattern Recognition. Proceedings, 1988. VII, 668 pages. 1988.

Vol. 306: M. Boscarol, L. Carlucci Aiello, G. Levi (Eds.), Foundations of Logic and Functional Programming. Proceedings, 1986. V, 218 pages. 1988.

Vol. 308: S. Kaplan, J.-P. Jouannaud (Eds.), Conditional Term Rewriting Systems. Proceedings, 1987. VI, 278 pages. 1988.

Vol. 310: E. Lusk, R. Overbeek (Eds.), 9th International Conference on Automated Deduction. Proceedings, 1988. X, 775 pages. 1988.

Vol. 313: B. Bouchon, L. Saitta, R.R. Yager (Eds.), Uncertainty and Intelligent Systems. IPMU '88. Proceedings, 1988. VIII, 408 pages. 1988.

Vol. 315: K. Furukawa, H. Tanaka, T. Fujisaki (Eds.), Logic Programming '87. Proceedings, 1987. VI, 327 pages. 1988.

Vol. 320: A. Blaser (Ed.), Natural Language at the Computer. Proceedings, 1988. III, 176 pages. 1988.

Vol. 329: E. Börger, H. Kleine Büning, M.M. Richter (Eds.), CSL '87. 1st Workshop on Computer Science Logic. Proceedings, 1987. VI, 346 pages. 1988.

Lecture Notes in Artificial Intelligence

Subseries of Lecture Notes in Computer Science
Edited by J. Siekmann

Lecture Notes in Computer Science

Edited by G. Goos and J. Hartmanis

Editorial

Artificial Intelligence has become a major discipline under the roof of Computer Science. This is also reflected by a growing number of titles devoted to this fast developing field to be published in our Lecture Notes in Computer Science. To make these volumes immediately visible we have decided to distinguish them by a special cover as Lecture Notes in Artificial Intelligence, constituting a subseries of the Lecture Notes in Computer Science. This subseries is edited by an Editorial Board of experts from all areas of AI, chaired by Jörg Siekmann, who are looking forward to consider further AI monographs and proceedings of high scientific quality for publication.

We hope that the constitution of this subseries will be well accepted by the audience of the Lecture Notes in Computer Science, and we feel confident that the subseries will be recognized as an outstanding opportunity for publication by authors and editors of the AI community.

Editors and publisher

Lecture Notes in Artificial Intelligence

Subseries of Lecture Notes in Computer Science
Edited by J. Siekmann

347

K. Morik (Ed.)

Knowledge Representation and Organization in Machine Learning

Springer-Verlag
Berlin Heidelberg New York London Paris Tokyo

Editor

Katharina Morik
Gesellschaft für Mathematik und Datenverarbeitung
Schloß Birlinghoven, 5205 Sankt Augustin, FRG

CR Subject Classification (1987): I.2.6

ISBN 3-540-50768-X Springer-Verlag Berlin Heidelberg New York
ISBN 0-387-50768-X Springer-Verlag New York Berlin Heidelberg

This work is subject to copyright. All rights are reserved, whether the whole or part of the material
is concerned, specifically the rights of translation, reprinting, re-use of illustrations, recitation,
broadcasting, reproduction on microfilms or in other ways, and storage in data banks. Duplication
of this publication or parts thereof is only permitted under the provisions of the German Copyright
Law of September 9, 1965, in its version of June 24, 1985, and a copyright fee must always be
paid. Violations fall under the prosecution act of the German Copyright Law.

© Springer-Verlag Berlin Heidelberg 1989
Printed in Germany

Printing and binding: Druckhaus Beltz, Hemsbach/Bergstr.

Preface

Machine learning has become a rapidly growing field of Artificial Intelligence (AI). Since the First International Workshop on Machine Learning held at Carnegie-Mellon University in Pittsburgh (USA) in 1980 [1], the number of scientists working in the field of machine learning has increased steadily, a fact indicated, e.g., by a new journal devoted to machine learning which has been appearing since 1986 [2]. This situation allows for specializing within the field. There are two types of specialization: on subfields of machine learning such as *learning from examples* or *learning from observation*, or, orthogonal to them, on themes of interest such as, e.g., *learning and logic* or *knowledge representation in machine learning*. This book follows the thematic orientation. It contains research papers, each of which brings to light the relation between knowledge representation, knowledge acquisition, and machine learning from a different direction. The book is based on the Workshop on Knowledge Representation and Organization in Machine Learning held in 1987 in Schloss Eringerfeld (Germany). It should be useful for researchers in the fields of knowledge representation, its application in knowledge-based systems, knowledge acquisition, and machine learning; for teachers and students of artificial intelligence as well as for developers of expert systems who are interested in new methods of knowledge acquisition and maintenance.

Before we give an overview of the content of the book and describe the topics more carefully, we will first give a short introduction to machine learning and clarify some technical terms.

Introduction to Machine Learning

The first question, of course, is: **What is Machine Learning?** Since the very earliest days of computer science, the need for machine learning as a prerequisite of intelligent machine behavior has been known. Turing, for instance, describes machine learning as using indexed problems and their solutions to solve new problems (Turing 59). The machine generates solutions to problems by trial and error, a human teacher then assesses the solutions, and the machine remembers the good solutions and uses them for further problems. Learning in this case is not only remembering a good solution but also accessing the solution when it is appropriate. From this point of view, the important ingredients of learning are

---

[1] This year's international workshop is the fifth one and was held at the University of Michigan in Ann Arbor (USA). In addition to the series of international workshops, a series of European Working Sessions on Machine Learning was started in 1985 at the Universite de Paris-Sud in Orsay (France). The International Meeting on Advances in Machine Learning held in 1986 in Les Arcs (France) was another event demonstrating both the increased interest in machine learning and the advances achieved in the field of machine learning.

[2] The journal "Machine Learning" appears quarterly and is published by Kluwer Academic Publishers.

- examples (here: problem-solution pairs),
- assessments of the examples by a teacher, and
- indexing or classifying the examples so that they can be accessed in future situations.

Turing did not claim that people learn in this manner or that machine learning simulates human learning, nor do most AI researchers nowadays. Rather, learning is viewed as a basic intelligent behavior observable among machines, animals, and, at the highest level, among human beings. A theory of learning should describe learning wherever it occurs and allow for pointing out the differences between human and machine learning or human and animal learning [3]. The definition of "learning" therefore should cover animal learning, human learning, and machine learning, each being a specialization of learning. Simon proposed such a definition:

"Learning is any change in a system that allows it to perform better the second time on repetition of the same task or another task drawn from the same population" (Simon 83).

This definition has been criticized for restricting itself to task performance. Michalski (86) argued that the notion of a goal has to be introduced explicitly into the definition. Under certain circumstances, decreasing performance can be the goal of the learning subject (e.g., in a labor camp, the workers learn to work less while appearing to do more). Michalski also argues that performance can be improved by means other than learning. A sharper knife cuts better, but sharpening the knife is not learning. Scott (83) also argues against Simon's definition. The usefulness of learned information need not be known at the time learning occurs. For instance, you may happen to notice the location of a library in a city without knowing that someone will ask you later in the street how to get to the library. However, now that you know where the library is you can answer the question. Thus, the knowledge turned out to be useful. Scott comes up with a definition very close to the one by Michalski:

"It is a process in which a system builds a retrievable representation of its past interactions with its environment" (Scott 83).

Whereas Scott restricts the definition to learning machines, Michalski puts it more generally:

"Learning is constructing or modifying representations of what is being experienced" (Michalski 86).

Ever since knowledge-based systems became an important paradigm in AI, the problem of acquiring the knowledge for such systems has been urgent (Hayes-Roth et al. 83). **Knowledge-**

---

[3] This is a typical AI view of intelligent behavior such as communication or language, problem solving or inferences, adaptation or learning. Whereas the notion of language has become independent from the human subject of that intelligent behavior, the notion of learning is just beginning to become a term describing a system of behavior in its own right.

based systems are those which perform their task on the basis of knowledge. Knowledge is explicable and represents a domain theory and problem solving methods in a form closely corresponding to human descriptions. The performance of the system increases with more (correct) knowledge. Knowledge is supposed to be more easily added or changed than a program can be changed to implement a new feature of a system. In this paradigm, the notion of **knowledge representation** is prominent. A representation is a mapping from a model of a part of the world to expressions of a representation language. The representation language is constructed by using a representation formalism which allows interpreting the language by the inverse mapping from expressions of the language to assertions of the model.

The paradigm of knowledge-based systems established a **need for machine learning.** Machine learning is now viewed as a means of

- automatically building up parts of a knowledge base for a knowledge-based system and
- enhancing a given knowledge base.

Corresponding to these two demands, there are two main approaches in the field of machine learning. One is often called **similarity-based learning.** Famous learning algorithms of this type are AQn (Michalski 83) and ID3 (Quinlan 83). From given instances of concepts, they learn the concepts. The concepts are then used in order to recognize a new object as an instance of a particular concept. They are similarity-based in that they detect the attributes which all instances of a concept have in common (what is similar among all instances?) and attributes which an object may not have in order to be an instance of that concept (what is dissimilar among instances and not-instances?). This approach has proved its applicability especially for acquiring knowledge in **heuristic classification** systems (Clancey 85). These are knowledge-based systems whose knowledge base consists of a classification of problems and already known solutions to them. A problem is solved by recognizing it as belonging to a certain class and applying the known solution to it. As is easily seen, from instances of classified problems, similarity-based learning algorithms can build up a classification of problems which can then be used by the knowledge-based system for solving new problems by heuristic classification.

The kernel inside similarity-based learning algorithms is **inductive inference.** From a finite set of examples a general concept is induced. Of course, this inference is not a safe one; it is not truth preserving but only falsity preserving (Michalski 86). Therefore, the learned concepts must be revisable, the domain of a concept must be narrowed in order to exclude counter-examples, or it must be widened in order to include new positive examples. Induction is a justified generalization from an instance to a class. There are always several generalizations possible [4]. Normally, the most specific generalization is looked for. The most specific generalizations

---

[4] For a careful analysis of generalization see (Kodratoff, Ganascia 86), (Kodratoff 88).

possible can be further restricted by concept quality measures (Michalski 83) and can be improved by using **background knowledge.** Background knowledge is knowledge about the domain which is used by the learning algorithm. A learning program is knowledge-intensive if it uses knowledge in addition to the examples for its learning task. **Closed-loop learning** is a particular way of using knowledge for learning. The learning program uses the knowledge it has already acquired, i.e. it feeds back the learning results into the background knowledge. Of course, knowledge-intensive approaches require a more ambitious knowledge representation than those which have different languages for the representation of the examples and for the representation of the learning results and do not use any more knowledge for learning. We have said that induction is a *justified* generalization. If the justification is purely statistical, it is more likely to verify arbitrary concepts. A theoretical justification, on the other hand, presupposes what was to be achieved: a domain model.

The other main approach in machine learning is **explanation-based learning.** Here, the justification for the new, learned concept is theoretically based. An explanation of why a certain example is a member of a certain concept is generalized to represent the concept (Mitchell et al. 86; DeJong, Mooney 86). Most often, the explanation is a proof, thus requiring the domain theory to be represented in (restricted) predicate logic. The main advantage is that one example together with the explanation is sufficient for acquiring an operational concept description. The example focuses the learning activity. As opposed to inductive learning, here most of the knowledge is already present. The learning step is to put the knowledge to use or, in other words, to find an *operational* representation for a concept. Explanation-based learning has been applied for enhancing knowledge bases in several scenarios. One scenario is represented by the LEAP system (Mitchell et al. 85). Whenever a rule in the knowledge base is missing and thus preventing the problem solver from coming to a solution, the user gives a solution to the problem. The learning system verifies the solution and then generalizes the verification (explanation). This produces a new rule for solving new problems of the same kind. Another scenario is presented by Wilkins in this book.

Overview of the Book

Above, we presented machine learning as a method to acquire knowledge and enhance knowledge bases. In this book, we consider machine learning embedded in the knowledge acquisition and maintenance process. Therefore, we first look at this context. We focus on knowledge representations which ease knowledge acquisition. Coming closer to machine learning in knowledge acquisition, we look at knowledge representation for machine learning. Here are the various aspects:

- The representation of the events from which a system learns. This representation determines what can be learned. How can this representation be enhanced?
- The representation of the learning results. What is necessary in order to enable the learning of complex concepts?
- Knowledge especially needed for a particular learning algorithm. How should this be represented? Moreover, how can it be acquired?
- The states of the learning program. How can they be represented?

The relation between knowledge representation and machine learning is two-fold: a suitable knowledge representation eases machine learning, and machine learning builds up representations of knowledge.

The knowledge acquisition problem demands explainable, maintainable, and learnable representations and therefore has led to new developments in expert systems. **William Swartout** and **Stephen Smoliar** show how the requirement for a maintainable knowledge base can be used as a guideline for an expert system's representation [5]. Their Explainable Expert System (EES) offers a KL-ONE-like representation formalism for building a representation language by which a domain model is expressed. This representation can then be compiled into a more performance-oriented representation. **Walter Van de Velde** also presents a two-level expert system: a representation for causal relations of a domain can be transformed into another one which is better suited for quick problem solving. As opposed to EES, his system transforms each solution found by reasoning on the causal model into performance-oriented rules, thus incrementally building up a rule base on the basis of a domain model.

The requirement of *learnable representations* exemplified by a vision system is discussed by **Michael Mohnhaupt** and **Bernd Neumann**. In vision systems, very complex examples have to be abstracted in order to find concepts. Mohnhaupt and Neumann describe a series of transformations from the original, close-to-pixel representation to a prototypical representation of car movements.

Even information retrieval systems set up a context for the *transformation of representations*. **Roy Rada and Hafedh Mili** reorganize different databases with different indexing schemata into one database. Their procedure is based on occurrences of the same term in both databases and uses analogy for mapping two indices.

The knowledge acquisition context is not restricted to systems. There is always a knowledge engineer, an expert, or an AI programmer involved. **David Littman** observed expert system designers at work and proposes some categories for cognitive entities and operations. A better understanding of knowledge engineers' cognitive processes when they represent knowledge

---

[5] Swartout's use of "explanation" is different from that in the context of machine learning: the system can produce explanations which make sense to a user. This requires the knowledge base to be well structured.

could also provide a guideline for adequate representation formalisms, and these, in turn, would ease knowledge acquisition.

With the context now established the next articles of the book consider knowledge acquisition with a closer look at learning. The introduction to this view is presented by **Katharina Morik**. A unifying view of knowledge acquisition and machine learning is developed thus allowing their integration. The reversibility of knowledge is stressed, and the conclusions for an integrated system are drawn. As an example of such a system BLIP is introduced.

The DISCIPLE system of **Yves Kodratoff** and **Gheorghe Tecuci** integrates knowledge acquisition by questioning the user, machine learning using various techniques (similarity-based learning, explanation-based learning, and learning by analogy), and a performance element.

The next section of the book focusses on *knowledge representation for machine learning*. **Werner Emde** examines requirements for knowledge representation formalisms posed by different learning tasks and demonstrates an inference machine which is specially designed to support incremental machine learning and knowledge revision. This deals with the last question of our list of topics above.

Sabine Thieme discusses the knowledge which a machine learning algorithm needs, thus contributing to the third topic of our list above. In her case, the learning algorithm is model-driven, i.e. the induction is restricted by models indicating what to look for. She presents not only the representation of these models but also a manual acquisition method for them.

The next papers all deal with particular learning algorithms. Similarity-based learning is looked at with respect to the representation of the examples and with respect to the representation of the learned concepts. **Maarten van Someren** discusses the dependency of the *representation of examples* from which the system learns and the learning results (the first topic from our list above). His careful description of problems for simple rule learning leads to an approach that uses knowledge about the domain in order to construct a more complex representation of the examples.

Michel Manago and **Jim Blythe** enhance Mitchell's version space method (Mitchell 82). As *representations of the concepts being learned*, disjunctive concept descriptions are allowed. This requires heuristics to avoid a combinatorial explosion of possible specific generalizations. Thus, the paper deals with the second aspect from our list above by showing the implications of enhancing the representation of the concepts to be learned.

Learning by analogy is investigated by **Christel Vrain** and **Yves Kodratoff** with respect to problem solving. If the structure of a new problem is similar to that of an already solved problem, how can the known solution be transferred to the new problem? This gives the notion of *similarity* in similarity-based learning a new meaning [6]. It can be used not only to generalize but also to directly transform a solution in order to transfer it to a new problem. The authors present similarity-based learning by analogy which makes good use of the dissimilarities of the analogous problems.

David Wilkins and Michael Pazzani describe two kinds of explanation-based learning. Stefan Wrobel presents a model-driven concept formation algorithm.

David Wilkins stresses the value of *learning for knowledge-base repair*. His system observes an expert at work and creates "explanations" for the expert's actions. If the system cannot derive a goal with respect to the problem state and the domain theory that corresponds to the expert's action - this being an explanation - then the knowledge base is suspected of being incomplete. Learning is then undertaken to complete the knowledge base by creating a rule that would help to explain the expert's action.

In his system OCCAM **Michael Pazzani** combines similarity-based learning and explanation-based learning. In his setting of story-understanding an explanation is a justification for a prediction of what will happen. Events have certain outcomes and to understand events also means to be able to predict these outcomes. Events are represented as schemata, which are acquired by similarity-based learning from input events and are used by explanation-based learning to explain new events. Thus, the *representation* needed *for explanation-based learning*, that is, the schemata as compact representations of goal-directed sequences of actions, is *built up by similarity-based learning*. In this respect, Pazzani contributes to the first aspect of knowledge representation for machine learning.

Stefan Wrobel applies model-driven rule-learning. He deals with both knowledge-base repair - as does David Wilkins - and the introduction of new concepts into the representation language of the domain theory - as does Michael Pazzani. The new concepts are used by further learning, thus enabling the system to learn rules that were previously excluded from the hypothesis space because of representational limits. In this respect, Wrobel's contribution refers to the first topic of our list above. In respect of knowledge repair it is an attempt to cope with the risk of inductive learning. Inductively acquired rules can be too general. They need to be restricted as soon as a contradiction indicates the overgeneralization of the rule. Explicitly representing the applicability of a rule allows for narrowing the rule's domain and thus for revising and working out the results of inductive rule learning (Emde, Habel, Rollinger 83).

All the papers of this book investigating particular learning algorithms are also contributions to the knowledge acquisition and repair problem in that the problem of knowledge acquisition is the problem of representing a domain and task, and the aim of machine learning is to build up a

---

[6] Similarity-based learning is commonly abbreviated SBL. Other common abbreviations are EBL for explanation-based learning and EBG for explanation-based generalization.

representation for a domain and/or task. Machine learning and knowledge acquisition meet at the topic of knowledge representation. The representation problem has to be confronted at various levels:

- the representation formalism has to be adequate for knowledge acquisition and machine learning as is discussed in this volume particularly by Emde and by Swartout and Smoliar;
- the representation language has to be adequate for machine learning and can be built up by machine learning as is particularly investigated by Manago, van Someren, Pazzani and Wrobel in this volume;
- the representation of domain knowledge is a complex process even if the representation language and formalism are given and adequate as is argued by Morik, Kodratoff and Tecuci, and Littman in this book.

The book by no means handles all the aspects of knowledge representation for machine learning and machine learning for knowledge representation. Nor does it fully cover the aspects it investigates, for this is impossible. However, a start is made, and the reader may feel inspired to think some more about the impact of representations on machine learning.

Acknowledgements

Without the support of the European Community's COST-13 project on "Machine Learning and Knowledge Acquisition", the workshop on "Knowledge Representation and Organization in Machine Learning " would not have been possible. The project, its vital leader Yves Kodratoff, and the scientific community it brought together supported the workshop in two respects: encouragement and financial support. Thanks also go to the project "Lerner", partially sponsored by the German Ministry of Research and Technology (BMFT) under contract ITW8501B1, in which scientists from Nixdorf Computer AG, Technical University of Berlin, and Stollmann GmbH have the opportunity to work on machine learning and knowledge acquisition. Thanks to all the colleagues!

Berlin, November 1988   Katharina Morik

References

Clancey, W.J.(85): "Heuristic Classification"; Artificial Intelligence 27, p.289-350, 1985

DeJong, G., Mooney, R. (86): "Explanation-Based Learning: An Alternative View"; Machine Learning, Vol.1, Number 2, p.145-176, 1986

Emde, W.,Habel, Ch.,Rollinger, C.R.(83): "The Discovery of the Equator (or Concept Driven Learning)"; In: Proc. IJCAI-83, Karlsruhe, 1983

Hayes-Roth,F.,Waterman, D.A., Lenat, D. (eds.): "Building Expert Systems"; Addison Wesley, London, 1983

Kodratoff, Y.,Ganascia, J.G.(86): "Improving the Generalization Step of Learning"; In: Michalski/Carbonell/Mitchell (eds.): Machine Learning, An Artificial Intelligence Approach, Volume II; Morgan Kaufmann, Los Altos, 1986

Kodratoff, Y. (88): "Introduction to Machine Learning"; Pitman, London, 1988

Michalski, R.S. (86): "Understanding the Nature of Learning: Issues and Research Directions"; In: Michalski/Carbonell/Mitchell (eds.): Machine Learning, An Artificial Intelligence Approach, Volume II; Morgan Kaufmann, Los Altos, 1986

Michalski, R.S., Stepp, R.E. (83): "Learning from Observation: Conceptual Clustering" In: Michalski/Carbonell/Mitchell (eds.): Machine Learning, An Artificial Intelligence Approach, Volume I; Tioga, Palo Alto, 1983, and Springer, Berlin, 1984

Mitchell, T.M., Keller, R.M., Kedar-Cabelli, S.T. (86): "Explanation-Based Generalization: A Unifying View"; Machine Learning, Vol.1, Number 1, p. 47-80, 1986

Mitchell,T.M.; Mahadevan,S.; Steinberg,L.I. (85): "LEAP: A Learning Apprentice for VLSI Design"; In: Proc. IJCAI-85, Los Angeles, CA, 1985.

Quinlan, R.J. (83): "Learning Efficient Classification Procedures and their Application to Chess End Games"; In: Michalski/Mitchell/Carbonell (eds.): Machine Learning, An Artificial Intelligence Approach, Volume I; Palo Alto, p. 463 - 482, 1983, and Springer, Berlin, 1984

Scott, P.D.(83): "Learning: The Construction of A Posteriori Knowledge Structures"; Proc. AAAI-83, Washington, 1983

Simon, H.A.(83): "Why Should Machines Learn?"; In: Michalski/Carbonell/Mitchell (eds.): Machine Learning, An Artificial Intelligence Approach, Volume I; Tioga, Palo Alto, 1983, and Springer, Berlin, 1984

CONTENTS

Preface...v

William R. Swartout, Stephen W. Smoliar
Explanation: A Source of Guidance for Knowledge Representation 1

Walter Van de Velde
(Re)Presentation Issues in Second Generation Expert Systems 17

Michael Mohnhaupt, Bernd Neumann
Some Aspects of Learning and Reorganization in an Analogical Representation 50

Roy Rada, Hafedh Mili
A Knowledge-Intensive Learning System for Document Retrieval.. 65

David Littman
Constructing Expert Systems as Building Mental Models or Toward a Cognitive Ontology for
Expert Systems.. 88

Katharina Morik
Sloppy Modeling.. 107

Yves Kodratoff, Gheorghe Tecuci
The Central Role of Explanations in DISCIPLE 135

Werner Emde
An Inference Engine for Representing Multiple Theories.. 148

Sabine Thieme
The Acquisition of Model-Knowledge for a Model-Driven Machine Learning Approach................. 177

Maarten W. van Someren
Using Attribute Dependencies for Rule Learning 192

Michel Manago, Jim Blythe
Learning Disjunctive Concepts... 211

Christel Vrain, Yves Kodratoff
The Use of Analogy in Incremental SBL 231

David C. Wilkins
Knowledge Base Refinement Using Apprenticeship Learning Techniques.. 247

Michael Pazzani
Creating High Level Knowledge Structures from Simple Elements.. 258

Stefan Wrobel
Demand-Driven Concept Formation.. 289

Explanation: A Source of Guidance
for
Knowledge Representation

William R. Swartout
Stephen W. Smoliar
USC Information Sciences Institute
4676 Admiralty Way Suite 1001
Marina del Rey, CA 90292-6695

ABSTRACT: In constructing an expert system, there are usually several ways to represent a given piece of knowledge regardless of the knowledge representation formalism used. Initially, all of them may appear to be equivalent, but as the system evolves, it often becomes apparent that some are better than others, leading to the need to revise representations. Such revisions can be very time-consuming and prone to error. In this paper, we argue that the additional constraints imposed by the addition of an explanation facility can guide the creation of a knowledge base in a manner that reduces the need to subsequently re-structure the knowledge base as the system's functionality increases. We describe criteria that may be applied after the knowledge base is constructed to reveal potential weaknesses as well as those that may be employed during knowledge base construction. Finally, we briefly describe an expert system shell we have constructed that embodies these guiding principles, the Explainable Expert Systems framework.

1. Introduction

It is frequently pointed out that current knowledge representation formalisms fail to capture adequately many types of knowledge, such as causality, time and space, and belief. Numerous research efforts have attempted to find a way to capture such knowledge. Ironically, while current formalisms fail to provide for the representation of some kinds of knowledge, they simultaneously provide *too many* ways to represent other kinds of knowledge.

In building an expert system, one is confronted with a plethora of choices. No matter what representation system is used, there are seemingly many ways that some kinds of knowledge can be represented. For example, the statement "smoking causes lung cancer" may be represented as a *relation*:

```
CAUSES(SMOKING, LUNG-CANCER)
```

It could be reified as a *concept* with attributes:

```
[CAUSE-47 (specializes CAUSE)
    CAUSER: SMOKING
    CAUSEE: LUNG-CANCER]
```

Or, the causal relation could be collapsed into a pair of primitive concepts focusing, respectively, on the symptom and the disease:

```
[SMOKING-THAT-LEADS-TO-LUNG-CANCER (specializes SMOKING)]

[LUNG-CANCER-CAUSED-BY-SMOKING (specializes LUNG-CANCER)]
```

While the system is being constructed, it is often difficult to find good criteria for deciding among these choices, so the knowledge engineer is forced to make many decisions arbitrarily. But as additional demands are placed on the expert system, some of these arbitrary decisions will turn out to be incorrect, leading to the need to revise the knowledge base. Such revisions can be very time-consuming and prone to error.

One solution to this problem is to provide knowledge representation frameworks that make it easy to modify a representation (as suggested by Morik's paper in this book). Another approach (that is compatible with the first) is based on the recognition that the knowledge representation problem is under-constrained if one is only concerned with the problem-solving behavior of a system. The solution is to find additional constraints that may be applied when knowledge is first represented. These should be constraints that help resolve choices among seemingly equivalent representations in such a way that the subsequent need to re-structure the knowledge representation is reduced. In this paper, we will argue that the constraints imposed by providing automated explanation can provide such guidance.

If a knowledge base is used to provide explanations *and* solve problems, then we are using that knowledge for multiple purposes, which means that we must satisfy the needs of both the explanation and problem solving components. Thus, in writing a plan to address some problem solving issue, we need a way of representing the plan that is "explanation predictive" that is, that assures us that the resulting representation will be explainable. Of course, these constraints apply only if the explanations and problem solving behavior are produced from the *same* underlying representation. Approaches to explanation that use separate representations for producing behavior and explanations (e.g. Lisp and "canned text") will not provide the needed constraints.

Is there anything special about explanation? Arguably, using a knowledge base in *any* additional way would add constraints that would limit the ways in which knowledge might be represented. We feel that explanation, in particular, provides constraints that reduce the need to re-structure the knowledge base as a system evolves and its functionality increases.

Our argument is as follows. To be useful, an explanation facility must present explanations in ways that are familiar to domain experts and practitioners, that is, it has to "talk" about problems the way they talk about them, using domain terms and expressions. These terms and concepts have been developed by the domain experts, based on their broad experience, to help them in conceptualizing problems to be solved and in communicating those problems and their solutions to other experts and practitioners. Requiring that an expert system produce explanations imposes constraints on the knowledge representation that tend to force it to be structured similar to the way experts talk about it. Hence, a representation that takes into account explanation will be more broadly based on the more extensive experience of experts, rather than "optimized" for some particular narrow problem. Thus, a system that is built taking into account explanation will have a structure that can handle an expanded range of problems with less extensive re-structuring.

It may appear that we are just advocating good knowledge engineering practice: one should try to capture a domain in the way experts seem to conceptualize it and talk about it. Dijkstra has pointed that out in the context of conventional programming:

> "If I judge a program by itself, my central theme, I think, is that I want the program written down as I can understand it, I want it written down as I would like to explain it to someone." -- [Dahl, Dijkstra and Hoare 72]

But we are saying more. The key is that mechanical explanation production imposes a strict "mental hygiene" on the knowledge representation process. If the knowledge base is structured inappropriately, either certain types of explanations will be unavailable, or the explanations that are produced will be difficult to understand or nonsensical. A mechanical explanation facility imposes these constraints with a consistency and rigor that would be difficult or impossible to achieve manually.

In the remainder of this paper, we will first give examples of the kinds of representation problems that can be revealed by an explanation facility once a knowledge base has been constructed and discuss how those problems can impact system evolution. We will then discuss the kinds of guidance that explanation provides in building a knowledge representation. Finally, we will briefly discuss the Explainable Expert Systems (EES) framework, an expert systems shell we have constructed taking into account the guidance that explanation provides.

2. Problems Revealed by Explanation

The representation problems that are revealed by explanation all stem from a common underlying source: the use of a low-level "compiled" representation in which important knowledge is either not represented or not explicitly identified. Although the problems share a common source, they manifest themselves in different ways and are remedied differently.

2.1. Missing Knowledge

If a system builder is solely concerned with creating a system that will solve a particular problem, he only needs to represent enough knowledge to support the solution of that problem. This approach can be short-sighted, however, leading to the need to extensively re-structure the knowledge base when the range of problems to be solved is expanded. From an explanation standpoint, the symptoms of this problem are that there will be certain important kinds of explanations that the system cannot offer.

As an example, consider the Digitalis Therapy Advisor [Swartout 77], a program designed to help physicians administer digitalis. A key task of the system was the reduction of the digitalis dose in response to any abnormal sensitivities to the drug. To *perform* correctly, the system merely needed to know what the sensitivities were, and to reduce the dose of digitalis if they were present. The causal relations that indicated why a particular parameter was a sensitivity were not represented because the program could perform correctly without them. As a result, that system was limited to the sorts of explanations that appear in Figure 2-1. While that explanation does indicate that serum calcium is a sensitivity, the system could not explain why, or even define what a sensitivity was, because that knowledge was not represented.

Because the causal relations that the code was based on were only present in the head of the system builder, it was more difficult to keep the system consistent and to maintain and evolve it. The system builder had to recall and manually apply those relations in all the appropriate places. As the system became larger, this became more difficult, and some inconsistencies did creep in (see [Swartout 83], page 318). Thus, the inability to offer certain important kinds of explanations can be a symptom that a system is not capturing knowledge that may seem insignificant initially but becomes important as the system grows.

WHAT IS THE LEVEL OF SERUM CALCIUM?

ENTER NUMERICAL VALUE ==> why?
*The user types "why?" indicating that he questions why he is being
asked to supply the value of serum calcium.*

MY TOP GOAL IS TO BEGIN THERAPY. ONE STEP IN DOING
THAT IS TO CHECK SENSITIVITIES. I AM NOW TRYING TO
CHECK SENSITIVITY DUE TO CALCIUM.

Figure 2-1: A Limited Justification for a Question

2.2. Confusing Explanations from Confounded Concerns

Another problem that stems from focusing on performance issues alone is that different
kinds of knowledge are not explicitly distinguished when they are represented. Thus, in a
single method or rule, some of the clauses may be concerned with domain reasoning, others
with the user interface, while still others may define terminology. In providing explanations to
various classes of users, not all of this information is appropriate; but because the different
kinds of knowledge are not distinguished in the representation, the explanation facility cannot
accommodate specific needs--it must present all the information. The results can be quite
confusing.

The Digitalis Therapy Advisor produced the text in Figure 2-2 to explain how it checked
for sensitivity due to serum calcium. It's reasonably clear from the explanation that the
system is performing a threshold test and making a reduction if the threshold is exceeded.
However, when we showed explanations like this to physicians, they were mystified by the
term "REASONS OF REDUCTION" and the steps that manipulated it. Those steps were part
of the internal record keeping mechanism of the Advisor, keeping track of the factors involved
in adjusting the dose. But that distinction was not explicit, so the explanation routines
displayed those steps along with the rest of the code. This is a reasonably mild example of the
kinds of problems that can result from confounding of knowledge, in part because the Digitalis
Advisor was a plan-based system and the plan structure tended to encourage the separation of
knowledge types. The problem can be more severe in rule-based systems due to their flat
structure (see for example [Clancey 83]).

Confounding different kinds of knowledge not only makes explanations difficult to
understand, it also makes the system more difficult to maintain and evolve. In part, this
results from the fact that confounding knowledge makes the system inherently more difficult
to understand--to maintainers as well as end-users. But it also indicates that the system is not

TO CHECK SENSITIVITY DUE TO CALCIUM I DO THE FOLLOWING
STEPS:

1. I DO ONE OF THE FOLLOWING:

1.1 IF EITHER THE LEVEL OF SERUM CALCIUM IS GRATER THAN 10
    OR IV CALCIUM IS GIVEN THEN I DO THE FOLLOWING
    SUBSTEPS:

1.1.1 I SET THE FACTOR OF REDUCTION DUE TO HYPERCALCEMIA
      TO 0.75.

1.1.2 I ADD HYPERCALCEMIA TO THE REASONS OF REDUCTION.

1.2 OTHERWISE, I REMOVE HYPERCALCEMIA FROM THE REASONS
    OF REDUCTION AND SET THE FACTOR OF REDUCTION DUE
    TO HYPERCALCEMIA TO 1.00.

Figure 2-2:   Confounding Concerns in an Explanation

modular. Because different concerns have been intertwined and distributed throughout the knowledge base, making a change will usually require making several modifications to different parts of the knowledge base. In a more modular design change is easier because it is more localized.

2.3. Inappropriate Conceptualization

As we mentioned in the introduction, a system builder is confronted with many possible ways to structure the concepts of the domain he is trying to capture. While many of these conceptualizations will lead to equivalent problem solving behavior, not all of them will offer equally good explanations or be equally easy to evolve.

One particularly problematic approach to knowledge representation is the use of what we will call "mega-concepts." These occur when one uses a single, non-decomposable concept to represent something that really should be represented as a composite of several domain concepts. Typically, these concepts are given long hyphenated names that describe what the concept is intended to denote. Unfortunately, most of the semantics for the concept resides in its name. Since such concepts have no substructure, as far as the system is concerned there is not much difference between the HAM-AND-CHEESE-SANDWICH-I-HAD-LAST-THURSDAY and RECENT-HISTORY-OF-ACUTE-MYOCARDIAL-INFARCTION. For explanation, the use of such concepts presents problems because the explainer has to present the entire phrase associated with the concept every time it refers to it since the concepts cannot be decomposed. This results in very stilted explanations (even if the hyphens are removed). For evolution, this is symptomatic of a failure to capture the appropriate underlying concepts of the domain.

Extensive use of mega-concepts is often a symptom that the knowledge representation lacks an adequate foundation. Such a lack usually makes it difficult to increase problem solving power without considerable re-structuring. The reason is that the terminology of the domain has evolved to facilitate reasoning about it and its description. If some of the domain concepts are not captured then certain kinds of reasoning may be difficult. As an example of this kind of problem, INTERNIST-1 made extensive use of mega-concepts to represent domain concepts. Caduceus, its successor, is capable of performing much more sophisticated reasoning, but it was not possible to create Caduceus without extensively re-structuring the knowledge base.

2.4. Missing Abstraction

The final problem we will consider is that many expert systems represent knowledge at a very specific level. General problem solving strategies are not represented, but instead a collection of specific rules covers the range of situations that should be handled by a single general strategy. This hampers both explanation and evolution.

For example, MYCIN [Davis, Buchanan, and Shortliffe 85] is sometimes able to determine the genus of the micro-organism infecting a patient but unable to determine its species. When this occurs, MYCIN just assumes that the species of the organism is the most likely one for the particular genus. This is a reasonable default rule. What is not reasonable is the way the rule is represented in MYCIN. The general heuristic is not represented at all. Instead, it is captured by a set of rules, each one specific to one of the genera MYCIN knows about. This is a problem for explanation, because the system cannot describe how it deals with the general problem of being unable to deduce the species of an organism. The best the system can do is present all the specific rules it has for each of the genera (which would probably overwhelm the user) or display one rule and hope that the user can generalize.

This overly specific representation of knowledge is also a major problem for system evolvability. From the standpoint of modularity, if one wanted to modify the general heuristic MYCIN employed, there is no single rule to modify. Instead, the system builder would have to locate and modify manually each of the rules that instantiated the general heuristic, with all the attendant possibilities for making a mistake. By forcing the system builder to express knowledge at an overly specific level, MYCIN also reduces naturalness, since the specific nature of the representation is an artifact and not what the system builder really intended to represent.

3. The Guidance that Explanation Provides

In the preceding Section we dealt with ways in which an explanation facility can be used to evaluate a knowledge base retrospectively. If the knowledge base is not structured well then certain kinds of explanations will not be available or the explanations that are produced will be poor. In this Section we discuss three ways in which explanation concerns can guide the construction of a knowledge base prospectively. First, consideration of the knowledge needed to support the kinds of questions that an explanation facility should be able to answer can help determine what kinds of knowledge need to be represented. Second, taking into account the linguistic concerns that arise from text generation can help in determining how to structure concepts and in identifying what concepts need to be represented. Third, explanation can help in determining how "deep" the knowledge base should be and in selecting an appropriate grain-size. In the remainder of this Section, we discuss each of these points in more detail.

3.1. Determining What Knowledge to Represent

By considering the kinds of questions that an explanation system should be able to answer, we have identified three different kinds of knowledge that an expert system should represent:

1. Domain descriptive knowledge

2. Problem solving knowledge

3. Terminology

We do not believe this list is exhaustive, but it can still be helpful to a knowledge engineer because it identifies kinds of knowledge that he should be looking for and that he should represent explicitly. Let us now consider these categories in greater detail.

3.1.1. Domain Descriptive Knowledge

This is knowledge that describes how the domain works. For example, in a medical domain it is basically physiological knowledge, including knowledge of physiological parameters, diseases, possible interventions, and related causal connections. This is typically the sort of knowledge that one finds in textbooks. Domain descriptive knowledge is needed to answer questions about the domain itself, such as:

- What does increased serum calcium cause?

- What are the presenting symptoms of a myocardial infarction?

It is important for an explanation facility to be able to answer such questions because they allow a user to assess the breadth and depth of the system's knowledge and thus help in determining its suitability for the user's needs. What is missing (and distinct) from domain descriptive knowledge is "how to" knowledge, which is our second category of knowledge.

3.1.2. Problem Solving Knowledge

This is knowledge about how tasks can be accomplished, e.g. how to perform a diagnosis or how to administer a drug. In our Explainable Expert Systems (EES) framework we have chosen to represent problem solving knowledge as plans, although other representations, such as rules, could also be used. In EES, plans have *capability descriptions* which describe what goals they can achieve. Each plan also has a *method* which is a sequence of substeps (which may themselves include subgoals) for accomplishing the goal. Problem solving knowledge allows the system to answer questions such as:

- How is the dosage level computed?

- Is the patient's age used in computing his ideal weight?

3.1.3. Terminology

This serves to describe the language used to express domain descriptive knowledge and problem solving knowledge [Swartout and Neches 86]. It constitutes the "language" that knowledge sources within an expert system use to communicate. In most expert systems, terminology is not explicitly defined; terms acquire their meaning based on how other parts of the system react to them. This has the undesirable effect that a modification to a portion of the problem solving knowledge may cause an unintended change in the definition of a term. If terms are explicitly defined, then answers may be given to questions such as:

- What does sensitivity mean?

- What is the difference between a symptom and a sign?

By providing distinct and separate representations for different kinds of knowledge such as these, the modularity of the system is increased. One part of the system may be modified without affecting others, easing maintenance and evolution of the system.

3.2. Guidance from Text Generation

If explanations are to be produced by paraphrasing the system's knowledge structures into natural language, that process will be facilitated if the knowledge structures reflect linguistic concerns. We have found that these concerns can provide guidance in creating a knowledge base in two ways. First, help is provided in representing concepts, both in determining what should *be* a concept and in *structuring* concepts. Second, linguistic concerns can provide help in determining how the upper levels of the knowledge base should be arranged.

Structuring Concepts

It is sometimes difficult to decide just what should be represented as a concept. In our discussion of "mega-concepts" (Section 2.3), we pointed out that if too much information was folded into an atomic concept, explanation would be difficult and the representation would not capture the domain very well, possibly impeding evolution of the system. To facilitate text generation, we have chosen to adopt the constraint that atomic concepts should correspond (roughly) to natural language words. Composite concepts are then constructed from atomic concepts and correspond to natural language clauses and phrases.

For example, in the EES framework we represent goals and plan capabilities as concepts that correspond to verb clauses. Thus, in one of the systems we have constructed using EES, a Program Enhancement Advisor (PEA), a goal that arises is for the PEA to enhance the readability of a program. This goal is represented as:

```
[ENHANCE
        object: [READABILITY
                     property-of: PROGRAM]
        actor: PEA-SYSTEM]
```

The "slots" on the verb ENHANCE correspond to the case slots in a case grammar (akin to [Fillmore 68]). By taking this approach, we avoid the temptation to represent the goal as an atomic concept like ENHANCE-PROGRAM-READABILITY. The advantage for explanation is clear, but there are also advantages from the standpoint of system construction. Because more of the underlying structure of this goal is captured, it is possible for both this goal and another goal to enhance the efficiency of a program to be implemented by the same general method for enhancing *characteristics* of programs, since both readability and efficiency are characteristics. It would be more difficult to capture such commonalities if the goals were represented atomically. Thus, by applying linguistic constraints for structuring concepts, we create a representation that is easier to explain, evolve and extend.

Representing the Upper Knowledge Base

Almost all current knowledge representation formalisms require the user to construct a knowledge base from scratch. That is, the user is only provided with some top-level concept (e.g., "THING") and a set of primitive operations for constructing new concepts. This imposes a significant burden on the system builder because he must create the entire top level of the concept hierarchy in addition to representing the domain knowledge. Creating the top level is hard, because the system builder is confronted by many seemingly arbitrary decisions; but it is also critical, because it provides the basis for the entire knowledge base. We have begun to partially relieve the system builder of this task by providing a reusable top-level knowledge base. This top-level knowledge base contains approximately 150 concepts. It provides a system builder with several layers of concepts beyond "THING", and aids system construction in several ways:

- **Easier system construction.** Knowledge for a new expert system is provided by *specializing* this existing knowledge base rather than constructing everything from scratch.

- **Greater potential for knowledge reuse.** Since systems will be constructed starting from the same underlying base, there should be greater opportunities for reusing knowledge across systems than would be possible if each system were constructed from a different (and arbitrarily structured) knowledge base.

- **Guidance for style.** The pre-defined top-level knowledge base acquaints a system builder with the appropriate style for using the knowledge representation.

This approach is similar to that taken by Sowa in his definition of a "conceptual catalog" in his book, *Conceptual Structures* [Sowa 84]. However, while Sowa's catalog appears to be simply a collection of entities arising from his experience in knowledge representation, we have tried to take a more systematic approach based on linguistic concerns for the structure of explanations. Thus, the knowledge base distinguishes (at a high level) among nouns, verbs, and modifiers of various sorts; and these, in turn, are further differentiated on the basis of sentence structures anticipated for explanatory text. This assures that the concerns of both problem solving and explanation will rest on a common foundation.

3.3. Guidance for Grain-size

A major problem in building a knowledge base is deciding when to stop. Modeling can be extended to capture the domain at increasingly finer levels of detail. When has enough been captured? When is the model sufficiently deep? Certainly one source of guidance stems from consideration of the system's intended problem solving capabilities. Knowledge must be represented at sufficient depth to support the system's problem solving behavior. We have found that another source of guidance comes from explanation. If experts appear not to use a particular piece of knowledge in explaining how they solve problems, it is often not necessary to represent that knowledge.

As an example, when re-implementing the Digitalis Advisor to provide better explanations, we were confronted with the problem of deciding how deeply to model the causal relations in the system. We modeled the fact that increased serum calcium causes increased automaticity in the heart, because physicians used that fact in justifying their decisions. However, that fact itself can be modeled in greater detail in terms of ion levels inside and outside the cardiac cell wall and cell wall de-polarization thresholds. Because the physicians told us that they never discussed clinical problems at that level of detail, we reasoned that it was not important to either reasoning or explanation at the clinical level; and, as a result, such detail could be left out of the model. Subsequent experience with the model has borne out that conjecture.

In this Section we have argued that explanation concerns can provide guidance during the construction of a knowledge base. This guidance can help in deciding what knowledge to represent, how concepts should be structured, and when to stop modeling. In the next Section we briefly present the Explainable Expert Systems framework which embodies these guiding principles.

4. The Explainable Expert Systems Framework

We have argued that an "uncompiled" declarative representation of knowledge will reduce the need to re-structure the knowledge base as a system evolves. But a system which always derives its behavior from "first principles" is likely to run very slowly. So, system builders currently hand-compile their representations, which unfortunately results in brittle systems that require much re-structuring as they evolve.

We created the Explainable Expert Systems (EES) framework[1] to address this quandary of how to have both an uncompiled representation and still achieve good performance. EES provides a development environment that encourages a system designer to represent knowledge

---

[1]See also [Swartout and Smoliar 87, Neches, Swartout, and Moore 85] for a more complete description of the EES project.

in an uncompiled fashion. EES's knowledge base provides explicit representations for domain descriptive knowledge, problem solving knowledge and terminology (as described in Section 3.1). An automatic program writer is then used to combine these different kinds of knowledge to produce an efficient implementation of an expert system. As it creates the expert system, the program writer records its design decisions in a design history. The design history links the compiled implementation of the system and the declarative representations it is based on, and it provides explanation routines with the rationale needed to justify the expert system's actions. Maintenance and evolution are then performed at a high level on the declarative representation, rather than the compiled implementation, as in current practice. New implementations are derived by the program writer.

EES's program writer creates an expert system using goal refinement and reformulation. Starting with a high level goal (such as "enhance program readability") the writer searches through its hierarchy of plans for those plans whose capability descriptions subsume (that is, match) the goal. It selects one of the matching plans and instantiates its method. This results in the posting of subgoals in the method as further goals to be implemented, and the program writer searches for plans to implement those goals in turn. The writer continues in this fashion until all goals have been implemented in terms of primitive constructs.

In the event that no plan is found for implementing a goal, the program writer attempts to reformulate, or transform, the goal into a goal or set of goals that *can* be implemented. This capability provides several benefits. Maintenance and initial system construction are easier because the program writer is able to bridge larger gaps between plans and goals. This also makes knowledge re-usable in a larger range of situations. We have provided for several different kinds of reformulations (see [Neches, Swartout, and Moore 85] for a detailed discussion).

As an example, let us consider how the program writer would combine problem solving, domain descriptive, and terminological knowledge to produce code to deal with sensitivities in the digitalis domain. Starting with a goal such as: `"compensate digitalis dose for digitalis sensitivities"` the program writer would combine a piece of general problem solving knowledge such as:

```
To compensate a drug dose for a drug sensitivity
  If drug sensitivities are present
    then reduce the drug dosage.
```

with the domain descriptive facts:

```
Increased serum calcium may cause dangerous heart
rhythms.
```

```
Digitalis administration may cause dangerous heart
rhythms.
```

and a definition of *sensitivity*:

```
    drug sensitivity: an observable deviation
    that causes something dangerous that is also caused by the drug
```

to derive a specific piece of problem solving knowledge:

```
If increased serum calcium is present
then reduce the dose of digitalis.
```

As the program writer creates the expert system, the design decisions it makes are recorded in the design history. For each goal that is posted, the design history records the following information:

- the plans that were found as candidates for implementing the goal.

- the plans that were attempted but failed to implement the goal, and the reasons for the failure

- any reformulations that were performed

- domain facts and terminology definitions involved

- the plan that actually implemented the goal, and

- the subgoals that were posted as a result of instantiating the plan

This recorded structure provides EES with the knowledge needed to provide richer explanations and justifications.

We have used the EES approach to implement demonstration-sized expert systems in four domains. We are currently in the process of selecting a domain for a much larger expert system.

5. Summary

Let us return briefly to the question of how to represent the statement "smoking causes lung cancer." Explanation concerns can help us decide. If we find that experts seem to talk about the relation as a simple link, without qualification, then a relational representation will suffice:

```
CAUSES(SMOKING, LUNG-CANCER)
```

On the other hand, if they frequently talk *about* the causal relation or qualify it, then representation as a concept with attributes is appropriate:

```
[CAUSE-47 (specializes CAUSE)
   CAUSER: SMOKING
   CAUSEE: LUNG-CANCER]
```

The third alternative of collapsing the relation into atomic concepts focusing on the disease and symptom is probably not a good representation because it involves the use of "mega-concepts."

The creation of a knowledge base is an under-constrained problem. Representations that initially appear to be valid often turn out to be incorrect, leading to the need to constantly revise a knowledge representation. In this paper we have argued that explanation concerns can provide guidance that tends to reduce the need to re-structure a knowledge base as an expert system evolves. We identified constraints that can be applied after the knowledge base is constructed to identify potential weak points, and ones that can be used while the knowledge base is being created to forestall later problems.

Acknowledgments

The research described here was supported under DARPA Grant #MDA 903-81-C-0335. We wish to thank Robert Neches and Johanna Moore for their significant contributions to the EES framework. We also wish to thank Robert Balzer, Lewis Johnson and David Wile for discussions and suggestions that contributed to our research.

References

[Clancey 83] Clancey, W., "The Epistemology of a Rule-Based Expert System: A Framework for Explanation ," *Artificial Intelligence* 20, (3), 1983, 215-251. Also in *Rule-Based Expert Systems: The MYCIN Experiments of the Stanford Heuristic Programming Project*, Buchanan, B., and Shortliffe, E., (eds.), Addison-Wesley, 1984.

[Dahl, Dijkstra and Hoare 72] Dahl, O.J., Dijkstra, E.W. and Hoare, C.A.R., *Structured Programming*, Academic Press, 1972.

[Davis, Buchanan, and Shortliffe 85] Davis, R., Buchanan, B, and Shortliffe, E., "Production Rules as a Representation for a Knowledge-Based Consultation Program," in Brachman, R. J., and Levesque, H. J. (eds.), *Readings in Knowledge Representation*, pp. 372-387, Morgan Kaufmann, Los Altos, CA, 1985.

[Fillmore 68] Fillmore, C., "The Case for Case," in Bach, E., and Harms, R. (eds.), *Universals in Linguistic Theory*, Holt, Rinehart and Winston, 1968.

[Neches, Swartout, and Moore 85] Neches, R., Swartout, W. R., and Moore, J. D., "Enhanced Maintenance and Explanation of Expert Systems Through Explicit Models of Their Development," *IEEE Transactions on Software Engineering* SE-11, (11), November 1985, 1337-1351.

[Sowa 84] Sowa, J. F., *Conceptual Structures: Information Processing in Mind and Machine*, Addison-Wesley, Reading, MA, 1984.

[Swartout 77] Swartout, W., "A Digitalis Therapy Advisor With Explanations," in *Proceedings of the Fifth International Conference on Artificial Intelligence*, pp. 819-825, Cambridge, MA., 1977.

[Swartout 83] Swartout, W., "XPLAIN: A System for Creating and Explaining Expert Consulting Systems," *Artificial Intelligence* 21, (3), September 1983, 285-325. Also available as ISI/RS-83-4

[Swartout and Neches 86] Swartout, W. and R. Neches, "The Shifting Terminological Space: An Impediment to Evolvability," in *Proceedings of the National Conference on Artificial Intelligence*, 1986.

[Swartout and Smoliar 87] Swartout, W., and S. W. Smoliar, "Explaining the Link Between Causal Reasoning and Expert Behavior," in *Proceedings of the Symposium on Computer Applications in Medical Care*, Washington, D. C., November 1987. Also to appear in *Topics in Medical Artificial Intelligence*, Miller, P.L. (ed.), Springer-Verlag, 1988.

(RE)PRESENTATION ISSUES
in
SECOND GENERATION EXPERT SYSTEMS

Walter Van de Velde

Artificial Intelligence Laboratory
Vrije Universiteit Brussel
Pleinlaan 2
B-1050 Brussels

ABSTRACT

This paper discusses representation issues for second generation expert systems. It provides a simple conceptual architecture of a second generation expert system. The realization of the model into an actual system requires several decisions to be taken. In the paper we illustrate how this has been done for a prototype second generation expert system called CONCLAVE. We discuss how a structural model of a domain is used for reasoning and indexing of knowledge gained from experience.

1. Introduction

This paper discusses some representation issues for second generation expert systems. In the first part I draw the overall sketch of a second generation expert system. The goal is to provide a framework which is simple, yet powerful enough to reveal the important characteristics of such a system. Moreover, discussion of these *presentational aspects* allows to clearly specify what has to be represented in an actual second generation expert system.

The second part deals with *representational aspects*. Actual implementation of a second generation expert system requires several decisions to be taken on how to represent and organize knowledge in accordance with the presentational sketch. It can be seen as part of the role of expert system technology to bridge the gap between the presentational and the representational level. It is shown how this is done for CONCLAVE, a prototype second generation expert system for the diagnosis of technical devices. The main contribution is to show how structural domain knowledge may be used, not only for problem solving, but also to generate rich abstraction hierarchies which are used for indexing learned knowledge. Its importance goes beyond the specific application in CONCLAVE, since it generalizes to any system in which deep models are constructed through specialization and composition of (abstract) components.

This research is supported by IWONL contract No. 4465, and a European COST-13 grant, project 19 on *Machine learning and knowledge acquisition*.

A formal and more thorough treatment of most of these issues may be found in [Van de Velde 88]. Admittedly, in this paper I rely a lot on the intuitions of the reader. CONCLAVE is implemented in KRS ([Van Marcke 88]), an object oriented knowledge representation system. The remainder is occasionally illustrated with KRS code. Its meaning is hoped to be straightforward.

1.1. Background: Second generation expert systems

Second generation expert systems (introduced in [Steels 84]) are an attempt to overcome the limitations of classical rule based ('heuristics only') expert systems. Many of these limitations can be traced back to lack of deeper knowledge at two levels (figure 1):

- *Problem solving knowledge*: an if-then rule implicitly encodes strategic knowledge. A body of rules exhibits a non-psychological strategy. Implicitly coded strategy decreases rule independence and knowledge base modularity. (see e.g. [Clancey 83]).

- *Domain knowledge*: the scope of heuristic rules is unknown as the underlying principles are not represented. It is not obvious when exactly an action applies, nor when a rule can be violated. Abrupt failure occurs when heuristics fail, for lack of knowledge to fall back on [Davis 82].

HEURISTIC RULE = DOMAIN KNOWLEDGE + PROBLEM SOLVING KNOWLEDGE

Fig. 1. Heuristic knowledge is but the surface of a complex underlying knowledge structures (from [Steels 87]). Second generation expert systems make all (more) of these explicit.

Second generation expert systems incorporate extra knowledge of both types. Deep knowledge is a primary source of power for a second generation expert systems. Practical problems (e.g. combinatorial explosion, time constraints) and epistemological factors (e.g. uncertainty, incompleteness) impose limitations on the usefulness of this deep reasoning. These are overcome by a suited inference strategy, and by a body of shallow knowledge. The latter is used whenever adequate, and reflects the conclusions from previous deep reasoning sessions. This is also the point where the learning comes in (e.g. [Van de Velde 88]).

1.2. An example: CONCLAVE

CONCLAVE is a prototype second generation expert system for the diagnosis of technical devices, like train engines, computer programs or power plants. A diagnostic problem consists of an indication of a discrepancy between observed and expected behavior of some device. The goal of problem solving is to find a diagnosis, that is an indication of one or more discrepancies between the actual and expected structure of the device, which, when present, cause the observed behavior to occur.

In its architecture CONCLAVE realizes a principled combination of deep and shallow reasoning. It contains the necessary machinery for diagnostic reasoning from first principles about technical devices (*constructive problem solving*), for acquiring experience on diagnosing them (*learning through progressive refinement*), and for using the accumulated experiencial knowledge (*classification problem solving*).

In CONCLAVE, constructive problem solving is based on a causal model of a device (figure 2). A causal model expresses paths of interaction between properties which describe aspects of a device. It can be used for diagnostic reasoning ([Van de Velde 85,88]), in much the same way as in the work of DeKleer and Williams (87) or Reiter (87). In CONCLAVE, the causal model is obtained from a structural model. The latter in turn is constructed by specializing and composing models of more primitive devices in ever more complex structures. For example, the model of a car may be composed of models of an engine, battery, lights, wires, etc. A store of such models is available in a concept library. Moreover, the structure of devices induces abstraction hierarchies on problems and solutions. These are used to index the problem solving knowledge gained from experience.

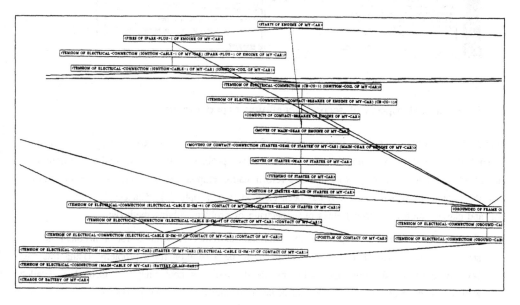

Fig. 2. Part of a causal model of the ignition function of a two-cylinder car, based on [Olyslager 72].

Figure 3 shows CONCLAVE's interface after a number of experience. The top window displays one of a number of heuristic rules which have been learned for repairing malfunctioning cars. These are used whenever possible, that is whenever the anomaly which is explained (displayed in the focus window middle-left) corresponds to the primary symptom of the rule, and the logical condition the association expresses is satisfied (*goal-directed rule invocation*, as in ACT* [Anderson 83]).

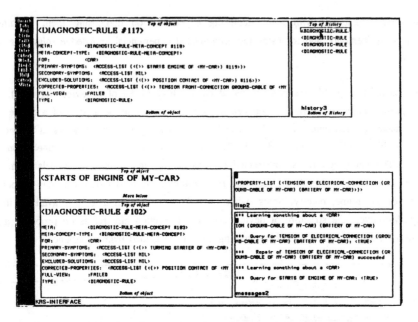

Fig. 3. CONCLAVE's interface after a number of experiences.

2. Presentational aspects of second generation expert systems

This section describes a simple abstract model of a second generation expert system. In the proposed framework deep reasoning is seen as constructive problem solving, and shallow reasoning as classification problem solving. Note that this reformulation emphasizes the reasoning *methods*, rather than the knowledge which is used. It has been claimed (a.o. [Pople 75], [Clancey 85]) that construction and classification are two extremes of a spectrum of problem solving methods:

- Constructive problem solving is at the 'rational' extreme. A solution for a problem is constructed based on knowledge of what it means to be a solution for a problem. Using this vast body of background knowledge, solutions are derived - without 'magic' - through a detailed analysis of the problem's structure, and pedantic assembly of bits and pieces.

- Classification problem solving is at the 'lazy' extreme of the spectrum. Solutions are predicted - by 'jumping-to-conclusions' - rather than rationally constructed. Predictive knowledge consists of a set of associations between problem and solution abstractions. Any problem (partially) described by the problem abstraction, is assumed to have a solution which is (partially) described by the associated solution abstraction.

The role of classification is to indicate a solution if it can, otherwise to narrow down the set of possible solutions so that construction can be intelligently focussed. This mechanism is put to use for each problem and subproblem the constructive problem solver may generate. The resulting hybrid behavior is closer to one extreme or the other depending on the 'predictive' power of the problem solver, thaty is, the effectiveness of classification.

2.1. Problem solving framework

A problem solver is viewed as a computational representation of a 'solution' relation between 'problems' and 'solutions'. Rarely this relation is explicitly known as a set of problem-solution pairs. Instead, it is decomposed through a structure of relations among problems, solutions, and any other type of object involved. The scheme of *inferential types* and *inferential relations* constitutes the *inference structure* of the method. A problem solver constructs a path through its inference structure from a problem to its solution. Additional knowledge is needed to recognize actual solution paths (i.e. leading to a solution for the problem) from mere inference paths.

The concept of inference structure is not new. For example, it occurs in [Clancey 85] to describe heuristic classification, in KADS [Breuker 85] as a guide for knowledge ellicitation and to describe the domain dependent reasoning patterns of expert systems, in [Tao, et al. 87] to formally estimate the performance of an expert system in the early stages of its development. However, the concept of inference structure has not been used as a general basis to describe problem solving methods.

Definition 2.1. A *problem domain* is a triple $\Omega = (P,S,Solution)$, where
P is the set of *problems* in Ω,
S is the set of possible *solutions* in Ω,
Solution is a relation between P and S, i.e. Solution $\subset$ P×S.
A *solution* for a problem p is any s in S such that Solution(p,s) holds. A problem p is *solvable* if it has at least one solution.

Usually problems can not be directly linked to their solutions. The problem solver then has to relate problems to their solutions in several steps. To express this I define the decomposition of a relation:

Definition 2.2. A *decomposition* of a binary relation R on sets A and B, consists of a number of sets E_i (i=1...n), with $E_0 = A$, $E_n = B$, and binary relations R_j (j=1...m) between some of these, such that R $\subset$ $\bigcup_j R_j \cup R_j^{-1}$.

Definition 2.3. An *inference structure* for a problem domain (P,S,Solution) is a decomposition of the Solution relation. The sets in the decomposition are called the *inferential primitives*, the relations *inferential relations* of the inference structure.

Notation: (Ω, E_i, R_j) denotes an inference structure for the problem domain Ω, with inferential types E_i (i=0...n), and inferential relations R_j (j=1...m). Since the exact values of n and m are seldom relevant, they are not mentioned in the notation.

Definition 2.4. A *problem solver* ρ for a problem domain $\Omega = (P,S,Solution)$ is specified by:
an *inference structure* (Ω, E_i, R_j),
a *competence theory* relating the relations R_j to the Solution relation.

Definition 2.5. An _inference path_ of $\wp$ with inference structure (Ω, E_i, R_j) is a sequence $(e_0, \ldots, e_r)$ such that each pair (e_{k-1}, e_k), $(k=1\ldots r)$ is in $\bigcup R_j \cup R_j^{-1}$.

A _solution path_ for a problem p is an inference path from p to one of its solutions.

A competence theory is thus a logical theory which uses the inferential relations to prove some instances of the Solution relation true. A problem solver uses this knowledge to find a solution path for any problem in its domain.

The definition of a problem solver may be used as the basis for discussing issues of competence and performance. The competence domain of a problem solver is the set of pairs in the Solution relation which it can in principle relate through a solution path:

Definition 2.6. The _competence domain_ $\langle \wp \rangle$ of a problem solver $\wp$ for a problem domain (P,S,Solution) is defined as follows:

$$\langle \wp \rangle = \{(p,s)\in P\times S \mid =_{\wp} \text{Solution}(p,s)\}$$

Finally, the complexity of an inference structure may be used to estimate the performance of the problem solver, based on such parameters as the number, size and characteristics of the inferential relations, the branching factor and the average length and the number of solution paths (comparable to [Tao, et al. 87]).

2.2. Constructive problem solving

Definition 2.7. A _constructive problem solver_ is specified by an inference structure with _problems_ P and _solutions_ S as inferential primitives, and as inferential relations:

Transformation$_i$, $(i=1\ldots n)$, binary relations between problems,

Primitive $\subset$ Solution,

Construction$_j$, $(j=1\ldots m)$, binary relations between solutions,

which it uses according to the following _construction axioms_ (for some pairs (i,j)):

$\forall p_1, p_2 \in P$; $\forall s_1, s_2 \in S$: Transformation$_i(p_1,p_2)$ $\wedge$ Solution(p_2,s_2) $\wedge$ Construction$_j(s_2,s_1)$ $\Rightarrow$ Solution(p_1,s_1)

The essence of constructive problem solving is that knowledge is present on how related problems have related solutions. More precisely, a solution s_1 for a problem p_1 can be constructed from the solution s_2 for a transformation p_2 of p_1 (figure 4(a)). Figure 4(b) shows the inference structure for constructive problem solving. The fact that there are inferential relations between elements of a single inferential type allows inference paths of arbitrary length. Obviously this has a negative impact on the expected performance.

From an analysis of the above formalization, it follows that the competence domain of a constructive problem solver is often explicitly known, but its performance depends on algorithms for efficiently exploring large search spaces for optimal or nearly optimal solutions. Unfortunately, for many problems the search space of possible transformations is just too large for exhaustive exploration (e.g.

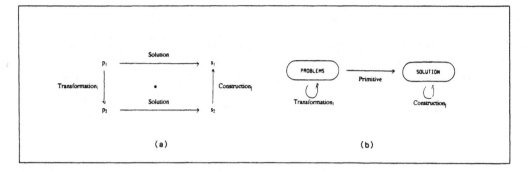

Fig. 4. Constructive problem solving.

Rubik's Cube, $4 \cdot 10^{19}$ states; or the 15-puzzle, about 10^{12} states). Moreover, the non-serializable problems ([Korf 85]) make it difficult to find local pruning criteria or search directives. Thus, competence of constructive problem solving is high, but performance may be unacceptable.

2.3. Classification problem solving

Notation: Let Δ_P be an abstraction hierarchy (boolean algebra of predicate expressions, [Touretsky 86]) on P with generalization relation $\leq_P$ (from specific to general). Δ_S is an abstraction hierarchy on S, with generalization relation $\leq_S$.
The set $\Delta_P \times \Delta_S$ of *associations* is denoted by Δ. Small Greek characters $(\alpha, \beta, \ldots)$ refer to associations. I write α_P for the problem abstraction of an association α, and α_S for its solution abstraction. Thus, we have $\alpha = (\alpha_P, \alpha_S)$.

Definition 2.8. A *classification problem solver* is specified by an inference structure with as inferential primitives *problems* P, *solutions* S, and:
   problem abstractions in an abstraction hierarchy Δ_P,
   solution abstractions in an abstraction hierarchy Δ_S,
and as inferential relations:
   Abstraction $= \{(p, \alpha_P) \in P \times \Delta_P \mid \alpha_P(p)\}$
   Match $\subset \Delta_P \times \Delta_S$,
   Refinement $= \{(\alpha_S, s) \in \Delta_S \times S \mid \alpha_S(s)\}$
which it uses according to the following *classification axiom*:
$$\forall p \in P; \ \forall \alpha \in \text{Match}: \ \alpha_P(p) \Rightarrow (\exists s \in S: \alpha_S(s) \land \text{Solution}(p,s))$$

Figure 5(b) shows the inference structure of the method. The pairs in the Match relation are called *associations*. Each association is such that, for each problem in its problem abstraction, the solution is known to be in the associated solution abstraction (figure 5(a)).

An important characteristic of classification problem solving is the weakness of the knowledge to distinguish solution paths from non-solution paths. The best that can be done is to limit the number of

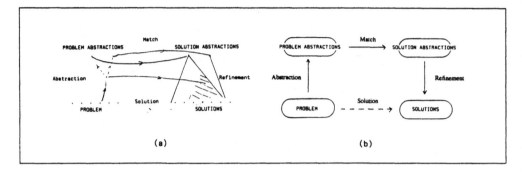

Fig. 5. Classification problem solving.

possible solutions. I will further assume that the following holds:

Single solution hypothesis: a classification problem solver finds at most one solution for each problem in its problem domain.

This hypothesis does **not** mean that each problem has at most one solution. It only says that a problem is 'in at most one way' in the competence domain of a classification problem solver. The single solution hypothesis is important because it allows an additional reasoning principle:

Reasoning principle (under single solution hypothesis): if a solution is known to exist in multiple solution abstractions then it is known to exist in the intersection of those.

Using this reasoning principle a classification problem solver may narrow down the set of possible solutions as much as possible. The differential of a problem is as far as it can get:

Definition 2.9. The *differential* Diff(Match,p) in a relation Match$\subset \Delta$ of a problem p is defined as follows:

$$\text{Diff(Match,p)} = \bigcap_{a \in \text{Match}, p \in a_p} a_S$$

A classification problem solver can do no more than reduce the set of possible solutions for a problem. If the number of possible solutions can be sufficiently reduced, exhaustive search of the differential may be possible (i.e. generate and test). Sometimes some rule of preference may be used to select one of the remaining possible solutions. Moreover, it is not always necessary to reduce the differential to a singleton. For example, in technical diagnosis the explanation for a malfunction has to be refined only as far as to distinguish between alternative repairs. Thus, though the competence of a classification problem solver is weak stricktly speaking, its partial results are useful, while performance is no problem.

2.4. Construction and classification combined

Classification and construction are perfect complements in terms of competence and performance. This explains why they have been described as extremes of a spectrum of problem solving methods. A combination of both may be expected to take the best of both worlds. The resulting inference structure is shown in figure 7.

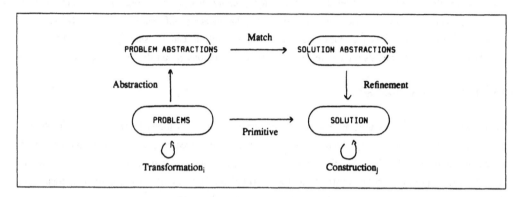

Fig. 7. The inference structures for constructive and classificatory problem solving can be combined. The solution for a problem may be found through a constructive, a classificatory, or a hybrid inference path.

Combination of competence theories has many advantages. Increased competence is the most obvious one. But the important advantage is one of *redundancy*: there may exist multiple solution paths for a single problem. This may be exploited in several ways:

Result caching: classificatory solution paths may be seen as convenient shortcuts for constructive solution paths. Instead of redoing a constructive search for previously encountered problems, classificatory solution paths are preferably used.

Intelligent focusing: classification may fail to narrow down the differential to a single problem, but it may arrive at useful partial results. Construction problem solving may benefit from these by focusing the search towards elements in these solution classes. Also, problems which are solvable by classification may serve as alternative targets for transformation in a hypothesis-directed inference strategy, thus virtually enriching the Primitive relation.

Flexible modality: construction and classification use different kinds of knowledge. Construction is *rational* and may be preferred if correctness of the answer is critical. Classification is *practical* and may be used if efficiency is important and errors can be easily detected and recovered from. A solution which is found by classification can be verified or explained by construction.

These advantages are closely related to the *cognitive economy* of intelligent systems. *'Cognitive economy is the degree to which a program is adapted to its environment'* ([Lenat 79]). The combination of construction and classification in one problem solver indicates a way to realize this in a principled way. For comparison, two things are worth mentioning.

- ✓ First, the approach unifies caching of computed results (*intelligent redundancy*) and expectation-filtering (*intelligent focus of attention*) in a single mechanism: preference for classificatory solution paths.

- ✓ Second, the use of multiple levels of abstraction (*intelligent knowledge organization*) turns out to be a central feature of the system. For one, classificatory inference paths can be seen as abstractions of constructive ones. But more importantly, it can be shown that the abstraction hierarchies induce an abstraction relation between associations ([Van de Velde 88]).

2.5. Learning from experience

Acquiring experience is viewed as learning to predict acceptable solutions for the relevant problems in an environment. Thus, the problem solver aims at acquiring predictive associations, the choice of which is ultimately justified by the usefulness for practical problem solving. As a result, if classification is preferred over construction (the 'normal' modality of the problem solver), then construction will become less important for practical problem solving (figure 8).

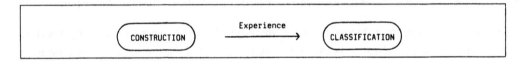

Fig. 8. With experience problem solving behavior changes from construction to classification.

The goal of learning may be paraphrased as bringing the problem solver in tune with the environment it is working in. It is thus highly dependent on the characteristics of the environment. If the environment changes then any learned information may be useless (*stability*). Rich environments may be more difficult to learn about (*diversity*), while in some environments the verification of solutions may be impossible or risky (*criticality*). Finally, the amount of *background knowledge* available considerably affects the learning situation.

A major concern of any learning theory is to understand the different qualities of alternative solutions to the learning goal, and the way in which these qualities are related to the characteristics of the environment. Michalski [86] discusses three criteria for evaluating the quality of a learned representation. *Correctness* refers to the degree of accuracy with which the representation fits the reality. It characterizes the precision of the mapping between the reality and the representation. *Effectiveness* attempts to capture the performance aspect of learning. It characterizes the usefulness of the representation for achieving a given purpose or goal. The more effective the representation, the better the performance of the system. *Abstraction level* reflects the scope, detail and precision of concepts used in the description. It defines the explanatory power of the representation.

Each of these criteria - correctness, effectiveness, abstraction level - is easily interpreted as an ordering on the set of associations (see [Van de Velde 88] for definitions). From their analysis it follows that they express largely incompatible concerns. The *bias* of a learning method ([Utgoff 84]) is a preference criterion on associations, which may be understood as preference for maximization in one of these orderings. For example explanation based generalisation ([Mitchell 86]) looks for the most effective association which is still correct. It finds this by using background knowledge. In the absence of background knowledge, it becomes simple caching. This form of learning however does not exploit the opportunities to maximize effectiveness when the environment is non-divers or non-critical.

Learning through progressive refinement (LPR) is the learning technique used in CONCLAVE. It also maximizes effectiveness, and keeps correctness as high as possible but only on the set of *practically relevant* problems. LPR follows an incremental and evolutionary learning scenario. First, the predictive knowledge - if any - is put to use on some relevant problem. If this is successful there is no need to learn. Failure can be due to the absence of an applicable association, or to an incomplete or unacceptable conclusion from applicable associations. Whenever this happens a full solution is obtained by construction. Learning then proceeds in two phases (figure 9):

- *Abstraction*: first the new problem-solution pair is reformulated as a predictive association, without considering those that were previously learned. This phase is a *deliberate overgeneralization*, but yields a very effective and abstract association.

- *Integration*: here the new association is added to the set of already existing ones. These are appropriately refined to cope with the new problem, as well as all the old ones. Integration is a phase of *forced specialization* which is responsible for keeping the set of associations practically consistent.

After a number of experiences, the overly general abstractions will be specialized just enough to correctly predict solutions for most practical problems, yet still general enough to make powerful inferential leaps in a wide variety of cases. This works best in a non-critical and non-divers environment.

2.6. Conclusion

A simple but powerful framework allows one to concisely formulate and reason about many problems and opportunities in second generation expert systems. Problem solving is viewed as an intelligent combination of construction and classification. The goal of learning, the spectrum of alternative solutions for it, and the merits of corresponding learning methods with respect to characteristics of the problem solving environment may be understood in the terms of this framework. This framework allows to express and reason about most of the important issues and opportunities in second generation expert systems.

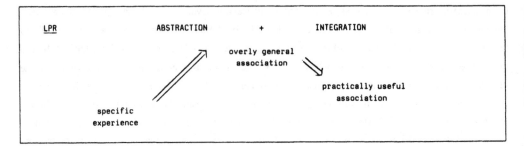

Fig. 9. Learning through progressive refinement proceeds in two phases. Abstraction is deliberate drastic overgeneralization of a specific experience. Integration is forced specialization of overly general associations.

3. The representational aspects of CONCLAVE

The problem solving and learning framework which has been described in the previous section specifies the kinds of things that need to be represented in a second generation expert system. The major goals of knowledge representation in such a system are the following:

- Support easy construction of domain models, in particular of the causal models used in CONCLAVE.

- Explain the relation between the representation of problems (resp. solutions) and problem abstractions (resp. solution abstractions).

- Provide flexibility for incremental construction of associations (abstraction and integration in learning through progressive refinement).

In this section it is shown how a structural model of a technical device serves as the basis for the representations in CONCLAVE. In particular it is shown how structure serves as a template for causal models, how it induces rich abstraction hierarchies on problems and solutions, and how the abstraction and integration are interpreted in terms of these abstraction hierarchies. These representation techniques generalize to any system in which deep models are constructed by specialization and composition of abstract components.

3.1. Structural and causal models in CONCLAVE

A *deep model* is intended to capture factual information about a domain. It consists of (abstract) *components* and *connections* between these (after [Bobrow 84]). Components are described by *properties*. Their values define the state of the components. The behavior of a component is a constraint on the states it can assume. A connection is an inter-component constraint. The possible states of the model follow solely from the interaction between the components through the connections specified (*principle of locality*). The constraints are *factual*. This means that they are known to hold under well defined assumptions (*environmental assumptions*). Thus, a deep model may be used to predict the behavior of the domain if the environmental assumptions hold (compare with heuristic knowledge!).

A *structural model* is a deep model which expresses physical connectivity of entities. The components of a structural model are physical parts of some system. Connections merely express that there is a physical connection between these parts. The components in a structural model for a technical system are *devices*. Each device has a number of distinguished slots to represent the connections. *Connections* are modelled as objects themselves (i.e. a dual representation). Devices and connections are described by *properties*. A library of devices and connections forms the basis for the construction of larger devices. Two means are available to construct models: *specialization* and *composition*.

- *Specialization*: a description is specialized, e.g. by adding or renaming properties, or specializing one of its models.

- *Composition*: a device is modelled by composing by means of connections, the models of other devices, its *subparts*.

A *causal model* is an extremely simple deep model. Its components are properties (or described by a single property) and have no behavior. A connection simply expresses that there is a constraint. Thus, change of one property changes an effect of it, assuming the connection is realized in the artifact which is modelled. The exact nature of the constraint is left open (*causality abstraction*). Then, no information is kept on which properties describe which components (*structural abstraction*), neither what is the exact nature of a property as a descriptor of aspects of the system (*property abstraction*).

Constructing a causal model from scratch is difficult and not practical. A realistic causal model may easily grow to contain a few thousand of properties (be it with a connectivity which is typically small). Remote parts of the model may represent similar mechanisms. Decisions need constantly be taken on how to represent certain aspects of a device, or even whether to represent them at all. Care has to be taken that these decisions are consistently enforced throughout the model. This is realized by taking a structural model as template for the construction of the causal model.

Only the properties of a device and its connections may be involved in a causal model of that device. Any other causal relation would violate the principle of locality. The properties of connections take part in the causal models of the devices they connect. All the causes of a property of a connection may be found by looking at the causal models of the devices it connects, and collecting the causes of it in these models. In a similar manner, the effects of a property may be found. Thus, it is sufficient to provide causal models for the primitive devices in the device library. The causal model of a complex device is then derived from its structural model.

3.1.1. Basic concepts

Devices and connections are the basic entities in a structural model. They are both described by one or several properties. Devices have a list of connections. A connection has a list of devices which it connects (its connects-what).

```
(defconcept STRUCTURAL-ENTITY)

(defconcept DEVICE
  (a structural-entity
    (properties (a property-list))
    (connections (a concept-list))
    (generalisations (a concept-list))
    (subpart-hierarchy (a concept-list))))

(defconcept CONNECTION
  (a structural-entity
    (properties (a property-list))
    (connects-what (a concept-list))))
```

A property has an observed-value and an expected-value. These are used to compute its observed-normality. Diagnostic reasoning (based on [Van de Velde 85]) is done entirely in terms of <normal> and <anomalous> values of properties. This decouples the finding of expected values from the construction of an explanation (as in [DeKleer and Williams 87]). The 'describes-what' subject holds the device or connection that is described by the property.

```
(defconcept PROPERTY
  (describes-what (a structural-entity))
  (observed-value (a value))
  (expected-value (a value))
  ((observed-normality
    (definition
      (a conditional
        (condition (>> (same (>> observed-value)) expected-value))
        (if-true normal)
        (if-false anomalous)
        (otherwise unknown))))))
```

A causal model is a binary relation. It is modelled as a set of causal links between properties:

```
(defconcept CAUSAL-MODEL
  (a relation
    (each-member (a effect-link))))

(defconcept EFFECT-LINK
  (a pair
    (cause (a property))
    (effect (a property))
    (definition [form (list (>> cause) (>> effect))])))
```

A property has a causes and an effects subject. The computation of the causes and effects is different depending on whether the property describes a device or a connection, and is therefore delegated to these.

```
(defsubject CAUSES of PROPERTY
  (>> (causes (>>)) describes-what))

(define-subject CAUSES of DEVICE
  (a subject
    (arguments [args ?property])
    (definition
      (a collect-and-transform
        (collect-from (>> causal-model))
        (collect-with [variable ?causal-link])
        (collect-when [form (>> (same ?property) effect of ?causal-link)])
        (transformer [form (>> cause of ?causal-link)])))))

(define-subject CAUSES of CONNECTION
  (a subject
    (arguments [args ?property])
    (definition
      (a transform-and-append
        (transform-what (>> connects-what))
        (transform-with [variable ?device])
        (transformer [form (>> (causes ?property) of ?device)])))))
```

Similar subjects are defined to compute the effects of properties.

3.1.2. Example

Consider the circuit in figure 10. It consists of three multipliers, M_1, M_2, and M_3, and two adders, A_1 and A_2.[1] At named places it is possible to measure a value. The drawing of the circuit corresponds closely to its structural model. Adders and multipliers are the components, and the wiring the connections. Because of this close correspondence it is fairly easy to construct a model.

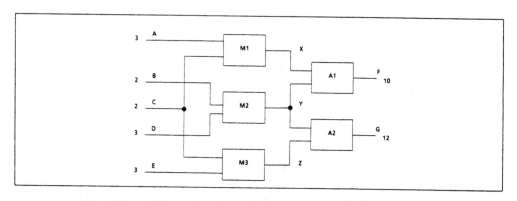

Fig. 10. A simple arithmetic circuit.

Adders and multipliers are modelled by the concept function-module. As a structural component, a function-module has three connections, in1, in2 and out. Viewed as functional entity, it computes a

---

[1] This device is used in [Davis 84], [Genesereth 84], and [DeKleer and Williams 87]. A similar one is used in [Reiter 87].

value of its out, from the values of its in1 and in2. A causal model is a simple abstraction of the functional one: the values on the inputs are the causes of the values of the outputs:

```
(defconcept FUNCTION-MODULE
  (a device
    (connections [concept-list ((>> in1) (>> in2) (>> out))]))
    (functional-view
      (a binary-function
        (inputs [concept-list ((>> value in1) (>> value in2))])
        (output (>> value out))
        ((to-compute
          (a subject
            (arguments [args ?in1 ?in2])
            (definition [form (a number)]))))))
    (causal-view
      [causal-model [effect-link (>> value in1) (>> value out)]
                    [effect-link (>> value in2) (>> value out)]])
    (in1
      (a data-connection
        (connects-what [set (>>)])))
    (in2
      (a data-connection
        (connects-what [set (>>)])))
    (out
      (a data-connection
        (connects-what [set (>>)])
        (expected-value
          (>> (to-compute (>> expected-value in1) (>> expected-value in2))
              functional-view))))))
```

Adders and multipliers are simple specializations of function-modules. Large libraries of function modules are easily constructed.

```
(defconcept ADDER
  (a function-module
    (functional-view
      ((to-compute
        (definition [form (>> (plus ?in2) of ?in1)]))))))
(defconcept MULTIPLIER
  (a function-module
    (functional-view
      ((to-compute
        (definition [form (>> (times ?in2) of ?in1)]))))))
```

Function modules communicate values through data-connections. A data-connection is described by a single property, its value. The expected value of (the value of) a connection may be calculated from the values of the inputs of the module for which the connection is an output. For example the expected value at X is the multiplication of the expected values at A and C. Some connections, like A, B, C, D and E, serve as inputs to the global circuit. We assume that their observed values are always as expected. Connections which serve as output of a circuit have no special behavior.

```
(defconcept DATA-CONNECTION
  (a connection
    (value
      (a property
        (observed-value (>> observed-value))
        (expected-value (>> expected-value))))
    ((output-of
      (a select-first
        (select-from (>> connects-what))
        (select-with [variable ?one-device])
        (selector [form (>> (same (>> out of ?one-device)))]))))
    (observed-value)
    ((expected-value
      (definition
        [form (clet ((?first-in (>> expected-value in1 output-of))
                     (?second-in (>> expected-value in2 output-of)))
                (>> (to-compute ?first-in ?second-in)
                    functional-view output-of))])))))

(defconcept INPUT-CONNECTION
  (a data-connection
    (expected-value (>> observed-value))))

(defconcept OUTPUT-CONNECTION
  (a data-connection))
```

The global circuit is described by the following concept:

```
(defconcept DEKLEER-DEVICE
  (a device
    (adder1 (a adder
              (in1 (>> x))
              (in2 (>> y))
              (out (>> f))))
    (adder2 (a adder
              (in1 (>> y))
              (in2 (>> z))
              (out (>> g))))
    (multiplier1 (a multiplier
                   (in1 (>> a))
                   (in2 (>> c))
                   (out (>> x))))
    (multiplier2 (a multiplier
                   (in1 (>> b))
                   (in2 (>> d))
                   (out (>> y))))
    (multiplier3 (a multiplier
                   (in1 (>> c))
                   (in2 (>> e))
                   (out (>> z))))
    (a (a input-connection
         (connects-what [set (>> multiplier1)])))
    (b (a input-connection
         (connects-what [set (>> multiplier2)])))
    (c (a input-connection
         (connects-what [set (>> multiplier1) (>> multiplier3)])))
    (d (a input-connection
         (connects-what [set (>> multiplier2)])))
    (e (a input-connection
         (connects-what [set (>> multiplier3)])))  ...
```

```
(f (a output-connection
     (connects-what [set (>> adder1)])))
(g (a output-connection
     (connects-what [set (>> adder2)])))
(x (a data-connection
     (connects-what [set (>> multiplier1) (>> adder1)])))
(y (a data-connection
     (connects-what [set (>> multiplier2) (>> adder1) (>> adder2)])))
(z (a data-connection
     (connects-what [set (>> multiplier3) (>> adder2)]))))))
```

Figure 11 shows the causal model of the device. It is obtained automatically from the structural model, and the causal models of the function-modules.

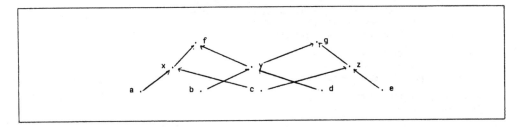

Fig. 11. The causal model of the example circuit.

Also note that, similar to the causal model, the local functional models fit together into a functional model of the device. Consider as an example the following state of the circuit (from [DeKleer 87]). The inputs are A=3, B=2, C=2, D=3, and E=3, and the outputs are measured showing that F=10 and G=12:

```
(defconcept DEKLEER-EX
  (a dekleer-device
    (a (observed-value [number 3]))
    (b (observed-value [number 2]))
    (c (observed-value [number 2]))
    (d (observed-value [number 3]))
    (e (observed-value [number 3]))
    (f (observed-value [number 10]))
    (g (observed-value [number 12])))))
```

Then a simulation is used to generate expectations for other values. For example:

```
(>> expected-value a of dekleer-ex)  -->  <number 3>
(>> expected-value f of dekleer-ex)  -->  <number 12>
(>> expected-value z of dekleer-ex)  -->  <number 6>
```

Observed normalities for properties follow from comparison with the observed value:

```
(>> observed-normality f of dekleer-ex)  --> <anomalous>
(>> observed-normality g of dekleer-ex)  --> <normal>
```

It is assumed that the values of data connections can be observed. Ease of observation is expressed in 'cost' subjects of the values of the connections. The causal reasoner prefers asking for observations which are easy to obtain.

3.2. Problems, solutions and abstractions

The first role of structural knowledge in CONCLAVE is to support the easy construction of large causal models. In this section it is shown that this is more than a knowledge engineering trick. Indeed, the structural model also accounts for the construction of rich abstraction hierarchies on problems and solutions. These abstraction hierarchies are used for indexing knowledge gained from experience in classification problem solving. The main point here is that representation decisions for problems and solutions induce representations for the abstractions thereof.

A diagnostic problem in CONCLAVE consists of a device type, an observation of some properties (contained in the device description) of an actual device of that type, and a focus, which is the property under investigation (i.e. the one which is being explained). It represents the task of explaining the normality or anomaly of the focus. Such an explanation, or diagnosis, is a list of properties which are 'malfunctioning', i.e. which disturb a chain of causal interaction.

Problem abstractions are ordered in an abstraction hierarchy which relates to the structural model of devices in several ways:

a) *Subsumption:* abstraction is made of certain features of a device. This is syntactic generalisation in which properties of a device are removed from consideration. For example, a start problem with a car of which the lights do not burn, is a start problem with a car.

b) *Type abstraction:* abstraction is made of the specific type or identity of a device. This corresponds to generalized subsumption [Buntine 86] with a type hierarchy as background knowledge. For example, a problem with spark-plug-1, is also a problem with a spark-plug, with a powered-device, or with a device.

c) *Part-of abstraction:* abstraction is made of the specific subpart structure of a device. This corresponds to generalised subsumption with a subpart hierarchy as background knowledge. For example, a problem with the left headlight of a car, is also a problem with a headlight.

Solution abstractions are obtained in much the same way. Solutions may be syntactically generalised, or abstracted through the type or subpart hierarchy of their device-type. Note that type- and subpart-abstractions may imply that certain properties need to be renamed, or even become meaningless.

3.2.1. Basic concepts

```
(defconcept DIAGNOSTIC-PROBLEM
  (device (a structural-entity))
  (focus (a property)))

(defconcept DIAGNOSIS
  (a property-list))
```

PROBLEM ABSTRACTIONS

A problem abstraction is described as a restriction on the type of the device, the normalities of its properties, or the focus of a diagnostic problem. These properties are referred to by means of their access, a form which represents an access-path. This form may be evaluated in a certain context. Accesses may be collected in an 'access-list'.

```
(defconcept PROBLEM-ABSTRACTION
  (device device)
  (primary-symptom (an access))
  (normal-properties (an access-list))
  (anomalous-properties (an access-list)))
```

The generalisation ordering ' $\leq$ ' among problem abstractions holds in each of the following cases:

a) *Subsumption:* a problem-abstraction a_P subsumes a problem-abstraction β_P (and therefore $a_P \leq \beta_P$) if both have the same device, the same primary-symptom when evaluated in context of their respective device, and the normal-properties (anomalous-properties) of a_P are a superset of those of β_P, when evaluated in context of their respective device.

b) *Type abstraction:* a problem-abstraction β_P is a type abstraction of a problem-abstraction a_P (i.e. $a_P \leq \beta_P$) if the device of a_P has the device of β_P in its type hierarchy, and the normal-properties (anomalous-properties) of a_P are a superset of those of β_P when evaluated in the context of the device of a_P.

c) *Subpart abstraction:* a problem-abstraction β_P is a subpart abstraction of a problem-abstraction a_P (i.e. $a_P \leq \beta_P$) if the device of a_P is a sub-part of the device of β_P, and the normal-properties (anomalous-properties) of a_P are a superset of those of β_P.

For all these forms of abstractions it is assumed that the accesses which are used for its formulation make sense for the device of the problem-abstraction. This may prevent certain abstractions, or require to change names of accesses (see examples). Consequently, though it may be easy to verify whether two abstractions are related in the lattice, it is not always easy to compute the abstractions of a given abstraction.

A problem abstraction describes a diagnostic problem if it is an abstraction of some problem abstraction whose device is in the type-hierarchy of the device of the diagnostic problem, whose primary-symptom yields the focus when evaluated in context of the device of the problem, and whose normal (anomalous) properties yield normal (anomalous) properties when evaluated in context of the device of the problem.

SOLUTION ABSTRACTIONS

A solution is a set of properties. An abstraction of this is specified by a device and a set of accesses.

```
(defconcept SOLUTION-ABSTRACTION
  (device device)
  (anomalies (an access-list)))
```

Solution abstractions yield a partial solution (i.e. lists of properties) when their anomalies are evaluated in a problem context, described by its device. An abstraction hierarchy similar to the one for problem abstractions exists for solution abstractions. Thus, solution abstractions are constructed by subsumption, type abstraction, and subpart abstraction.

ASSOCIATIONS

An association is a pair of problem and solution abstraction. It applies to a problem if its problem abstraction describes it. The solution is then found by evaluating the solution abstraction in context of the device of the problem. Associations will be looked at in the following form:

```
(defconcept ASSOCIATION
  (a pair
    (problem-abstraction (a problem-abstraction))
    (solution-abstraction (a solution-abstraction))
    (device (>> device problem-abstraction))
    (primary-symptom (>> primary-symptom problem-abstraction))
    (normal-properties (>> normal-properties problem-abstraction))
    (anomalous-properties (>> anomalous-properties problem-abstraction))
    (corrections (>> solution-abstraction))))
```

PROBLEM SOLVING

Associations are indexed by the device they apply to. Therefore all those which apply to the same device are grouped in a list of associations. CONCLAVE verifies its expectations following the strategy of *structural focusing*. It is summarized by the following principles:

- ✔ an anomaly with a device is expected to be a problem specific for the entire device, rather than for a subpart of it.

- ✔ an anomaly with a device is expected to be a problem specific for the actual device rather than for one of its types.

Following these principles CONCLAVE first tries the associations which are specific to the device of a problem or one of its types (in that order). Then, it looks at the largest subpart which is also described by the focus, and tries to solve the problem as if it were for that device. Thus it structurally zooms in on the focus of a diagnostic problem. This strategy of *structural focusing* is illustrated in figure 12.

3.2.2. Examples

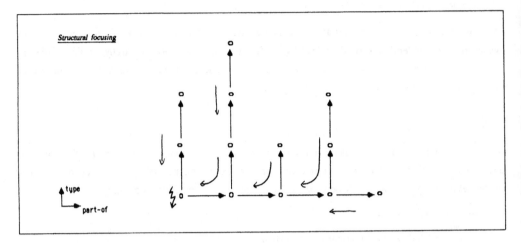

Fig. 12. CONCLAVE's strategy for retrieving associations applicable to a problem is determined by the type- and subpart-structure of the device which the focus describes.

PROBLEM ABSTRACTION

The diagnostic problem for the device in the previous example is the following:

```
(defconcept DEKLEER-PROBLEM
  (a diagnostic-problem
    (device dekleer-ex)
    (focus (>> value f of dekleer-ex))))
```

The most specific problem abstraction describing it is the following:

```
(defconcept DEKLEER-ABSTRACTION
  (a problem-abstraction
    (device dekleer-ex)
    (primary-symptom [>> value f])
    (normal-properties
      [access-list ([>> value a] [>> value b] [>> value c]
                    [>> value d] [>> value e] [>> value g])])
    (anomalous-properties
      [access-list ([>> value f])])))
```

Some abstractions of this problem abstraction:

Subsumption: this is a straightforward form of generalisation:

```
(a problem-abstraction
  (device dekleer-ex)
  (primary-symptom [>> value f])
  (normal-properties
    [access-list ([>> value a])])
  (anomalous-properties
    [access-list ([>> value f])]))
```

Note that there has to be at least a device and a primary-symptom for there to be a diagnostic problem at all. Thus, the most general abstraction through subsumption is the following:

```
(a problem-abstraction
  (device dekleer-ex)
  (primary-symptom [>> value f]))
```

Type abstraction: this is a little more complicated than subsumption. In a first step the device is generalised:

```
(a problem-abstraction
  (device dekleer-device)
  (primary-symptom [>> value f])
  (normal-properties
    [access-list ([>> value a] [>> value b] [>> value c]
                  [>> value d] [>> value e] [>> value g])])
  (anomalous-properties
    [access-list ([>> value f])]))
```

This is perfectly acceptable. However, pulling up the device one more step higher, i.e. to device, makes all accesses senseless. Therefore, the type-hierarchy of dekleer-ex does not allow a further type abstraction.

Subpart abstraction: this is the most intriguing form of abstraction. The following is an example:

```
(a problem-abstraction
  (device adder)
  (primary-symptom [>> value out]))
```

Indeed, the primary-symptom is equivalent to [>> value out adder1]. It is thus legitimate to replace the device by its 'adder1', and the primary-symptom by [>> value out]. Since there are no further subparts, no more subpart-abstraction is possible. In this case, the dekleer-abstraction may be further abstracted by a type-abstraction:

```
(a problem-abstraction
  (device function-module)
  (primary-symptom [>> value out]))
```

Further abstraction is not possible, as it then becomes impossible to express the primary-symptom.

SOLUTION ABSTRACTION

A solution to the problem with the dekleer-ex, may be the following:

```
[solution (<x of dekleer-ex> <f of dekleer-ex>)]
```

This solution may be described in various ways. The most specific description is the following:

```
(a solution-abstraction
  (device dekleer-ex)
  (anomalies [access-list ([>> value x] [>> value f])]))
```

This may be abstracted in several ways:

Subsumption

```
(a solution-abstraction
  (device dekleer-ex)]
  (anomalies [access-list ([>> value x])]))
```

Type abstraction

```
(a solution-abstraction
  (device dekleer-device)]
  (anomalies [access-list ([>> value x])]))
```

Subpart abstraction

```
(a solution-abstraction
  (device adder)
  (anomalies [access-list ([>> value in1] [>> value out])])))
```

ASSOCIATIONS

Associations are no more than pairs of problem and solution abstractions. For example, consider the following association:

```
(an association
  (problem-abstraction
    (device dekleer-device)
    (primary-symptom [>> value f])
    (normal-properties
      [access-list ([>> value a] [>> value b] [>> value c]
                    [>> value d] [>> value e])]))
  (solution-abstraction
    (device dekleer-device)
    (anomalies [access-list ([>> value x])]))))
```

This association expresses the knowledge that a diagnostic problem which is described by its problem abstraction has the value of x in the explanation (but possibly other properties as well). It is also written in the following form:

```
(an association
  (device dekleer-device)
  (primary-symptom [>> value f])
  (normal-properties
    [access-list ([>> value a] [>> value b] [>> value c]
                  [>> value d] [>> value e])])
  (corrections [access-list ([>> value x])]))
```

This association applies to the dekleer-problem. The class of solutions it describes are all explanations which contain <value x of dekleer-ex>. Note that the same effect would be obtained with the following, more abstract association:

```
(an association
  (device adder)
  (primary-symptom [>> value out])
  (corrections [access-list ([>> value in1])]))
```

This association also describes the dekleer-problem, viewed as a problem with its adder1, and thus will indicate the in1 of its adder1 as one of the culprits. This association however is more general, as it will also apply to a problem in which anomalous g would be explained by anomalous y. Of course, this association might apply to any problem, not only those with some dekleer-device.

3.3. Learning

Heuristic associations in CONCLAVE are derived from experience with constructive problem solving. The specific context of the experience has to be abstracted in order to get an association which is useful beyond the specific case from which it was learned. In CONCLAVE the device structure is used for indexing. It has to be determined with which device type a new association is to be stored. CONCLAVE uses learning through progressive refinement as learning strategy. It thus uses the abstraction hierarchies to drasticly overgeneralize a specific experience. With these hierarchies, CONCLAVE's abstraction theory amount to the following (non-factual) assumptions:

✔ An anomaly with some device which is explained once by some explanation is always explained by it.

✔ A correct association for a device that can be interpreted for its type is correct for that type. In other words, the specific identity of the device is irrelevant.

✔ A correct association for a device that can be interpreted for one of its subparts, is correct for that subpart. Thus, the way a device is embedded in a larger one is irrelevant.

Consider an example. One day, my car does not start. Some deep reasoning learns me that the battery is flat. Learning through progressive refinement tells me to learn a rule as general as possible, i.e. as if living in a world in which the only problem that will ever occur is a flat battery. But then, do I learn the rule for my car, for a Dyane, for cars, or for vehicles, or devices in general? For vehicles will not work because they do not all have a battery, and the rule would not make much sense. So we learn it for the most general generalisation for which the rule makes sense.

This is but half of the story. Take another example. The left headlight of my car does not burn, and the bulb turns out to be broken. What do I learn from this? Something for my car, or something for headlights? Or something for bulbs in general? Here the most general abstraction is obviously to lamps. The only properties involved in the formulation of the experience are properties of the lamp, so that is what we learn something for: if a lamp does not burn then it may be broken. Note however, that the braking of the lamp could be specific to left headlights in a Dyane-6. However, if for another car some light does not burn, it still makes sense to check whether the bulb is ok.

With this form of abstraction, transfer of experience is guaranteed. A device for which an association is learned may be part of several type- or subpart hierarchies, so that it will be retrieved for solving problems in totally different contexts than those in which it was learned. However, this abstraction theory almost certainly leads to drastic overgeneralization of experiences, and subsequent refinement will be required. Integration uses a factual theory based on the causal model of a device. Discrimination is not required when two associations are orthogonal, i.e. explain a different anomaly (the primary symptom). If two associations explain the same primary symptom, then CONCLAVE uses the following principles to find a discriminating property. The first two principles are used when an existing association did not apply, and therefore has some normal or anomalous property which prevented it from applying.

  ✔ if a normal property in an existing rule is anomalous in the current experience then it can be used for discrimination.

  ✔ if an anomalous property in an existing rule is normal in the current experience then it can be used for discrimination.

The other principles are used when an existing association applied but wrongly indicated a solution. They all follow from the general principle that a property which is relevant but not mentioned in an association must have been normal in the experience from which it originates, or an effect of some of the corrections.

  ✔ a correction in an existing rule which is normal in the current experience can be used for discrimination (i.e. add it as normal property to the new abstraction, as anomalous property to the old).

  ✔ a correction in the current experience which is not a correction in the existing rule may be used for discrimination unless it is an effect of some of the old corrections.

  ✔ if a correction in an existing rule is anomalous in the correct experience, but not one of the corrections then a property which explains it in the current experience can be used for discrimination.

In any case, a discriminating property can be found. Integration always succeeds by specializing problem abstractions. In case of several possibilities CONCLAVE uses the property which is cheapest to observe. In summary then, integration in CONCLAVE is causally discriminating conflicting associations, and indexing them at the abstraction level where they can still be discriminated.

3.3.1. Basic concepts

The associations which CONCLAVE acquires are all of type 'experience-abstraction', 'refined-association', or 'integrated-association', three specializations of 'association':

Experience abstraction: this is a direct abstraction of some experience.

Refined association: this is the result of adding an extra condition to an existing association which was in conflict with a new canonical abstraction.

Integrated association: this is the result of adding extra conditions to a new abstraction which was in conflict with existing ones.

An important feature of the implementation is that it exploits the KRS programming by definition style to construct new associations. For example, instead of using a procedure which computes a refinement of an association, and then creates the proper instance, it uses several types of associations which themselves have the proper subject definitions to fill in their own subjects. The result is not only a clean piece of code. In addition, each association automatically keeps its own history. For example, a refined association knows why and how it has been refined, and from what abstraction it originates.

An experience is a problem and its solution as found by the combined effort of construction and classification. It is abstracted in two steps (figure 13). First its canonical form is generated, which is the most effective but least abstract formulation of the experience under the abstraction theory mentioned above. Then, by structural abstraction, this canonical form is formulated as abstractly as possible.

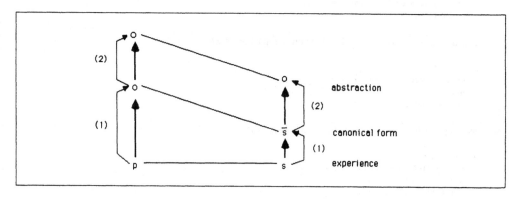

Fig. 13. An experience is abstracted in two steps to obtain a most effective and abstract description of it which is correct under the assumptions of some abstraction theory AT.

Integration of a new association in the Match-relation requires to restrict the application of the overly general associations. This is done by adding to them one or more extra conditions (normal or anomalous properties). As mentioned before, a refined association knows where it comes from, and how it is being constructed. These features are important for the generation of convincing explanations (or rather justifications) of the association's form ([Smith 85]), but are not yet fully exploited in the current system.

Instead of providing details of the implementation, the following section shows some illustrative examples of structural abstraction and integration.

3.3.2. Examples

An example of structural abstraction

Take the following example from the car domain:

```
(defconcept example-problem
   (a diagnostic-problem
      (device my-car)
      (focus (>> burns left headlights of my-car))))
```

Causal reasoning locates the malfunction in the light bulb of the left headlight:

```
(>> diagnosis of example-problem)
   --> [diagnosis (<burns left headlights of my-car>)]
```

This experience may be expressed with the single property <burns left headlights of my-car>. The most specific abstraction is therefore

```
(a association
   (device my-car)
   (primary-symptom [>> burns left headlights])
   (corrections [>> burns left headlights]))
```

This can be stated at an abstract level, using subpart-abstraction:

```
(a association
   (device <headlights of my-car>)
   (primary-symptom [>> burns left])
   (corrections [>> burns left]))
```

and one step further, again using a subpart-abstraction:

```
(a association
   (device <left headlights of my-car>)
   (primary-symptom [>> burns])
   (corrections [>> burns]))
```

Of course, no further subpart-abstraction can be made here. The abstraction hierarchies are climbed higher by two type-abstraction:

```
(a association
   (device headlight)
   (primary-symptom [>> burns])
   (corrections [>> burns]))

(a association
   (device light-bulb)
   (primary-symptom [>> burns])
   (corrections [>> burns]))
```

The next type-abstraction is more complex. It requires to take a closer look at the definition of the light-bulb:

```
(defconcept light-bulb
   (a powered-device
      ((burns
         (a synonym-subject
            (synonym-for [symbol major-effect]))))))
```

Thus, the association can be reformulated in more abstract terms:

```
(a association
  (device light-bulb)
  (primary-symptom [>> major-effect])
  (corrections [>> major-effect]))
```

Now, a final type-abstraction becomes possible:

```
(a association
  (device powered-device)
  (primary-symptom [>> major-effect])
  (corrections [>> major-effect]))
```

The type of powered-device is device, for which the property major-effect can not be interpreted. Therefore no further abstraction can be made. The final association applies to any powered-device of which the major-effect is anomalous. It locates the malfunction in the device itself, i.e. it is broken.

Thus, transfer of experience is large. The association can be applied in a lot of cases totally different from the one it was learned from. If later the lamp on my desk does not burn, it could be used to recommend to check whether the light-bulb is broken. Or, if some electro-motor does not turn, it may be malfunctioning (instead of getting no power). Clearly, experience is transferred to a lot of cases in which it fails.

An example of integration

Consider the following electrical devices:

```
(defconcept electrical-connection
  (a connection
    (properties [property-list ((>> tension))])))
(defconcept powered-device
  (a device
    (connections
      [connection-list ((>> power) (>> ground))])
    (properties
      [property-list ((>> major-effect))])
    (causal-model
      [causal-model ([causal-link (>> power) (>> major-effect)]
                     [causal-link (>> ground) (>> major-effect)])])
    (major-effect (a property))))
(defconcept switch
  (a powered-device
    (connections
      [connection-list ((>> power-in) (>> power-out))])
    (properties
      [property-list ((>> position))])
    (causal-model
      [causal-model ([causal-link (>> tension power-in) (>> tension power-out)]
                     [causal-link (>> position) (>> tension power-out)])])
    (position (a property))))
```

```
(defconcept switchable-device
  (a powered-device
    (subparts
      [device-list ((>> switch))])
    (causal-model
      [causal-model ([causal-link (>> tension power-out switch) (>> major-effect)]
                     [causal-link (>> ground) (>> major-effect)])])
    (switch
      (a switch
        (power-in (>> power)))))))
```

The causal models of powered and of switchable device are shown in figure 14.

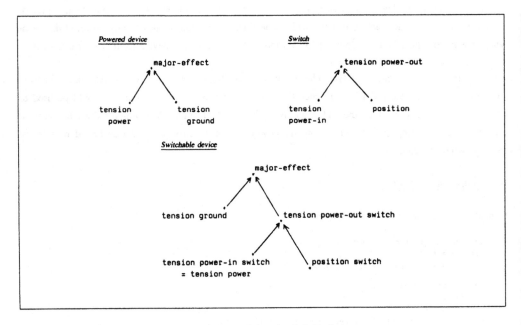

Fig. 14. The causal models of powered-device, switch and switchable-device.

Suppose the following sequence of experiences.

```
experience-1
  device: <switchable-device>
  focus: <major-effect of switchable-device>
  correction: <tension power of switchable-device>
```

The association learned herefrom is the following:

```
association-1
  abstraction-of: <experience-1>
  device: <powered-device>
  focus: [>> major-effect]
  correction: [>> tension-power]
```

With this experience tension of power will be the expected failure for every powered-device and every switchable-device. It applies to, but does not account for the following experience:

```
experience-2
  device: <switchable-device>
  focus: <major-effect of switchable-device>
  correction: <position switch of switchable-device>
```

The reconstruction of experience-1 with this new experience says that the switch must have been in the good position, or the device has no switch. In the second case, the set of associations is practically consistent because the old experience is not described by the new abstraction. For the first possibility, the property <position switch> may be used for discrimination, at the level of switchable-devices. Thus, association-1 has to be pulled down a level of abstraction for discrimination to become:

```
association-2
  device: <switchable-device>
  focus: [>> major-effect]
  normal-property: [>> position switch]
  correction: [>> tension power]
```

and the new experience becomes the following association:

```
association-3
  device: <switchable-device>
  focus: [>> major-effect]
  anomalous-property: [>> position switch]
  correction: [>> position switch]
```

Association-1 is still useful at the level of powered-device. It may still be adequate for explaining non-turning electro-motors or so. The effect is now that first the position of the switch is checked, and later the tension of the power.

Note that the same story works for part-of abstraction. The reconstruction of an experience says that either the subpart was part of another device than in this case, or of the same device but with a different explanation. For the first case, the set of associations is practically consistent as is; for the second case, the abstraction is pulled down to apply to larger devices, and causally discriminated.

If the experiences would have occurred in reverse order a similar but not quite the same result is obtained. Thus differences in the sequence of experiences may give rise to subtly different sets of associations.

3.4. Conclusion

The role of structural knowledge in CONCLAVE is threefold. First it serves as a powerful guide for knowledge acquisition. Second, it is used to support the construction of large causal models. Third, it induces rich abstraction hierarchies on problems and solutions, which may be used for indexing knowledge acquired from experience. These results generalize to any system in which deep models are constructed through specialization and composition from a library of components.

4. Conclusion

We summarize the major contributions of this paper to second generation expert systems technology:

- A simple but powerful model, based on a study of problem solving methods, illustrates the basic features of a second generation expert system.

- A structural model can be used as the basis for a second generation expert system for the diagnosis of technical devices.

With respect to knowledge representation and organization in learning systems, we tried to show the following:

- Structure-based indexing of associations is a powerful means to realize transfer of experience.

- Explicit representation of the history and role of conditions in associations is useful both for explanation and refinement.

References

Anderson, J. (1983) *The Architecture of Cognition*. Harvard University Press. Cambridge, MA.

Bobrow, D.G. (1984) Qualitative Reasoning about Physical Systems: an Introduction. In *Artificial Intelligence Journal*, 24(1-3). North Holland Pub. Amsterdam.

Breuker, B.J. and Wielinga, J.A. (1985) KADS: Structured Knowledge Acquisition for Expert Systems. In *Proceedings of the Fifth International Workshop on Expert Systems*. Avignon, France.

Clancey, W.J. (1983) The Epistemology of a Rule-Based Expert System: A Framework for Explanation. In *Artificial Intelligence Journal*, 20(3). North Holland Pub. Amsterdam.

Clancey, W.J. (1985) Heuristic Classification. In *Artificial Intelligence Journal*, 27(4). North Holland Pub. Amsterdam.

Davis, R. (1982) Expert Systems: Where are we? and Where do we go from here? AI memo 665. Massachusetts Institute of Technology. Cambridge, MA.

Davis, R. (1984) Diagnostic Reasoning Based on Structure and Behavior. In *Artificial Intelligence Journal*, 24(1-3). North Holland Pub. Amsterdam.

DeKleer, J. (1976) Local Methods of localizing faults in electronic circuits. AI memo 394, MIT. Cambridge, MA.

DeKleer, J. and Williams, B.C. (1987) Diagnosing multiple faults. In *Artificial Intelligence Journal*, 32(1). North Holland Pub. Amsterdam.

Genesereth, M.R. (1984) The Use of Design Descriptions in Automated Diagnosis. In *Artificial Intelligence Journal*, 24(1-3). North Holland Pub. Amsterdam.

Korf, R.E. (1985) Macro-operators: a Weak Method for Learning. In *Artificial Intelligence Journal*, Vol 26, number 1. North Holland Pub. Amsterdam.

Lenat, D.B., Hayes-Roth, F., Klahr, P. (1979) Cognitive Economy. Working paper, HPP-79-15. Stanford University, California.

Michalski, R.S., Carbonell, J.G. and Mitchell, T.M. (1986) *Machine Learning - An Artificial Intelligence Approach. Volume II*. Palo Alto, Tioga Publ. Co.

Mitchell, T.M., Keller, R.M., Kedar-Cabelli, S.T. (1986) Explanation-based Generalization: A Unifying View. In *Machine Learning*, Vol 1, number 1. Kluwer Academic Publishers, Boston.

Olyslager, P. (1972) Vraagbaak Dyane-6. Kluwer, Amsterdam.

Pople, H.E. et all. (1975) DIALOG: a Model of Diagnostic Logic for Internal Medicine. In *Proceedings of the Fourth International Joint Conference on Artificial Intelligence*. Tbilisi, Georgia, USSR.

Reiter, R. (1987) A theory of diagnosis from first principles. In *Artificial Intelligence Journal*, 32(1). North Holland Pub. Amsterdam.

Smith, R.G., Mitchell, T.M., Winston, H.A., Buchanan, B.G. (1985) Representation and Use of Explicit Justification for Knowledge Base Refinement. In *Proceedings of the Ninth International Joint Conference on Artificial Intelligence*. Los Angeles, California.

Steels, L. (1984) Second Generation Expert Systems. Conference on future generation computer systems, Rotterdam. Reprinted in *Future Generation Computer Systems*, 1(4), 1985. North-Holland Pub. Amsterdam.

Steels, L. (1987) The Deepening of Expert Systems. In *AI-communications*. Vol 1(1). North Holland. Amsterdam.

Tao, Y., Zhijun, H., Ruishao, Y. (1987) Performance Evaluation of the Inference Structure of Expert Systems. In *Proceedings of the Tenth International Joint Conference on Artificial Intelligence*. Milan, Italy.

Touretzky, D. (1986) The mathematics of Inheritance Systems. Morgan Kaufmann Pub., Inc., Los Altos, California.

Utgoff, P.E. (1984) *Shift of Bias for Inductive Concept Learning*. Doctoral dissertation. Rutgers University, New Brunswick, NJ.

Van de Velde, W. (1985) Naive Causal Reasoning For Diagnosis. In *Proceedings of the Fifth International Workshop on Expert Systems and their Applications*. Avignon.

Van de Velde, W. (1988) *Learning from Experience*. PhD Thesis. Also as technical report. VUB AI-Lab, Brussels.

Van Marcke, K. (1988) *The Use and Implementation of the Knowledge Representation System KRS*. PhD Thesis. Also as technical report. VUB AI-Lab, Brussels.

Some Aspects of Learning and Reorganization in an Analogical Representation

Michael Mohnhaupt, Bernd Neumann,
University of Hamburg,
Department of Computer Science,
Bodenstedtstr. 16, D-2000 Hamburg 50,
West Germany.

mohnhaupt@rz.informatik.uni-hamburg.dbp.de
neumann@rz.informatik.uni-hamburg.dbp.de

1   Introduction

This paper is concerned with learning and reorganization in an analogical representation of time-varying events. Current research in machine learning deals mainly with different aspects of acquiring knowledge for propositional representations in traditional machines (see *Michalski + Carbonell + Mitchell 83* and *Michalski + Carbonell + Mitchell 86*), or with learning problems in parallel distributed architectures (see *Rumelhart + McClelland 87*).

We discuss several aspects of learning with respect to analogical representations, because we believe in the usefulness of analogical representations for certain tasks. Theoretical considerations (see e.g. *Levesque 86, Sober 76, Palmer 78* and *Selman 87*), practical considerations (see e.g. *Larkin + Simon 87*) and experiments with the human cognitive system (see e.g. *Block 81, Kosslyn 80, Finke 85*) support this assumption.

Some aspects of categorization in our work are related to work by *Drescher 87* and *Phelps + Musgrove 85*, but our main focus is investigating learning in analogical representations.

Our representation deals with observed trajectories of moving objects. By modelling such spatio-temporal events we want to support certain tasks involving knowledge about typical object motion such as trajectory prediction. We consider this problem in the context of a natural-language guided scene analysis task where simple questions like:

Did a car turn off Schlueterstreet?

are used to initiate top-down controlled image sequence analysis. In order to control the vision processes effectively it is essential to provide knowledge about the spatio-temporal constraints implied by the verb 'turn-off' and other verbs for that matter. For a detailed discussion of the analogical representation involved in solving these problems see *Mohnhaupt + Neumann 87, Mohnhaupt 87*.

The main purpose of this paper is to describe processes, working on an analogical representation, which realize certain learning objectives. The problems we want to tackle are:

- learning a representation from examples,

- generalizing information from examples, abstracting relevant information from irrelevant details and adapting information to slightly different situations in the same environment,

- reorganizing the representation by computing analogies to solve similar problems in a different environment.

In Section 2 we discuss advantages and disadvantages of 'empirical' and 'analytic' representations. We believe that such a dichotomy is useful to distinguish between different knowledge representation schemes. Roughly speaking, in an 'empirical' representation, knowledge is seen as accumulated and abstracted from examples (concrete observations). On the other hand, we call a representation 'analytic', if it results from a theoretical model of the domain.

A representation for object motion, which we call 'Trajectory Accumulation Frame' (TAF), will be developed in Section 3. We show how concrete observations are recorded and how abstractions, generalizations and small adaptions are computed by local operations.

In Section 4 we describe ideas on reorganizing the representation in order to apply the representation to similar problems in a different context. If, for example the representation for a 'turning right' event was recorded in a particular geometric environment, we want it to be applicable to similar events involving streets of different shape. This reorganization can also be seen as computing analogies to make experience gained in a particular environment to be applicable to different geometric surroundings. Extracting invariant.event properties is very important for this kind of reorganization. We discuss the role of perceptual primitives for the computation of invariants.

Finally, Section 5 serves to summarize the main ideas and to sketch some unsolved problems.

The representation has been implemented on a Symbolics 3640 and examples are simulated to illustrate the performance of the proposed model.

2 'Empirical' and 'Analytic' Representations

Knowledge representation schemes are often characterized along different dimensions such as 'procedural' vs. 'declarative' and 'local' vs. 'distributed'. We want to point out in this section that a distinction between 'empirical' and 'analytic' might also be useful. We call a representation 'empirical' if it is accumulated and abstracted from concrete observations, whereas we call a representation 'analytic' if it is motivated by a theoretical model of the domain. To be more concrete, we turn to a clarifying example.

Let us consider the problem of predicting the path of a thrown baseball. If one knows something about elementary physics, one should be able to calculate the path without ever having seen a throw before. By using a theoretical model which takes into account the initial forces, gravitation, the initial angle of elevation, the weight of the ball and so on, one could build a representation which calculates the path of any ball, given the necessary initial data. The relevant theoretical model on which this calculation is based is a result of a careful analysis of the problem domain. Hence we call this representation 'analytic'.

On the contrary, one could solve the prediction problem in a completely different way. By observing a certain number of instances of thrown balls, one can build a representation which relies only on concrete observations and operations operating on observed data. Generalizations and abstractions are needed in cases where the current prediction situation differs from the set of stored observations. If, for example, the initial angle of elevation differs in a prediction task from the observed and stored examples, one can use some kind of interpolation or 'blurring' (generalizing the information to slightly different situations) between the two closest examples to calculate a prediction. Knowledge is seen as accumulated and abstracted from experience in this class of representations. Hence we call the representation 'empirical'.

Comparing the two different solutions, it is important to note the following:

- A theoretical analysis and therefore a complete understanding of the domain is not needed for an empirical representation, whereas for an analytic representation a theoretical understanding is a necessary precondition. One can think of many situations where a theoretical understanding is advantageous. On the other hand, there are problems which cannot be modelled theoretically, due to an overwhelming complexity or due to the lack of a theory. In both cases an empirical solution can be the only way to tackle the problem. In cases where the time constraints imposed on the problem are very hard an empirical solution may be the only way, under the assumption that it is less complex. Some kinesthetic tasks belong to this kind of problems: We doubt that a robot can walk through an unknown environment with appropriate speed, or play tennis (besides other unsolved problems), by solving the standard kinematic and dynamic equations of robot motion. We believe that in these cases an empirical solution is more adequate.

- An empirical represention may lead to an explanation how problem solving strategies have evolved through evolution. An empirical representation has a natural transition from concrete observations to accumulated experience. There is striking evidence that empirical representations are favored by biological systems, because their representations have evolved through evolution. But empirical representations are also important for technical systems, by two reasons. First, as biological systems are often very powerful and sophisticated, typical biological solutions may inspire the development of technical systems. And second, we believe that technical systems cannot solve a certain class of problems without being able to learn and act based on experience with their environment.

- A representation should reflect the perceptual capabilities, if it models parts of the visual world. An empirical representation may implicitly lead to a natural connection between visual processes and learned behavior. In an analytic represention this connection has to be formalized explicitly. A similar argument concerns the representation of prototypes. Prototypes may easily be explained as accumulated and processed observations in an empirical representation. Again, this requires careful modelling in an analytic representation.

We argued that it is useful to distinguish between analytic and empirical knowledge representation schemes. Criteria to evaluate how adequate a representation is for a certain task are still far from being clear in the knowledge representation literature. The term 'adequate' is used to say that the knowledge base should be tractable (*Levesque 86* use the word 'vivid' to characterize a certain form of adequate knowledge bases). Dimensions like procedural, declarative, analogical, propositional, local, distributed etc. help to distinguish between different representations, but do not imply adequacy criteria. Empirical is another useful characterization. It might turn out that a representation has to be empirical for a certain class of problems to be adequate.

3   Trajectory Accumulation Frames

In this section we describe a computational model for learning from observations in an analogical representation. We describe local operations to compute generalizations and abstractions of the accumulated experience. Finally, we show how to adapt the representation to constrained situations (e.g. obstacles in the street traffic domain). We introduce a TAF as the basic data structure for recording trajectories (i.e. object motions) in a fixed environment. Our domain of interest is street traffic, hence we will restrict ourselves to planar motion. TAFs can be viewed as event models for object motion.

A TAF is a four-dimensional accumulator array $C(x, y, d, v)$ covering a certain subfield of the xy-plane. For each xy-pair there are counter cells for all possible velocity vectors, each represented by direction d and speed v. The vector $S = (x\ y\ d\ v)$ describes the motion state of an object at a given time. Note that it is composed of quantities which may be perceived by the observer of a visual scene. For each object trajectory, a trace of state vectors is registered in the TAF by incrementing the associated counters. As more objects are entered, more cells (possibly the same) are incremented without discriminating between different objects.

Let us consider now the recall of individual trajectories from a TAF. Given a starting cell the obvious operation to perform is to look for a nonzero counter in the four-dimensional vicinity. This reflects the assumption that the trajectory has been continuous and sufficiently densely sampled. Hence successive state vectors must be similar. Note that not all xy-neighbors may be reached if the velocity direction is restricted to vary smoothly. Details of the prediction algorithm can be found in *Mohnhaupt 87* and *Mohnhaupt + Neumann 87*.

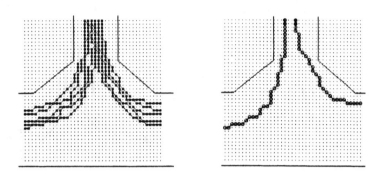

Figure 1: A TAF with ten trajectories (left). Two recalled trajectories (right)

The left illustration in Figure 1 shows the xy-projection of a TAF containing ten trajectories. Note that cells with equal xy-location but different velocities are distinct in a TAF but cannot be distinguished in the figure. The right illustration in Figure 1 illustrates the recall of two trajectories given two starting points (solid).

The number of individual trajectories that may be recalled from a single TAF depends on the similarity of the trajectories as compared with the coarseness of the quantization. Trajectories are inseparable if they meet in state space, i.e. have similar velocities at close locations. In this case the recall algorithm may continue with the 'wrong' trajectory. As we are interested in predicting typical behavior rather than individual trajectories, we do not worry about this and turn to the multiple trajectory situation.

3.1 Typical Trajectories and Prototypes

Now we consider the case where trajectory predictions are no longer determined by individual examples but depend on the experience gained from observing a possibly very large number of trajectories. We shall also introduce a blurring operation which spreads out the counter function over a local neighborhood. The combined effect of having many trajectories and of blurring will produce a counter function which is nonzero throughout the approximate area covered by the observed trajectories. Hence the TAF may be considered a four-dimensional density field with high values indicating experience supported by many observations.

In addition we shall discuss a convergence operation. This operation computes an abstraction of the current TAF by emphasizing trajectories with high probability and by suppressing trajectories with lower probability.

Traces along density maxima define a pattern of typical behavior, called the skeleton of the TAF. Predictions will essentially follow this pattern. In the remainder of this section we outline the general ideas.

Blurring:

Blurring is a generalization operation to the effect that experience represented by a counter cell is propagated to its neighbors. This is accomplished by replacing the value of each cell by the weighted average of all neighbors orthogonal to the direction of motion. Cells along the direction of motion contribute according to their positive difference.

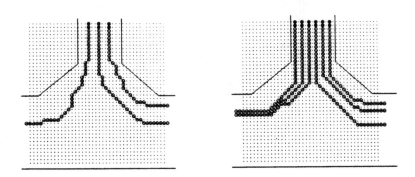

Figure 2: Predictions after single blurring (left). Predictions after triple blurring (right)

Figure 2 shows predictions after different degrees of blurring. Note that predictions are possible at coordinates where no experience was accumulated and that predictions do not necessarily follow any of the recorded individual trajectories (compare to Figure 1). The amount of blurring depends on the resolution of the representation in its different dimensions and the validity of a homogeneity criterion (blurring across the street is useful, but blurring from the street across the sidewalk should be avoided).

Convergence:

While blurring is an operation which generalizes information into the neighborhood, convergence is an operation which abstracts the most relevant information from TAFs by suppressing details and making the most important information explicit. Roughly speaking, to apply the convergence operation, each cell **S** adds weight to all neighboring cells from where the cell **S** can be reached. The weight is proportional to neighboring counter values. Therefore cells with higher values get more additional support than cells with lower values.

We show the effects of the convergence operation after discussing why skeletons play an important role for our representation.

Skeletons:

Predictions are computed by picking maximum counter value cells for successors, hence cells which are local maxima play a special part. They form a pattern of typical trajectories in the sense that they outline distinct paths which are maximally supported by experience. We call this pattern a skeleton.

Figure 3 demonstrates the different effects of the blurring and the convergence operations. The

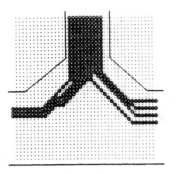 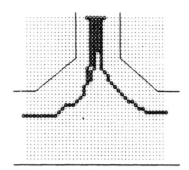

Figure 3: Skeleton of the TAF in Figure 1 (triple 'blurring'). Skeleton of the same TAF after single 'convergence' (right)

skeletons show typical behaviour regardless of starting points. The left illustration in Figure 3 shows that the blurring operation has generalized the information by propagating it into the neighborhood. After applying the convergence operation in the right illustration one obtains the skeleton that makes the most important paths explicit. It is interesting to note that the skeleton can be segmented into two conceptual clusters ('turning right' and 'turning left').

3.2 TAFs in constrained situations

Now we want to show how TAFs can be adjusted to cope with slightly different situations, e.g. situations with obstacles. We assume that obstacles were absent when the experience was accumulated. We show that a TAF is flexible enough to allow meaningful predictions in situations which are slightly different from the underlying experience.

An obstacle is a subspace of the 4-dimensional TAF where activities are not allowed, for example, due to a parking car or due to a forbidden range of velocities (in case of snow on the street). We introduce an obstacle into the TAF by setting the counter values of the appropriate subspace to zero. Then we propagate this information through the TAF by using a local inhibition operation.

Inhibition:

We inhibit a cell **S** by setting its counter value to zero under the following conditions:

- All the counter cells which can be reached from **S** are equal to zero,

- or all the counter cells from which **S** can be reached are equal to zero.

This operation is performed repeatedly for all cells until no more changes occur. Thus, one is sure that all cells which have no active predecessor or no active successor are set to zero. We demonstrate the inhibition operation with examples.

The left illustration of Figure 4 shows the TAF of Figure 1 after introducing two obstacles. The effects of the inhibition operation are visible in the right illustration. All trajectories which would pass through the obstacle are inhibited. Hence the representation is adapted to the constraint situation.

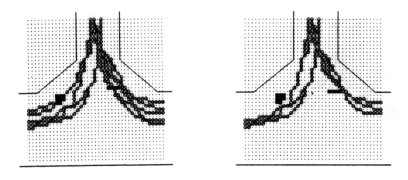

Figure 4: Skeleton for the TAF in Figure 1 with obstacles (left). The same skeleton after inhibition (right)

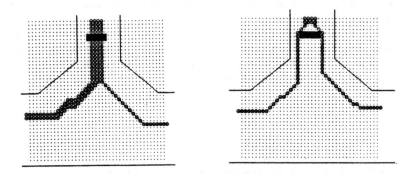

Figure 5: A skeleton with an obstacle (left). The same skeleton after inhibition (right)

The left illustration of Figure 5 shows a skeleton of a TAF after introducing an obstacle that does not allow for any of the prototypical paths. The effects of the inhibition operation are visible in the right illustration. The computed trajectories avoid the obstacle. The limits of the inhibition operation are given by the set of observed and generalized examples. If none of the stored paths allows for obstacle avoidance, a meaningful prediction is impossible.

4 Reorganizing the Representation

We now turn to consider how information derived from the experience acquired in a particular environment could be reorganized to make relevant information available when confronted with similar, albeit novel, situations. In particular, we want to make the experience accumulated at a particular street intersection applicable to another intersection with a different shape, as we cannot have direct perceptual experience for every possible geometric environment. This reorganization can also be seen as computing analogies.

4.1 Invariant event properties

The key idea is to make certain characteristic properties of an event-type explicit, where they were previously only implicit in the TAF. Thus we express descriptive properties common to all events of a given event-type, hence called invariant event properties. Such invariants form the necessary and sufficient conditions for the classification (categorization) of an event. The aim is to derive a particularly convenient set of descriptive primitives given the tasks of interest.

Invariant event properties are based on a subset of the rich repertoire of perceptual primitives exploited by perceptual systems in general. As such they help to identify events, to make predictions about, and to reason over, the visible world. Selecting invariant event properties can also be viewed as a first step from concrete image-like perceptions to more abstract (possibly propositional) descriptions. For example, they may contain predications about quantitative attributes of an event-type.

The set of invariant event properties should:

- facilitate tasks (be useful for the later stages of processing),

- be robustly and efficiently accessible from the data,

- provide a complete representation with respect to the tasks for which they are needed,

- be relatively independent.

Some of the primitives might not be independent in a strict sense. Rather independence is defined only in terms of the information explicit (see *Levesque 86*), i.e. the information accessible with little or no computation according to the primitive operations available in the system. Therefore independence means not easily derivable within the time available. For example, we would call velocity and acceleration of an object to be independent although information about the speed of an object over time contains information about its acceleration, but only implicit.

Hence, we believe that the following features constitute a useful subset of perceptual primitives for characterizing time-varying events in terms of invariants, independent of a particular geometry:

- relative orientation between different objects,

- distance between important objects,

- relative speed between different objects,

- absolute speed,

- direction of velocity relative to a reference object,

- orientation change,

- orientation change relative to a reference object.

The repertoire of perceptual primitives also contains absolute modalities like orientation and position, which are obviously not invariant over different geometries for the time-varying events we are discussing. We choose absolute speed to be in the set of possible invariant properties, however, as we assume a stationary observer.

It is interesting to note the similarity between these primitives and the primitive events proposed for bottom-up event recognition from a geometric scene description by *Neumann + Novak 83, Neumann + Novak 86, Neumann + Mohnhaupt 88*. They derive primitive events by analyzing natural language motion verbs, which are taken to define complex events. These qualitative primitives can be computed from a quantitative scene description involving exactly the same quantities as in this repertoire of perceptual primitives. Constant values (like constant velocity or constant motions), restricted values (like 'parallel', 'close to' or 'beside'), comparative values and constant derivatives (like constant acceleration) form a basic set of primitives in their framework. Their main concern is to generate a natural language description of time-varying scenes. Therefore a propositional event description based on such primitives is a useful intermediate representation. Because our goal is to use event descriptions in an image-like context, our representations looks different. Nevertheless, both cases have strong similarities with respect to the set of perceptual primitives and the process of abstraction.

After discussing the need for useful perceptual primitives, we turn now to the different computational steps necessary to reorganize the representation.

4.2 Computing the spatial analogues

The main steps necessary to reorganize the representation to compute the spatial analogues are summarized in Figure 6:

Following the four boxes in Figure 6, we discuss now how the original TAF is extended, how a generic event description is computed, and how this generic description is adapted to the new environment.

- **Event model for observed environment**

  A detailed description of the original TAF was already given in Section 3. In the case of 'turning-off', the TAF contains the dimensions (x, y, d, v). These dimensions were chosen because of their general usefulness for the description of time-varying scenes. Without knowing much about the events to be detected, the location and the velocity of the objects form a very general first description.

- **Extended event model**

  The extended event model contains the original dimensions (x, y, d, v), as well as all dimensions which could in principle be invariant for time-varying events. They are listed in Section 4.1.

  In our example we use only a reduced repertoire of perceptual primitives from which some are found to be invariant. For example, we do not consider the orientation of an object relative to a reference object as possible invariant feature because the objects are currently represented by their respective centers of mass.

  The information in the additional dimensions was already implicit in the original TAF (under the assumption that the stationary backround is known). This information is now made explicit to be able to compute generic event models.

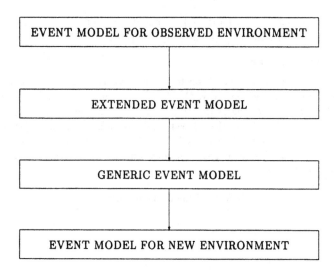

Figure 6: Transforming an event model

• **Generic event model**

The next step is to compute a generic event description by abstracting the extended event model from dimensions which vary over different event instances. In the case of 'turn-off', the spatial dimensions and the orientation of velocity are variant, because they change with the particular geometry. We choose as a first approximation the following dimensions as invariant event properties for 'turn-off' events:

− speed (v),
− relative orientation between car and sidewalk (ro),
− distance between car and sidewalk (di).

Hence, the abstracted TAF for 'turn-off' contains only the dimensions (v, ro, di). The other dimensions depend on the particular geometry of the intersection.

The abstracted information can be collected from a single geometric environment (e.g., the closest example according to some criterion) or possibly a large number of environments.

We are currently separating invariant from non-invariant dimensions interactively. In principle, this could be done automatically by observing the statistical behavior of the different dimensions over a number of observed examples, but this is left for future work.

The generic description contains data about the relative orientation between car and sidewalk and about the distance between car and sidewalk irrespective of the xy-location. This reflects the observation that these primitives are approximately constant over the intersection for a single 'turning-off' event. Therefore the generic event model stores less information than relative orientation of velocity and distance to the sidewalk for each cell (roughly speaking the values of its dimensions are 'averaged' over xy-locations). It might turn out that this description is too weak for a more detailed model, but it is a good first approximation.

- **Event model for new environment**

  Finally one has to adapt the generic information to a new instance (the new geometric environment) by reintroducing the dimensions (x, y, d), which depend now on the new intersection. The final TAF has the same dimensions as the original TAF. Each point in the TAF for the new intersection has a certain distance to the sidewalk and a certain orientation relative to the sidewalk. Its value is set according to the activity in the generic description for this combination of coordinates. After filling the new TAF, the local operations 'blurring', 'convergence' and 'inhibition' are applicable.

The following examples demonstrate the effects of the transformation:

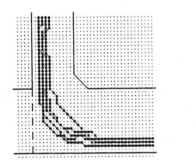 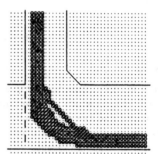

Figure 7: A TAF with five trajectories (left). Skeleton of this TAF after single 'blurring' and no 'convergence' (right)

The left illustration in Figure 7 shows the xy-projection of a TAF containing five trajectories. The right illustration shows the skeleton of the same TAF after single 'blurring'. The skeleton is not very narrow because no 'convergence' operation was applied. The 'blurring' operation spreads the information in areas where no experience was accumulated (see Section 3).

The left illustration of Figure 8 shows the skeleton of the transformed TAF obtained from the street shape in Figure 7. This is the main result in this section. Information collected in a particular environment in space-time has been transformed to be applicable in a different environment by conserving event dependent information and abstracting away irrelevant information. This figure can also be interpreted as showing the computed visualization of 'turning-right' events on intersection 2 in analogy to observed 'turning-right' events on intersection 1. The analogy is computed by using invariant event properties which were chosen from a rich set of perceptual primitives.

The right illustration in Figure 8 demonstrates the 'inhibition' operation after introducing obstacles in the transformed TAF. The local operations are applicable to image-like representations like TAFs, regardless whether they are a result of direct observation or a reorganization for a particular purpose.

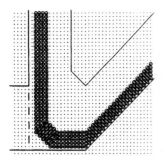 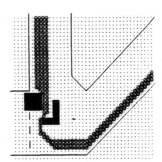

Figure 8: Skeleton of the transformed TAF (left). Skeleton after introducing obstacles and 'inhibition' (right)

5   Summary and Discussion

We have considered several aspects of learning and reorganization in analogical representations. We believe that learning, reorganizing knowledge, and having an analogical representation are essential to build an adequate representation for a certain class of perceptual and cognitive tasks.

We have introduced the dichotomy of 'empirical' vs. 'analytic' as a useful characterization of a knowledge representation scheme. A representation is empirical if the knowledge is seen as abstracted and accumulated from concrete observations, whereas a representation is analytic if it is the result of a theoretical model of the domain. An empirical representation is advantageous in various situations. It provides for a natural transition from individual examples to accumulated experience. There is no epistemological discontinuity between concrete examples and prototypical knowledge. In addition, it leads to a possible explanation how a problem solving strategy has evolved through evolution. Furthermore, there are problems which cannot be modelled in other than an empirical way, due to a lack of understanding, due to an inherent complexity or due to constraining time conditions.

A TAF and its associated local operations have been proposed as an empirical computational model for:

- learning an analogical representation from concrete observations,

- generalizing information from examples, abstracting relevant information from irrelevant details and adapting information to slightly different situations

- computing analogies by reorganizing the representation to solve similar problems in a different context.

The model has the following interesting properties:

First, in a TAF one can distinguish between typical and atypical behavior, thus it captures an important dimension of experience. In the context of top-down controlled image sequence analysis, for example, high-value areas of a TAF can be used to define primary search areas for - say - discovering a turn-off event.

Second, a TAF can be used for generalizing observations w.r.t. location and velocity. These are essential means to help apply experience to novel but similar situations. TAFs are also able to deal with obstacles which were not present during knowledge acquisition.

Third, a TAF may be characterized by abstracted information (its skeleton) and by the trajectory prototypes as defined by the skeleton. This provides the possibility to refer to and reason about typical motion behavior in terms of a finite set of alternatives.

Fourth, TAFs can be used to compute analogies by reorganizing the representation appropriately. 'Turn-off' events have been predicted for an intersection where no examples have been observed. The prediction has been computed in analogy to 'turn-off' events observed at an intersection with different geometry. Hence an important aspect of reasoning about experience has been modelled.

Fifth, the transition from event descriptions gained in particular environments to generic event models was achieved by using a subset of perceptual primitives to characterize invariant information. We feel that the set of perceptual primitives we have discussed plays an important role for several perceptual and cognitive tasks.

The flexibility of the representation was achieved by using an analogical, 'scenic' mapping from the world into the model and by applying local operations to make certain information explicit. We believe that an analogical representation is needed for efficient solutions in the domain discussed in this work.

Several aspects of the problem area will be investigated in the near future. One is the relation between analogical image-like representations and more abstract propositional representations. How can we learn propositional descriptions from observations? Are image-like representations a useful intermediate representation for the computation of propositions?

Another problem concerns the limits of separability. How can one attain the separation of trajectory bundles which share common parts? One way to deal with this problem is to extend the state vector S to contain other useful features such as object characteristics or - to improve separation - global trajectory characteristics. As the usefulness of such features would depend on the situation, a theory of how to select useful features must be developed. This, again, is left for future work.

A third problem we want to tackle was already mentioned in Section 4. We want to distinguish variant from invariant information automatically by looking at the distribution of information in different dimensions over a variety of observed examples.

Finally, the role of different characteristics of representations (like empirical and analytic) is not completely understood. Can we develop systematic criteria to evaluate the adequacy of a certain representation?

Acknowledgements

This work has been financially supported by DFG (German Science Foundation). We thank David Fleet for valuable comments on Section 4.

References

[Block 81]
>   *Imagery.*
>   Ned Block(Ed.).
>   MIT Press, Cambridge, Mass. 1981.

[Drescher 87]
>   *A Mechanism for Early Piagetian Learning.*
>   Gary L. Drescher.
>   Proc. Nat. Conf. on Art. Intell. AAAI-6, 1987, 290-294.

[Finke 85]
>   *Theories Relating Mental Imagery to Perception.*

Ronald A. Finke.
Psychological Bulletin **98** (1985) 236-259.

[Kosslyn 80]
Image and Mind.
Stephen M. Kosslyn.
Harvard University Press, 1980.

[Larkin + Simon 87]
Why a Diagramm is (Sometimes) Worth Ten Thousand Words.
Jill H. Larkin, Herbert A. Simon.
Cognitive Science **11** (1987) 65-99.

[Levesque 86]
Making Believers out of Computers.
Hector J. Levesque.
Artificial Intelligence **30** (1986) 81-108.

[Michalski + Carbonell + Mitchell 83]
Machine Learning I.
Ryszard S. Michalski, Jaime G. Carbonell, Tom M. Mitchell.
Tioga Publishing Company 1983.

[Michalski + Carbonell + Mitchell 86]
Machine Learning II.
Ryszard S. Michalski, Jaime G. Carbonell, Tom M. Mitchell.
Morgan Kaufman Publisher 1986.

[Mohnhaupt 87]
On Modelling Events with an Analogical Representation.
Michael Mohnhaupt.
Proc. German Workshop on Artificial Intelligence GWAI-11, 1987, 31-40.

[Mohnhaupt + Neumann 87]
Szenenhafte Modelle für zeitabhängige Ereignisse.
Michael Mohnhaupt, Bernd Neumann.
Technical Report, FBI-B-127, Fachbereich Informatik, University of Hamburg, February 1987.

[Neumann + Mohnhaupt 88]
Propositionale und analoge Repräsentation von Bewegungsverläufen.
Bernd Neumannn, Michael Mohnhaupt.
Künstliche Intelligenz **1** (1988) 4-10.

[Neumann + Novak 83]
Event models for recognition and natural-language description of events in real-world image sequences.
Bernd Neumann, Hans-Joachim Novak.
Proc. Int. Joint Conf. on Art. Intell. IJCAI-8, 1983, 724-726.

[Neumann + Novak 86]
NAOS: Ein System zur natürlichsprachlichen Beschreibung zeitveränderlicher Szenen.
Bernd Neumann, Hans-Joachim Novak.
Informatik Forsch. Entw. **1** (1986) 83-92.

[Palmer 78]
> *Fundamental Aspects of Cognitive Representation.*
> S. P. Palmer.
> in: E. Rosch, B.B. Lloyd (Ed.): Cognition and Categorisation, Hillsdale, N.Y.: Erlbaum Press 1978.

[Phelps + Musgrove 85]
> *A prototypical approach to machine learning.*
> R. I. Phelps, P. B. Musgrove.
> Proc. Int. Joint Conf. on Art. Intell. IJCAI-9, 1985, 698-700.

[Rumelhart + McClelland 87]
> *Parallel Distributed Processing I + II.*
> David E. Rumelhart, James L. McClelland and the PDP research group.
> MIT Press, Cambridge, Mass. 1987.

[Selman 87]
> *Analogues.*
> Bart Selman.
> Technical Note CSRI-47, University of Toronto, Department of Computer Science, March 1987.

[Sober 76]
> *Mental Representations.*
> Elliot Sober.
> *Synthese* **33** (1976) 101-148.

A KNOWLEDGE-INTENSIVE LEARNING SYSTEM
FOR DOCUMENT RETRIEVAL

Roy Rada
Department of Computer Science
University of Liverpool
Liverpool L69 3BX, England

Hafedh Mili
Department of Electrical Engineering and Computer Science
George Washington University
Washington, D.C. 20052, U.S.A.

Abstract

Our learning system supports repeatable experiments in which practical problems related to document indexing and retrieval are addressed. Knowledge bases are typically critical to the document indexing and retrieval. In our experiments, one knowledge base is augmented with knowledge from another knowledge base, and at the first level this augmentation is an instance of similarity-based or analogy-based learning. But the overall system is tuned by interaction with a person so that changes in the representation of the knowledge base and in the performance and evaluation components of the learning system can lead to demonstrably improved performance. We provide evidence that small changes in structure or representation should correspond to small changes in function or meaning. Furthermore, all the components of the learning system depend in some way on detecting similarities and exploiting differences, and the move from similarity to analogy in learning exploits a second-order difference.

1. Model

In a simple model of a learning system the environment supplies some information to the learning element, the learning element uses this information to make improvements in an explicit knowledge base, and the performance element uses the knowledge base to perform its task (see Figure 1).[11] In our experiments the environment provides documents and queries to the performance element (see Figure 2). The performance element relies on a knowledge base and outputs documents to those who generate the queries. The learning element operates on the knowledge base so as to produce better

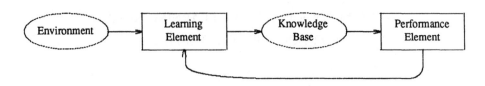

Figure 1: A Simple Model of Learning Systems.

knowledge.

The knowledge bases which are used in document storage and retrieval systems are often referred to as thesauri. The characteristics of a thesaurus allow it to also be called a semantic net, a classification language, or an ordering system.[8] For our purposes these semantic nets (sns) may be formally represented as directed, labeled graphs $G = \{V, E\}$ where vertices $V=\{v_0,v_1, \ldots \}$ and where edges $E=\{(v_i,v_j,l_k) \mid v_i,v_j \in V; \; l_k \in labels; \; i, j, k \in N\}$ with labels=\{is-a, part-of, cause, \ldots\}.

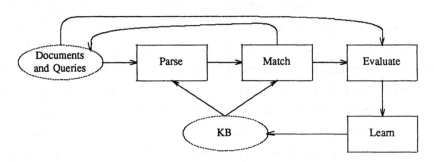

Figure 2: Knowledge-Base (KB) and Learning System in Document Retrieval Model

In information systems documents are represented as sets of concepts from a semantic net (sn). Queries are represented as boolean combinations of concepts from the sn. The system parses documents and queries into subgraphs of the sn. The system then matches the query to documents based on these parsed representations (see Figure 3).

There are hundreds of different thesauri supporting hundreds of information retrieval systems, and each thesaurus has its own idiosyncratic structure. We take these thesauri and parse them into sns. Then part of one semantic net is inserted into the other semantic net by the learning algorithm (see Figure 4). A robust system would automatically develop new methods of uniting semantic nets (see Simon's[39]

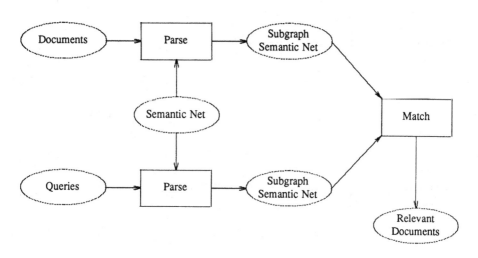

Figure 3: Role of semantic net in parsing and matching.

definition of machine learning) but a system that interacted with a person in the course of refining some of its basic strategies would be one approach to man-machine learning. This might be the first step towards a meta-learner component which would itself observe the behavior of the remainder of the system and suggest changes. In the context of the learning system for knowledge-based document retrieval, the human "meta-learner" would get feedback from the evaluation element and would be able to intervene in the functioning of the performance element, the learning element, and the evaluation element (see Figure 5).

A series of experiments will be presented. First hierarchical semantic nets will be compared with one another as concepts from one sn will be inserted into their appropriate position in the other sn. The hierarchical relationship includes such relationships as is-a and part-of.[40] Then the addition of associative relations from one sn into another will be explored. The associative relation includes the causal relation, the side-effect relation, the carried-by relation, and more. Finally, the effect of adding simultaneously hierarchical and associative relations from one sn to another will be considered with richer patterns of similarity and difference becoming evident. In all cases the interplay between the learning element and the other components of the learning system will be stressed.

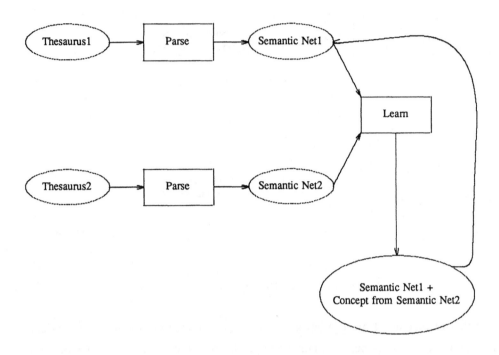

Figure 4: Closer look at input and output of the learning component.

2. Literature Review

Our work borrows from the theory of genetic algorithms, of explanation-based learning, of learning by analogy, of sloppy modeling, and more. Our focus has been on how changes to one component of the learning system are related to changes in another component.

The genetic algorithm takes advantage of the general phenomenon that good things should combine to form newer, yet better things.[19] This principle underlying the genetic algorithm is at the base of the algorithms explored in this paper. In our work two sns are examined, each of which is supposed to be good, and a part of one is inserted into the other. While the genetic algorithm is robust across many search spaces,[3] it should have heuristics to help guide it in its determination of which parts of one sn to insert into another sn.[24, 32] Recent extensions of the genetic algorithm look at ways to more richly distribute reward and to find q-morphisms that guide changes.[20] Our work takes advantage of existing knowledge to push the refinement of

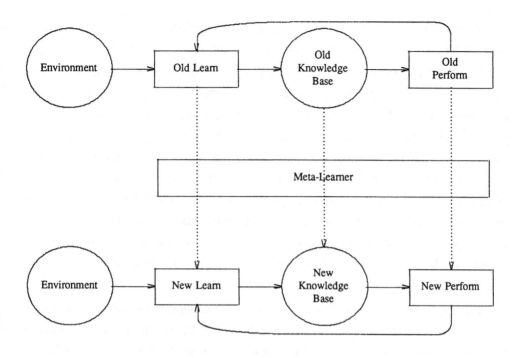

Figure 5: The meta-learner changes components of the learning system.

knowledge--all this occurring at a cognitively understandable level.[12] We are applying some aspects of the genetic algorithm to sns that have been routinely used in information systems.

There are, at least, two major types of learning for generalizations--one is learning from many instances a single generalization and the other is learning from one example by applying substantial domain knowledge to guide a generalization. In either case there has been substantial interest in the development of hierarchies of generalizations. UNIMEM[23] and COBWEB[16] both take instances and add them one by one to hierarchies. New generalizations are not created unless a body of instances have led to some condition which isn't well handled by the existing hierarchy of generalizations. This kind of learning from instances is different from the conceptual clustering done by Michalski[26] in, among other ways, that it is incremental in nature, whereas Michalski's conceptual clustering first collected all instances before classifying them. In most of our work, the existing conceptual classes have been labelled from the beginning, but the challenge is to properly order them. One of our experiments involved a best-first search for the most specific class in a way not dissimilar from work with, for instance,

UNIMEM. Also our latest work with analogical inheritance can discover new relationships or generalizations that didn't exist in any of the sns which we were connecting.

The BLIP approach to machine learning allows knowledge to be entered as predicate logic statements but otherwise allows relative flexibility to the user in expressing knowledge. The BLIP system then learns from the input and structures further information.[29] The approach advanced in this paper looks at existing knowledge bases--less complex than natural language but more robust than unstructured examples--and asks how they can be put together. This allows a flexibility or adaptability in representation related in some ways to the flexibility that those working with BLIP call sloppy modeling. Furthermore, by combining existing semantic nets each of whose structure reflects a particular domain of knowledge, the learning system is able to shift bias[42] from one view to another as other components of the learning system indicate that such a shift is appropriate.

The importance of a smooth structure-function relationship in learning is illustrated in work where gray-codes and hierarchies both were instrumental in creating structures to which small changes could be made that resulted in small changes in function.[7] The similarity metric of Carbonell[5] or the decomposability algorithm of Pearl[30] are two of the many, many other examples of approaches that hinge on the gradualness or regularity or continuity in a search space.

We are interested in modifying through time all the components of the learning system. The utility[37] or goal served by the semantic net must be changed hand-in-hand with the learning strategy. The evaluation, performance, knowledge base, and learning components of the learning system are intricately connected and one can not be changed without impacting on the other.

One of our arguments in this paper is that the learning system should be interactive so that a person can provide guidance for the changes that need to be made. In learning by watching or apprentice learning interactive dialog leads to amendments to the knowledge base;[10] this method has advanced to include sophisticated models of the user and the domain. Our approach is embryonic in its computer-supported interactive component, but takes advantage of a rich experimental situation within document retrieval systems.

3. Hierarchical

3.1. Method

The Medical Subject Headings (MeSH) is a thesaurus used to classify medical literature. The Systematized Nomenclature of Medicine (SNOMED) is used in hospital information systems to classify patient records. The Computing Reviews Classification Structure (CRCS) is used to classify the literature of the Association of Computing Machinery. MeSH contains about 100,000 concepts in a large hierarchy that goes 11 levels deep (see Figure 6).[1]

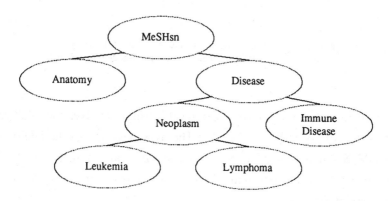

Figure 6: Sample of MeSH hierarchy beginning with the root MeSHsn.

This hierarchy is a tangled one as a concept may have more than one broader-than concept. SNOMED has about 50,000 concepts in a tree where the first level represents: topography, morphology, function, and etiology.[43] CRCS has about 1000 concepts in a 4-level tree. Its subtrees cover such topics as software, hardware, and theory of computation.[38]

If x, y, and z are concepts and x is narrower than y and y is narrower than z, then x is narrower than z. This transitivity phenomenon can be applied as follows: first, two concepts v_2 in sn V and w_1 in sn W are determined to be similar. Then the children of w_1 are copied to v_2 (see Figure 7). This is a kind of incremental learning from classified examples.

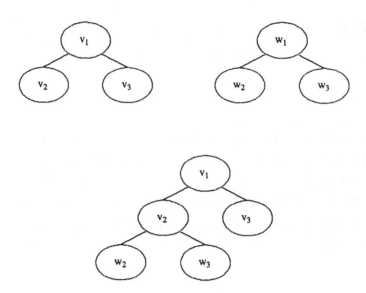

Figure 7: Example of merged semantic nets. Given that $v_2 = w_1$, the two, 3-node semantic nets become the one, 5-node semantic net.

In our experiments incremental, hierarchical learning involves the addition of concepts from SNOMED or CRCS to MeSH. The hypothesis is that the addition of these concepts to MeSH makes a better sn. To test this claim a measure of "better" is needed--the measure is the extent to which MeSH versus augmented-MeSH supports automated indexing or parsing.

The National Library of Medicine supports about 100 full-time indexers whose job is to scan articles in the biomedical literature and to assign a handful of MeSH concepts to each article. The product of this indexing is stored on the computer and thus becomes available not only for searchers around the world but also for anyone wishing to do experiments. With the indexing is also stored other basic information about each article such as its title.

The indexing of the human experts is considered to be a gold standard against which a computer program can be benchmarked. We developed a simple computer parser which would match the terms in titles to the terms representing the concepts in

MeSH. Each time there was a match, the computer would suggest that that MeSH concept should be assigned to the document with that title. After the automatic parsing had occurred, the results of the automatic parsing were compared to the results of the human indexing.

After MeSH was augmented with a concept x from another sn, the automatic parser might find a match between a title and x. By pointing from x to the hierarchically nearest MeSH concept, the computer parser might succeed in duplicating the indexing that the human indexers had achieved with MeSH. In other words, the augmented sn might support improved automatic parsing.

3.2. Result

3.2.1. Similar Domains

Subtrees were isolated in SNOMED, and synonyms between the root of these SNOMED subtrees and MeSH concepts were determined. The synonym test was basically a check for lexical match. SNOMED subtrees were then connected to the MeSH concepts with the mechanism illustrated in Figure 7.

The automatic indexer was applied to 247 bibliographic records randomly selected from 6 million document records on the National Library of Medicine computer database called MEDLINE. In the assessment of parsing robustness the concepts assigned by the automatic parser were compared to the concepts assigned by the human indexer for each article. The evaluation showed the performance to be the same both with MeSH and augmented-MeSH (MeSH+SNOMED). This was explained by a variety of factors, including, that there was limited flexibility in the lexical match. Also, the SNOMED terms not already in MeSH proved to not occur in the titles of MEDLINE documents.

To bypass the weakness of lexical matches between SNOMED and MeSH concepts, the synonyms in MeSH were considered to be newly entered concepts from another sn which pointed to their appropriate MeSH concept. To our surprise the automatic parser again did not show a significant change in it parsing when used with or without the synonyms. While some synonyms often helped the automatic parser, such as "cancer" as a synonym to "neoplasm", some synonyms misled the automatic parser due to the ambiguity of the synonym without context. For instance, in MeSH "dressing" is considered a synonym to "bandage", which makes sense when one is talking about "surgical dressing" as a "bandage". But the MEDLINE article "Allergic Reaction to Salad Dressing" was incorrectly mapped by the computer to the MeSH concept "bandage" because of the ambiguity of the meaning of "dressing". The problem is not with the learning element but with the performance element which needs to consider context when doing parsing.

3.2.2. Dissimilar Domains

The foregoing led us to want:

1) a more constrained domain where the context might cause less difficulty and

2) another sn for which the concepts did not occur in MeSH but did occur in the MEDLINE.

Computer science is both a relatively small area within the context of biomedicine and also a rapidly growing area. When this experiment started, there were many computer concepts which MeSH was missing but that it could benefit by having.

For various reasons knowledge from different contexts may conflict. For instance, at one time "artificial intelligence" was considered a subset of "pattern recognition" whereas at another time "pattern recognition" was considered a subset of "artificial intelligence". A non-cumulative[14] learning strategy may be needed rearrange a sn in the course of augmenting it and resolving conflicts.

A conflict resolution strategy was developed[27] which gives preference to the placement of a concept which comes from the deepest hierarchical structure. For the case of directly contradicting hierarchical relationships, the heuristic is to make the two conflicting concepts siblings. Figure 8 shows a case where concepts v_1 and v_3 have opposite relations to one another in two sns and the resultant merge. If one were to define v_3 is-a v_1 as $v_3 \supseteq v_1$, the preceding conflict resolution strategies would be inappropriate. For instance, if $v_3 \supseteq v_1$ and $v_1 \supseteq v_3$, then there are only two possibilities: either $v_3 = v_1$ or there is an error. But in "real" sns the is-a relation is not a subset relation.[4]

MeSH and CRCS were united with the conflict resolution strategy. Automatic indexing was then done on titles from MEDLINE about computers and medicine. Using an "Average Hit Proportion", there was no evidence of improvement in indexing with the augmented MeSH, but to the human observer the new sn seemed clearly

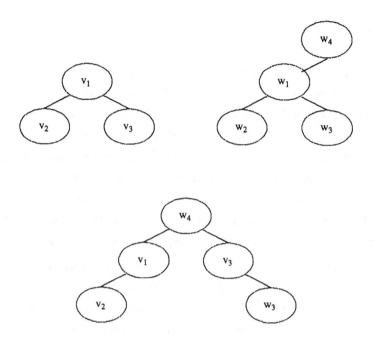

Figure 8: Conflict resolution. Given that v_1 equals w_2 and v_3 equals w_1, the merged semantic net changes the relationship of v_3 to v_1.

better. Accordingly, a more sensitive assessment of parsing performance was sought.

The notion of a distance between two concepts in the sn was introduced and applied to the evaluation. When the automatic parser produced no output it was considered to be arbitrarily far from the gold standard. If the automatic parser produced a concept x that was an instance of concept y and the human indexer chose y, then the automatic parser was considered to be close to correct. A formal elaboration of this strategy was devised and applied to the performance of the automatic parser on MeSH and MeSH+CRCS. The augmented MeSH now proved to support parsing significantly better than the unaugmented MeSH. The results of this merging of sns also led to some practically useful sns.[34]

3.3. Related Literature

Hierarchical insertion is like similarity learning but may also be compared to explanation-based learning. In similarity-based learning a program takes a number of instances, compares them in terms of similarities and differences, and creates a generalized description based on this structural analysis. Much of the similarity work has been based on comparing instances syntactically.[11] An explanation-based learning program takes a single instance, builds an explanation of how the various components relate to each other using domain-dependent understanding or planning methods, and then generalizes the properties of various components of the instance.[22] This generalized description of the instance can then be applied in understanding further instances.

An explanation-based learning system constructs an explanation in terms of a domain theory that proves how a training example satisfies a goal concept definition. Then a set of conditions under which the explanation structure holds is stated in terms that satisfy an operationality criterion.[28] Our case goes beyond similarity learning because we use two sns rather than arbitrary instances. These nets provide simultaneously the domain theory and the training example. The goal concept is to connect the nets and the operationality criterion is that consistency be maintained and that document processing be improved. The explanation first comes in the form of possible positions for a concept from sn_2 with respect to the information in sn_1. The generalization that occurs comes in the conflict resolution which removes those relations which would not support the operationality criterion.

4. Associative

The concepts in a sn should have more than hierarchical relations among them. Uniting associative relations from one sn with hierarchical relations from another sn should provide for a better sn. This section advances a method for doing and evaluating such uniting. The results of the experiments show a surprising aspect of spreading activation.

4.1. Method

The sn to be used as the source of associative relations in the experiments to be discussed here is CMIT. CMIT is produced by the American Medical Association and contains about 4000 disease descriptions.[15] Each disease has 11 attributes, including etiology, symptoms, signs, and prognosis. The values of these attributes are represented in a noun-phrase format (see the disease description in Figure 9).

AYERZA SYNDROME
　　See also Polycythemia, secondary;
　　Hypertension, pulmonary, secondary.
at Arrillaga-Ayerza syndrome; Black cardiac
　　disease; Pulmonary arteriosclerosis syndrome.
et Primary disease of pulmonary artery and
　　branches; arterial, arteriolar sclerosis; syphilis;
　　congenital hypoplasia of pulmonary artery.
sg Onset at about age 40; persistent cyanosis;
　　dyspnea; enlargement of liver, spleen.
lb Blood: RBC increased.
cr Prognosis: unfavorable; right-sided heart
　　failure.

Figure 9: Description of Ayerza Syndrome from CMIT publication.

Various parsing strategies were used to translate these attributes into concepts from MeSH. The similarity learning algorithm would map a CMIT disease name to a MeSH concept, and then the relation which connected the CMIT attribute to the CMIT disease was added to MeSH.

We have combined the notion of spreading activation with that of conceptual distance. If one concept is related to another concept, then the two are close. If instead many relations separate two concepts, they are not close. This observation has been generalized to sets of concepts so that a metric called DISTANCE on sets has been defined.[17]

The strategy for applying DISTANCE in evaluating a sn started with a query and a set of documents. Experts were asked to score each document for its conceptual similarity to the query. Then DISTANCE was applied to the same query and documents. From the scores were generated ranks, and the ranks by people were compared to the ranks by DISTANCE. If the hypothesis was that sn_1 was better than sn_2, then the expectation was that the document ranking with sn_1 would be significantly like those of people but the ranking based on sn_2 would not significantly agree with human ranking.

4.2. Result

MeSH supported the ranking of documents in a way that significantly agreed with the ranking of experts. And yet more surprising, MeSH augmented with CMIT associative relations led to rankings by DISTANCE that did not significantly correlate with the rankings of experts.

Our learning algorithm inserted non-hierarchical relationships such as "x causes y". But, the additional relationships did not improve retrieval. DISTANCE treated the hierarchical relationships no differently than it would handle the non-hierarchical relationships. This is consistent with the work of Collins and Loftus,[6] where activation went across all relationships equally.

We revised DISTANCE to take advantage of some of the different kinds of relationships that exist in augmented MeSH. This new DISTANCE or neo-DISTANCE can only follow an associative relationship when the query which is being processed contains an appropriate reference to that relationship. The application of neo-DISTANCE to augmented-MeSH produced good rankings. We were also able to show examples where augmented-MeSH with neo-DISTANCE could make useful rankings that DISTANCE on MeSH or augmented-MeSH couldn't.[31]

In the context of knowledge acquisition these experiments show the need for structure-function linkage. An additional structural unit (such as an edge saying that x causes y) does not help unless its corresponding functional significance is appreciated. When the reasoning or DISTANCE algorithm was modified to account for the difference between the original "is-a" edges in MeSH and the variety of added edges, then the knowledge acquisition effort proved more effective.

5. Inheritance

5.1. Direct Inheritance

Two diseases may be said to be similar to one another if they have overlapping attributes. An equation for similarity was empirically derived for representing similarity between two diseases. A best-first search algorithm (BFSA) was implemented for searching the MeSH+CMIT disease hierarchy.

In the BFSA a set of concepts describing a disease is first evaluated for similarity to each of the children of the top node in the disease hierarchy. Each of these children represents an entire class of diseases and is described by the union of all the attributes of all its children. The algorithm determines which class of diseases is most "similar" to the given set of concepts and makes that the new parent. The process is then repeated looking at the children of the new parent, each of which represents a subclass of diseases, and so on down the hierarchy until a situation is encountered in which the children are all less similar to the set of concepts than the parent. Comparable strategies have been used in a variety of other learning systems.[21]

To evaluate the nature of inheritance in the augmented MeSH hierarchy, it was hypothesized that if properties are inherited, then the BFSA will find a disease to be most similar to itself. To test this hypothesis, ten CMIT ocular diseases which had already been merged with the MeSH hierarchy were arbitrarily selected. Initially, these ten diseases were mapped with the BFSA based on all properties combined. The algorithm found nine of ten of the diseases to be most similar to themselves.

Next, the same experiment was repeated but only a single axis was used for the hierarchy traversal. The results of this experiment are shown in Figure 10.

Field	Correct	Close
All fields used:	9	1
Etiology:	6	1
Symptoms:	3	0
Signs:	4	1
Labs:	2	4
Path:	4	0
Course:	0	0
Xray	0	0

Figure 10: Number of correct and "close" proposed MeSH locations when mapping ten diseases into MeSH+CMIT. "Close" means correct answer was algorithm's second choice.

Based on these results, etiology was the most inherited property. From this data, one might speculate that the MeSH hierarchy is primarily etiology oriented. This suggests the possibility of having the computer propose possible etiologies for a given disease based on the etiologies of its neighbors in the hierarchy.

Given the cognitive nature of the decisions which need to be made in augmenting sns, an interactive system may be valuable. We stored MeSH, CMIT, and SNOMED in a relational database management system on an Apollo workstation. Programs were developed to propose to a physician similarities among terms based on various lexical and morphosemantic criteria.[33, 25] A disease concept from CMIT was proposed for insertion into the MeSH disease hierarchy based on patterns of inheritance in

MeSH+CMIT. The physician would interactively decide whether the proposed place was a good one. Each time a CMIT disease concept was inserted in MeSH, its attributes were also embedded in MeSH, and there was more data available for subsequent analysis of inheritance patterns. Our experiments proved that after an insertion, the likelihood increased that the next proposed insertion would be an accurate one.[35]

5.2. Analogical Inheritance

To say that a concept inherits the attributes of its broader-than concept is to only characterize the attributes which the two concepts have in common and says nothing about why the relationship is unidirectional. We argue that there is a structure-function relationship in knowledge bases which allows a special kind of inheritance that we call analogical inheritance.

Given $f(x) = x'$, $f(y) = y'$, broader-than$(x) = y$, and broader-than$(x') = y'$, analogical or isomorphic inheritance means that broader-than$(f(x)) = f($broader-than$(x))$. In an ideal knowledge base--one built according to the principles of direct and analogical inheritance--each concept x would for each attribute $f(x)$ either directly inherit the value $f(y)$ or analogically inherit the value y'. This principle could be used to guide the development of sns. It could be evaluated by testing the extent to which sns in the real world maintain the property of analogical isomorphism. It could also be a guideline for inserting concepts into a hierarchy.

An example of how this insertion might occur is in the placement of the "Chairman of the Mathematics Department" into the hierarchy of knowledge about the administration of the university (see Figure 11). If we know that the "Chairman of the Mathematics Department" has an office in the "School of Natural Sciences", then we might expect that the Chairman reports to the "Dean of the School of Natural Sciences" rather than to the "Dean of the School of Engineering".

A merge of part of MeSH with part of an Oncology sn provides another example of the role of analogical inheritance.[36] In MeSH "rectal neoplasms" is broader-than "anal neoplasms". In the Oncology sn "anal neoplasms" and "rectal neoplasms" are both narrower-than the same concept. Since the Oncology thesaurus is, in general, more specific in oncology than is MeSH, its relationship and not the MeSH relationship is hypothesized to be better. More careful examination of MeSH reveals, however, another problem. In the anatomy section of MeSH "rectum" is broader-than "anal canal". MeSH has maintained an isomorphism (across the "located-in" relation)

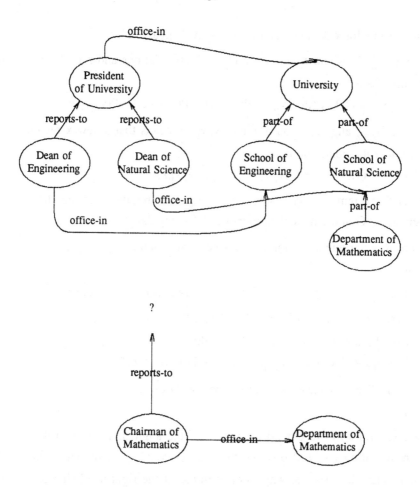

Figure 11: To whom should the "Chairperson of Mathematics" report?
Reasoning by analogical inheritance.

between the disease and anatomy sections. Thus to change the MeSH neoplasm section without also changing the MeSH anatomy section, would destroy the isomorphism and introduce an inconsistency.

We have formalized aspects of analogical inheritance in several ways, and an example of one follows.

Definitions:

* $P(v_i, v_j, l_k)$ is a predicate which is true, if and only if, $(v_i, v_j, l_k) \in E$.

* $\cap$ represents logical "and", and $\cup$ represent logical "or".

* Regular$_{x,y,z}$ G where x and y are hierarchical relations and z is a non-hierarchical relation means

  $(\forall v_i,v_j,v_{i'},v_{j'} \in V)\ (P(v_i,v_j,x)\cap P(v_i,v_{i'},z)\cap P(v_j,v_{j'},z))\rightarrow P(v_{i'},v_{j'},y)$.

* Regular $G_{x,y,z}$ augmentation through $(v_i,v_{i'},z)$ means that a new x relation is added to G under the condition that

  $(\exists\ v_j\exists v_{j'}P(v_{i'},v_{j'},y),\ P(v_j,v_{j'},z))\rightarrow$ create (v_i,v_j,x).

* To say that augmentation is sound with respect to regularity means that:

  (regular$_{x,y,z}$ G and augmentation creates G')$\rightarrow$regular$_{x,y,z}$G'.

* Claim: Regular augmentation is not necessarily sound.

  Proof:

  1) The new edge (v_i,v_j,x) makes possible
     $P(v_i,v_j,x)\cap P(v_i,v_{i'},z)\cap P(v_j,?,z)\rightarrow P(v_{i'},?,y)$.

  2) Could there be any value of ? such that
     $P(v_i,v_j,x)\cap P(v_i,v_{i'},z)\cap P(v_j,?,z)$ is true but not $P(v_{i'},?,y)$.

  3) Yes. We may have $(v_j,v_{j'},z)$ but not $(v_i,v_{j'},y)$.

  Q.E.D.

There are several ways to extend the power of the augmentation algorithm. The augmentation algorithm could also create the edge $(v_i,v_{j'},y)$. "Unknown" values in the sn could be handled in a special way. For example, if the right-hand side of the implication in the definition of "regular$_{x,y,z}$G" is or-ed with $P(v_{i'},$ unknown, $y)$, then an uncertain value for $v_{i'}$ will allow regularity to hold where it otherwise might not. With these kinds of extensions we have developed augmentation algorithms which are both sound and complete (but the topic of another paper).

5.3. Related Literature

One investigation into ways to assure that concept acquisition leads to consistent results has relied on results from path algebra. A path algebra has binary operations with certain properties, such as associativity and distributivity. Given "a-kind-of", "part-of", and "causes" relations, methods have been developed for integrating a new relation and concept so that the properties of a path algebra are retained.[2]

Inheritance takes advantage of similarity, while analogy is a kind of second-order similarity. The kind of inheritance which we have defined as analogical inheritance can also be considered analogical learning. An analogy is a mapping of knowledge from a base domain into a target domain. Objects in the base are placed in correspondence with objects in the target (Map: $base_i \rightarrow target_i$). When predicates are mapped, the mapped relations are determined by systematicity, which means that higher-order constraining relations exist (e.g., cause (push ($base_i, base_j$), collide ($base_j, base_k$))$\rightarrow$ cause (push ($target_i, target_j$), collide ($target_j, target_k$))).[18] The work with analogical learning has tended to use a small number of richly connected concepts.[9] Our work applies the analogical paradigm to massive semantic nets that have a strong hierarchical backbone.

Our augmentation algorithms which are sound and complete relative to regularity show how complex changes in a sn may need to be. This is, on one hand, the problem of stability and cost.[16] The possible need for substantial restructuring of a sn is addressed by methods for non-cumulative learning[14] which allow for dramatic restructuring. The authors of this paper have explored methods for non-cumulative learning from the perspective of hypercycles[13] and population dynamics.

6. Discussion

6.1. Augmentation

As more sets of documents, each with its own sn, become available, the utility of augmented sns becomes more evident. If, for instance, a physician in his office wants to retrieve a patient record and also desires published literature that might be relevant to the patient's problem, then the sn that was used to classify the patient records should be connected to the sn that was used to classify the medical literature.

Our experiments have taught us several things about how to augment and connect sns. The conventional, artificial intelligence, software tools are not prepared to deal with the size of the sns that are available and useful. An attempt to store MeSH in a frame-based language called FRAMEKIT and in KEE failed due to memory overflow problems.[35] Database management systems can readily store large sns. Since algorithms do not exist which can reliably build or connect sns, human intervention is required. On the other hand, there are many steps which a computer can take hand-in-hand with the person which facilitate sn improvement.

We have explored methods of adjusting weights on rules to guide improved intelligent computer behavior[32] but dealing with higher-level semantic constructs from existing sns is a richer domain. In uniting sns the simple rule of thumb has been to determine similarities and exploit differences. Given that the knowledge in sns is complex and strict rules of inheritance don't apply, how does one resolve the conflicts that may arise when different perspectives lead to different determinations of what concept is broader than what other concept? One possible guideline is analogical inheritance which dictates that a concept inherit attributes in a pattern that reflects the hierarchies in which the attributes of its parent are embedded--these are second-order similarities and differences, as they are in analogical learning.

6.2. Performance and Evaluation

One has to develop performance and evaluation tools that are sensitive to the evolving character of the sns. We have appended algorithms onto information systems for parsing and matching documents and queries. We are able to take advantage of the millions of encoded documents that have been manually created and which have been stored on the computer.

We have noted that spreading activation is a powerful means for taking advantage of the relations in sns--both in parsing and matching information. We have built a metric on graphs that uses spreading activation to arrive at conceptual distances. We have discovered that the hierarchical relations are powerful supporters of decisions about conceptual similarity. The non-hierarchical relations should only be traversed when the searcher has explicitly stated an interest in that type of non-hierarchical relation.

We have recently become very interested in multi-user hypertext creation systems. We feel that there is great opportunity for engaging here in performance and evaluation with users who are interested in sns that turn a document into a knowledge base. In the process of creating hypertext, people need interactive knowledge acquisition guidance.

Our experiments have shown such things as:

1) The performance element should exploit differences in edge types (such as causal versus hierarchical).

2) The performance element should exploit similarities of context in the environment (the ambiguity of synonyms led to this conclusion).

3) The evaluation element should be sensitive to small differences in performance as that difference can be reflected in the distances in the semantic net.

A user of the learning system can operate as a "meta-learner" who is shown how the learn, perform, and evaluate elements are responding to the knowledge base and environment and who suggests refinements to keep the changes in one in tune with the changes in the other. Our approach at the meta-level has been informal and creates specializations from generalizations (in contrast to other work[41] which at the meta-level is formal and creates generalizations from specializations). The basic representational scheme for knowledge and data in our experiments has been directed, labeled graphs. The general rule guiding hypothesis generation has been that shifts in structure should be gracefully linked to shifts in function.

Acknowledgements: Many people have contributed to the research reported here. The collaboration of Ellen Bicknell, Lindley Darden, Steve Lester, and Brian Martin is particularly appreciated. This work was supported by the American National Science Foundation under Grant ECS-8406683 and by the American National Library of Medicine.

References

1. Joyce Backus, Sara Davidson, and Roy Rada, "Searching for Patterns in the MeSH Vocabulary," *Bulletin of the Medical Library Association, 75, 3*, pp. 221-227, July 1987.

2. Rene R Bakker, "Knowledge Graphs: Representation and Structuring of Scientific Knowledge," *PhD Dissertation*, Department of Informatics, University of Twente, Twente, Netherlands, 1987.

3. Albert Bethke, "Genetic Algorithms as Function Optimizers," PhD Thesis, Dept Computer and Communication Sciences, University Michigan, Ann Arbor, Michigan, 1980.

4. Ronald Brachman, "What IS-A Is and Isn't: An Analysis of Taxonomic Links in Semantic Networks," *Computer 16, 10*, pp. 30-36, 1983.

5. Jaime Carbonell, "Learning by Analogy," in *Machine Learning*, ed. T Mitchell, pp. 137-161, Tioga Publishing, Palo Alto, CA, 1983.

6. A M Collins and E F Loftus, "A Spreading Activation Theory of Semantic Processing," *Psychological Review, 82*, pp. 407-428, 1975.

7. Jonathan H Connell and Michael Brady, "Generating and Generalizing Models of Visual Objects," *Artificial Intelligence, 31*, pp. 159-183, 1987.

8. Ingetraut Dahlberg, "Conceptual Compatibility of Ordering Systems," *International Classification, 10, 1*, pp. 5-8, 1983.

9. Lindley Darden and Roy Rada, "Hypothesis Formation via Interrelations," in *Analogica*, ed. Armand Prieditis, pp. 109-128, Pitman Publishing, London, 1988.

10. Randall Davis, "TEIRESIAS: Applications of Meta-Level Knowledge," in *Knowledge-Based Systems in Artificial Intelligence*, ed. D Lenat, pp. 229-491, McGraw-Hill, New York, 1982.

11. Thomas Dietterich, Bob London, Kenneth Clarkson, and Geoff Dromey, "Learning and Inductive Inference," in *Handbook of Artificial Intelligence, Vol 3*, ed. E Feigenbaum, pp. 323-511, William Kaufman, Inc, Los Altos, CA, 1982.

12. Thomas G Dietterich, "Learning at the Knowledge Level," *Machine Learning, 1*, pp. 287-316, 1896.

13. Manfred Eigen and Peter Schuster, "Abstract Hypercycle," *Die Naturwissenschaften 65, 3*, pp. 7-41, 1978.

14. Werner Emde, "Non-Cumulative Learning in Metaxa.3," *Proceedings of the Tenth International Joint Conference on Artificial Intelligence*, Morgan Kaufmann Publishers, Los Altos, California, 1987.

15. A Finkel, B Gordon, M Baker, and C Fanta, *Current Medical Information and Terminology*, American Medical Association, Chicago, 1981.

16. Douglas H Fisher, "Knowledge Acquisition via Incremental Conceptual Clustering," *Machine Learning, 2*, pp. 139-172, 1987.

17. Richard Forsyth and Roy Rada, *Machine Learning: Expert Systems and Information Retrieval*, Ellis Horwood, London, 1986.

18. Dedre Gentner and Cecile Toupin, "Systematicity and Surface Similarity in the Development of Analogy," *Cognitive Science, 10*, pp. 277-300, 1986.

19. John Holland, *Adaptation in Natural and Artificial Systems*, University Michigan Press, Ann Arbor, Michigan, 1975.

20. John Holland, Keith Holyoak, Richard Nisbett, and Paul Thagard, *Induction: Processes of Inference, Learning, and Discovery*, MIT Press, Cambridge, Massachusetts, 1986.

21. Janet Kolodner, *Retrieval and Organizational Strategies in Conceptual Memory*, Lawrence Erlbaum, Hillsdale, NJ, 1984.

22. Michael Lebowitz, "Integrated Learning: Controlling Explanation," *Cognitive Science, 10*, pp. 219-240, 1986.

23. Michael Lebowitz, "Experiments with Incremental Concept Formation: UNIMEM," *Machine Learning, 2*, pp. 103-138, 1987.

24. Douglas Lenat, "The Role of Heuristics in Learning by Discovery," in *Machine Learning*, ed. T Mitchell, pp. 243-306, Tioga Publishing, Palo Alto, CA, 1983.

25. Brian Martin and Roy Rada, "Building a Relational Data Base for a Physician Document Index," *Medical Informatics, 12, 3*, pp. 187-201, July-September 1987.

26. R Michalski and R Stepp, "Automated Clustering of Classifications: Conceptual Clustering Versus Numerical Taxonomy," *IEEE Transactions on Pattern Analysis and Machine Intelligence, 5, 4*, pp. 396-409, 1983.

27. Hafedh Mili and Roy Rada, "Merging Thesauri: Principles and Evaluation," *IEEE Transactions on Pattern Analysis and Machine Intelligence, 10, 2,* pp. 204-220, 1988.

28. T M Mitchell, R M Keller, and S T Kedar-Cabelli, "Explanation-Based Generalization: A Unifying View," *Machine Learning, 1, 1,* pp. 47-80, 1986.

29. Katharina Morik, "Acquiring Domain Models," *International Journal of Man-Machine Studies, 26,* pp. 93-104, 1987.

30. Judea Pearl, "On the Discovery and Generation of Certain Heuristics," *AI Magazine 4, 1,* pp. 23-34, 1983.

31. Roy Rada, Susanne Humphrey, and Craig Coccia, "A Knowledge-base for Retrieval Evaluation," *Annual Proceedings Association Computing Machinery,* pp. 360-367, Oct 1985.

32. Roy Rada, "Gradualness Facilitates Knowledge Refinement," *IEEE Transactions on Pattern Analysis and Machine Intelligence, 7, 5,* pp. 523-530, September 1985.

33. Roy Rada, Florence Lu, John Eng, and Brandon Brylawski, "Augmentation and Evaluation of a Medical Classification Structure Through Morphosemantic Analysis," *Proceedings MEDINFO '86,* pp. 1096-1100, North-Holland: Amsterdam, Holland, October 26-30, 1986.

34. Roy Rada, Bruce Blum, Edith Calhoun, Hafedh Mili, Helmuth Orthner, and Sarah Singer, "A Vocabulary for Medical Informatics," *Computers and Biomedical Research 20,* pp. 244-263, 1987.

35. Roy Rada and Brian Martin, "Augmenting Thesauri for Information Systems," *ACM Transactions on Office Information Systems, 5, 4,* pp. 378-392, 1987.

36. Roy Rada, "Connecting and Evaluating Thesauri," *International Classification, 14, 2,* pp. 63-69, 1987.

37. Larry Rendell, "A General Framework for Induction and a Study of Selective Induction," *Machine Learning, 1,* pp. 177-226, 1986.

38. Jean Sammet and Anthony Ralston, "The New (1982) Computing Reviews Classification System--Final Version," *Communications of the Association for Computing Machinery, 25, 1,* pp. 13-25, January 1982.

39. Herbert Simon, "Why Should Machines Learn," in *Machine Learning,* ed. T Mitchell, pp. 25-38, Tioga Publishing, Palo Alto, CA, 1983.

40. Barry Smith and Kevin Mulligan, "Pieces of a Theory," in *Parts and Moments: Studies in Logic and Formal Ontology,* ed. Barry Smith, pp. 15-109, Philosophia Verlag, Munich, Germany, 1982.

41. Sabine Thieme, "The Acquisition of Model-Knowledge for a Model-Driven Machine-Learning Approach," *Proceedings Knowledge Representation and Knowledge (Re-)Organization in Machine Learning,* 1988. (appears in this book)

42. Paul E Utgoff, *Machine Learning of Inductive Bias,* Kluwer Publishers, Boston, Massachusetts, 1986.

43. F Wingert, "An Indexing System for SNOMED," *Methods of Information in Medicine, 25, 1,* pp. 22-30, 1986.

Constructing Expert Systems as Building Mental Models
o r
Toward a Cognitive Ontology For Expert Systems

David Littman
Department of Computer Science
Yale University
New Haven, CT
USA

Introduction: Motivation and Goals

For the last few years we have been investigating the ways in which software designers construct large computer programs. Three of the main results of this work are:

Finding 1: Littman & Soloway, 1986   Software designers build and use multiple mental representations when they design software.

Finding 2: Littman, Pinto & Soloway, 1986   Software designers make extensive use of mental simulation during the design process to coordinate their multiple mental representations.

Finding 3: Littman, 1987   Expert systems designers exhibit seven recurrent mental activities which appear directed toward the construction of mental models.

Though suggestive, in many respects the analyses of software design behavior provided in the work noted above were superficial --- that is, the analyses did not satisfactorily describe either a) the mental objects or b) the mental actions that software designers employ when they design complex software such as expert systems. In my current work on the cognitive activities that underlie the design of expert systems I have, therefore, attempted to go below the surface and to move toward an understanding of the process of designing expert systems that would be deep enough to serve as the basis for writing an AI computer program that could, itself, design expert systems. The reason for wanting to write an AI program that could design expert systems is that to do so is to prove that the description of the phenomenon has reached a level at which it can be described in computational terms. That is, such a description would be a well-defined theory of the mental activity of building expert systems. There are several reasons that such a computational theory is desirable and we will return to this issue in the final section.

In this paper I will describe the context in which I am doing this research, providing a brief description of how we came to the three findings stated above. Following the description of past work, I will concentrate on clarifying the following two assertions, which are the main concern of this paper:

Assertion 1 Building an expert system is nothing more, or anything less, than building a mental model of the world that has the property that, when the mental model is represented as a running computer program, it solves some problem that its designers intended it to solve.

Assertion 2 There is an identifiable set of mental objects, and actions on those objects, that underlie the process of building the kind of mental models referred to in 1, above.

The bulk of the paper will focus on supporting arguments for these two assertions.

Background For Current Research

For several years, our research group has studied professional software designers with the goal of developing a cognitive, and computational, model of software design. Since we are interested in how "real live" designers perform their tasks when they are "on the job", we have shied away from highly controlled studies of software design, which typically present programmers with very small programs and ask them to perform highly constrained tasks such as filling in a line of code that has been omitted from a program. While such studies can be of value in studying the microstructure of the software design process, we have been primarily concerned with exploring the cognitive activity that occurs when designers are confronted with reasonably complex tasks; if not as complex as the most difficult that they encounter on their jobs, at least as complex as their typical tasks.

Thus, in our studies of software design, we present designers with a task that requires them either to develop a complex piece of software or to modify an existing piece of software. To this end, we have developed several tasks for programmers. These tasks usually require at least three hours to solve and, thus, require programmers to use the kinds of problem solving activities that they use in their daily work. In all cases, we present the programmer with the task, encourage him or her to talk aloud while they are doing the task, encourage them to make drawings or notes, and videotape the entire design session.

The three findings noted in the introduction derive from three separate studies with professional grade programmers. The first and third studies presented programmers with a problem to solve that required writing a new program; in the second study programmers were required to enhance an existing program. The following is a brief description of the tasks, the programmers, and the main findings of the studies as they bear on the topic of this paper.

Finding 1: <u>Littman & Soloway, 1986</u> *Multiple Mental Representations* --- 6 professional programmers at a major telecommunications company (ITT) were asked to design an electronic mail system that could run on a computer which was largest enough so that processing speed and memory were not significant design constraints. The programmers, all with several years of professional experience, were given commands that the mail system should provide e.g., READ, REPLY, DELETE, mail messages. The designers were asked to produce pseudocode solutions if they had time or just high level design specifications if there was not enough time. The designers worked for several hours and produced around 10 sheets of design specification and pseudocode.

As they designed their solutions, we saw that designers did not maintain a single perspective on the design of their programs. For example, several designers constructed, and used, the following two representations of the mail system:

-- a <u>finite state automaton</u> in which the user starts in the "READY" state, issues a command (e.g., READ a message), receives the results of the processing, moves to another state (e.g., DELETE a message) and so on. In this representation, the designer is concerned with the logical structure of the flow of events at a very high level of abstraction. For example, one designer who reasoned about a finite state automaton said:
"Think of it as a big state machine. ... O.K. Let me start looking at the *states* of a user first of all. ... He starts out with some state ... let's call it an *initial state* ... Let's look at a reception scenario ... he becomes capable of receiving mail ... either there is mail or there is not mail ... this brings him to a *new state* where he knows what mail he has. He can *choose at this state* to exit ... "

As this quotation shows, the designer is reasoning in terms of states of a system that the user moves through by making choices about what action to take. Indeed, one designer who reasoned in terms of such a state transition model drew a finite state automaton on his design sheets and fleshed it out as he reasoned through various user scenarios.

-- a <u>system in which there are two agents</u>, the user and the mail system. In this representation, designers imagined scenarios in which the user and the system exchanged commands and information of various kinds, such as desired commands and error messages. The designers used this representation to determine what functionalities the user interface should have, what kinds of error protection the system should provide, and so forth. For example, one designer said the following when reasoning at a very abstract level about how the system would interact with a user:

"We are sending and receiving messages through the mail system. The input (from the user to the system) is a message; the output (from the system to the user) is ... some kind of response. If it (the user's goal) is a RECEIVE operation then it (the system's response) is either a message or an empty message."

Here we see the designer reasoning explicitly about the user and the mail system as collaborative agents exchanging instructional messages through a narrow bandwidth interface.

Thus, as these examples show, during the process of designing their electronic mail systems, the designers used different representations for different purposes. Of course, they were then faced with the task of coordinating the mental representations to produce their solutions. That, however, is another story.

Finding 2: <u>Littman, Pinto & Soloway, 1986</u> *Mental Simulation* --- 10 professional programmers working at Jet Propulsion Laboratories (JPL) were asked to modify a FORTRAN program that implemented a simple data base for personnel records for e.g., a small business. The unmodified program permitted standard transactions on database records e.g., ADD, DELETE, UPDATE, SHOW. The programmer's task was to add code that would implement the function RESTORE so that a user could return to the database any record that had been deleted during the session. All the programmers produced some FORTRAN code for their solutions. The amount of code was small --- between 5 and 20 lines. The small amount of code produced resulted from the task: an enhancement task that was intended to leave the rest of the program untouched as much as possible.

As the programmers engaged in their enhancement task, they realized that they would have to understand how the unmodified program was constructed, and how it behaved, before they could reasonably begin to rewrite the program to perform the RESTORE function.

One of the most prevalent, and time consuming, activities that the programmers performed was mental simulation of the program. That is, the programmers spent a great deal of time "playing computer" and running in their heads the code of the program. Mental simulation appeared to serve the goal of building a mental model of the program that contained a basis for reasoning about how the parts of the program interacted. For example, one subject, who exemplified this use of simulation, said:

"I'm tracing through the main program to see the flow of the main program through its subroutines ..."

Thus, mental simulation was used to build a mental model of how the parts of the program were connected. With this mental model of the connections and interactions of the parts of the program the software designer could modify it with a clear awareness of how the modification affected the previous interactions that had to be preserved to leave the program's function undisturbed. Thus, it was through the process of mental simulation that the programmers constructed their mental models of the program in both its unmodified and modified forms.

Indeed, a main finding about mental simulation was that programmers who produced successful RESTORE routines, i.e., solutions that did not interfere with the functioning of the original program, spent much more time engaged in mental simulation than programmers who produced unsuccessful RESTORE enhancements. But that, too, is another story, told in Littman, Pinto, & Soloway (1986).

Finding 3: Littman, 1987 *Recurrent Activities in Design* --- Six experienced designers of AI programs, all advanced graduate students in the AI program at Yale University, were asked to design an interactive tutoring system, using AI methods, that could help people learn about causes of weather in various regions of the world. As a constraint on their designs, the programmers were provided with a hypothetical dialogue between a user and the program that their AI systems should be able to support. The designers produce high level specifications for some of the components of the complex system and some designers produced some initial sketches of knowledge representations. None of the designers actually produced code.

Part of the hypothetical dialogue is presented in Figure 1. Notice that the conversation revolves around the tutor's strategy of asking the student questions and then following up the student's answers with either another question or an acknowledgement that the student's response is correct. As they analyzed the full dialogue, which contained approximately 10 exchanges between the tutor and the student, the programmers came to the realization that they would have to design their tutoring systems to integrate a sophisticated strategy for maintaining a question based dialogue with a representation of the knowledge of weather that they wished to communicate. For example, it was clear from the hypothetical dialogue that the program should be able to use questions to lead a user to understand the reasons that it rains so much in the northwestern part of the United States instead of simply giving the user the reasons.

Instead of finding that all designers behaved differently, it was clear that, even though the particular AI methods they chose might have been different, there was a great deal of consistency in what the designers did. In fact, it was possible to identify seven major similarities in the behavior of all the designers (Littman, 1987). For example, all of the designers seemed to focus on a "touchstone", an issue that represented a key problem that, when solved, would lay the groundwork for constructing a major part of the design. For example, one designer focused on the interaction shown in Figure 1. As he considered the interaction he came to the conclusion that, if he could identify representations for the domain knowledge and dialogue strategies that could support the tutor's reasoning about the effect of the Japan Current on weather in the northwestern United States that then he would be "home free" and able to construct a program that would handle the entire dialogue.

Of particular relevance to the current argument that constructing expert systems is constructing mental models is the finding that all the designers performed extensive mental simulation of both their mental models of the weather domain and their emerging designs. They used mental simulation of their mental models of the weather domain and the tutorial interactions to determine what knowledge they *should* represent in their programs; they used mental simulation of their designs to determine what knowledge they *could* represent at any given stage in the development of their designs and, hence, what representational techniques appeared to be promising and which needed modification.

TUTOR: How do you think the Japan Current along the northwest coast affects rainfall there?

STUDENT: It's probably rainy.

TUTOR: Yes. There are rain forests in Washington.

STUDENT: Then the Japanese Current is warm.

TUTOR: Right.

STUDENT: And the wind blows in from the sea.

TUTOR: What happens to the moist air blown over Washington and Oregon by the winds?

STUDENT: It condenses and rains because the moist air cools and cannot hold the water. It cools when the wind blows it and it lowers from the sky.

Figure 1: Sample Dialogue Between Tutor and Student

For example, one designer of the ITS said this during a period of simulation of the weather patterns off the northwest coast of the United States said:

"I'm inferring that the Japan Current is cold. If I make (this) assumption about the Current's path, then the Current *starts out* in Japan, which is fairly far north, and *goes even farther north*. So, it probably *gets very cold* when it *comes down the coast* and probably makes Washington and Oregon a fairly cold place."

The words in italics are intended to show that the designer is simulating a mental model of the Japan Current's travel past the northwest United States and discovering, through the simulation, that the Current gets colder as it moves north. In fact, the current actually makes the northwest United States quite temperate, and rainy --- the point is that this incorrect conclusion was derived by mental simulation of a model of the domain. In addition to simulating the domain, the designers simulated their program designs, using the same kinds of strategies used by the designers in the foregoing two examples.

The reasons AI designers depended so heavily on mental simulation appear to be the same as the reasons designers of conventional software do so: All use mental simulation as a way of gathering data about the ways in which their current designs meet high level goals for the design. When mental simulation yields evidence that the current design is inadequate, the design is revised using knowledge that we have not yet identified. Sometimes designers conclude that they had an entirely mistaken view of the problem, throw away their designs, and begin again. This process of constructing a tentative design, "running" it mentally, evaluating the result, and modifying the design appropriately is the process of constructing a mental model of a mechanism that can achieve the high level goals of the design task.

In summary, the picture that begins to emerge form these studies of the program design process is that mental models, and strategies such as mental simulation for manipulating them, are somehow key aspects of the cognition that supports design of computer programs. In the next section we consider the possibility that the process of building computer programs and, by extension, expert systems, *is* the process of constructing and manipulating mental models.

Supporting The Two Assertions

In what follows I will sketch the arguments for the two assertions identified above. In discussing Assertion 1, we will consider some implications of the notion that designing expert systems is identical to the process of building mental models. In considering Assertion 2, we will attempt to describe the objects and actions, i.e., the cognitive ontology, that support the construction of expert systems and, by extension, other classes of designed artifacts, of which all computer programs are examples. In forging arguments to support both assertions I will appeal to empirical observations of designers of various kinds of software, including expert systems.

Assertion 1: Building expert systems is building mental models.

The argument for the assertion that building expert systems is building mental models has two parts, an *in-principle* part and an *in-practice* part. We now consider arguments for each.

<u>In-Principle:</u> If an expert system designer is given a task to build a system that is not exactly like one that he or she has built before, then the designer must *construct* the solution. In essence, the process of designing expert systems is one of invention. But invention of what?

Suppose that an expert system designer must build an expert system to determine what is wrong with large diesel engines. Suppose further that the designer has access to a human expert troubleshooter for diesels. To build such a system, the designer not only must construct a model of diesel engines that can support reasoning about their behavior under faulted, and unfaulted, conditions; he or she must also construct a model of the process of diagnosing faults in diesel engines that the expert troubleshooter uses. The model of the diagnostic process must address issues such as how diagnostic hypotheses are selected, how data relevant to the selected hypotheses are collected, how the data are evaluated, how the results of the evaluation are used to modify diagnostic hypotheses, and so forth. In short, the designer must invent a model of the diesel and a model of the diagnostic process which can be implemented in a programming language, e.g., OPS5.

Since the models that lie at the center of expert systems are not built out of physical materials, and since the cognitive activities identified in the previous section e.g., mental simulation, play a central role in this kind of design, it is apparent that the construction of mental models plays a central role in developing the model of the diesel and the model of the diagnostic process. Indeed, it is hard to see how an expert system designer could build such an expert system without at the same time building mental models.

In essence, then, an expert system that runs on a computer is a translation of a designer's mental models of a domain, its tasks, and relevant problem solving processes into an algorithmic language, such as OPS5 or Prolog or LISP. How this translation occurs is not well understood, but it is likely that it is governed by the same principles that govern programming activities in other domains (cf. Adelson & Soloway, 1984). Thus, the process of building an expert system depends fundamentally on a) constructing a mental model of the objects and processes in the problem domain, b) building a mental model of problem solving techniques that are used in the domain, and c) "translating" these mental representations into a computer program.

<u>In-Practice:</u> In my work on the cognitive activity underlying the design of expert systems I have repeatedly observed that different designers solve the "same problem" in different ways. For example, when I gave several

experienced AI designers the task of constructing a tutoring system that could teach about weather systems, differeni designers selected different representations for the knowledge of the weather domain that their programs would have to manipulate. That is, different designers built different mental models of the weather domain. An example comparing two designers of an expert system illustrates what I mean.

Subject 1 decided to use a causal chain representation for the weather domain. For example, in explaining why it rains so much in the Northwestern region of the United States, Subject 1's representation tied together, in sequence, 1) the accumulation of evaporated ocean water in clouds, 2) the heating of this water by the sun and by warm ocean currents, 3) the stacking of the clouds against the mountain ranges in the Northwest US and 4) the saturation of clouds with moisture. The result of this process, of course, is that it rains a lot in the Northwest US. Thus, Subject 1 constructed a mental model of the interactions of different physical aspects of weather in which the semantics of causality between distant parts of weather systems was represented by ordered sequences of actions where Action $n-1$ is said to be the cause of Action n. Finally, Subject 1's design for a computer program to solve the task reflected his mental model and encoded causality as causal chains.

Subject 2 constructed a different mental model of weather systems. For Subject 2, knowledge about weather was represented in frames which had slots that identified attributes of the frame that he wanted his program to manipulate. For example, Subject 1 constructed a frame for the climate in a region. The climate frame for a region had slots for such attributes as temperature and humidity. Subject 1 intended that the frames representing knowledge about weather would be manipulated with rules that supported causal inferences.

A fundamental difference between the solutions of Subject 1 and Subject 2 lies in the mental models they had of weather. Subject 1's mental model of weather was **dynamic**; to reason about it he imagined sequences of events that connected some initial state with a resulting state. Subject 2 constructed a mental model that had a large component that was <u>static</u>. Subject 2's mental model contained much information in frames which contained slots with content knowledge, such as temperature, that he could reason about independently of how it participated in the dynamic activity of a weather system.

Of course, I have tried to paint Subject 1 and Subject 2 to be as different as possible. Their mental representations had some elements in common, such as causal rules for determining what the effects of one state of affairs would be after some period of time. Even in the case of causal rules, however, Subject 1 and Subject 2 differed. Causal rules *were* Subject 1's mental model of weather.

Subject 2 *used* causal rules to make inferences in his frame-based mental model of knowledge about weather. Since there is such apparent diversity in the mental models constructed by designers of software, it seems reasonable to try to understand the underlying elements out of which they are built. In the next section, therefore, we begin to lay out the different kinds of mental objects that designers of artifacts such as computer programs use when they build mental models.

Assertion 2: There is a cognitive ontology for building mental models.

What does this assertion mean? In brief, this assertion means that the cognitive activities that comprise the process of designing expert systems depend upon a set of mental objects and mental operations. These mental objects and operations are the cognitive ontology --- the mental "stuff" that forms the basis for constructing mental models.

My work on identifying the stuff of such mental models has produced an initial taxonomy of the aspects of cognition that support the design of complex artifacts such as expert systems. This taxonomy was developed from the studies described earlier in the paper. I will just outline the taxonomy here, giving examples where appropriate. The taxonomy has two major components, Mental Model Types and Cognitive Activities On Mental Models.

I. Mental Model Types

I have identified two main dimensions of the mental models that are used by designers of software. First, mental models can be simple or mental models can be complex. Second, mental models can be static or they can be dynamic. The following examples illustrate this taxonomy. These examples are drawn from our experience studying expert software designers who were given the task of designing an electronic mail system and Figure 2 displays the examples which are described in more detail below.

Static & Simple: A mental model of a single user of the electronic mail system is a static, simple mental model. The mental model is static because the user is not doing anything, though s/he has potentials for doing so which are inherent parts of the mental model. Thus, simple mental models are typically structured representations that have many attributes that cohere in some frame-like representation. As one designer said:

"What are the *things* we are dealing with?   Objects.   We've got *users* ..."

As the italicized words show, the designer has identified "users" as a complex data type which is manipulated during program development.

Static & Complex: A static, complex representation is similar to a static, simple representation except that it is a composed object.   A composed object is one with many components that are not bound together in any inherent structure, such as a "person".   Thus, the hallmark of a complex object is that components of it can be deleted without fundamentally compromising the integrity of the object.   This cannot be done with a simple object, such as a person.   An example of a static, complex mental representation is a group of users of the electronic mail system.

Dynamic & Simple: A dynamic, simple mental model is one that represents an action that is simple in the sense that it is not composed of separable components.   An example of a dynamic, simple mental model is a single user action, such as requesting an electronic mail system to display unread messages. Requesting the system to display unread messages is simple because it does not have any components.   Of course, the individual finger motions required to type the string display are components of the action, but from the point of view of the designer of the mail system display is a unitary, simple action.   For example, one designer said:

"Let me look back at my *primitives* ... READ ...."

This quote shows that, for the purposes of designing a system to *coordinate* the various actions of the mail system, each can be viewed as a dynamic, simple action that results in a well-defined event (and thus is dynamic) when the user evokes it by performing some action.

Dynamic & Complex: Dynamic, complex mental models are ones that represent actions and have several decomposable parts which are, themselves, either complex or simple mental models.   An example of this kind of mental model would be of a particular user scenario of interaction with the electronic mail system in which the user issues several commands and the system responds to them.   Examples are given in the first two quotations in this paper.

In sum, there there appear to be at least two dimensions of mental models that designers of software use.   Software designers use, and construct, mental models which appear to be built out of components that have these two dimensions. In the next section we consider some of the cognitive operations that can be applied to such mental models in the course putting them together into a complex design.

II. Cognitive Activities On Mental Models

If software designers had ready-made solutions to all of their design tasks, then they could simply retrieve one from memory and implement it as a computer program. In most cases of design, however, it is not possible to retrieve an off-the-shelf solution. Rather, designers must build a complex mental model that achieves an overall design goal out of components that they either have stored in memory or can construct from design requirements generated before, or during, the design process. In this section we describe two classes of cognitive activities on mental models, Build Activities and Operate Activities.

	SIMPLE	COMPLEX
STATIC	SINGLE USER	GROUP OF USERS
DYNAMIC	USER'S SINGLE ACTION	SCENARIO OF USER'S ACTIONS

Figure 2: Two Dimensions of Mental Models

I. Build Activities

Build activities result in the addition of components of a mental model. There are seven main kinds of build activities. We now describe and present examples of each of them.

Identify: Identification of mental models is to determine one or more candidate mental models that might be appropriate for a subgoal of a design task.   For example, in constructing the tutoring system for the weather domain, some tutors identified both a causal chain representation for the knowledge of the weather domain and a frame-like representation.   They then used other criteria to select which one to use for their designs as the next paragraph and quotation show.

Select: Selection of a mental model is just what it seems.   Out of several choices that have been identified, the designer selects one that seems most appropriate. For example, a designer might select a causal chain representation of the weather domain over a frame-based representation.   For example, one designer settled on a frame representation and observed:

"If there's a climate frame, one of its slots is going to have to be temperature."

The reasons for selecting one representation over another are an important topic for research.

Tailor: Tailoring of mental models occurs when a mental model has been selected that "almost works" but needs to be modified for the current design task. The term tailoring is due to James C. Spohrer who has been studying the ways in which novice programmers generate solutions to simple programming assignments.   A very simple example of tailoring is the addition of a buffer management scheme to the nearly-completed electronic mail system.   As one designer observed:

"This brings up an important question.   How to keep track of buffers that are already destined for other users and buffers that are empty. "

This is an example of tailoring of mental models because the designer had already developed a fairly complete solution to the electronic mail design problem but was required to alter it just a bit to manage the problem of buffers.

Compose: Composition of mental models is one of the primary activities of experienced software designers, whether they are building conventional software or expert systems.   Composition is the process of "stitching together" separable mental models.   For example, in building a mental model of an interaction scenario between a tutoring system and a student, a designer composes mental models of the student and the tutoring system which takes into account the requirements of each.   There are several composition operations that can be used to compose mental models. Three of the most common are abutment, nesting, and merging. These terms were invented by James Spohrer to describe the behavior of novice programmers when they must compose several plans to solve a complex goal. We use the terms here both because they seem to apply to the problem of composing mental models and because the cognitive activity of composing several plans to achieve a complex goal may, in fact, be the result of the composition of mental models.

Abutment occurs when two mental models share information only at their boundaries; this might occur in a mental model of the electronic mail system when the user produces a command, the system executes it, and the user views the result; or when the designer of the mail system adds actions to the state transition diagram of the mail system.

Nesting occurs when one mental model is "placed inside" another. For example, a mental model of the operating system routine that allocates space for mail messages might be nested inside the mental model of the behavior of the routine send by which a user sends a message to another user. The mental model of space allocation is nested inside the mental model of the action of the send routine because it is "invisible" from other mental models, say the mental model of the read routine.

Merging occurs when two or more mental models share a common mental model. For example, when he was constructing his RESTORE routine for the personnel database program, one designer discovered that records are not really deleted from the database. He then deduced that it would be necessary to prevent the routine that searches for the record the user wants to restore from returning an active record, i.e., one that had never been deleted. His solution to this problem was to merge the search process with the mechanism for preventing the return of an active record. As he said:

"We know the command at this point (when the search process is called). So, what I would do is put a check at this point (in the search subroutines) to check if the command is a RESTORE."

If the command were RESTORE, then the designer's solution would require that search return either an *inactive* record or no record at all. Thus, the designer merged his model of the the search process with his model for how to satisfy the constraint on the RESTORE subroutine and constructed a single mechanism for satisfying a constraint on the record search mechanism.

Construct: Construction of mental models occurs when the designer knows what general purposes a mental model should serve but does not have one in his or her memory that 1) fits the requirements exactly or b) can be tailored to do so. Construction typically occurs when a designer confronts a problem that he or she has not solved before. Several of the designers of the intelligent tutoring system for weather had very poor mental models of weather and actually constructed them during the process of designing their systems. For example, one said:

"Obviously my model of weather is off. It's a confounding factor. The first thing I'd do in building (this) AI system would be to get out some books on weather and *understand what is really going on.*"

Transform: Transformation of mental models occurs when knowledge that is represented in one way is re-represented in another way. For example, a designer who converted a causal chain model of the weather domain into a frame-based model of the weather domain would be performing a transformation of the mental model. Of course, that would be a fairly radical transformation of a mental model.

Augment/Diminish: Augmenting and diminishing are just what they seem --- the addition and elimination of elements of a mental model. For example, a designer of the electronic mail system might add new commands to the mail system e.g., copy-to-file or might eliminate existing commands e.g., reply, because it is redundant with the combination of read and send.

II.   Operate Activities

Operate activities provide the designer with information about the behavior of a mental model and its relation to design specifications. There are two major kinds of operate activities, inspect and evaluate.

Inspect: A designer inspects mental models to generate information that can be used to evaluate whether it meets the goals that it should. Several inspection techniques appear to be common.   A very common inspection technique used by designers is to simulate their mental models to determine how it behaves when it "runs". This topic is considered in depth in Littman, Pinto, Letovsky, and Soloway (1986) and several examples are presented earlier in this paper.   As well, a designer can inspect a mental model from different perspectives.   For example, designers of the electronic mail system inspected it from the point of view of the user, the point of view of the operating system, and so forth.   As one designer said when thinking about the electronic mail system from the point of view of the user:

"How in the world is this going to be seen from the (point of) view of the user?"

Evaluate: Designers evaluate their mental models to determine whether the designs they have constructed meet the design goals set for them. The evaluation process proceeds by applying evaluation heuristics to the results of inspection operations, such as running the mental model. For example, a designer of the intelligent tutor for the weather domain might decide that a consistent representation for weather knowledge outweighs certain considerations of efficiency at run-time. For example, one of the designers of the ITS for weather performed some of the evaluation of his design using the following strategy:

"So I guess I am playing this game, predicting what the interviewer is trying to say (and then seeing if his design could generate that statement)."

Adelson & Soloway (1984) discuss the evaluation process in some detail.

In sum, we have described two aspects of the process of building mental models --- construction and evaluation. In evaluating this description it should be kept firmly in mind that it is intended only as an initial attempt. There are several problems with this description, most notably the following: The description lacks at least two kinds of information that would be necessary to permit it to serve as a basis for constructing an AI program to perform the activities of constructing mental models that we have described here.

First, we have not specified, in detail, the actual knowledge required to build mental models of programs in a given domain. An example of an attempt to do so is provided by the dissertation work of Stanley Letovsky who is representing the knowledge needed to understand a 250-line database program that carries out transactions such as creating, deleting, and modifying records. (See Letovsky, 1986 for an excellent account of how he identifies this kind of knowledge.)

The second kind of information that is missing is *under what conditions* each of the kinds of activities is appropriate. In essence, what is needed is a process model of design of expert systems which identifies the kinds of knowledge used and when it is used. In the area of general software design, Adelson and Soloway (1984) have proposed such a process model --- it seems important to try to construct one for the area of expert systems as well. This should be a main focus for future research in this area.

Concluding Remarks and Implications

The current paper is intended to do little more than point the way to some possible directions for research into knowledge representation. The goal of the paper is to provide a taste of the work I have been doing to understand the types of cognitive activity that we call "designing expert systems". I have suggested that designing an expert system is nothing more, or less, than constructing a mental model of a process in the world. The process in the world that is represented by the mental model has the attribute that, when it "runs" in the form of a computer program, it behaves in a way that solves problems of the kind that expert systems are intended to solve --- this is what makes it an expert system. I have further suggested that the construction of the mental models that are represented in the world as expert systems are built out of an identifiable set of cognitive objects which can be manipulated by an identifiable set of cognitive actions.

The main implications of this work are twofold. First, from the theoretical point of view, a complete, explicit, computational theory of the kinds of mental models there are, and the pieces out of which they are built, might provide part of the requirements of an AI program that could simulate the human activity of designing expert systems --- it would be arguably useful to have computer programs which could, themselves, build expert systems.

Second, if we understand how humans build the kinds of mental models that are represented in the world as expert systems, then we may be able to build very intelligent support tools that can effectively assist humans in the process of building expert systems because, in a deep sense, these tools can be endowed with an understanding of the thought processes of the humans using the tools.

For both reasons, it seems worthwhile to continue to pursue this line of research.

Acknowledgements

As always, I would like to express my heartfelt thanks to Dr. Elliot Soloway for his support of my work. In addition, I would like to thank Dr. Katharina Morik for inviting me to present this work at the 1987 International Workshop on Knowledge Representation and Knowledge Organization in Machine Learning

(KROML) and for making many constructive suggestions about the paper.

References:

Adelson, B. & Soloway, E. A model of software design. Technical Report #342, Department of Computer Science, 1984.

Letovsky, S. Cognitive processes in program comprehension. In E. Soloway & S. Iyengar (Eds.) Empirical studies of programmers. Ablex, Norwood, NJ, 1986.

Littman, D., Pinto, J., Letovsky, S., & Soloway, E. Mental models and software maintenance. In E. Soloway & S. Iyengar (Eds.) Empirical studies of programmers. Ablex, Norwood, NJ, 1986.

Littman, D. & Soloway, E. Mental simulation of programs: Some Data and some theory. Unpublished paper (1986) available from the author.

Littman, D. Modelling human expertise in knowledge engineering: Some preliminary observations. IJMMS 1987.

Sloppy Modeling

Katharina Morik

Technical University Berlin

Project Group KIT

Sekr. FR 5-8

Franklinstr.28/29

D-1000 BERLIN 10

<MORIK@DB0TUI11.BITNET>

Abstract

In this paper, I would like to present a unifying view on knowledge acquisition and machine learning. In this view, knowledge acquisition systems should support the user in doing the modeling of a domain, and machine learning systems are those which perform part of the modeling autonomously. Taking the notion of modeling as the central point, some aspects of modeling along with their impact for building knowledge acquisition and machine learning systems are discussed. In particular, reversability at all levels is claimed to be supported by the system.

As a result of the unifying view, a new way of integrating machine learning into knowledge acquisition is presented and exemplified by the system BLIP [1], a system which supports the user in domain modeling and at the same time takes part of the work off the user's back by modeling autonomously. Since all decisions regarding the model can be revised and revision is supported by the system, we call this way of modeling "sloppy modeling"; the user may start with a sloppy model which can be revised and enhanced.

1 Knowledge Acquisition as Transfer

Knowledge acquisition and knowledge engineering has been viewed as a transfer process for a long time (Hayes-Roth, Waterman, Lenat 83). This view is best illustrated by the bottleneck metaphor cited all over the literature: knowledge acquisition is the bottleneck of building expert systems. Knowledge engineering then means extracting knowledge out of the expert and pushing a completed model into the expert system. We can assign two interpretations to this metaphor: on the one hand, the expert system is the bottle, and the problem is to get the knowledge in. On the other hand, the expert is meant by the bottle, and the problem is to get the knowledge out.

---

[1]   BLIP is currently under development at the Technical University Berlin, project KIT-Lerner; KIT-Lerner is partially supported by the German ministry for research and technology (BMFT) under contract ITW8501B1. Industrial partners are Nixdorf Computer AG and Stollmann GmbH.

1.1 The Expert System as a "Bottle"

First-generation expert systems (like MYCIN) offer the user only one data structure to represent knowledge about a domain, knowledge about a task, and knowledge about consultation strategy: the production rule. Knowledge engineering within this framework means encoding diverse types of knowledge as production rules. In order to support the knowledge engineer, tools such as knowledge editors, debuggers, and menu interfaces have been developed.

These tools are supposed to serve as "funnels." They are built to offer an additional functionality to the expert system shell. In particular, they should provide for
- inspectability of the knowledge base,
- explainability of system behavior, and
- changeability of the encoded knowledge.

However, as will be shown in the next section of this paper, tools cannot help the knowledge engineer more than the expert system's representation language allows them to.

1.1.1 Tools don't help

In this section, the shortcomings of knowledge acquisition with respect to first-generation expert systems are discussed using three examples: goal integration, representation at the most specific level (object level), and uniform representation of diverse knowledge types. The examples have already been discussed with respect to explainability of expert systems (Swartout 83; Neches, Swartout, Moore 85; Clancey 86). Here, I want to recall this discussion and point out its impact on knowledge engineering.

The problem of goal integration or integration of action parts of production rules has been raised by Mostow and Swartout (86). Usually, different derivations of the same conclusion are integrated by strengthening the certainty factor of the conclusion using Shortliffe's (Shortliffe 76) formula

$$1-\prod_{i=1}^{n}(1-x_i),$$

where xi are the certainty factors of the single conclusions.

This formula is only applicable if the premises of the rules are mutually independent. Swartout takes this example and proposes an explicit representation of goals and methods. I do not want to go that far here, but only indicate consequences for tools. Adding a new rule thus requires checking all rules with the same action part, looking for specialization relations between premises, and preventing these relations. Since the system has no epistemic knowledge of super- and subconcepts, it is up to the knowledge engineer to take care that the premise of the new rule is independent of already existing premises with the same conclusion. A knowledge acquisition tool can display all rules with the same action part. It cannot, however, watch over the independence of premises. This example already shows that a tool cannot offer a really additional functionality to the expert system shell. In fact, a good tool requires functionality on the part of the expert system shell itself; here: epistemic knowledge of super- and subconcepts.

The representation at the most specific level in EMYCIN-alike systems has been criticized by, among others, Clancey (86). The prominent example is the representation of heuristics in MYCIN. MYCIN behaves as if there were the following heuristic:

> *If the genus of a micro-organism can be determined but not its species*
> *then take the most probable species for that genus.*

This behavior, however, is a result of rules which give the most probable species for a genus. The heuristic is encoded as the level of "genus" and "species". Therefore, the heuristic cannot be found and changed at one place in the knowledge base. Moreover, the system cannot collect all rules involved in the heuristic in order to display them to the user as it could - in the first example - show all rules with the same action part. Neither can the user express her/his wish to change the heuristic nor can the system determine the set of rules corresponding to the heuristic. Another consequence of this representational framework is that changing a rule on species may cause a new system behavior in a way the user is not aware of. No tool can support the user in changing the heuristic or call the user's attention to consequences of changing innocent-looking rules for the system's overall behavior.

The uniform representation of consultative, problem-solving, and domain knowledge prevents the user from changing just one type of knowledge. For example, the strategy of questioning the advice-seeking user cannot be changed as such. Moreover, changing a rule system behavior in an unforeseen way. The well-known rule of MYCIN:

> *If the age of the patient is greater than 17 and*
> > *the patient is an alcoholic*
> *then Diplococcus might be causing infection.*

is of the same form as

> *If the age of the patient is less than 7*
> *then remove Tetracycline from the list of drugs under consideration.*

(Clancey 86). The intention behind introducing the age of the patient into the left-hand side of the rule, however, is different. In the first rule, younger patients are not asked whether they are alcoholics because of the first premise. In the second rule, Tetracycline are not prescribed to children, because Tetracycline can do harm to their teeth and bones. If child alcohol abuse increases so that the question of whether the patient is an alcoholic is also applicable to the 12-year-olds, a rule on Diplococcus but not a similar looking rule on Tetracycline has to be changed. How can the knowledge engineer find the rules to be changed? How could a tool find them for him?

In addition, the knowledge engineer inspecting knowledge about Diploccocus may well delete the age-premise of the first rule, regarding it as nonsense. He then changes the questioning behavior, without intending it and neither the system nor a tool can warn him.

As these examples show, even tools with high polished interfaces using window and mouse techniques cannot compensate for representational deficiencies of the expert system shell. In terms of the metaphor: building funnels is no solution if the bottle is the problem.

1.1.2 Newer Acquisition Systems

The discussion sketched in the previous section has led to newer developments in expert systems. As tools turned out to be inappropriate, work concentrated on developing expert system shells which ease knowledge acquisition by their representation forms. The goal is to offer representational constructs which match the expert's concepts. It is the standard AI goal of representing knowledge in the "human window" (Michie 82). Where production rules were first viewed as corresponding to expert's concepts they now are classified as "implementation-level primitives" to a domain ontology (e.g. "disease process taxonomy") and epistemological distinctions. The underlying assumption with respect to knowledge acquisition is: if there is no mismatch between representational constructs offered by the system and mental concepts to the expert, knowledge acquisition is more or less a direct typing-in process.

A system which allows the user to type her/his knowledge into the system in the same way as s/he used to write it on paper is OPAL (Musen, Fagan, Combs, Shortliffe 87). The system acquires oncological reports like with spread-sheets. This is possible because the oncological knowledge is already fully represented. The domain model is used to guide the acquisition dialog. Turning it the other way around: the hard problem of domain modeling must have been solved before the easy knowledge acquisition such as filling in forms becomes applicable. Similarly, the KRIMB system (Cox, Blumenthal 87) reduces knowledge acquistion to the specification of an already prepared model. For instance, it is already known that animals eat food, that cats are animals, that fish is food, and that cats eat fish. The system is then capable of acquiring the fact that a particular cat eats a particular fish. Calling the specification process "model building" is misleading.

A more general knowledge acquisition tool is MOLE (Eshelman, Ehret, McDermott, Tan 87). MOLE also exploits assumptions about the world. These assumptions, however, are much more general than those of OPAL or KRIMB. It is presupposed that
- the task of the new domain is of the heuristic classification type,
- there are hypotheses which cover symptoms,
- there are symptoms which differentiate between hypotheses, and
- there is knowledge about the combination of hypotheses.

This general structure is adequate for a wide range of domains. It enables the system, e.g. to check whether hypotheses can be differentiated in principle, to supply default support values, to discover intermediary concepts between symptoms and hypotheses. In a second phase of knowledge acquisition, the knowledge base is interactively refined. In this framework, the knowledge engineer is regarded an AI programmer. He is offered a workbench with which he can encode a knowledge base. This is analogous to the environment of a programming language. As is the case there, the model (algorithm) has to be constructed by the knowledge engineer (programmer); only the encoding is supported. In fact, model building is not at all supported by these systems but rather presupposed.
Figure 1 shows the transfer view of knowledge acquisition.

The newer approaches differ from the tool approach in the integration of knowledge acquisition and the performance element. The two approaches do not differ, however, in the sequential procedure of

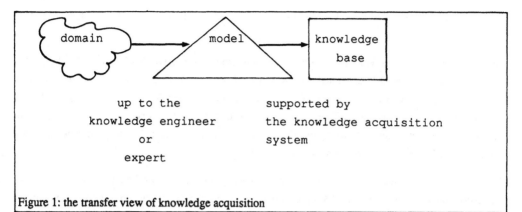

Figure 1: the transfer view of knowledge acquisition

knowledge acquisiton. Building a model for a domain is an activity which is neither supported nor even recognized by both approaches. The model is viewed as given in a more or less completed form. The problem is then to transfer the given model from one representation form (on paper, in the head) into another (the representation form of the system). The influence of the representations and the influence of the encoding phase back to the model building cannot be dealt with in this paradigm. In terms of figure 1, the arrow back from the knowledge base to the model and model building is missing.

In particular, revision of the model based on experience with the system's performance is restricted to refinement. Only belief revision in the knowledge base is supported by the system, but changing the granularity or reorganizing the taxonomy - to name just two examples - is not handled by these systems. However, from observing users of a knowledge acquisition system, it becomes quite obvious that very often the user first chooses inappropriate representations. For instance, the decision whether a concept should be represented as an object (or event), as an attribute, or as a value determines further expressability of facts. Revising such a decision should be supported by the system. Only then can it be called a system supporting modeling.

This point will be discussed in more detail in section 2.4. Here, it suffices to point out that even advanced knowledge acquisition systems still fit into the transfer as opposed to the modeling view.

1.2 The Expert as a "Bottle"

Another way to interpret the bottleneck metaphor is to identify the expert with the bottle. The problem of knowledge acquisition is then to elicit the knowledge from the expert. Knowledge elicitation techniques such as interview techniques, content and protocol analysis, and the application of the personal construct theory (Kelly 55) are psychological means to this end. The way from the model supposedly in the expert's head of the expert to a knowledge base is divided into two steps: the elicitation and the encoding step. Often it is argued in favor of a mediating or intermediate representation between both steps, (e.g. Johnson 87; Young, Gammack 87).

How far the first step can be supported by a system is an open question. Knowledge elicitation primarily deals with the interaction of expert and knowledge engineer. This interaction requires social and communicative skills which cannot be ascribed to computers today. Manual knowledge elicitation therefore still remains the most broadly used method for the first step of knowledge acquisition (LaFrance 87).

Knowledge acquisition systems stressing the elicitation step are, e.g. AQUINAS (Boose, Bradshaw 87), KSS0 (Gaines 87), and KRITON (Diederich, Ruhmann, May 87). These systems interview the expert or knowledge engineer and form a representation of the knowledge which can then be transferred to an expert system. The user is guided through an acquisition dialog, in which s/he enumerates the objects of the domain, their relations and properties. The interfaces are so constructed as to please the user, thus compensating for lacking human communicative abilities.

Knowledge elicitation techniques take into account interview effects such as the influence of the form of a question to the answer. LaFrance (87) points out that asking the expert questions is like a search: the answer is in the mind of the expert but it might be missed by a question following the wrong path. This clearly shows that knowledge elicitation also presupposes the model itself to be fixed and complete in the head of the expert. Therefore, modeling is taken to be accomplished before the acquisition starts, and knowledge elicitation systems do not support the modeling phase.

2 Knowledge Acquisition as Modeling

In this section we want to inspect the modeling process and discuss some properties of the model which the expert has in mind. Is the model already completed in the head of the expert or is knowledge acquisition (including knowledge elicitation) the process of creating that model interactively? First, we argue that expertise need not rely on a model. Therefore, a good task-performer need not have a good model of the domain which could be elicited. Second, we describe the modeling process as scientific investigation. Psychological and sociological theories cast light on the nature of the modeling process. They also point out the interactive nature of modeling, which is the third point to be discussed. Finally, we derive from the discussion of models and the modeling process a view on knowledge acquisition as modeling. In order to make clear what is required of a system supporting modeling, modeling is contrasted with stepwise refining knowledge acquisition.

2.1 Knowledge vs. Skill

Knowledge is explicable and more or less conscious [2]. Skill is not explicable or conscious. This short characterization points to different types of expertise: one based on knowledge, and one based on skills. Good task performance need not rely on knowledge but may well rely on skills. Take for an example the arts. Ask composers, artists, poets how they came to create the composition, the picture, the poem - most often you will get a better answer from a critic. Where the artist is the expert in the sense of the person who is able to perform a task perfectly, the critic is the expert in the sense that he has a theory

---

[2] "More or less" because the implications of knowledge are not always conscious, too, and one knows not always what one knows.

explaining the result of the task performance. This distinction is important because elicitation techniques are only applicable to interviewing the theoretician, not to interviewing the task-performer.

Another example will make this point evident. Let us take natural language as the domain. Native speakers are the experts for their mothertongue in the sense of task-performers. Their linguistic competence is their skill. In a language knowledge base we want to have (at least) a grammar, a lexicon, semantic rules, word meanings, and morphological information. Now, imagine how manual elicitation as the one presented by LaFrance look like if we apply it to this domain.

"Could you describe the kinds of things that native speakers do?"

"Are there different types of native speakers? Is speaking a subtype of some other kind of communication?"

"You said that thinking about what to say occurs before speaking. Why is that the case?"

"Let me play devil's advocate. What if you were thinking while speaking?"

"What are the basic objects in natural language?"

All these questions raise points of great theoretical interest: the first question could be the starting point for discussing speech act theory or communication and action theory; the second in addition points to variation in language; the third and fourth are heatedly discussed in natural language generation; the last question can be viewed as the root of all linguistic research for centuries. Of course, the native speaker is not aware of the theoretical implications of the questions. Before being interviewed, he may well have never thought about it. So he just starts with developing explanations for his own behavior, probably using what he has learned in school, some general explanation patterns, and introspection. Analogous to "naive physics", the model which people produce if they have to explain their expertise in dealing with the physical environment efficiently, a "naive linguistics" is developed. It is merely a rhetorical question, whether we want to build a knowledge base with naive linguistics for a knowledge-based natural language system. We surely do not! This example shows that skills cannot be elicited by the methods of knowledge elicitation and that the best task-performer is not necessarily the right person interviewed if we want to get knowledge about a domain. What the good task-performer (here: the native speaker) is good at is providing and assessing examples of task-performance (here: example sentences).

Figure 2 shows the relation between knowledge and skill with respect to knowledge-based systems. The important point is that people's skills are *described* for knowledge-based systems. Describing competence is a scientific task. In our linguistic example, describing adequately the linguistic competence can viewed as the central task of linguistics. We call the process of describing competence **modeling.** For knowledge-based systems, we demand, in addition, that the model must be operational, i.e. the system should be able to produce good taskperformance with the help of the model. In our above example, generative linguistics satifies this requirement: the grammar is not only descriptive but, at the same time, can produce or analyze sentences. A **model** is an explicit, explainable, and operational theory of a domain. The two lines of Artificial Intelligence research, the more application oriented and

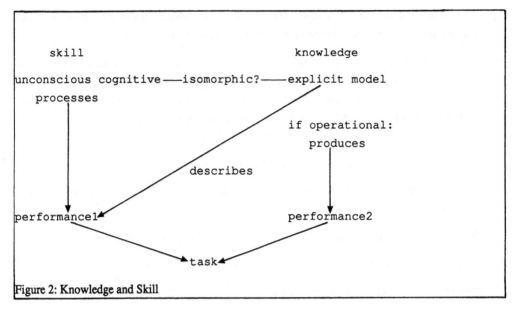

Figure 2: Knowledge and Skill

the cognitive oriented one, correspond to whether the model is claimed to be an isomorphic representation of the human competence and performance (Newell, Simon 72) or to whether it is sufficient that the model gives a good performance (Waterman 86).

2.2 Scientific vs. Naive Theories

The native speaker example in the section above already indicated that modeling is a scientific process. This does not exclude common-sense theories. The same cognitive processes are involved in building scientific and every-day life theories. As phenomenologists and symbolic interactionists have shown, constructing a model of reality is always embedded into the context of every-day life and its social reality (Schütz 62:256). The activity of producing knowledge which selects and explains the relevant observations, thus providing a basis for social interaction, is the same for common sense reasoning as for scientific reasoning (Garfinkel 67:279). Both kinds of theories are always provisional, although both are taken for granted in order to elaborate the theory. The main difference between every-day life and scientific theories is that scientific theories are systematically exposed to doubt and counter-examples. Institutions such as conferences with their refereeing procedure for acceptance and the discussions after talks guarantee that counter-examples or arguments against a theory are brought up and lead to a revision of the theory built up so far. This makes scientific theories more robust with respect to unforeseen events.

If we want to know how people normally build models, we may also look at naive psychology and its scientific investigation. In the field of perception of other people and in the field of attribute theory (derived from balance or dissonance theory) we find interesting results concerning introspection: the self-image is made up by the very same attribution process as is the image of other people. Herkner (80:46ff) reports a number of experiments which give evidence for this thesis. We learn from this that there is no direct link to inner processes of the self. Therefore, experts produce an explanation of their own behavior just in the same way as they would produce it for other people with that behavior [3]. If an expert is expert at performing a certain task and not at producing explanations for this task-performance, s/he will produce a naive theory. The naive theory - as it is not tested by counter-examples and systematic doubt - is just the first approach to modeling. The danger for knowledge acquisition following from the sociological and psychological theories just alluded to is that we build systems with "naive knowledge bases" and confuse this with a knowledge acquisition problem!

2.3 Interactive Nature of Modeling

It has often been reported that experts changed their own thinking after working with a knowledge engineer (e.g. Turkle 84). They developed a model of their own expertise. Moreover, they adapted to the computer model which became their conscious model of what they were doing. This again gives evidence that the acquired model was not in the head of the expert before the acquisition process started, but was built up during the knowledge acquisition.

Modeling is driven by a need for explanation. Facts which are normally overseen become an object of attention if a crisis or conflict occurs or if the person starts thinking - regardless of why - with a theoretical attitude (Garfinkel 73). Interviewing somebody can well be regarded as engendering a theoretical attitude. Note also the stress LaFrance (87) is laying on playing the devil's advocate in interviewing: confronting the evolving model with counter-examples enhances its quality. In science, we can presuppose the theoretical attitude. But even there, the interaction between the scientists drives the scientific evolution. The commonly agreed upon assumptions underlying a theory as well as objections against the theory are a matter of interactive agreement. Taking this statement of phenomenologists and interactionsists seriously we also regard the process of knowledge acquisition as an interactive one. The model of the domain is not already in the head of the expert but is interactively constructed by the expert and the knowledge engineer. This view corresponds exactly to the observation mentioned above.

2.4 The Modeling Cycle

Let us now summarize what we have learned about models and the process of making them.
1. Good task-performance need not rely on an explicable model of the domain.
2. The expert who is a good task-performer is not necessarily also an expert who knows about the domain.
3. A model can be an operational one.
4. Modeling is a scientific process.
5. Interviewing task-performers may start their modeling activity.

---

[3] The main difference between the self-image and the image of other people lies in the parameter "distance": the self is always close to itself, while other people can be distant or close. Closeness gives a positive bias to the explanation forming.

6. A model which is not exposed to counter-examples and doubt sytematically and over a longer period of time is a naive theory.

7. Modeling is an interactive process.

Applying these points to knowledge acquisition we get the following picture:

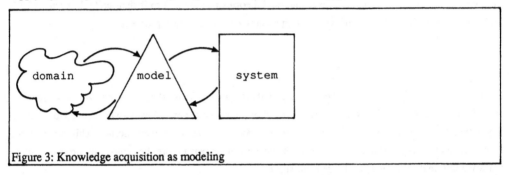

Figure 3: Knowledge acquisition as modeling

The important difference as compared to the transfer view is that the feedback is present from the system to the model-building activity and from the model to observations or experiments in the domain. That is, modeling - as science - is a cyclical, not linear process.

A closer look at the modeling cycle reveals three phases and three types of revisions. This cycle is independent of whether computers are involved or not. It corresponds to the cycle in scientific research. In the first phase, the framework of the model is laid out. It is determined which aspects of the domain are relevant and are to be included in the model, the vocabulary for describing phenomena of the domain is chosen, and some semantic relations between concepts, properties, or states are taken as basic assumptions. Normally, we write this framework down on paper before we choose an appropriate computational representation for it. The step from the domain to the model, especially the creation of the first tentative representation, is not system-supported.

In the second phase, facts and rules are filled into the framework. By working out the framework, it becomes finer grained and more complex. More and more semantic relations are established, and more and more observations of the domain are represented. If there are observations in the domain which are considered to be important but cannot be reflected within the framework, the framework has to be revised. Due to the great difficulty of this revision the step from the domain to the model is normally not system supported. The framework is the basis on which the model is built. Changing the basis, of course, effects changes in the model. In fact, desired changes of the model are the reason for changing the representational framework. The problem is to formulate the effects in a language which itself is subject to change. People, however, seem to be able to reformulate, reorganize, restructure, and refine a model - and systems should be able to support them in doing it! In the next section, an example for this kind of revision is discussed, indicating the requirements of a system supporting the revision.

In the third phase, the model built-up so far is evaluated. In order
- to test the model,
- to clarify conflicts which cannot be resolved with the given information, and
- to fill in underdeveloped areas of the model

experiments are designed. Experiments make new observations available. The new facts may then be used to validate the model.

Evaluating the model implies revisions of facts and rules. This type of revision can be supported by a system, today [4]. Consequences of retracting a fact are determined and the consistent state of the knowledge is maintained.

However, the third phase involves also another revision. It may turn out that some basic assumptions have to be retracted which, in turn, invalidates a lot of facts and rules. If we do not want an empty model again, facts and rules should be adjusted to new basic assumptions [5].

An intermediate representation on paper of the model, which is then encoded in a computational representation language, is necessary if the system which maintains the knowledge cannot handle the three revisions of the modeling cycle. The revisions are then performed on the model, and the encoding is undertaken when no major revisions are expected. In contrast, a system supported modeling cycle integrates intermediate representations into the system (see figure 4). The challenge for a system supporting the modeling cycle lies in the reversability of facts and rules as well as terminology and basic assumption.

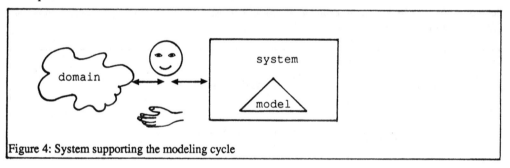

Figure 4: System supporting the modeling cycle

Because today's hand-eye technology does not allow for direct observations and experiments in a domain, a person mediates domain and system, but this is not relevant for our concern. The important point is that the person builds up and revises the model from the first phase to the third and then entering the first phase again with the help of the system.

2.5 Modeling vs. Stepwise refinement

In this section I discuss two examples in order to contrast the system support for modeling with the support today's knowledge representation (acquisition) systems offer. Today's knowledge representation systems acquire knowledge in a stepwise restricting manner: each definition restricts the space of further

---

[4] Of course, belief revision is also not a solved and fixed problem!

[5] Emde (87a) presents a learning program, METAXA.3, which re-classifies facts because of theory revision.

possible definitions, facts, and rules. It is impossible to retract a definition because of incoming new definitions or - even worse - new facts. Instead, the conflicting new definitions or facts are rejected. The advantage of stepwise restriction is the sound logical basis. The disadvantage is that it forces the user to a top-down procedure in acquisition: defining terminology from the most general to more specific terms, then giving rules and facts which are controled by the terminology [6]. This procedure is adequate in some cases, namely when a well defined terminology already exists. In situations, however, where the user develops the terminology with respect to facts, this procedure is not helpful. In particular for revision, a system-supported way back from the more specific entries to the more general ones is missing. In practice, the user first models the domain on paper or with a text editor. There, the user is allowed to proceed from the more specific to the general as well as from the general to the more specific. The user revises the evolving model by hand until the terminology is almost completed. Then, the user enters the domain model into the acquisition system starting with the terminology. If additional revisions are necessary, the knowledge base is loaded into an editor, revisions are made by hand, and the edited knowledge base is loaded back into the system. Thus, the user is responsible for all effects of the changes because a text editor has no ability of revision and maintenance.

Typical examples for stepwize restricting knowledge acquisition are KL-ONE-like systems (Brachman, Schmolze 85). Let us look at an example of upwards revision in the terminology. Figure 5 shows an excerpt of a T-Box.

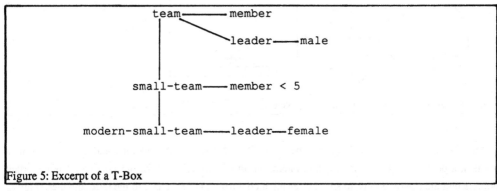

Figure 5: Excerpt of a T-Box

A *team* is a primitive concept with the roles *member* and *leader*. The leader is assumed to be *male*. A *small-team* is defined as a *team* with at most 4 *members*. Let there be the rule that *small-teams* which are guided by a woman get a special grant from an equal-rights-fund. We now want to define a *modern-small-team* as a *small-team* with a *female leader*. This new definition would be rejected by stepwise restricting acquisition systems because it contradicts the definition of the superconcept *team*. However, it is often the case that we are very convinced of a definition of a more particular concept and want to change the superconcept definitions accordingly. This is quite natural, since we cannot think of all consequences beforehand and therefore often take default definitions for general concepts. These

---

[6] Terminology controls facts and rules in that it defines the semantics of the objects, attributes, and relations which are used to write facts and rules.

definitions must be overwritable when more specific definitions come in. Of course, there are several possibilities to change the T-Box as to allow the definition of the *modern-small-team*. We could retract the superconcept-relation between *modern-small-team* and *small-team*, create a new concept *female-guided-team* and put *modern-small-team* below it. This, however, would require doubling the restriction of the number of *member*. Less changes are necessary if we change the restriction of *leader* in the concept *team* to *human*. Note, that changing the restriction to *female* would affect the definition of *small-team* in an undesired way: it would become the same concept as *modern-small-team* and no *small-teams* with a male leader would remain. This rather simple example shows what a system must be capable of in order to support modeling. It must detect contradictions, find possible ways to resolve the contradiction, compute the consequences of the resolution, and choose the possibility with the least changes.

To make things even more complicated, let us look at a second example. Here, a definition is to be changed because of facts. Let us imagine a typical bureaucratic situation: it is known that grants are given to *modern-small-teams*, and we thought that *modern-small-teams* are always guided by a woman. Now, however, we hear of a team which got the grant but is guided by a man. We know the facts, and want to adjust our definitions to them. Figure 6 shows an excerpt of a T-Box and an A-Box.

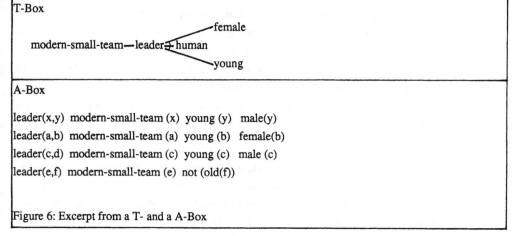

Figure 6: Excerpt from a T- and a A-Box

In order to be able to enter the team x and the team c, we can change the definitions in the T-Box in different ways. If we regard all the teams which got the grant, we find that they have in common that the leader is young or at least not old. Changing the definition accordingly requires not only the change of the particular value *female* into *human* but also the introduction of another role, namely *age*. Changing the definition in this **bottom-up** way is, in fact, a **learning** step. Because observations are what is most certain, definitions should be reversable - we cannot change the observations to fit to our definitions! This demands, however, for the definition of revising operations, the computation of all consequences and a selection algorithm which chooses the best change. Before this is achieved, no system can fully support the modeling cycle developed in a top-down as well as a bottom-up manner, but rather must stick to the stepwise refining paradigm. This is to say that **modeling** should not be taken as a new word for an old thing but to indicate the work that has to be done in order to support modeling.

3 Machine Learning as Automatic Modeling

In the field of Machine Learning, many aspects of modeling have been investigated, and prototype systems which perform some tasks of the modeling cycle have already been built. In this section, we give some examples of machine learning programs which perform part of the modeling task. Viewing machine learning as automatic modeling and knowledge acquisition as a modeling task, it is an obvious idea to integrate machine learning into knowledge acquisition. A new way of integration is then exemplified by the system BLIP.

3.1 Aspects of Modeling in Machine Learning

It would take too much space to report on all the efforts to automate parts of the modeling cycle or on all the work on theory formation (which can be viewed as another word for model-building) which has been undertaken in the field of machine learning. However, pointing to some example system may make clear that, in fact, machine learning is an attempt to operationalize modeling.

Finding the concepts with their defining properties and deleting irrelevant parts of object descriptions corresponds to an early step in the first phase of modeling. Having a system perform this task has long been a goal of machine learning. Going further, taxonomies of concepts have been automatically built up. Techniques for concept formation and learning class descriptions have been developed by Michalski (Michalski 80; Michalski, Chilausky 80; Michalski,Stepp 83), Winston (75), and Mitchell (82) - to name but a few. Learning classification trees (or rules) which can be regarded as concept formation from another point of view is also a task of the first modeling phase (Michie, Bratko 78; Quinlan 86).

Discovering regularities, generating hypotheses, testing them, and using them to create a knowledge base with a considerable coverage is performed - by very different techniques - by systems such as INDUCE (Dietterich,Michalski 81), SPARC/E (Dietterich,Michalski 85), BACON (Langley, Bradshaw, Simon 83) and META-DENDRAL (Buchanan,Mitchell 78). Here, part of the second phase of the modeling cycle is automated. Discovering laws (Lenat 77, Langley 81) is, probably, the most evident correspondent of machine learning to the development in science. In the scientific process, the theory built up so far is used to guide further research. Analogeously, a theory-driven approach has now been followed by discovery programs (Michalski, Falkenhainer 87, Kokar 87).

Enhancing problem-solving performance by chunking operators (Laird, Rosenbloom,Newell 86) or creating a knowledge structure from primitive elements (Pazzani 87) is an aspect of re-representing in modeling.

Refining rules because of conflicts (Michalski 85, Wrobel 87c) or failures (Schank 82; Rajamoney, DeJong, Faltings 85), or master's advice (Mitchell, Mahadevan, Steinberg 85, Kodratoff, Tecuci 87b) are other tasks out of the second modeling phase which are operationalized by machine learning programs.

Finding explanations for observations has become a hot topic in machine learning (Rajamoney,DeJong,Faltings 87; Wilkens 86; Pazzani 86). Of course, all rules or laws found by a program should explain the facts and predict new facts. Thus, just as science is always creating explanations, so do learning programs (cf. Kodratoff 86). However, at an early stage of the scientific proces one is bound to empirical discovery, whereas with a better developed model it becomes possible to learn a lot from just one example.

Taking remembered solutions as a basis for a new model to be built or for a problem to be solved is dealt with in learning by analogy (Carbonell 83).

The third modeling phase deals with theory as such, as opposed to single concepts or rules. Forming a theory (Amarel 86) as well as revising it (Emde 87a, Rose, Langley 86) is part of the third phase. Validating the model and gathering new data by conducting experiments is another part of this phase. In the field of knowledge acquisition and machine learning, some attempts are now being made to design experiments automatically (Wisniewski,Winston,Smith,Kleyn 86; Rajamoney,Dejong, Faltings 87; Dietterich 86).

As opposed to stepwise restricting acquisition systems, learning systems proceed from extensions to the intension of sets. Definitions are built up incrementally and can be changed and enhanced baised on new facts. This well suits the demand for reversibility. However, machine learning also faces the problem of changing the representation which was taken as a starting point - yet at another level. The examples - whether selected by a teacher or coded observations - have to be represented so that the learning program can use them to form concepts, taxonomies, or definitions, which in turn can be used to express more facts and rules about the domain. Choosing the appropriate description language for the examples determines the possible outcome of the learning program. Revising the description language because of unsatisfactory learning results is a most challenging approach for meeting the reversibility requirement (Amarel 68). Today, this task is left either to a teacher in most similarity-based learning programs, or to the knowledge engineer who has built the knowledge base which is refined by explanation-based learning.

3.2 Integrating Machine Learning into Knowledge Acquisition

Machine learning has been successfully applied to building large parts of knowledge bases. Examples of such successful learning programs are ID3 (Quinlan 83) and AQ11 or INDUCE (Michalski 80). Most often, the learning system and the performance system are linked **serially**: the learning system acquires rules independently from the knowledge which is already stored in the expert system. It delivers rules (or facts, or tables) to the performance system without getting or using any feedback from it. Another way of putting learning programs to good use in knowledge acquisition is shown by apprenticeship-learning, where the learning program **interacts** with the expert system. It compares the performance system's solution with a solution given by an expert, explains the difference, and changes the knowledge base accordingly. An example of such a system is LEAP (Mitchell, Mahadevan, Steinberg 85). Together with the expert system VEXED, the architecture of the system shows that both system and user work on the same knowledge, in this case a rule (see figure 7).

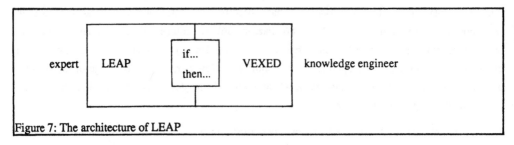

Figure 7: The architecture of LEAP

However, LEAP is restricted to the end of the second phase of the modeling cycle.

Another interactive knowledge acquisition system of an architecture similar to LEAP's is DISCIPLE (Kodratoff, Tecuci 87b). As does LEAP, DISCIPLE learns from one rule given by the user and, therefore, needs a verification for the step from this one example to a general rule. Verification in DISCIPLE is explanation. In contrast to LEAP, DISCIPLE does not presuppose a strong domain theory. Instead, the system integrates the user into the verification process: it selects the possibly interesting explanations for a rule, forms necessary conditions for the rule, and generates examples for the generalized application condition of that rule, each time asking the user to classify the system's results. The outcome of the learning process is a qualification for a rule which can be a disjunction. However, also DISCIPLE relies heavily on the quality of the domain theory. Whether explanations can be found and whether they are interesting depends on the expertise of the knowledge engineer who encodes objects, properties, and relations. The material for an explanation is a pattern of - possibly indirect - relations among the objects involved in the user's rule. Part of the generalization of the applicability condition is performed with the help of theorems which lead from a specific relation to a more general one. The domain theory may be weak, but it must have a rich structure and carefully constructed theorems giving a hierarchy of relations. The construction of the domain theory itself is not system-supported. The outcome of the learning program is not fed back into the domain theory.

A third way to integrate machine learning into knowledge acquisition is **balanced cooperative modeling.** A knowledge-acquisition system supports the user in modeling and, at the same time, enhances this model by learning. The user is the person who builds up the domain model, the knowledge engineer. It is not a person showing skills in problem solving, but a person providing the system with *knowledge* - and thus perhaps showing some skills in describing phenomena. The role of the user is that of a scientist who writes down observations, structures them, and finds rules which cover the phenomena. The role of the system is that of an assistant looking over the user's shoulder, compiling information, taking care of the book-keeping, and cleaning-up consequences of the user's changes, pointing to hidden conflicts, and recommending enhancements for the model. The enhancements include new rules induced from the user's notices, new concepts, and structuring of the objects into classes. Of course, the user is also free to reject the recommendations of the system. Figure 8 shows the architecture of such a system.

A consequence of this approach is that the learning part of the system has to cope with an incomplete and probably wrong domain theory because building up the theory and learning from it takes place at the same time. Another implication of this is that the domain model must be reversible at all points because either the user or the system can make a mistake. BLIP is an example of the balanced cooperative modeling approach. We call this approach "sloppy modeling" in order to point out that the user may start with a very tentative (sloppy) layout of the model and then change and enhance it with the help of the system.

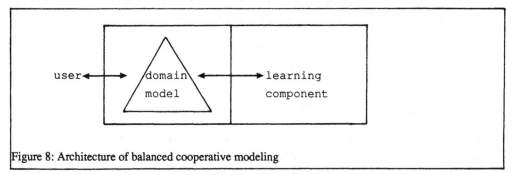

Figure 8: Architecture of balanced cooperative modeling

3.3 The BLIP System

BLIP is a system which supports the modeling activity of the user through the first two phases by a convenient interface, a coordinator of different knowledge sources, and by watching consistency and integrity. The user may easily follow the bottom-up procedure or the top-down procedure of acquisition. Terminological knowledge can also be changed; the system manages the consequences of the revisions. BLIP is also an active modeling system which is designed to enhance the model by learning and revising. Moreover, the same procedures which integrate the new facts, rules, or objects given by the user also incorporate those given by another part of the system, the learning component.

Relating BLIP to our results about modeling (cf. 2.4), an important point is that BLIP is not a skill acquisition system, nor does it acquire knowledge from observing skilled task-performance, nor does it suppose the user is a good task-performer. The BLIP user is supposed to deal with explicable knowledge. However, this explicable knowledge need not be the rules (laws) of the domain; it can also be observed, factual knowledge. The modeling activity of user and system is regarded as a scientific process, as contrasted to the training process of expertise.

The question of whether the model built up by BLIP is an operational one needs a little more explanation. BLIP is *not* a consultative system or integrated into a consultative system. Of course, deductions can be made by BLIP's inference engine. Viewing this as problem solving (as is done, e.g. for the DISCIPLE system), the user can solve problems using BLIP. In this sense, the domain model of BLIP is an operational one. However, for a consultative system, many more capabilities are required: an efficient and explicit strategy for asking the user for the specification of his problem (cf. the MYCIN rule with the implicit age limit quoted above), an explicitly represented strategy for problem solving (cf. the MYCIN heuristic quoted above), and explanation capabilities. None of these capabilities are present in BLIP. In the sense of a consultative system, BLIP's domain model is not operational.

BLIP does not generate possible counter-examples in order to present them to the user (as is done by DISCIPLE). Thus, it is the user's task to test and verify the evolving domain model. The third phase of the modeling cycle is not supported by BLIP.

The insight that modeling is an interactive process was the guideline for the system design of BLIP. The terminal screen can be viewed as the scratch-pad for system and user. The important point here is that the system really processes on the epistemic or ontological level the inputs and changes of the learning part and the user with all consequences - as opposed to an editor which only handles strings.

In this section, an overview of the BLIP system is presented. We then concentrate on revising possibilities in BLIP and show some examples.

3.3.1 Knowledge Representation of BLIP

Knowledge in BLIP is represented by **facts** and **rules.** Facts are expressed by predicates with constants as arguments. Syntactically, predicates are declared to have arguments of a certain **sort.** Each constant belongs at least to one sort. Rules may include negation and conjunction and have only one conclusion. Rules whose predicate's arguments are variables are written as **meta-facts.** Thus, meta-knowledge in BLIP has nothing to do with strategic knowledge, but is knowledge about the domain itself. It is a declarative representation for rules. Meta-facts are expressed by **meta-predicates** with predicates as arguments. Meta-predicates are defined by associating the predicate with a rule-schema.

The step from a meta-fact to a rule is performed by a rule-generating rule which uses the meta-predicate's declaration (cf. Emde 87b). The declarative representation of rules as meta-facts provides for reasoning about rules, checking the consistency of rules, and deriving rules from other rules. The means for that are **meta-rules.** Meta-rules are rules with predicates as arguments of higher-order predicates. Also meta-rules can be represented redundantly as facts, namely meta-meta-facts (cf. Thieme 87). The type restriction (the predicate must always be of a higher type than its arguments) is obeyed.

BLIP uses higher-order concepts. It does not realize, however, a full higher-order logic because that would result in unacceptable computational properties of the knowledge representation. As Wrobel (87b) has shown, BLIP's representation language is fact-complete and allows for answering any query within a time that is polynomial to the size of the knowledge base.

3.3.2 BLIP's Architecture

The main components of BLIP are the **coordinator,** the **modeler,** the **inference engine,** and the **interface.** The components interact with each other by sending and receiving notifications. This is the reason why the user's input is treated in the same way and handled by the same processes as the "input" of the modeler: the notifications sent to the coordinator are of the same form. The coordinator is the module which maintains the integrity of diverse knowledge sources. It can be viewed as the environment of the knowledge sources which represent the domain model (Morik 87). It also includes a program which acquires and (re-)organizes the sorts and syntactic declarations of predicates and maintains the membership of constants to sorts (cf. example below). The modeler is the component which evolves the domain model automatically. It includes a program which acquires meta-knowledge (cf. Thieme 87), a program which learns new rules, and a program which forms concepts (Wrobel 87c). The inference engine stores facts and rules from the object level as well as those from meta-levels (Emde 87b).

Rule-learning in BLIP is, in fact, learning meta-facts. The procedure is based on experience with the learning system METAXA (Emde 84). Hypotheses of possible meta-facts are generated and tested against the facts known so far to the system. The space of hypotheses is limited by syntactical restrictions which are attached to meta-predicates. These restrictions concern the argument sorts of predicates of a rule. Heuristics select the hypotheses to be actually generated and tested. Hypotheses are tested with the help of **characteristic situations.** Characteristic situations are search patterns which collect verifying and falsifying facts for a rule-schema. Verified hypotheses become known meta-facts and the rule-generating rule enters the corresponding rule into the inference engine. The rule, in turn, is used to derive new facts. In this way, induction and deduction work together to enlarge the domain model. BLIP is a closed-loop learning system.

The interface reacts immediately, showing the user all consequences of an action - be it performed by the user or by the modeler. Compared to the edit-and-compile behavior of many systems, this immediate feedback is an advantage for the user. The system can quickly be learned, a mental model of the system can be built very easily and naturally, and the processes become transparent and inspectable. For more details about the interface see Wrobel(87a).

3.3.3 Modeling with BLIP

In general, modeling with BLIP means interactively defining concepts and finding rules. Inference rules in BLIP can be terminological rules (those which express the semantics of a concept or relation) or empirical rules (those which describe or summarize a set of facts). When starting to build up a domain model with BLIP, the system contains nothing but meta-knowledge (the user can choose among several sets of meta-knowledge). The user then has to declare the predicates s/he wants to use in order to represent facts and rules. This is the very first phase of defining a terminology. The following part is to establish the semantics of the predicates by finding meta-facts concerning them. BLIP does not support the third phase of the modeling cycle: no experiments for evaluating alternative domain models are designed. However, the first and the second phase being fully reversible, the reorganization of a model needs no particular phase in its own right but is integrated into the first and second modeling phase.

In the following, we discuss how BLIP supports the first and second phase of the modeling cycle with a specific focus on the reversibility options.

3.3.3.1 Layout of representational framework

In this section, the interactive layout of the representational framework for a domain model is described. Four typical types of inappropriate modeling are differentiated, and it is shown how BLIP helps to recover from inadequate first modeling attempts,. thus illustrating the sloppy modeling approach.

BLIP supports the declaration of the predicates and - if needed - the introduction of additional meta-(meta-)predicates. The declarations can be performed in a bottom-up manner and are fully reversable. The system support for declaring meta-(meta-)representations is described in Thieme (87). The system support for predicate definitions is based on collecting all constants together with their membership to a sort. Thus, if a predicate is declared and facts are inputted, a new predicate with (some of) these sorts need not be declared, but rather corresponding facts with known constants can immediately be entered. The predicate declaration for the new predicate is then automatically built. The more important use of the collected constants is the automatic and reversible arrangement of the sorts. Sorts with their intersections are transferred into classes which are arranged in a lattice. With more and more facts, the intersections and subset and superset relations between sorts can change, and, accordingly, the lattice of classes is revised. Thus, also in this respect, the user may largely follow a bottom-up routine (i.e. entering facts) and the system signs responsible for necessary revisions (Kietz 88). Further work on sorts will deal with sort predicates; if for each sort there is a corresponding predicate, the granularity of the model can be changed from objects taken as sorts to objects taken as predicates. Furthermore, the meta-facts about sort-predicates can then be learned.

With the syntactic declaration of predicates, the user decides which entities are to be represented as objects, as object classes, as predicates, or as rules. This choice determines the adequacy of the model with respect to its further use. It also determines the applicability of BLIP's learning. BLIP learns about predicates. Thus, the most interesting things should be represented as predicates. However, it may well happen that the user first chooses an inappropriate representation. Our demand for reversibility means, in this context, that the system should be able to do something about it.

What are inappropriate first modeling attempts and how does BLIP support the recovery from them? We want to discuss four widespread problems of laying out the representational framework, thus illustrating the BLIP approach. As an example domain, let us take hepatitis. To make the example simple, we just want to express that a yellow skin color indicates that the liver is disturbed in its function. The first attempt of a user to represent this could be writing the following rule:

color (yellow) -> disturbed (liver)

In this attempt, no general, i.e. all quantified, rule is possible:

color (x) -> disturbed (z)

does not make any sense, because z is "unbound". All that is interesting is expressed by constant terms. We call this type of inadequate modeling the **case of the unbound variable.** The user recognizing the inappropriateness of this representation might change it by introducing a new predicate

relation (<color>, <organ>)

and change the rule into

relation (x,z) & color (x) -> disturbed (z).

In this case, no revision of accepted entries into the fact base are to be made. Some new facts can be entered relating the color of the skin to disfunctions of organs.

However, this is not a clever way to model the subject, either. One of the problems with this attempt is the **case of the missing argument.** All facts which could be entered in this framework would implicitly refer to the same patient who can only be yellow, pale, red, etc. Thus, different cases cannot be represented. A quantification over a set of patients is needed. This, in turn, requires the predicates *color* and *disturbed* to have one more argument. We could then write

relation (x,z) & color2 (x,y) -> disturbed2 (z,y)

and enter facts such as

  color2 (yellow, tim), color2 (pale, tom), disturbed2 (liver, tim).

In order to introduce the new two-place predicates, we could write

color (x) & patient (y) -> color2 (x,y)

disturbed (x) & patient (y) -> disturbed2 (x,y)

and give the name of the one (former implicit) patient by

patient (tim).

But this rule is not appropriate in general because it links any patient and any symptom. It only serves as a transformation of a fact base which models implicitly one patient's case. Such a transformation should be performed by changing the predicate's definition. Now, however, editing the predicate definition of *color* makes the already entered facts syntactically ill-formed, and there is no way for the system to insert the appropriate term into the second place of the predicate. Thus, the only solution here is to put a dummy symbol into the second place and leave it to the user to replace it.

The model developed so far expresses the interesting concepts *yellow* and *liver-disturbed* as constant terms. Thus, BLIP cannot learn about these concepts. This is an example of the **case of the interesting constants.** Using BLIP is much more effective if we represent the central concepts of a domain as predicates. Here, these predicates are

yellow (<patient>)

and

liver-disturbed (<patient>).

The symptom-to-disease relation is then expressed by the rule

yellow (x) -> liver-disturbed (x).

This representation makes the predicate *relation* superfluous which, in fact, is quite specialized since there are only a few diseases recognizable by skin color. Expressing symptoms by predicates, we can have other symptoms besides skin color for other disfunctioning organs besides the liver. If we want to maintain the already given facts but change the representation we can write

color2 (yellow, x) -> yellow (x)

and

disturbed2 (liver, x) -> liver-disturbed (x).

Modeling can go on with the new predicates, learning about them is enabled, and analogous relations between symptoms and diseases fit into this framework.

The fourth case we want to discuss here is the **case of the missing predicate.** It is quite common for the user to forget to introduce a predicate which discriminates different cases. Perhaps the user did not even realize that there are different cases. So far, changes in the representational framework were performed by the user and supported by BLIP. However, we expect a learning system to change the representation autonomously if the facts give reason to do so. And, in fact, BLIP is capable of introducing new predicates. BLIP recognizes that a predicate is missing by exceptions to a rule which show that the rule applies in too many cases. The rule must thus be restricted by discriminating the cases where it should apply from those where it should not. As opposed to DISCIPLE, where just one rule is qualified by an applicability restriction, BLIP exploits exceptions for forming concepts which are not only used to restrict the particular rule but are also available for all processes. In particular, relations between the new predicate and other predicates can then be learned. The process of concept formation is described in Wrobel (87c).

The user need not restart modeling from scratch after recognizing that the first attempt to lay out the representation was more adequate; as has been illustrated, the model evolves from the **sloppy** first attempt to the more appropriate one without a loss of the already typed-in facts. The first phase of modeling can be reentered at any point, i.e. it is fully reversible in the sense discussed above.

3.3.3.2 Elaboration of the framework

The second phase of the modeling cycle is performed with BLIP by entering facts and rules. BLIP deduces additional facts and induces additional rules. Here, too, we want to concentrate on reversibility. To illustrate revise with BLIP, we take the BACK example from above (cf. 2.5). First, we assume that the user modeled a situation corresponding to that of figure 5 and show how with the support of BLIP the user can overwrite the definition of the superconcept. Handling contradictions at the meta-level as well as at the object level is demonstrated. Then we present the more effective use of BLIP: entering the facts corresponding to figure 6, BLIP learns the appropriate rules.

In order to model the T-Box behavior of BACK, we need the meta-meta-predicates that realize inheritance of value-restrictions and the meta-predicates realizing the superconcept relation and the set of disjoint values concerning a role. The meta-level predicates can be presupposed by the user, i.e. they need not be entered by the user, but can be chosen loading the KL-ONE-METAPRED set. Note that the different sets of meta-level predicates model different system behavior at the inferential level. If the user does not want to have value-restrictions inherited because this is considered too restrictive, another meta-(meta-)predicate set should be chosen. The rule expressing the superconcept-relation is

inclusive(p,q): p (x) -> q (x)

The rule expressing disjoint concepts is

opposite(p,q): p (x) -> not (q (x))

where because of

symmetric (opposite)

also

opposite(q,p): q (x) -> not (p (x))

holds. By writing the meta-fact

inclusive (modern-team, team)

the user establishes *modern-team* as subconcept of *team*[7]. By writing the meta-fact

opposite (male, female)

---

[7]   The number-restriction of the member role is not representable in BLIP.

the user expresses disjoint concepts. For value restrictions we introduce the meta-predicate

valr (p, q, r): p (x,y) & q (y) -> r (x)

and for another constellation of predicates

valr2 (p, q, r): p (x, y) & q (x) -> r (y).

The T-Box mechanism can then be described by two meta-rules:

mm1 (inclusive, valr): inclusive (p, q) & valr (l, m,q) -> valr (l, m, p)

mm2 (inclusive, valr, opposite): inclusive (p, q) & valr (l, m, q) & opposite (m, n) ->

$$not (valr (l, n, p)).$$

The first meta-rule inherits the value-restriction, the second ensures consistency between rules. By writing

R1;valr (leader, male, team): leader (x, y) & male (y) -> team (x)

and

R2;valr2 (leader, team, male): leader (x, y) & team (x) -> male (y)

the user defines the concept *team* corresponding to the definition in the KL-ONE example above. If the user now wants to enter

R3;valr (leader, female, modern-team): leader (x, y) & female (y) -> modern-team (x)

R4:valr2 (leader,modern-team,female): leader (x, y) & modern-team (x) -> female (y)

we get a contradiction between meta-facts. BLIP therefore first rejects the entry and informs the user of the contradiction and of the possibility of entering the same contradictory meta-fact again. If the user then selects the same entry-menu as before, thus insisting on the second definition, it is stored in the inference engine as a contradictory rule. Up to now, the knowledge revision on the meta-level has to be done by the user; s/he has to decide which of the conflicting meta-facts is to be changed or deleted. If the user decides to delete the rule which was restricting teams to groups with male leaders, the facts derived from this rule are retracted. The user could also delete the responsible meta-rule so that the derived meta-fact

not (valr (leader, female, modern-team))

is retracted. The inference engine is capable of keeping track of the derivations at the object level as well as at the meta level (Emde 87b).

As meta-rules watch consistencies between rules, rules are watching consistency between facts. Thus, if the user wants to enter

modern-team (kit-back)

leader (kit-back, kai)

male (kai),

BLIP first refuses to store *male (kai)* and informs the user of the contradiction. But if the user is really convinced of the fact and inputs the fact again, knowledge revision starts in order to solve the conflict. Here, there is not enough known to revise autonomously. Therefore, BLIP asks the user whether s/he wants to provide a better support set for R4 or to delete the rule. If R4 is deleted and, as the user expects, all facts derived by R4 are retracted, we don't have a proper definition of *modern-team* any more. Of course, the user can give another defintion by typing in a meta-fact. However, the easier way is to input the facts and let BLIP find the appropriate value-restriction defining the concept *modern-team*. From the following facts *male (kai)*, *male (michael)*, *female (christa)*, *female (katharina)*,

modern-team (kit-back), *modern-team (kit-natan)*, *modern-team (kit-fast)*, *modern-team (kit-lerner)*,

young (kai), *young (michael)*, *young (christa)*, *young (katharina)*,

leader (kit-back, kai), *leader (kit-natan, michael)*, *leader (kit-fast, christa)*, *leader (kit-lerner, katharina)*.

BLIP learns - among other meta-facts -

$$valr\ (leader,\ young,\ modern\text{-}team)$$
and
$$valr2(leader,\ modern\text{-}team,\ young)$$

Thus, the best way to use BLIP for modeling is to enter facts, look at the results of BLIP's learning, correct them by giving negated facts or by editing the meta-facts or rules, and leave all the rest up to the system.

Meta-meta-facts, meta-facts, and facts can easily be retracted, and BLIP maintains consistency by retracting all **deduced** (meta-)facts. The problem of how to determine which meta-facts were **induced** from the retracted facts remains open. It would cost too much space to index and store the set of facts which instantiated a characteristic situation and thus helped to verify or (falsify) a hypothesis.

Modeling with BLIP is restricted to building up a domain model, corresponding to the first and the second phase of the modeling cycle. Because of revision possibilities, however, modeling need not be performed in sequential phases. Reorganization of the model, even of the representational framework, is always possible and is always system-supported. Thus, the infinite and cyclical nature of modeling is taken into account. Moreover, BLIP autonomously enriches the representation by forming new concepts and enhances the model by learning new rules. Thus, BLIP is an example for balanced cooperative modeling.

The user interacts with BLIP in different ways.

BLIP uses learned or given rules to deduce new facts, and if the user denies those facts, knowledge revision tries to modify the corresponding rules. The derived facts can be regarded as predictions, and the user judges whether they are accurate or not. Here, the user represents the 'real world' to the system.

Of course, the user, having all comforts of an inference engine, can ask BLIP questions about its knowledge. In this sense, a domain model in BLIP is an operational one. The user employs the system as a domain encyclopedia with inferential capabilities.

The typical user-system constellation, however, is that of a scientist and his assistant: a cooperative and interactive process of model-building guided by the scientist.

In addition to stepwise refinement, BLIP allows for a bottom-up procedure of modeling: starting with known facts and developing concepts and definitions on that basis. Changes in the fact base lead to changes of definitions and concepts.

4 Conclusion

If one views the activity of modeling as the central issue for both knowledge acquisition and machine learning, the integration of machine learning into knowledge acquisition follows naturally. By inspecting the properties demanded of systems which support and perform modeling we can conclude:

- Modeling is an interactive process, thus the system should be interactive at all points in the modeling process
- Models can be operational, thus the system should not only store the model but also answer questions about the knowledge
- Modeling is a scientific process, thus the system's behavior can be designed along the lines of theory formation: gathering data, laying out a representational framework, finding regularities (laws), predicting facts, verifying the predictions, and starting all over again.

The most important implication of our observations on modeling is the need for **reversibility** because of the tentative character of layout and even laws. Starting with a sloppy model and then improving with revisions it has been illustrated by examples from BLIP, a system designed to meet the modeling requirements.

Acknowledgements

I'd like to warmly thank Bernhard Nebel, with whom I discussed the possibilities of change in KL-ONE alike systems, Marianne LaFrance who frankly spoke about her experience in knowledge elicitation at last year's workshop in Banff Knowledge Acquisition for Knowledge-based Systems, Brigitte Bartsch-Spoerl, who encouraged me when I first thought about the sloppy modeling paradigm, and all participants of the workshop on Knowledge Representation and Organization in Machine Learning, who enriched my understanding of the modeling issue by lively discussions.

REFERENCES

Amarel, S.(68): "On Representation of Problems of Reasoning about Actions"; In: B. Meltzer, D. Michie (eds.): Machine Intelligence, Vol. 3, pp. 131-171, Edinburgh University Press, Edinburgh, 1968

Boose, J.H., Bradshaw, J.M. (87): "Expertise Transfer and Complex Problems Using AQUINAS as a Knowledge Acquisition Workbench for Expert Systems"; In: International Journal of Man-Machine Studies, Vol. 26, No. 1, pp. 3-28, January 1987

Brachman, R.J.; Schmolze, J.G. (85): "An Overview of the KL-ONE Knowledge Representation System"; In: Cognitive Science 9, 2, pp.171-216.

Buchanan, B.G.; Mitchell, T.M. (78): "Model-Directed Learning of Production Rules"; In: D.A. Waterman, F. Hayes-Roth (eds.): Pattern-Directed Inference Systems, pp. 297-312, Academic Press, New York, San Francisco, London 1978

Carbonell, J.G. (83): "Derivational Analogy and its Role in Problem Solving"; In: Proceedings of the AAAI, Washington, D.C. 1986, pp. 64-69

Clancey, W.J. (86): "From GUIDON to NEOMYCIN and HERACLES"; In: The AI Magazine, Vol. 2, No. 3, pp. 40-60

Cox, L.A.; Blumenthal, R. (87): "KRIMB: An Intelligent Knowledge Acquisition and Representation Program for Interactive Model Building"; In: Proceedings of the first European Workshop on Knowledge Acquisition for Knowledge-Based Systems, p.E3, Reading University, UK, September 1987

Dietterich, T.G. (86): "The EG Project: Recent Progress"; In: T.M. Mitchell, J.G. Carbonell, R.S. Michalski (eds.): Maschine Learning, a Guide to Current Research, pp. 51-54, Kluver Academic Press, Boston, Dordrecht, Lancaster 1986

Diederich, J.; Ruhmann, I.; May, M. (87): "KRITON: a knowledge-acquisition tool for expert systems"; In: International Journal of Man-Machine Studies, Vol. 26, No. 1, pp. 29-40, January 1987

Dietterich, T.G.; Michalski, R.S. (81): "Inductive Learning of Structural Descriptions: Evaluation Criteria and Comparative Review of Selected Methods"; In: Artificial Intelligence, Vol. 16, No. 3, pp. 257-294, July 1981

Dietterich, T.G.; Michalski, R.S. (85): "Discovering Patterns in Sequences of Events"; In: Artificial Intelligence, Vol. 25, No. 2, pp. 187-232, February 1985

Emde, W. (84): "Inkrementelles Lernen mit heuristisch generierten Modellen"; Technical University Berlin, Department of Applied Computer Science, KIT-Report No. 22

Emde, W. (87a): "Non-Cumulative Learning in METAXA.3"; In: Proceedings of the 10th IJCAI-87, Milano 1987, pp. 208-210

Emde, W. (87b): "An Inference Engine for Representing Multiple Theories"; (In this Volume)

Eshelman, L., Ehret, D., McDermott, J., Tan, M. (87): "MOLE: A Tenacious Knowledge Acquisition Tool"; In: International Journal of Man-Machine Studies, Vol. 26, No. 1, pp. 41-54, January 1987

Gaines, B.R. (87): "Knowledge Acquisition for Expert Systems"; In: Proceedings of the first European Workshop on Knowledge Acquisition for Knowledge-Based Systems, p.A3, Reading University, UK, September 1987

Garfinkel, H. (67): "Studies in Ethnomethodology"; Prentice-Hall, Englewood Cliffs, N.J.

Garfinkel, H. (73): "Das Alltagswissen über soziale und innerhalb sozialer Strukturen"; In: Alltagswissen, Interaktion und gesellschaftliche Wirklichkeit; rororo studium, Reinbeck bei Hamburg, pp. 189-262, 1973

Hayes-Roth, F.; Waterman, D.A.; Lenat, D. (83): "Building Expert Systems"; Addison-Wesley, Reading, Massachusetts, 1983

Herkner, W. (Hg.) (80): "Attribution - Psychologie der Kausalität"; Hans Huber Verlag, Bern, Stuttgart, Wien 1980

Johnson, N. (87): "Mediating representations in Knowledge Elicitation"; In: Proceedings of the first European Workshop on Knowledge Acquisition for Knowledge-Based Systems, p.A2, Reading University, UK, September 1987

Kelly, G.A. (55): "The Psychology of Personal Constructs"; Norton, New York, 1955

Kietz, J.-U. (88): "Incremental and Reversible Acquisition of Taxonomies"; in: Proceedings of the European Knowledge Acquisition Workshop (EKAW 88), p.24, GMD-Studien, Bonn, June 1988

Kodratoff, Y. (86): "Is AI a Sub-Field of Computer Science? Or AI is the Science of Explanations"; Universite de Paris-Sud, Laboratoire de Recherche en Informatique, Report No. 312

Kodratoff, Y.; Tecuci, G. (87a): "DISCIPLE-1: Interactive Apprentice System in Weak Theory Fields"; In: Proceedings of the 10th IJCAI-87, Milano 1987, pp. 271-273

Kodratoff, Y., Tecuci, G. (87b): "The Central Role of Explanations in DISCIPLE" (in this volume)

LaFrance, M. (87): "The Knowledge Acquisition Grid: a method for training knowledge engineers"; In: International Journal of Man-Machine Studies, Vol. 26, No. 2, pp. 245-256, February 1987

Laird, J; Rosenbloom, P.; Newell, A. (86): "Universal Subgoaling and Chunking"; Kluver Academic Publishers, Boston, Dordrecht, Lancaster, 1986

Langley, P.; Bradshaw, G.L.; Simon, H.A. (83): "Rediscovering Chemistry With the BACON System"; In: T.M. Mitchell, J.G. Carbonell, R.S. Michalski (eds.): Maschine Learning, an Artificielle Intelligence Approach; pp. 307-330, Tioga Publ., Palo Alto, CA, 1983

Michalski, R.S. (80): "Knowledge Acquisition through Conceptual Clustering: A Theoretical Framework and an Algorithm for Partitioning Data into Conjunctive Concepts"; In: University of Illinois, Urbana-Champaign, Dept of Computer Science Report No. 80-1026 (1980)

Michalski, R.S., Chilausky, R.L.(80): "Learning by Being Told and Learning from Examples: An Experimental Comparison of the Two Methods of Knowledge Acquisition in the Context of Developing an Expert System for Soybean Disease Diagnosis"; International Journal of Policy Analysis and Information Systems, Vol. 4, No. 2, pp. 125-161, 1980

Michalski, R.S./Stepp, R.E.(83): "Learning from Observation: Conceptual Clustering" In: T.M. Mitchell, J.G. Carbonell, R.S. Michalski (eds.): Maschine Learning, an Artificielle Intelligence Approach; pp. 331-364, Tioga Publ., Palo Alto, CA, 1983

Michie, D. (82): "Game-playing Programs and the Conceptual Interface" In: SIGART Newsletter, No. 80, pp. 64-70, 1982

Michie, D.; Bratko, I. (78): "Advice Table Representations of Chess End-game Knowledge"; In: Proceedings of the AISB/GI Conference on Artificial Intelligence, Hamburg 1978

Mitchell, T.M. (82): "Generalisation as Search"; In: Artificial Intelligence, Vol. 18, No. 2, pp. 203-226, March 1982

Mitchell, T.M.; Mahadevan, S.; Steinberg, L.I. (85): "LEAP: A Learning Apprenticeship for VLSI Design"; In: Proceedings of the 9th IJCAI-85, Los Angeles 1985, pp. 573-580

Morik, K.J. (87): "Acquiring Domain Models"; In: International Journal of Man-Machine Studies, Vol. 26, No. 1, pp. 93-104, January 1987

Mostow, J.; Swartout, B. (86): "Towards Explicit Integration of Knowledge in Expert Systems: An Analysis of MYCIN's Therapy Selection Algorithm"; In: Proceedings of the AAAI-86, Philadelphia 1986, pp. 928-935

Musen, M.A.; Fagan, L.M.; Combs, D.M.; Shortliffe, E.H. (87): "Use of a domain model to drive an interactive knowledge-editing tool"; In: International Journal of Man-Machine Studies, Vol. 26, No. 1, pp. 105-121, January 1987

Nebel, B., von Luck, K. (87): "Issues of Integration and Balancing in Hybrid Knowledge Representation Systems"; In: Morik (ed.): Proceedings of the GWAI-87, 11thGerman Workshop on Artificial Intelligence, Guericke; pp. 114 - 123, Springer Verlag, Berlin, 1987

Neches, R./Swartout, W.R./Moore, J.(85): "Enhanced Maintenance and Explanation of Expert Systems through Explicit Models of their Development"; In: IEEE Transactions on Software Engineering, Vol. SE-11, No. 11 November, pp. 1337 - 1351, 1985

Pazzani, M.J. (86): "Explanation-Based Learning for Knowledge based Systems"; In: International Journal of Man-Machine Studies, Vol. 26, No. 4, pp. 453-472, January 1987

Pazzani, M.J. (87): "Creating High Level Knowledge Structure from Primitive Elements"; (in this volume)

Quinlan, R.J. (83): "Learning Efficient Classification Procedures and their Application to Chess End Games"; In: T.M. Mitchell, J.G. Carbonell, R.S. Michalski (eds.): Maschine Learning, an Artificielle Intelligence Approach; pp. 463-482, Tioga Publ., Palo Alto, CA, 1983

Quinlan, R.J. (86): "Induction of Decision Trees"; In: Maschine Learning, Vol. 1, No. 1, pp. 81-106, 1986

Rajamoney, S.; DeJong, G.; Faltings, B. (85): "Towards a Model of Conceptual Knowledge Acquisition through Directed Experimentation"; In: Proceedings of the 9th IJCAI-85, Los Angeles 1985, pp. 688-690

Rose, D.; Langley, P. (86): "STAHLp: Belief Revision in Scientific Discovery"; In: Proceedings of the AAAI 86, Philadelphia 1986, pp. 528-532

Schank, R.C. (82): "Looking at Learning"; In: Proceedings of the ECAI-82, Orsay Paris 1982, pp. 11 - 18

Schütz, A. (62): "Collected papers"; Nijhoff, Den Haag, 1962

Shortliffe, E.H. (76): "Computer-Based Medical Consultations: MYCIN"; American Elsevier Publishing Company, 1976

Swartout, W.R. (83): "XPLAIN: A System for Creating and Explaining Expert Consulting Programs"; In: Artificial Intelligence, Vol. 21, No. 3, pp. 285-325, September 1983

Thieme, S. (87): "The Acquisition of Model-Knowledge for a Model-Driven Machine Learning Approach"; (In this Volume)

Turkle, S. (84): "The Second Self. Computers and the Human Spirit"; Simon and Schuster, New York, 1984

Wilkens, D.C. (86): "Knowledge Base Debugging Using Apprenticeship Learning Techniques"; In: J. Boose, B. Gaines (eds.): Proceedings of the Knowledge Acquisition for Knowledge-Based Systems Workshop, Banff, Canada, 1986

Winston, P.H. (75): "Learning Structural Descriptions from Examples"; In: P.H. Winston (ed.): The Psychology of Computer Vision; McGraw-Hill, New York, 1975

Wisniewski, E.; Winston, H.; Smith, R.; Kleyn, M. (86): "Case Generation for Rule Synthesis"; In: J. Boose, B. Gaines (eds.): Proceedings of the Knowledge Acquisition for Knowledge-Based Systems Workshop, Banff, Canada, 1986

Wrobel, S. (87a): "Design Goals for Sloppy Modeling Systems"; In: J. Boose, B. Gaines (eds.): Proceedings of the 2nd Knowledge Acquisition for Knowledge-Based Systems Workshop, Banff, Canada, 1987, (to appear in Int. Journal of Man-Machine Studies)

Wrobel, S. (87b): "Higher-order Concepts in a Tractable Knowledge Representation"; In: Morik (ed.): Proceedings of the GWAI-87, 11thGerman Workshop on Artificial Intelligence, Guericke; pp. 129 - 138, Springer Verlag, Berlin, 1987

Wrobel, S. (87c): "Demand Driven Concept Formation"; (In this Volume)

Young, R.M.; Gammack, J. (87): "Role of Psychological Techniques and Intermediate Representations in Knowledge Elicitation"; In: Proceedings of the first European Workshop on Knowledge Acquisition for Knowledge-Based Systems, p.D7, Reading University, UK, September 1987

THE CENTRAL ROLE OF EXPLANATIONS IN DISCIPLE

Yves Kodratoff

U.A. 410 du C.N.R.S., Laboratoire de Recherche en Informatique

Bat.490, Université de Paris-Sud , 91405 Orsay Cedex, FRANCE

Gheorghe Tecuci

Research Institute for Computers and Informatics

71316, Bd. Miciurin 8-10, Sector 1, Bucharest ROMANIA

Abstract

DISCIPLE is a Knowledge Acquisition system that contains several learning mechanisms as recognized by Machine Learning. The central mechanism in DICIPLE is the one of **explanations** which is used in all the learning modes of DISCIPLE.

When using the *Explanation-Based* mode of learning, an explanation points at the most relevant features of the examples.

When using the *Analogy-Based* mode of learning, the explanations are used to generate instances analogous to those provided by the user.

When using the *Similarity-Based* mode of learning, the explanations are "examples" among which similarities are looked for.

The final result of DISCIPLE is the description of the validity domain of the variables contained in the rules. Since the users always provides totally instantiated rules, the system must automatically variabilize them, and then must find the validity domain of these variables by asking "clever" questions to the user. Given a particular (instantiated) rule by its user, the system will look in its Knowledge Base for possible explanations of this rule, and ask the user to validate them. The set of explanations validated by the user is then used as a set of (almost) sufficient conditions for the application of the instantiated rule.

1. Introduction

Knowledge Acquisition tools are expected to perform a wide range of tasks in order to help the human expert to give a computer-usable form to his knowledge. These tasks include decomposing problems, combining uncertain information, testing, help in defining data types, help in the expansion, refinement, and deficiencies recovery of the knowledge base, use of multiple sources of knowledge, changes in knowledge representation, development of models of the expert knowledge (see the series of special issues of International Journal of Man-Machine Studies).

Surprisingly enough, the classical methods developed in order to improve the knowledge of the system by the AI approach to Machine Learning (ML) have been little used. To the best of our knowledge, there are three exceptions to this rule. One is BLIP (Morik, 1987) that maintains a base of deuctions drawn from meta-rules and observed facts. The second is DISCIPLE that integrates some of the ML mechanisms such as Explanation-Based Learning, Analogy-Based Learning, and Similarity-Based Learning (see references). The third, and most famous one, is LEAP (Mitchell, Mahadevan & Steinberg, 1985). The differences between LEAP and DISCIPLE are as follows.

LEAP utilizes Explanation-Based Generalization:

- it produces a justifiable generalization from a single example;

- it is able to reject incorrect training examples;

- it relies on a strong domain theory.

DISCIPLE utilizes a combination of Explanation-Based Learning, Analogy-Based Learning, and Learning from large sets of instances.

- it relies on an incomplete and/or weak domain theory;

- it relies on user to reject incorrect training instances;

- it produces justifiable generalizations from examples.

While DISCIPLE is presented in detail in (Kodratoff & Tecuci, 1986), in this paper insist on what is an *explanation* for DISCIPLE.

2. The problem solving method

We shall restrict our exemplification to the assembling techniques, specifically: manufacturing techniques for loudspeakers.

This technique design problem can be characterized as follows: given the constructive design of a loudspeaker, design the actions needed to manufacture the loudspeaker.

The design of technologies is viewed here as a successive decomposition (or specialization) of complex operations into simpler ones, and better defining these simpler operations by choosing tools, materials or verifiers, which are in turn successively refined.

Let us consider designing the manufacturing of some given loudspeaker. We start with the following top-level operation, which can be seen as the current goal:

MANUFACTURE loudspeaker

DISCIPLE will try to solve this problem by successive decompositions (or specializations), thus reducing it to a sequence of primitive problems. This process is illustrated in *Figure 1*.

In order to achieve the goal:
    MANUFACTURE   loudspeaker
achieve the sub-goals:

1.   MAKE   chassis-assembly

In order to achieve this sub-goal, achieve in sequence the sub-sub-goals:
1.1.   FIX   upper-flange   ON   chassis
                In order to achieve this sub-sub-goal, achieve the specialization:
                1.1.1 FIX upper-flange ON chassis WITH an automatic press
1.2.   MOUNT   magnet, lower-flange   AND   bolt

2.   MAKE   membrane-assembly

3.   ASSEMBLE   chassis-assembly   AND   membrane-assembly

4.   PERFORM   ultimate-operations   ON   loudspeaker

Figure 1. Problem solving operations: decompositions and specializations of problems.

3. Inputs and outputs of DISCIPLE.

When DISCIPLE is unable to satisfactorily decompose or specialize a problem, it will ask for a solution from the user. Once this solution is given, a learning process will take place which can be described by its inputs and its outputs.

The following are given to the system: An incomplete domain theory (types of objects with properties, inference rules, and problem solving operators, i.e. decomposition and specialization rules), a problem to be solved, and a particular solution to the problem.

The following is issued by the system: A general rule indicating how to decompose (or specialize) problems *similar* to the given one.
Consider the following specialization, indicated by the user:

Example-1:

        In order to solve the problem
    CLEAN entrefer
        solve the more specialized problem
    CLEAN entrefer WITH air-sucker

Figure 2. An example of a specialization indicated by the user.

This specialization is interpreted by DISCIPLE as an instance of a general rule indicating a way of specializing the CLEAN action. The learning of the general rule will be based on an "understanding" of *Example-1*, as in Explanation-Based Learning. Notice however, that the domain theory contains only shallow and/or incomplete knowledge concerning this specialization, knowledge consisting here in some of the properties and the relations of the objects from the specialization, as well as some rules for inferring new properties and relations.

DISCIPLE shows that even such a weak theory can provide (shallow) explanations and can guide learning. From *Example-1*, the domain theory, and user's answers to its questions, DISCIPLE was able to learn the following general rule:

IF

      (x HAS z) & (y ISA cleaner) & (y REMOVES z) & NOT (y DESTROYS x)

THEN

        solve the problem

    CLEAN x

        by solving the specialization

    CLEAN x WITH y

Figure 3. A general specialization rule.

4. Exemplification of the learning process stages.

Rule learning takes place in three stages which are illustrated in *Figure 4.*, and explained in the following:

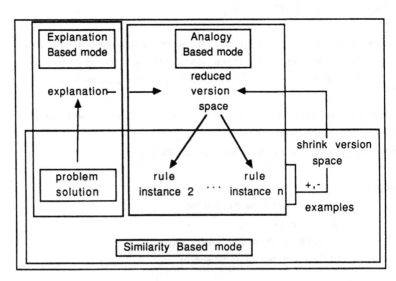

Figure 4. The learning method of DISCIPLE.

First DISCIPLE finds a shallow explanation of user's solution. Then it formulates a reduced version space for the rule to be learned. Each rule in this space covers only instances which are analogous with the user's example. DISCIPLE carefully generates analogous instances to be characterized as positive examples or as negative examples by the user. These are used to further narrow the version space.

4.1. Explanation-Based mode.

The system will try to explain to itself why the solution indicated by the user is a good one, relying on its incomplete theory, partly illustrated in *Figure 5*.

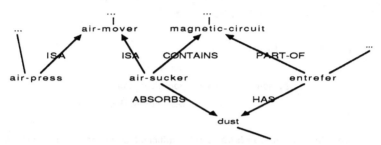

Figure 5. An incomplete knowledge base.

An essential hypothesis in DISCIPLE is that an explanation of an example is always expressible in terms of the links connecting the objects referred at in the example. DISCIPLE will therefore propose these links to the user as pieces of explanation of the example. It is the user's duty to validate them as explanations.

A piece of explanation of an example rule is therefore a link (or a succession of links) in the hierarchical semantic network of DISCIPLE. DISCIPLE will ask the user questions in order to distinguish between the relevant and the irrelevant links of the above network.

Example (continued).

The system ask the following question, user's answers are in boldface.

Does your solution work because

entrefer PART-OF magnetic-circuit & magnetic-circuit PART-OF air-sucker ? *No*

entrefer HAS dust & air-sucker ABSORBS dust ? *Yes*

Figure 6. Generation of pieces of explanation. All the pieces of explanation marked by a user's "Yes" form the explanation of the example rule .

Explanation-1:

> entrefer HAS dust &
> air-suc!:er ABSORBS dust

Notice that this explanation may be incomplete. This is due partly to the incompleteness of the domain theory and partly to the heuristic used to find explanations (DISCIPLE looks only for the relations between objects, ignoring their properties). However, the found explanation evidentiates some causal features of the objects, features justifying *Example-1*.

DISCIPLE takes *Explanation-1* as a sufficient condition for the application of *General-rule-1*, and generate the following rule in which dummy variables have been introduced through the ISA links. Notice that no actual generalization has still been taking place.

> IF   *(sufficient condition)*
>   (x ISA entrefer) & (y ISA air-sucker) & (z ISA dust) &
>   (x HAS z) & (y ABSORBS z)
>   THEN
>
> *General-rule-1*:   *solve the problem*
>   CLEAN x
>   *by solving the more specialized problem*
>   CLEAN x WITH y

DISCIPLE over-generalizes *Explanation-1* sufficient condition to the most general expression which may still be accepted by the user as an explanation of *General-rule-1*.
To this purpose, DISCIPLE first turns all the objects from Explanation-1 into (real) variables:
>   (x HAS z) & (y ABSORBS z).
In practice, the reader can see that this over-generalization is performed simply by isolating the parts of the sufficient condition that do not contain ISA links.
Then it will try to further generalize this expression by using its domain theory. Indeed, the property of absorbing z is only the manifestation of a more general property of y, that of cleaning z. The generalization of ABSORBS to REMOVES is suggested by the following theorem:
>   (y ABSORBS z) -> (y REMOVES z)
Notice however that there could be other theorems, suggesting other generalizations. For instance, the theorem
>   (y ABSORBS z) -> (y GETS z)
suggests the generalization of ABSORBS to GETS.
In such a case, DISCIPLE will ask the user if the interesting property of y is that it REMOVES z or that it GETS z.
The over-generalized explanation obtained in this way is in general a simple approximation of a necessary condition for the application of General-rule-1, this is why we call it an almost-necessary condition.

> IF   *(almost-necessary condition)*
>   (x HAS z) & (y REMOVES z)
>   *(sufficient condition)*
>   (x ISA entrefer) & (y ISA air-sucker) & (z ISA dust) &
>   (x HAS z) & (y ABSORBS z)
>   THEN
>   *solve the problem*
>   CLEAN x
>   *by solving the specialization*
>   CLEAN x WITH y

The rule to be learned has an applicability condition which is postulated to be less general than the almost-necessary condition and which is more general than the sufficient condition. The next phases will be devoted to the improvement of these conditions.

4.2 - Analogy-Based mode.

Since the object features from **Explanation1** causally imply **Example-1**, DISCIPLE deduces (reasoning by analogy) that objects having *similar* features could replace the objects from **Example-1**, yielding an analogous example.

DISCIPLE will generate instances of the rule to be learned by replacing the variables x, y, and z with objects satisfying the almost-necessary condition (over-generalized explanation). These instances are analogous with **Example 1**. This means that, in DISCIPLE's present state, analogy is defined: Two examples are analogous iff they are common instances of the same almost-necessary condition. This definition is still somewhat crude, and is under improvement.

Let us increase the semantic net of figure 5 by the following.

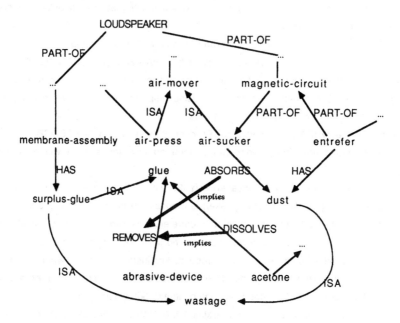

Figure 6. A more detailed semantic net.

Let us consider the following knowledge about membrane-assembly, acetone, and surplus-glue contained in our semantic net. It tells that 'membrane-assembly HAS surplus-glue' and 'acetone DISSOLVES surplus-glue' which satisfies the over-generalized explanation. DISCIPLE will therefore generate the following instance analogous to the first one.

Instance-2:   *In order to solve the problem*

             CLEAN membrane-assembly

             solve the more specialized problem

             CLEAN membrane-assembly WITH acetone

4.3 - Empirical learning from examples mode.

Using analogy, DISCIPLE may find new examples or counter-examples of the rule to be learned. The user has to characterize such system-generated instances as positive or negative examples of the rule to be learned. In this way, DISCIPLE discovers new positive examples of the rule, as well as some "real-life" negative ones.

4.3.1 - Positive instances

Each positive example shows an explanation of an example rule. All these explanations are generalized and used as a new sufficient condition. The set of sufficient conditions is then seen as a set of examples, and we apply classical generalization techniques to it, like those described in earlier sections of this chapter.

Suppose that the user validates Instance-2, then DISCIPLE will ask him to validate also the explanations it will obtain as above. From the above semantic net the reader can understand how the following explanation is possible.

$$(x \text{ ISA membrane-assembly) \& (y ISA acetone) \&}$$
$$(z \text{ ISA surplus-glue) \& (x HAS z) \& (y DISSOLVES z)}$$

which is a sufficient condition to the rule contained in Instance-2. Let us now compare the two sufficient conditions and generalize them, by using empirical or contructive learning from examples. Recall that the sufficient condtion for rule 1 was

(x ISA entrefer) & (y ISA air-sucker) & (z ISA dust) & (x HAS z) & (y ABSORBS z)

From the semantic nets, the reader can understand how the system will generalize these two expressions to

(x PART-OF loudspeaker) & (y ISA cleaner) & (z ISA wastage) & (x HAS z) & (y ABSORBS z)

The generalization (x PART-OF loudspeaker) is proposed to the user since it is the only link between the to concepts of 'membrane-assembly' and 'entrefer'. It is kept if the user validates it. In case the user rejects this generalization or when there are no links between two concepts, their generalization is emtpy, the corresponding term is then dropped. For instance, if there would be no links between 'membrane-assembly' and 'entrefer' then DISCIPLE would ask its user if he knows of any link between the two. If the user does not provide a link, the generalization would become

(y ISA cleaner) & (z ISA wastage) & (x HAS z) & (y ABSORBS z).

Therefore, from the generalization of the two sufficient conditions of each rule, we obtain a new almost-sufficient condition for the two rules

Explanation-2:   IF   *(almost-necessary condition)*

                (x HAS z) & (y REMOVES z)

                (almost-sufficient condition)

                (x PART-OF loudspeaker) & (y ISA cleaner) &

                (z ISA wastage) & (x HAS z) & (y ABSORBS z)

        THEN

                solve the problem

                CLEAN x

                by solving the specialization

CLEAN x WITH y

We insist that the new lower bound is 'almost-sufficient' since from these two examples we may have been over-generalizing because our generalization process can never prove its minimality. Only a disjunction of the two sufficient condition would stay really sufficient. The following negative example will show how much important is the above remark.

4.3.2 - Negative instances

Each negative example shows the incompleteness of *Explanation-2* and of its over-generalization. The explanation of why this instance is a negative example points to the features which were not evidentiated by *Explanation-2*. These new features are used to update both the necessary condition and the sufficient one.

Let us consider now the following knowledge of the domain theory.

membrane-assembly HAS surplus-glue & abrasive-device REMOVES surplus-glue.

DISCIPLE will therefore generate the following instance:

In order to solve the problem

CLEAN membrane-assembly

solve the more specialized problem

CLEAN membrane-assembly WITH abrasive-device

This instance is rejected by the user. The explanation of why this is not a valid specialization is 'abrasive-device DESTROYS membrane-assembly'. This explanation does not come from the semantic net, but is directly provided by the user. We skip here DISCIPLE behaviour when faced to the new concept of 'DESTROYS' and the question then asked to the user.

Given this information from its user, DISCIPLE will update both boundaries by adding to them the predicate "NOT (y DESTROYS x)". The rule issued from the negative example becomes

IF

(almost- necessary condition):

(x HAS z) & (y REMOVES z) & NOT (y DESTROYS x)

(almost- sufficient condition):

(x PART-OF loudspeaker) & (y ISA cleaner) &

(z ISA wastage) & (x HAS z) & (y ABSORBS z) & NOT (y DESTROYS x)

THEN

solve the problem

CLEAN x

by solving the specialization

CLEAN x WITH y

One will notice that the almost-necessary condition is particularized due to the negative example, like in the Version Spaces approach. Unlike this approach, the almost-sufficient condition is particularized as well in ours.

The learning process always decreases the distance between the almost-necessary condition and the almost-sufficient one. Since the domain theory is weak and/or incomplete, we must expect however that the system will not always find a necessary and sufficient condition. Therefore, we will preserve as explanation two conditions, the almost-necessary and the almost-sufficient one, instead of a single necessary and sufficient condition. We propose to define such a case as being typical of an *uncertain explanation* (in which uncertainty is not expressed by numerical means).

5. Case of a decomposition rule.

We shall briefly illustrate the learning of a decomposition rule.

Example-3:

> *In order to solve the problem*
> ATTACH sectors ON chassis-membrane-assembly
> *solve the sequence of sub-problems*
> APPLY mowicoll ON sectors
> PRESS sectors ON chassis-membrane-assembly

Explanation-3:

> mowicoll GLUES sectors
> mowicoll GLUES chassis-membrane-assembly

General Rule-3:

> *Solve the problem*
> ATTACH x ON y
> *by solving the sequence of sub-problems*
> APPLY z ON x
> PRESS x ON y

Rule to be used by hte analogy:

> IF
>> *G: ((almost) necessary condition)*
>> (z GLUES x) & (z GLUES y)
>> *S: ((almost) sufficient condition)*
>> (x ISA sectors) & (y ISA chassis-membrane-assembly)&
>> (z ISA mowicoll) & (z GLUES x) & (z GLUES y)
>
> THEN
>> *solve the problem*
>> ATTACH x ON y
>> *by solving the sequence of sub-problems*
>> APPLY z ON x
>> PRESS x ON y

Learned rule:

> I F
>> (z ISA adhesive) & (z TYPE fluid) & (z GLUES x) & (z GLUES y)

THEN

    solve the problem
ATTACH x ON y
    by solving the sequence of sub-problems
APPLY z ON x
PRESS x ON y

6. Conclusion.

This paper shows how explanations of different kinds are used in DISCIPLE. They can be summarized by the following set of *definitions*.

A piece of explanation of an example rule is a link (or a succession of links) in the hierarchical semantic network of DISCIPLE.

All the pieces of explanation validated by the user constitute *the explanation of the example rule.*

An explanation of a (generalized) rule is a generalization of explanations of example rules. It describes the validity domain of the variables contained in the rule.

A perfect explanation is a necessary and sufficient condition for the application of a generalized rule.

An uncertain explanation is a set of (disjoint) necessary conditions and sufficient ones for the application of a generalized rule.

DISCIPLE is still far from being in its achieved form, and many improvements are under way. The one that will be completed first is the merge of our program OGUST (see Vrain's paper in this volume) into DISCIPLE so that the almost-sufficient conditions might be generalized fully using the available well-formalized background knowledge, if any. An other improvement, more relevant to this paper, concerns a definition of a piece of explanation of an example rule, better than the one given just above. Since the semantic net mixes together lots of different kinds of knowledge, it may happen that the system will be explosive relative to the number of pieces of explanation generated for a given rule instance. Nevertheless, before being too much bothered by this potential explosion, one must notice that it is very difficult to decide in advance what may or may not be a piece of explanation. For instance, the reader may wonder why the glue named 'mowicoll' has been used by the designer of the original knowledge base for loudspeakers. The actual reason is that the designer is romanian, and due to all the problems met in socialist countries, 'mowicoll' is the best one available. Now, the set of links hidden under the expression 'all the problems met in socialist countries' depends of so many factors, as for instance of the political opinions of the semantic net designer, that the real explanation may well need to be sorted out of a huge collection of useless ones. On an other hand, it may also happen that the user considers as uninteresting explanations that refer to concepts outside a given range. He could then provide some "cutters" that will reject all potential pieces of explanations going through the concept said to be a cutter. If the knowledge is organized by contexts, with different micro-worlds, the system can be told which micro-worlds are relevant. Our opinion is that rather than fearing too many explanations (that can always be displayed in a friendly way) one should rather fear too few of them.

References

Burstein, M. H. (1986). Concept formation by incremental analogical reasoning and debugging. In R. S. Michalski, J. G. Carbonell, T. M. Mitchell (Eds.), *Machine learning: An artificial intelligence approach* (Vol. 2). Los Altos, CA: Morgan Kaufmann.

Carbonell, J. G. (1986). Derivational analogy: a theory of reconstructive problem solving and expertise acquisition. In R. S. Michalski, J. G. Carbonell, T. M. Mitchell (Eds.), *Machine learning: An artificial intelligence approach* (Vol. 2). Los Altos, CA: Morgan Kaufmann.

Cohen, B., & Sammut, C. (1984). Program synthesis through concept learning. In A. W. Biermann, G. Guiho, & Y. Kodratoff (Eds.), *Automatic program construction techniques.* Macmillan Publishing Company.

DeJong, G. F., (1981). Generalizations based on explanations, In *Proceedings of the Seventh International Joint Conference on Artificial Intelligence* (pp. 67-70). Vancouver, British Columbia, Canada: Morgan Kaufmann.

DeJong, G. F., & Mooney, R. (1986). Explanation-based learning: an alternative view. *Machine Learning 1,* 145-176.

Kedar-Cabelli, S. T. (1985). Purpose-directed analogy. In *Proceedings of the Cognitive Science Society* (pp. 150-159). Irvine, CA.

Kodratoff, Y. (1983). Generalizing and particularizing as the techniques of learning. *Computers and Artificial Intelligence,* 4, 417-441.

Kodratoff Y., & Ganascia J-G. (1986). Improving the generalization step in learning, In R. S. Michalski, J. G. Carbonell, T. M. Mitchell (Eds.), *Machine learning: An artificial intelligence approach* (Vol. 2). Los Altos, CA: Morgan Kaufmann.

Kodratoff Y. (1986). Learning expert knowledge and theorem proving. In C-R. Rollinger & W. Horn (Eds.) *GWAI-86 und 2. osterreichische artificial-intelligence-tagung.* Berlin: Springer-Verlag.

Kodratoff, Y., & Tecuci, G. (1987). Techniques of design and DISCIPLE learning apprentice. *International Journal of Expert Systems,* 1, 39-66.

Lebowitz M. (1986). Integrated learning: controlling explanation. *Cognitive Science,* 10.

Michalski, R. S. (1983). A theory and a methodology of inductive learning. *Artificial Intelligence, 20,* 111-161.

Michalski, R. S., Mozetic, I., Hong, J., & Lavrac, N. (1986). *The AQ15 inductive learning system: An overview and experiments.* (Internal Paper). Univ. of Illinois at Urbana-Champaign.

Mitchell T. M. (1978). *Version spaces: An approach to concept learning.* Doctorial dissertation, Department of Electrical Engineering, Stanford University, Stanford, CA.

Mitchell, T. M., Mahadevan, S., & Steinberg, L. I. (1985). LEAP: a learning apprentice system for VLSI design. In *Proceedings of the Ninth International Joint Conference on Artificial Intelligence* (pp. 573-580). Los Angeles, CA: Morgan Kaufmann.

Mitchell T. M., Keller R. M., & Kedar-Cabelli S. T. (1986). Explanation-based generalization: a unifying view, *Machine Learning,* 1, 47-80.

Morik K. (1987). Acquiring domain models. *Int. J. Man-Machine Studies* 26, 93-104.

Mostow J., Bhatnagar N. (1987). Failsafe -- A Floor Planner that Uses EBG to Learn from its Failures. In *Proceedings of the Tenth International Joint Conference on Artificial Intelligence* (pp.

249-255). Milan: Morgan Kaufmann.

Rajamoney S., DeJong G. (1987). The classification, detection and handling of imperfect theory problems. In *Proceedings of the Tenth International Joint Conference on Artificial Intelligence* (pp. 205-207). Milan: Morgan Kaufmann.

Russell, S. J. (1987). Analogy and single-instance generalization. In Langley, P. (Ed.), *Proceedings of the Fourth International Workshop on MACHINE LEARNING*. Irvine, CA: Morgan Kaufmann.

Sammut C., Banerji R.B. (1986). Learning concepts by asking questions. In R. S. Michalski, J. G. Carbonell, T. M. Mitchell (Eds.), *Machine learning: An artificial intelligence approach* (Vol. 2). Los Altos, CA: Morgan Kaufmann.

Silver, B. (1983). Learning equation solving methods from worked examples. *Proceedings of the Second International Machine Learning Workshop* (pp. 99-104). Urbana, IL.

An Inference Engine for Representing Multiple Theories

Werner Emde

Technische Universität Berlin
Fachbereich Informatik, Projektgruppe KIT
Sekr. FR 5-12
Franklinstr. 28/29
1000 Berlin 10, F.R.G.

Abstract

The objective of this paper is to discuss some general requirements for knowledge representation formalisms used in learning systems. Some general examples of learning tasks are examined, and it is discussed how the extent of these tasks determines the requirements which must be fulfilled by the knowledge representation used in the learning program. It is argued that learning tasks in which the output of one learning stage is "looped back" as input to the next brings about specific requirements for the knowledge representation and for the maintenance of knowledge. A logic-based system is described which fulfills these requirements, allows the representation of the epistemological states of a learning program, and offers mechanisms necessary to solve "real world" learning tasks. As a case study, the possible use of a multiple theory representation is described in more detail.

1 Introduction

In the early days of Machine Learning, many knowledge representation issues were neglected. One of the main interests was to develop generalization techniques, and, therefore, almost simple knowledge representation languages and formalisms were very often used (cf. [Dietterich/Michalski 83]). By doing so, people disregarded the fact that a learning program will be only one component in a larger system with specific and distinctive requirements for the knowledge representation. Furthermore, restricted representation formalisms and languages for the hypothesis space were used as an implicit generalization bias to focus the learning program's attention and to achieve the desired kind of generalizations ([Utgoff 86]). As a consequence, the application of these generalization techniques within a larger system with a more elaborate representation scheme is difficult.

Since that time, a number of efforts have been made to understand more about the influence of the knowledge representation on the efficiency and effectiveness of learning. For example, Holte [86] examined the significance of alternative knowledge representation formalisms in learning systems and showed that formalisms which are well suited for a performance task can lead to inefficiency in the learning task and vice versa. Flann and Dietterich [86] distinguished different types of representations (namely, structural, functional and behavioral representations) as a determining factor for the suitability of a representation. To solve the difficulty which arises if the "natural" representations for the learning task and the performance task are of a different type, they have proposed a "multiple representation strategy".

In trying to support the construction of consultation systems with machine learning techniques, various people have recognized the separation of different kinds of knowledge (e.g. "problem solving knowledge", "domain theories") as advantageous ([Emde/Morik 86], cf. [Neches/Swartout/Moore 85]). The process of combining these different kinds of knowledge from several explicit, but inefficient, forms into one more efficient form has also been studied in Machine Learning under the heading 'knowledge compilation' ([Dietterich 86], cf. [Emde/Rollinger 86]).

A number of other people have addressed the problem of how a learning system can automatically change and extend representation languages and formalisms as a result of learning processes and/or as a prerequiste of (further) processes (e.g. [Lenat 83], [Someren 88], [Wrobel 88]). All these efforts - the description above is by no means exhaustive - are concerned with the problem of how knowledge must be represented in a learning system and how representations can be transformed accordingly.

In this paper, we will take a somewhat different perspective on knowledge representation in Machine Learning. Instead of dealing with the question of how knowledge should be represented to ensure that generalization techniques can be applied to this knowledge efficiently, this paper discusses requirements for the knowledge representation formalism brought about by the learning task from the viewpoint of the epistemological states which occur in learning programs.

It is argued that a continuously ongoing and complex process (including generalization, knowledge revision, and the application of induced knowledge) brings about specific requirements for the knowledge representation formalism and for the maintenance of knowledge. The objective of the paper is to discuss some general requirements for the knowledge representation of integrated learning systems. A logic-based system is described which fulfills these requirements and offers mechanisms necessary to solve "real world" learning tasks.

The paper is organized as follows. First, some examples of learning tasks are presented, and we discuss how the extent of these tasks determines the requirements which must be fulfilled by the knowledge representation used in the learning program. Some general requirements entailed by "real world" learning tasks are also examined. Then, the representation formalism of IM-2, an inference engine for integrated learning systems, is introduced and it is described how the requirements are met by the representation used in IM-2. As a case study, this representation is then used to give some examples of how a multiple theory representation can be utilized in machine learning systems.

2 Requirements for the representation formalism

The requirements brought about for the knowledge representation formalism and the knowledge maintenance program are determined by the extent of the learning task. A "simple" learning task requires no or only a few special representational constructs. A more sophisticated representation scheme is needed if a "complex" learning task has to be solved with many activities, e.g. the generalization of descriptions, the formation of new concepts, and the revision and maintenance of knowledge. Therefore, the extent of the learning task, determined by the function of the learning component for the overall system it is embedded in (either really or virtually), has to be defined before it is possible to derive general requirements for the representation formalism. In the following, we will take a look at different kinds of learning tasks with increasing complexity and will discuss the corresponding requirements which are entailed by these tasks.

2.1 Rote learning

The task of rote-learning programs is to memorize some input descriptions, e.g. the class membership of objects (cf. [Holte 86]) or, to give a more specific example for a program playing the game checkers, board positions with their computed scores ([Samuel 59]). In rote-learning, restricted resources possibly limit the amount of knowledge which can be stored and limit the time to retrieve information. Therefore, it is necessary to have an efficient storing schema for statistical information about the frequency of use of the knowledge entries so as to ensure that the most important information is remembered quickly. A hierachical organization of knowledge has proven to be useful to achieving storage and retrieval-time economy ([Collins/Quillian 72]).

However, rote-learning does not lead to the generation of additional knowledge (beyond statistical information) during the learning process. Therefore, no extra representational constructs are needed in the learning component for this kind of learning task.

2.2 Simple generalization tasks

Non-inductive learning tasks are not the only ones which are so undemanding. The same is valid for non-incremental learning-from-example tasks which have been studied by numerous AI researchers [1]. In learning from examples, the program must generalize low-level information about specific instances of a concept in order to form a concept description which can guide the actions of a performance component. The learning is called non-incremental if the program is not required to update its hypotheses when additional training examples become availible.

Thus, the real task is restricted to the production of generalizations: The set (or sequence) of positive and negative examples are made available by the environment, and furthermore, the overall system is responsible for controlling the usage of the generalizations, that is, the learning program does have not to supervise the validity of generalizations. No additional knowledge which is necessary to fulfill the task is generated during the learning process. Therefore, no general requirements for the knowledge representation formalism are brought about.

2.3 Incremental learning

Now, let's take a look at a more complex kind of learning task bringing about some requirements: A program continuously receives information about a domain and is supposed to induce a model about the domain by looking for regularities in the data. After each input, the program outputs a new model which has been extended or otherwise modified according to the new input.

---

[1]   e.g. Hayes-Roth's SPROUTER or Vere's THOTH (cf. [Dietterich/Michalski 81])

The term 'incremental learning' has been used to describe this kind of learning, in which information learned at one stage can be revised to accomodate new facts provided in subsequent stages. Some examples of incremental learning programs are INCREMENTAL-AQ ([Reinke/Michalski 85]), STAGGER ([Schlimmer/Granger 86]), UNIMEM ([Lebowitz 87]) and COBWEB ([Fisher 87]).

2.3.1 Representation of uncertain and incomplete knowledge

Incremental learning requires passing the induced knowledge and the original inputs to the next learning stage [2]. For this purpose, a representation formalism for the original input and a formalism for the representation of generalizations will be sufficient. However, the learning program should additionally be able to use partially confirmed and incomplete hypotheses in the next learning stage. Partially confirmed (uncertain) hypotheses may occur, if e.g. a generalization is based on a small number of examples. In the next learning step, the system should prefer partially confirmed hypotheses for closer inspection over other "similar" (so far unconfirmed) hypotheses. The degree of (dis-)confirming evidence can be used (as one factor among others) to determine the ordering and efficient processing of subtasks in learning. Lenat's AM can be mentioned as one example of a learning program in which the number of positive examples of concepts is used to compute the numerical rating of reasons supporting a task on the agenda [Lenat 82].

Incomplete knowledge can arise for the same reasons as uncertain knowledge does. If the system is able to identify the incompleteness, e.g. through the use of an appropiate generalization method, this additional knowledge can be used to choose informative experiments (cf. [Mitchell/Utgoff/Banerji 83]).

This requires that the representation scheme used in the learning program allows the representation of the intermediate results and knowledge states which occur during learning processes (cf. [Rendell 85]). The representation formalism of an incremental learning system should allow distinguishing between induced statements and intermediate hypotheses. Furthermore, the representation of uncertainty should be supported by the representation formalism [3]. The reader may ask why the latter is necessary. What prevents one from representing uncertainty using the representation at hand, e.g. by simply adding another slot if a frame-based language is used [4]? If the program has to acquire multiple concepts, it should be able to take advantage of dependencies among concepts. If some evidence for a hypothesis has been discovered, the evidence should be propagated to dependent hypotheses. For example, if a program has induced some evidence for the transitivity of the 'smaller-than' relation, and it is known that 'taller-than' is the inverse-relation of 'smaller-than,' then the system should be able to utilize the positive evidence which can be inferred for the related transitivity of 'taller-than'. Thus, the answer to the

---

[2] The latter is necessary only if the new model has to be consistent with all previous inputs.

[3] It is important to note that the requirement for the representation of uncertain knowledge is independent from the specific learning task, e.g. the uncertainty of input data and the necessity to deal with noise (cf. [Rendell 85]).

[4] The 'Number-of-good-Examples'-Slot in AM may be regarded as an example for representing "(un)certainty" using an additional slot.

question above is that uncertain knowledge should be represented in such a way that the component responsible for making inferences propagates (un)certainty automatically instead of leaving this job to the learning component. An example how uncertain knowledge might be represented and used in inferential processes will be given in section 3.

2.3.2 Modification of knowledge

Another requirement arises from the fact that in incremental learning the acquired knowledge is subject to modifications. The representation formalism should facilitate the correction of induced rules by supporting different kinds of modifications and by allowing certain changes to be made explicitly. In the literature, several methods for modifying inference rules have been described ([Hayes-Roth 83]). The premises and the conclusion can be modified, new premises can be added, and premises can be replaced. The disadvantage of these methods is that changes are not explicitly represented. If a few exceptions of a regularity have been discovered, it can be appropiate to prevent a rule application by remembering these exceptions. Instead of hiding this information in additional premises, exceptions should be represented explicitly. This allows generalizing exception conditions and forming new concepts when more exceptions and/or more information about the exceptions become available ([Emde/Habel/Rollinger 83]). An explicit representation of exception conditions may support the development of a new and better rule ([Michalski/Winston 86]) and, furthermore, the improvement of the structure of the rule set using new concepts ([Wrobel 88]).

2.4 "Closed-loop" learning

Common to all the incremental learning programs mentioned above is that the learning result is not applied to new incoming data in the sense that new descriptions of objects are derived which serve as a basis for new generalizations [5].

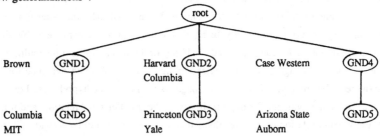

Figure 1: A memory structure of UNIMEM [Lebowitz 87]

Let's take the example of UNIMEM's university domain [Lebowitz 87] to make this point clear. At

---

[5] COBWEB and UNIMEM apply induced concept descriptions in the sense that with each input objects are classified according to their descriptions along these induced concepts.

one stage, UNIMEM has generalized the concept 'GND2' (described as 'quality of life' liberal arts school). Later, the program has processed and classified a description of Columbia University as one instance of this concept (Figure 1). UNIMEM is able to use this classification of Columbia as a 'GND2' to produce sub-generalizations of 'GND2'. However, the description of 'Columbia' is not enriched, e.g. by an additional feature 'GND2-NESS' with the value "yes". As a consequence, UNIMEM is not able to make full use of the induced knowledge at later stages of the learning process. Features like 'GND2-NESS' will not be available if e.g. other sub-generalizations of 'GND6' (with Columbia University as one instance) would be appropiate using 'GND2-NESS' as an determining feature. Furthermore, the information about the concept membership of an instance is not utilized to infer unknown values of features. For example, an unknown feature value of Columbia University would not be inferred from known values for the same feature of other 'GND2'-universities.

This kind of utilization of induced knowledge is regarded as natural (and necessary) in continuously ongoing "real world" learning processes. The output of one learning stage has to be "looped back" as input to the next. The term "closed-loop learning" (adopted from K. Haase) is used to describe this kind of learning. In the rest of this section, some difficulties of closed-loop learning are examined, and the requirements for the knowledge representation caused by these difficulties are discussed. Mainly, we will be concerned with knowledge revision problems that have been studied with the development of the closed-loop learning system METAXA.3 ([Emde 87]) [6].

2.4.1 Representation of contradictory knowledge

The advantage of applying induced knowledge in later steps is that learning can be become more efficient and effective. The advantage of NOT applying induced knowledge is that knowledge revision becomes easier. If a generalization process is based only on incoming data, there are only two possibilities in the case of an inconsistency among a new input, an earlier input, and a generalization: an input can be rejected or the generalization can be modified. However, if induced knowledge is applied to the incoming data, the learning program may have to decide which generalization should be modified. Suppose a program has successively applied several induced rules to infer unknown feature values. In the next step, the learning program is supplied with new descriptions about the objects in the domain, and some of them contradict previously inferred descriptions. In such a case, the system has to decide which generalized rules have to be blamed and how the generalizations have to be modified ([Wrobel 88], [Emde 86]).

The process of computing possible candidates and selecting one (or more) of them may lead to the generation of new contradictions. The number of remaining contradictions and the number of contradictions additionally generated for each candidate may be used as one criterium for the selection of a modification. Therefore, the representation formalism should allow the representation of contradictory knowledge. This would also allow retaining "less important" contradictions if the

---

[6] cf. [Haase 86] and [Wrobel 88] for a treatment of problems which occur with concept formation in closed-loop learning.

resources available to the learning program are very restricted [7]. Nevertheless, the effect of inconsistencies should always be limited to the smallest possible knowledge entities. If, for example, the information about one attribute of an object is contradictory, the effect of the inconsistency should be limited to the corresponding assertion in the knowledge base.

2.4.2 Representation of data dependencies

There is another consequence arising from the application of induced knowledge to incoming data. Because the knowledge revision sub-component of the learning system must be able to track down the origin of a contradiction, a structure describing the dependencies between entered, deduced and induced data must be available, and a data dependency maintenance program is necessary to maintain these dependencies.

2.4.3 Representation of multiple theories

So far, we have been concerned with only one method of applying induced knowledge to incoming data: the use of induced knowledge to make learning more effective and efficient. However, there is another possible and necessary application of induced knowledge: the classification of incoming data into (different kinds of) "noisy" and correct data for further learning processes and performance tasks. Of course, a number of programs are able to learn in noisy environments (e.g. UNIMEM, COBWEB, etc.), but in these programs, the classification is not an application of induced knowledge in the sense that the result is used in further processing. If induced knowledge is applied to classify incoming data in a closed-loop learning program, the knowledge revision problem becomes much harder since learning in complex domains requires the learner to restrict the search for a model of the domain, e.g. to use a confirmatory strategy and/or a hill-climbing strategy in generalization processes and conservatism in knowledge revision processes ([Langley/Gennari/Iba 87]). Unfortunately, the program then risks running into a dead-end (local optimum), a process accelerated by presence of "noise" because each faulty rule may lead to a classification of "correct" data into "noisy" and vice versa (strengthening the learner's "belief" in its model) ([Emde 86]).

It seems that it is not always possible for a learning program to avoid dead ends if resources are restricted. Therefore, the learning system should be capable of escaping such dead-ends. Several solutions have been proposed and discussed. In Samuel's checkers player (described in [Dietterich et al. 82]), staying on local maxima is prevented by making arbitary changes to the polynomial evaluation function. Michalski has discussed the "revolutionary approach" of knowledge revision, which is simply to throw away a piece of knowledge and develop another one from scratch ([Michalski 85]). A similar idea has been used in the GALATEA program, in which "paradigms" are used to restrict the learner's view of the world ([Brebner 85]). If a "paradigm" fails, the program discards all data accumulated during experiments and tries another one. A constructive approach which takes advantage of parts of

---

[7]   Retaining some minor contradictions also seems to be natural in human learning and scientific processes.

the old knowledge has been proposed by the author ([Emde 87]). In his METAXA.3 program, a model developed in a "cumulative learning mode" is utilized to create a new one by making some radical changes to the model.

However, if a learning program has tried to leave a dead end (local optimum) by making radical changes, nothing is guaranteed. It is possible that the program has improved its model or will be able to do so by refining the new model, or it is possible that the program has induced an alternative model which covers different aspects about the domain or is advantageous for different kind of application. It is also possible that the program has made a change for the worse (e.g. in the sense that fewer inputs are "explained" by the program's model). The learning program must be able to estimate the (supposed) improvement achieved by the shift from one model to another in order to decide if the old or the new model should be kept. This may require comparing, selecting, and ranking these models, as well as handling these models as objects in themselves. Furthermore, it may be necessary to give each model the same input data and then to see what the set of valid assertions are and what exceptions and "noisy data" the model produces. Another requirement entailed for the knowledge representation formalism in closed-loop learning is therefore, that the learning program is able to represent "multiple theories" instead of having just one unstructured homogenous body of knowledge (cf. [Brazdil 87]).

It should be mentioned that such a formalism (and the corresponding mechanisms) can also be used to organize the knowledge base, e.g. to separate background knowledge from induced knowledge and general knowledge from specific knowledge. This is especially important for logic-oriented representation schemes, which are known to have the disadvantage, that means for the organization of knowledge are not naturally present.

Some examples of the possible use of a multiple theory representation will be given in part 4 of this paper after a knowledge representation has been introduced which fulfills the requirements for incremental and closed-loop learning described above: a representation which allows the representation of uncertain and contradictory knowledge, which facilitates the repair of induced rules, which allows a program to maintain the data dependencies, and which allows the representation of multiple theories.

3 An inference engine for "closed-loop" learning systems

In this section, the knowledge representation formalism of the inference engine IM-2 is described [8]. IM-2 is designed as a knowledge representation and maintenance component for integrated closed-loop learning systems. The general task of IM-2 can be stated as follows: First, the inference engine is supposed to explicate the meaning of sequentially incoming facts by using a changable set of inference

---

[8] The knowledge representation formalism of IM-2 can be regarded as an offspring of the Berlin Semantic Representation Language (SRL). SRL has been developed in various projects concerned with question-answering and text-understanding systems (cf. [Habel 82], [Habel 86], [Rollinger 84]). With respect to the inference mechanism and the data dependency maintenance procedures, IM-2 can regarded as a successor to the inference engine IM-1 ([Emde/Schmiedel 84]). IM-1 was especially designed to reason about uncertain knowledge and has been successfully used to implement the learning program METAXA and a user modeling system ([Morik/Rollinger 85]).

rules. Second, IM-2 is supposed to answer queries by using input and inferred facts and by applying inference rules. Third, IM-2 is responsible for maintaining the inferential and assertional knowledge if an input fact (or a inference rule) is retracted or if an input (or deduction) results in a contradiction making earlier inferences invalid.

In contrast to AI programming languages like CONNIVER ([McDermott 83]) or MULTILOG ([Kauffman/Grumbach 86]), logic programming/reasoning systems like MRS (cf. [Russell 85]) and RUP ([McAllester 82]), and meta-level extensions of PROLOG (cf. [Bowen 85]), the inference engine IM-2 does not offer the usual constructs of a programming system, e.g. control mechanisms which are necessary to write problem solving programs. The inference engine IM-2 is not intended as a programming system, but as knowledge representation system. One main difference of IM-2 from other reasoning systems (RUP, MRS etc.) is that it is able to deal with higher order concepts like "transitivity" (cf. [Attardi/Simi 84]) and to use such concepts to reason about inferential knowledge. However, IM-2 is not able to deal with assumptions and equalities which systems like RUP can deal with. As a consequence, IM-2 does not require a truth maintenance system (A/TMS) to track down and handle the assumptions which underlie contradictions.

In the closed-loop learning system BLIP (cf. [Morik 88], [Wrobel 87a], [Morik 87], [Emde/Morik 86]), the inference engine IM-2 is responsible for memorizing the assertional and inferential (object-, "meta"-, and "meta-meta"-) knowledge, making inferences, and maintaining the assertional and inferential knowledge by recording dependency networks between these knowledge entities [9].

In this paper, we will be concerned only with the knowledge representation formalism implemented in IM-2. This representation is based on the distinction between assertional and inferential knowledge. First, the basic concepts for the representation of assertional and inferential knowledge are introduced. Then, more advanced facilities will be described, and it will be shown how IM-2 fulfills the requirements discussed in part 2 of this paper.

3.1 Assertional knowledge in IM-2

The formalism for the representation of assertional knowledge allows the description of attributes of and relations among objects of the world. As is usual in logic-oriented representation formalisms, assertions are represented with formulas formed with the aid of 'formula-making' constants, e.g. predicates. Possible arguments of such constants are terms, formulas and predicates (but not variables!). Formulas are used to represent attributes of and relations among objects. Terms are used to refer to single objects as well as compound objects (e.g. sets) in the world. A term is constructed with a 'term-making' constant (function symbol). In addition, all natural numbers are regarded as terms. Presupposing

---

[9]   This requires a note about the relation between the knowledge representation in BLIP and IM-2. Because IM-2 is designed as general tool, it is not very surprising that BLIP's knowledge (re)presentation differs from the knowledge representation made available by IM-2. BLIP's sorted, higher-order knowledge representation with types ([Wrobel 87b]) is realized using IM-2. The knowledge representation formalism of IM-2 allows the representation of higher-order assertions, but terms are not sorted and predicates are not typed.

a set of constants and a description of the results (i.e. formula or term) and the arguments of these constants, it is possible to define the set of well-formed expressions. We will restrict ourselves to look at some examples. This should suffice to give an intuitive understanding about the expressive power of the IM-2 representation formalism.

In figure 2, some examples of 'term-making' constants and terms constructed with these constants are given. A quadrupel $<e,k,l,m>$, called the degree (DEGREE) of these constants, describes the result and the required arguments of the constants [10]. The first value of DEGREE describes whether the constant is a 'term-maker' or a 'formula-maker'. The remaining values are used to describe the number of terms (k), the number of formulas (l), and the number of predicates (m) demanded as arguments.

	DEGREE	Term	
aspirin	$<ter,0,0,0>$	aspirin	(1)
bufferin	$<ter,0,0,0>$	bufferin	(2)
producer	$<ter,1,0,0>$	producer(aspirin)	(3)
;	$<ter,2,0,0>$	(peter, novalgin); (john, aspirin)	(4)
set	$<ter,1,0,0>$	set(novalgin)	(5)
all_of	$<ter,0,0,1>$	all_of(single_substance_drug)	(6)
all	$<ter,0,0,0>$	all	(7)
excl	$<ter,2,0,0>$	all_of(single_substance_drug) excl set(aspirin)	(8)

Figure 2: Some examples of terms

It is assumed that distinct terms describe distinct objects in the world. All 0-place term-making constants, e.g. 'aspirin' and 'bufferin', are interpreted as names. The constant 'producer' in figure 2 is declared as one-place 'term-maker'. It might be used to refer to producers of medical drugs.

A special pre-defined meaning is assigned to the term-makers ',', ';', 'set', 'all_of', 'all', and 'excl'. In contrast to other (user-specified) constants the meaning of this pre-defined term-makers is not given by inference rules (see section 3.2), but predetermined by the inference mechanism (see section 3.2.2 for how these special term-makers are used).

The two-place (infix-) operators ',' and ';' are predefined to describe explicitly tupels and sets of objects. For example, the term (4) in figure 2 refers to a set consisting of two pairs, one which might refer to a person Peter and the drug Novalgin, and another, which might refer to a person John and the drug Aspirin. The constant 'set' takes one term as an argument and is used to refer to the set containing the corresponding object as the only member (5).

The term-maker 'all_of' takes an predicate p as argument and then refers to the set of objects for which the corresponding formula 'p(x)' is true. For example, the term (6) may be used to refer to all single substance drugs. The set of all objects is described by the term 'all'. The infix-operator 'excl'

---

[10]   Actually, DEGREE is not used in IM-2, but is introduced here for expository purposes.

corresponds to the relative complement operator of set theory. It takes two arguments t_1, t_2 and refers to a set which contains all objects contained in t_1 except those objects also contained in the set described by t_2. For example, the term (8) describes the set of single substance drugs except the drug Aspirin. In the following, 'all_of' and 'set' will be omitted as part of the arguments of 'excl' if there is no risk of confusion.

	DEGREE	Formula	
single_substance_drug	<for,1,0,0>	single_substance_drug(aspirin)	(1)
contains	<for,2,0,0>	contains(aspirin,asa)	(2)
inverse_2	<for,0,0,2>	inverse_2(contains,is_contained_in)	(3)
m_symmetrical	<for,0,0,1>	m_symmetrical(inverse_2)	(4)
body_temperature	<for,2,0,0>	body_temperature(jonas,37)	(5)
believes	<for,1,1,0>	believes(iris,body_temperature(jonas,39))	(6)
transitive	<for,1,0,1>	transitive(west_of,(all_of(loc_in_europe),	
		all_of(loc_in_europe),all_of(loc_in_europe)))	(7)

Figure 3: Some examples of well-formed formulas

Figure 3 shows some examples of well-formed formulas, which may be used to represent the facts in figure 4. Attributes of and relations among predicates can be described using higher-order predicates, which are predicates taking predicates as arguments ((3), (4) of figure 3). This allows a declarative representation of inferential knowledge as "meta-(meta-)facts" and the ability to reason about inferential knowledge (see section 3.2.2). Similar, assertions about statements (6) can be represented using formula-makers consuming formulas as arguments. The possible use of the predefined term-makers will be discussed in section 3.4; for now, formula (7) gives an example of how these terms are used. The relation 'west-of' is stated as transitive if 'west-of' is applied to locations in Europe. The second argument is a 3-place tupel interpreted as cartesian product of three domains for the variables used in the corresponding inference rule.

Aspirin is a single-substance drug.	(1)
Aspirin contains ASA.	(2)
The relation 'contains' is the inverse relation of 'is contained in'	(3)
The relation 'inverse' is symmetrical.	(4)
The body temperature of Jonas is 37° C.	(5)
Iris believes that the body temperature of Jonas is 39° C.	(6)
The relation 'west of' is transitive if applied to locations in Europe.	(7)

Figure 4: A natural-language representation of figure 3

So far, the basic constructs for the representation of assertional knowledge are described. It is important to note that no logical operators (e.g. the connectives ' $\land$ ' and ' $\lor$ ', the negation '$\neg$', or quantifiers) are predefined [11]. In the next section, the representation of the inferential knowledge in IM-2 is presented. Afterwards, the formalism for the representation of assertional knowledge is extended to fulfill the requirements discussed in the second part of this paper.

3.2 Inferential knowledge in IM-2

The meaning of constants used to build formulas is described by inference rules. Inference rules are applied to the assertional knowledge to make explicit what is implicitly represented in assertions. Whereas assertions are used to describe objects in the world, inference rules are regarded as transformation rules between assertions. Inference rules are NOT assertions about the world, like "All men are mortal" is a statement about the world with a particular "truth value" [12], to which inference rules can be applied. In contrast to implication rules, inference rules are not applicable to determine the truth value of a premise if the truth value of the conclusion is known to be false. Thus, inference rules may be regarded as the logical equivalent of productions rules [13].

By adding inference rules to the rule base of IM-2, the interpreter for the assertional knowledge is changed. These "non-logical" inference rules are the only ones used in the current version of IM-2. The "usual set of inference rules" (e.g. modus ponens, modus tollens, etc.) is not necessary because no logical operators are defined in the assertional language of IM-2.

In logic, the usual notation of inference rules is:

$$p_1$$
$$\vdots$$
$$p_n$$
$$\overline{}$$
$$c$$

In an inference, the formulas $p_1 .. p_n$ are called the premises and c is the conclusion. A more economical notation with the symbol '-->' (to separate the premises and the conclusion) and the symbol '&' (to concatenate premises) is used in IM-2. Some examples of inference rules which can be described in IM-2 are shown in figure 5.

The list of premises and the conclusion are preceded by a declaration of the variables in the inference rule. The declaration (in front of the separator '::') determines which symbols in the rule have to be interpreted as variables [14]. In addition, the range of the variables can be specified in the rule. In figure 5, all variables are unrestricted, and a range specification is omitted. For example, rule (1) describes the

---

[11] The symbols ' ∧ ' and ' ∨ ' may be defined as non-logical operators. The representation of negated assertions is described in section 3.3.

[12] Statements like this could be represented if the language for representing assertions contained quantifiers and variables.

[13] This approach of representing inferential knowledge in non-logical inference rules has been adopted from SRL (cf. [Habel 82], [Rollinger 83], cf. also Reiter's default logic [Reiter 80]).

[14] Variables are not typed.

x,y,z	::	cheaper(x,y) & cheaper(y,z) --> cheaper(x,z)	(1)
x,y	::	contains(x,y) --> is_contained_in(y,x)	(2)
p1,p2	::	inverse_2(p1,p2) --> inverse_2(p2,p1)	(3)
p1,p2	::	transitive(p1) & inverse_2(p1,p2) --> transitive(p2)	(4)
pers, temp	::	body_temperature(pers,temp) & gt(temp,38) --> has_fever(pers)	(5)

Figure 5: Some examples of inference rules

transitivity of the operator 'cheaper', with 'x', 'y' and 'z' as variables.

Rule (3) may be used to reason about (the declarative representation of) inferential knowledge, given 'inverse_2' is defined as taking predicates as arguments (s. formula (3) in figure 3). Generally, all formula-making operators can be used to build premises and conclusions. Additional built-in predicates are predefined which can be used to compare terms (e.g. 'eq(_,_)' (equal), 'ne(_,_)' (not equal), 'lt(_,_)' (lower than)) and to check or make arithmetic computations (e.g. 'prod(_,_,_)' (multiplication), 'add(_,_,_)' (addition)).

3.2.1 Rule generating rules

Up to now, we have been concerned with inference rules capable of transforming one or more assertions into other assertions. We will now make an extension which allows transforming assertions into rules. In figure 2, some examples for the declarative representation of inferential knowledge (called "metafacts" in BLIP) were given, and inference rules which allow reasoning about inferential knowledge have been described. The declarative representation of inferential knowledge can be very useful in knowledge acquisition and learning, but it doesn't make too much sense if the declarative representation of the rules is not connected to the rules themselves. In the inference engine of the METAXA programs, attached procedures were used to generate rules if corresponding facts were added to the knowledge base. Unfortunately, the maintenance of data dependencies necessary for knowledge revision becomes very tricky for this solution. Therefore, the representation formalism of inference rules is extended in such a way that assertions, i.e. metafacts, can be transformed into inference rules. In addition to formulas, rule schemes as well are allowed as conclusions. Inference rules with a rule schema as conclusion are called "rule generating rules".

p :: transitive(p) --> (x,y,z :: p(x,y) & p(y,z) --> p(x,z))	(1)
p,q :: inverse_2(p,q) --> (x,y :: p(x,y) --> q(y,x))	(2)
p,q,c :: thresh_max(p,q,c) --> (x,y :: p(x,y) & gt(y,c) --> q(x))	(3)
p,q :: m_symmetrical(p) --> (x :: p(x,y) --> p(y,x))	(4)

Figure 6: Examples of rule generating rules

In figure 6, some examples of rule-generating rules are given. If such rules are applied to a corresponding assertion, the rule schemta are instantiated, and the resulting rule is added to the set of applicable rules [15]. For example, if rule (1) is applied to

---

[15] Rule generating rules are only applied in the forward chaining mode.

transitive(cheaper),

the rule:

x,y,z :: cheaper(x,y) & cheaper(y,z) --> cheaper(x,z)

is added to the "rule base".

3.2.2 Support sets: restricted domains of variables

It was already mentioned at the beginning of section 3.2 that the domain of variables in inference rules can be restricted. The symbol 'elem' behind the variables in the rule header marks a following "support set description", the description of the domains of the variables in the rule. Support sets are intended to specify the domain to which the rule is applicable. Originally, support sets were proposed as an annotation of higher-order assertions to overcome some problems with the (local) transitivity of particular predicates (e.g. 'west-of') ([Habel/Rollinger 82]). Later, an successful attempt was made to use support sets for learning concepts which are useful to describe the valid application domain of induced rules ([Emde/Habel/Rollinger 83]) [16]. However, an appropiate representation of support sets was not realized by the inference engine used in the learning program; instead, support sets were translated into additional premises by the learning program ([Emde 87]). In the following, a more general notation of support sets as used before is described and, moreover, introduced into the rule representation. This new rule representation facilitates the correction of induced rules in incremental learning as demanded in section 2.3.2.

x,y,z elem (all,all,all) ::   cheaper(x,y) & cheaper(y,z) --> cheaper(x,z)   (1)
pers,temp elem (all_of(adult), all) ::
                            body_temperature(pers,temp) & gt(temp,37) --> has_fever(pers)   (2)
x elem (all excl (novalgin;metamiz_2000)) ::
                            single_substance_drug(x) --> suitable(x)   (3)
x elem all_of(metamizol_drug) ::
                            single_substance_drug(x) --> suitable(x)   (4)
x,y elem ((all,all) excl ((drug_77,drug_78); (drug_94,drug_13)))::
                            contains_less_cortisone(x,y) --> better(x,y)   (5)
x,y,z elem (all_of(loc_in_europe), all_of(loc_in_europe), all_of(loc_in_europe)) ::
                            west_of(x,y) & west_of(y,z) --> west_of(x,z)   (6)

Figure 7: Some examples of rules with restricted variable domains

The symbol 'all' can be used if the domain of a variable is not restricted. For example, rule (1) in figure 7 is equivalent to rule (1) in figure 5. The restricted domain of variables is described by the symbols 'all_of', 'set', 'excl', ';', and ',', which were also introduced as term-makers (section 3.1). The

---

[16]   In the METAXA program, only one domain description (for usually one variable) of each rule could be defined as "the" support set of the rule. An induced rule was modified by changing this domain description. Thus, a bias towards particular modifications was implemented in METAXA's knowledge representation. In the BLIP system, a more general notation which will be described below is used ([Wrobel 88]).

symbol 'all_of' in rule (2) of figure 7 is used to restrict the domain of the variable 'pers' to terms which refer only to objects described as adults because infants tend to have a higher body temperature than adults.

Rule (3) and (4) are taken again from the domain of drugs. The domain of the variable 'x' in rule (3) is extensionally restricted to the set of all objects with exception of the drugs named 'Novalgin' and 'Metamiz_2000'. This rule might be generated by a learning program after a few exceptions from the regularity "all single substance drugs are suitable" were observed. The restriction might be refined at a later learning stage after more exceptions of the regularity are found, thus enabling the learning program to form the concept of drugs containing the dangerous substance 'Metamizol' (rule 4).

The symbol 'excl' may also be used to specify explicitly listed exception tupels, e.g. if the set of known exceptions of a regularity is too small to produce a reasonable generalization of the exceptions ([Emde/Habel/Rollinger 83], [Wrobel 88]). For example, the support set of rule (5) is restricted only by a set of two exception tuples, but the single domains of the variables are not restricted. The rule will not be applied if the variable 'x' is bound with the term 'drug_77' **and** 'y' is bound with the term 'drug_78' or if the variable 'x' is bound with the term 'drug_94' **and** the variable 'y' with 'drug_13'.

Support set descriptions are treated differently from logically equivalent premises. If a new assertion matching with premises of inference rules is added, these rules will (usually) be applied in the forward-chaining mode. In contrast, a rule will not be triggered if its intensionally described support set (using 'all_of' and 'excl', and 'all') has grown. A rule is only applied in the forward-chaining mode to explicate the meaning of incoming assertions matching a premise. For example, if a drug is stated to be a Metamizol drug using the operator 'metamizol_drug', rule (4) of figure 7 would not be triggerd [17].

In contrast to the "rule censors" approach described in ([Michalski/Winston 86]), inference rules with support set restrictions do not indicate expectations about the outcome of an inference if the premises are verified unless the support set condition has been proven. Therefore, support sets are not appropriate for controling the reasoning if resources are restricted. Support sets, unlike rule censors, cannot be ignored in situations in which rapid response is critical.

In the declarative representation of rules which is possible in IM-2 (in contrast to the declarative representation offered by BLIP), the support set is described as an additional argument of the corresponding predicate. An example of a support set description has already been presented in figure 3:

transitive(west_of, (all_of(loc_in_europe),all_of(loc_in_europe),all_of(loc_in_europe)))

The transitivity of 'west_of' is restricted to objects which are elements of the set described by the term 'all_of(loc_in_europe)', which means that the variables in the corresponding rule can only be instantiated by terms known also as instances of 'loc_in_europe'. The reason why support set descriptions are

---

[17]   However, if the support set of a rule becomes smaller, the data dependency procedures will take care of updating the assertional knowledge.

represented as an additional argument is that this allows the program to easily reason about inferential knowledge even if the support sets are restricted. The support set argument of a meta-fact is translated into domain restrictions for all variables in the rule using a corresponding rule-generating rule. As an example, the following rule-generating rule can be used for 'transitive':

p,s :: transitive(p,s) --> (x,y,z elem s :: p(x,y) & p(y,z) --> p(x,z))

This rule can be applied to assertions with a support set argument. If the rule is applied to:

transitive(west_of, (all_of(loc_in_europe), all_of(loc_in_europe), all_of(loc_in_europe)))

the following rule will be added to the set of applicable rules:

x,y,z elem (all_of(loc_in_europe), all_of(loc_in_europe), all_of(loc_in_europe)) ::
            west_of(x,y) & west_of(y,z) --> west_of(x,z)

If a higher order assertion (a "meta-(meta)-fact") is deleted, the data dependency maintenance procedures of the inference engine are responsible for deleting the corresponding rule. Furthermore, all applications of this rule will be retracted.

So far, the basic constructs for the representation of the assertional and inferential knowledge have been introduced. In the next section, we will turn to the question of how the remaining requirements stated in section 2 of this paper are fulfilled.

3.3 Attributions of formulas and rules

In section 3.1, the syntax of well-formed terms and formulas was informally described, and we noted that no connective for the representation of negated facts is defined. Thus, the very basic requirement that it should be possible to represent negated facts is not (yet) met. Further, the requirements mentioned in section 2 for the representation of uncertain and contradictory knowledge and multiple theories have yet to be dealt with. These requirements are treated in this section by the introduction of the concept of attributed formulas, which is adopted from SRL ([Habel 82], [Habel 86]).

A set of attributes is attached to the formulas to represent the attitudes of the learning program or any other "user" of IM-2 towards these propositions. Now that we have introduced the notion of attributes, the assertional knowledge ASSERT can formally be described by the set of formulas FORMULA attributed by a set of attributes A-ATT. The inferential knowledge INFER is given with the set of rules RULE (as used above) attributed by a set of rule attributes R-ATT.

$$ASSERT \subseteq FORMULA \times A\text{-}ATT$$
$$A\text{-}ATT = ID \times EP \times KT \times UR \times W$$
$$INFER \subseteq RULE \times R\text{-}ATT$$
$$R\text{-}ATT = ID \times KT \times UR \times W$$

Five attributes are used in IM-2: a unique name for the assertion or rule (ID), a two-dimensional evidence rating (EP), a description of the origin (justification) of this evidence or rule (a "knowledge trace", KT), a description about the use of the assertion or rule in further inferences (the use record, UR), and a description of the context ("world", W) in which the assertion or rule is known. In the following, the evidence attribution EP and the world attribution W are described in more detail.

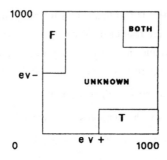

Figure 8: The evidence space

3.3.1 Negation, uncertainty, and contradictions

In order to represent negated statements, uncertain knowledge, and contradictory information, a two-dimensional evidence rating is attached to formulas. The use of two-dimensional evidence values was originally proposed in [Rollinger 83] (cf. [Rollinger 84]) [18]. Instead of having a binary truth value, formulas have the attribution of an "evidence point" in a two-dimensional "evidence space" (figure 8) which is formed by the dimensions "evidence for" (ev+) and "evidence against" (ev-) a proposition. An evidence point EP is determined by the positive and negative evidence entered and inferred for a proposition. The maximum value for the positive and negative evidence is 1000, the minimum value is 0.

$$EP = [0,1000] \times [0,1000]$$

The evidence points [1000,0], [0,1000], [1000,1000], and [0,0] correspond to Belnap's [Belnap 76] epistemic truth values T (told true), F (told false), BOTH (told both true and false), and UNKNOWN (told neither true nor false), respectively. The interpretation of other evidence points in IM-2 is determined by three parameters which are similar to the threshold parameter used in MYCIN ([Shortliffe 76, p. 102]). The parameter 'min_confirm_evidence' specifies the minimum positive (negative) evidence which is necessary for an assertion to be regarded as "true" (or "false", respectively). The value of 'max_counter_evidence' determines the maximum negative (positive) evidence for an assertion still to be regarded as "true" (or "false", respectively). An evidence point is interpreted as a "contradiction" if both positive and negative evidence are greater than the value of the parameter 'contradiction_threshold'.

These parameters are also used in inferential processes to determine if premises are "verified". As 'target evidence points' for premises, only [1000,0], [0,1000] and [1000,1000] are allowed [19]. They are

---

[18]   The proposal was implemented in the inference engine IM-1 ([Emde/Schmiedel 83], cf. [Morik/Rollinger 85]).

[19]   The original proposal of C.-R. Rollinger is more general and allows all points of the evidence space as target points. Furthermore, the deviations allowed from the target point must be specified with each premise, e.g. it is possible to specify that a particular premise is "verified" if the evidence point of the matching proposition is equal to (or in "a certain neighborhood" to) the evidence point [500,500].

specified using the additional symbols 'not' and 'both'. A premise of the form 'not(p)' requires an evidence point of [0,1000], and a premise of the form 'both(p)' requires an evidence point of [1000,1000]. A premise of the form p requires an evidence point of [1000,0]. If all premises of a rule are "verified", then the evidence point of the conclusion is computed by applying the minimum function to the ratings of the quality of all premise verifications (conjunctive combination). Afterwards, the maximum function is applied to all positive and negative evidence values inferred for an assertion to compute the evidence point (disjunctive combination). A function strengthening the final evidence of several uncertain inferences is not used, because the use of such a function requires knowledge about the independence of the single evidence values. This knowledge is not available if IM-2 is part of a learning system whose task is to acquire a model of a domain.

Thus, the following interpretations of an evidence point EP are possible:
(1) The assertion is regarded as "true"; a premise p is verified.
(2) The assertion is regarded as "false"; a premise not(p) is verified.
(3) The truth value of the assertion is "unknown"; a premise is not verified.
(4) The information about the truth value of a proposition is contradictory; a premise both(p) is verified.

In figure 9, a trace of some inputs to the inference engine is shown. Attributions are attached to an input (using the symbol '---'). The evidence point attribution is preceded by the symbol 'ep:'. If no evidence is specified, an EP of [1000,0] is assumed. As an abbreviation for the evidence point [0,1000], formulas can be "negated" with the symbol 'not'. For convenience, this notation is also used for the rest of this paper. Assertions and inference rules are added to the knowledge base using the interface function 'im_tell'. A question about the assertional knowledge is asked using the function 'im_ask'. The question is answered on the basis of the assertions which have been entered, which have been inferred, or which can be deduced using the inferential knowledge. The function 'im_retract' retracts an assertional or inferential input and all dependent knowledge entities which are not supported otherwise. User inputs are following the symbol '?-', all other lines are trace messages of the inference engine about changed evidence points and new inference rules.

The trace illustrates what has been said about the capabilities of IM-2 to reason about uncertain knowledge. The drug 'paracetamol_100' is described as a single substance drug with some positive (600) and a little negative (100) evidence. At first, nothing is inferred from this assertion using rule 'r1' because there is to little positive evidence [20]. However, a later input increases the positive evidence to 800, the corresponding threshold is passed, and it is inferred that 'paracetamol_100' is a suitable drug with a positive evidence of 800. The negative evidence is not carried over.

To summarize, this extension enables representing negated statements with the evidence point [0,1000], representing and reasoning about uncertain knowledge, and representing contradictory

---

[20] Following threshold parameters are used in the sample run: 'min_confirm_evidence' = 750, 'max_counter_evidence' = 250, 'contradiction_threshold' = 800.

```
?- im_tell((single_substance_drug(aspirin)---ep:[1000,0])).
 New EP: f4  single_substance_drug(aspirin) --- ep: [1000, 0]
?- im_tell((single_substance_drug(arantil)---ep:[0,1000])).
 New EP: f5  single_substance_drug(arantil) --- ep: [0, 1000]
?- im_ask(suitable(aspirin)).
 Nothing is known about this!
?- im_tell(((x::single_substance_drug(x)-->suitable(x)))).
 New rule: r1  x :: single_substance_drug(x) --> suitable(x)
?- im_ask((suitable(aspirin))).
 New EP: f6  suitable(aspirin) --- ep: [1000, 0]
 Yes, suitable(aspirin)
?- im_tell(single_substance_drug(ben_u_ron)).
 New EP: f7  single_substance_drug(ben_u_ron) --- ep: [1000, 0]
 New EP: f8  suitable(ben_u_ron) --- ep: [1000, 0]
?- im_tell(single_substance_drug(paracetamol_100) --- ep: [600,100])).
 New EP: f9  single_substance_drug(paracetamol_100) --- ep: [600, 100]
?- im_tell((single_substance_drug(paracetamol_100) --- ep: [800,100])).
 New EP: f9  single_substance_drug(paracetamol_100) --- ep: [800, 100]
 New EP: f10  suitable(paracetamol_100) --- ep: [800, 0]
?- im_tell(((p::both(p)-->contradictory_prop(p)))).
 New rule: r2  p :: both(p) --> contradictory_prop(p)
?- im_tell((suitable(paracetamol_100) --- ep: [0,1000])).
 New EP: f10  suitable(paracetamol_100) --- ep: [800, 1000]
 New EP: f11  contradictory_prop(suitable(paracetamol_100)) --- ep: [800, 0]
?- im_retract(f9).
 New EP: f9  single_substance_drug(paracetamol_100) --- ep: [0, 0]
 New EP: f10  suitable(paracetamol_100) --- ep: [0, 1000]
 New EP: f11  contradictory_prop(suitable(paracetamol_100)) --- ep: [0, 0]
```

Figure 9: A sample trace

knowledge with the evidence point [1000,1000] [21].

3.3.2 Organization of knowledge: Worlds

A well-known disadvantage of logic-oriented representation schemes is that no means for the organization of knowledge are naturally present. This is also true for the basic representation scheme of IM-2. By the introduction of another attribution, called W(orld)-attribution, for assertions and rules, means for the organization of knowledge are made available.

A-ATT = ID x EP x KT x UR x W
R-ATT = ID x KT x UR x W
W = TERM

---

[21]   Note that the number of contradictions which can be represented is not restricted to 16 as is the case in the MONK-PLUS system ([Adams 88], p.5).

The W-attribution is used to collect assertions and inference rules which "belong together" in larger knowledge entities called "worlds". All assertions and rules are attributed by a term, the designation of a world. Knowledge entities with the same designation are stored in the same world. Every world can be extended and modified by adding new assertions and rules. In general, the assertions and rules are only known within one world. The knowledge of one world can be incommensurable and incompatible to the knowledge stored in another world without inconsistencies coming to light in either of these worlds [22]. For example, the following contradictory assertions are stored in different worlds:

> better(aspirin, bufferin) --- ep: [1000,0], w: side_effects_of_pain_killers1
> better(aspirin, bufferin) --- ep: [0,1000], w: side_effects_of_pain_killers2

Each world can have its own specific evidence threshold parameters described in the previous section and parameters controlling the maximum search depth in forward chaining and backward chaining inferences. The parameters are defined by adding a corresponding assertion to the world 'system', which contains all system specific information about worlds. For example, the threshold parameters for the sample run presented in figure 9 were asserted for the world 'user', which is the default world.

The organization of knowledge into worlds is augmented by the possibility of defining inheritance relations between worlds and by an extension of the functionality of inference rules which allow transfering assertions and rules between worlds. An inheritance mechanism is made available with the world-mechanism which allows giving access to information stored in other worlds. This is necessary if, e.g. worlds are used to separate general (background) knowledge from specific knowledge. In IM-2, inheritance relations can be specified by adding a corresponding assertion to the world 'system'. For example, with the input

> inheritance(effects_of_drug_substances,side_effects_of_pain_killers1) --- w: system

all assertions and rules of the world 'effects_of_drug_substances' will also be available in the world 'side_effects_of_pain_killers1'.

The use of the inheritance mechanism is not appropiate if a selective transfer of informations has to take place or if worlds are used to separate knowledge of different levels of abstraction, e.g. to separate declarative knowledge from procedural knowledge. In section 3.2.1 (describing rule-generating rules), we have already dealt with inference rules transforming declarative knowledge into a more procedural form. The separation of these kinds of knowledge is supported by an extension of the scheme of inference rules used so far: conclusions can be attributed with a name of a world. This allows storing the declarative representation of inferential knowledge ("metafacts") in one world and the corresponding inference rules in a different world. For example, if the following rule is added to the world 'mp':

> p,q,s :: inverse_2(p,q, s) --> ((x,y elem s :: p(x,y) --> q(y,x)) --- w: object_level)

and applied to an input:

> inverse_2(contains,contained_in, (all,all))

---

[22] Nevertheless, it is possible to represent contradictory knowledge within one world using the evidence point [1000,1000] attached to one (or more) single assertions.

then the generated rule:

x,y elem (all,all) :: contains(x,y) --> contained_in(y,x)

will be added to the world 'object_level'. This way, the interpreter for the assertional knowledge of a world can be changed by delivering inference rules from another world. The data-dependency maintenance of IM-2 takes care of updating the assertional and inferential knowledge across worlds in both cases: whether the inheritance mechanism or inference rules with attributed conclusions are used. In the next section, some examples of how organizing knowledge in worlds can facilitate closed-loop learning are given.

The world mechanism of IM-2 is similar to the context mechanisms used in various AI programming languages like QA4 or CONNIVER ([McDermott 83]). The most important difference to these approaches is that in IM-2 several worlds can be accessed at the same time without it being necessary to use special operations to switch from one current data/knowledge base to the next. Meta-level extensions of PROLOG based on an incorporation of a provability relation for the object level language allow the representation of multiple theories ([Bowen 85]), assertions about theories, and the organization of knowledge. In contrast to IM-2, the provability relation (e.g. called 'demo') also allows reasoning about the abilities of theories (e.g. the ability to answer a particular question ([Brazdil 87])). [Bowen 85] illustrates how meta level extensions might be used to **implement** different representations (including representations capable to deal with uncertainty), non-standard control mechanisms, and reason maintenance mechanisms.

IM-2 worlds are also similar to the viewpoints of OMEGA ([Attardi/Simi 84]). The most notable difference between worlds and viewpoints is that information can be only added but not changed within viewpoints. If a description in OMEGA must be changed, then a new viewpoint has to be created. This may be regarded as a disadvantage of the world mechanism because IM-2 is contrained in its abilities to keep the history of the development of a model. Last but not least, a very similar mechanism is made available in the logic programming system MRS. The main difference here is that "theories" in MRS cannot be used to represent information which is partially contradictory. The same statement can be made about the relation between IM-2 worlds and worlds in the logic programming language MULTILOG.

4 Multiple theories

In the following, some examples will be given to demonstrate the necessity of a multiple theory representation in a closed-loop learning system. First, it is shown how the representation formalism can help to organize different kinds of knowledge into different worlds. The organization of object-, meta-, and meta-meta knowledge in the current version of the BLIP system is chosen as example. Second, it is described how competing models about a domain may be represented using in IM-2.

4.1 Multiple theories in BLIP

As mentioned in the previous sections, IM-2 is used to implement the higher-order knowledge representation used in the BLIP system ([Wrobel 87b]). The most important difference between the representation offered with BLIP and the representation made available by IM-2 is that the BLIP representation is typed. Formulas built up with a predicate of type 1 are called facts, formulas built up with predicates of type 2 (metapredicates) are called metafacts, and formulas constructed with predicates of type 3 (metametapredicates) are called metametafacts. Metafacts are used to describe properties of predicates and metametapredicates describe properties of metapredicates. The meaning of a meta(meta)predicate is given by meta(meta)predicate definitions which associate a rule schema with the meta(meta)predicate to be defined, such as

transitive(p): p(x,y) & p(y,z) --> p(x,y)

where p is a predicate variable and 'transitive' is the metapredicate to be defined.

Metametafacts and the corresponding metarules (rules of type t=2) can be regarded as the backgroud knowledge in inductive processes performed by BLIP to support the modeling of a domain. Whereas this knowledge is acquired using a special acquisition component (described in [Thieme 88]), metafacts are induced, and facts are entered by the user of the system.

In figure 10, an example is given how these different kinds of knowledge are organized in IM-2 using the world-attribute. Metametapredicate definitions (realized with rule-generating rules) are gathered in the world 'mmp', metametafacts are added to the world 'meta_meta_level_world', and metapredicate definitions reside in the world 'mp'. The declarative representation of object-level rules is stored together with meta-rules in a meta-level world, e.g. the two 'inverse_2'-facts in the world 'meta-level-world1' describe declaratively the rules stored in the world 'object_level_world1'.

The reason for separating meta(meta)predicate definitions from meta(meta)facts is simple: defintions are more general and can be used more the once. For example, the definitions stored in 'mp' are used to generate the rules described in 'meta_level_world1' (and stored in 'object_level_world1'). The same definitions are also used to generate the rule stored in 'object_world2'. Definitions are inherited to the corresponding (meta-)meta-level world. Whenever a metametafact or metafact is stored, the corresponding rule-generating rule is applied: the generated rule is added to all worlds which are defined as 'subworlds' of a meta-level world. This also explains the 'subworld' entries. Note, that 'sw' is declared as variable in the rule-generating rules. When these rules are applied the variables are bound sequentially by all names of subworlds specified in the corresponding meta-(meta)-level world. For example, when 'm_symmetrical(inverse_2)' was added to 'meta_meta_level_world', the 'inverse_2' rule was added to both meta-level worlds shown in figure 10. The inferred facts and rules are printed in italics.

Let's summarize what is achieved by this organization. Specific knowledge is separated from general knowledge. Knowledge belonging to different models (or domains) can also be separated. Furthermore, different parameters can be specified for different worlds. For example, a low maximum search depth is specified for forward chaining processes on the object level because it is assumed that it is not necessary

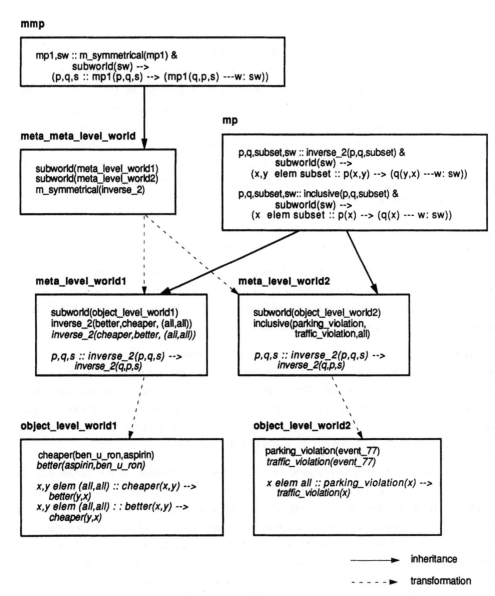

Figure 10: Organization of knowledge in BLIP

to show all consequences of an input to the user. A higher value is specified for the meta-level because the meta-rules are used to check the consistency of the object-level rules.

4.2 Competing theories

In section 2, the necessity of simultaneously representing several theories about a domain at the same time was discussed. It was argued that a learning program must be able to represent competing theories about a domain in order to compare, rank, and select these theories, as well as to run a competition between alternative theories. The aim of this section is to give an illustration of how competing models and the knowledge about competing models can be represented and how such a representation can facilitate the learning process.

global

```
goal(theory_3,causes_harmless_side_effect)
goal(theory_4,causes_harmless_side_effect)
background_knowledge(background_knowledge_1,theory_3)
background_knowledge(background_knowledge_1,theory_4)
rating(theory_3,world_5,800)
rating(theory_4,world_5,950)
qualitative_model(model_2,theory_3)
knowledge_revision_strategy(theory_3,conservative_strategy_1)
knowledge_revision_strategy(theory_4,work_out_strategy_1)
competition(theory_3,theory_4)
rejected_theory(theory_1)
last_shift(theory_3,theory_4,t-14)
```

Figure 11: A simple description of competing theories

For example, two simple theories, 'theory_3' and 'theory_4', about a very small sub-domain of 'side-effects of drugs' are presented. Some information about these theories is represented in the world 'global' (figure 11). Both theories are supposed to allow the determination of drugs causing only harmless side-effects. The learning program is referred to the world 'background_knowledge_1' for the background knowledge necessary to fulfill the learning task, e.g. information about the severity of particular side-effects, the components of sample drugs, the dosage of substances, and the side-effects of substances.

The description of the competing theories also contains the rating computed for each theory with respect to a particular application. The rating of 'theory_3', for example, is 950 with respect to its application in 'world_5'. Further, it is noted that the world 'model_2' contains a qualitative model supporting 'theory_3'[23]. The knowledge revision strategy to be used if a theory must be revised is specified for each theory, e.g. the learning program is referred to a set of heuristics collected under the name 'conservative_strategy_1' if 'theory_3' has to be revised. These entries may be changed by the learning program. If a new theory, e.g. like 'theory_4' has been worked out and gained enough explanatory power, it may be useful to change over to the use of a conservative knowledge revision strategy.

Both theories are shown in figure 12 along with the background knowledge and the noisy data which has been produced by the learning program using the theories in order to classify the input data into "noisy" and "correct" data. The theories are very simple but should be sufficient to illustrate some basic ideas about the representation of competing theories. The first theory ('theory_3') about side-effects of

---

[23]   The contents of 'world_5' and 'model_2' will be described in a forthcoming paper.

background_knowledge_1

```
severity(head_ache,10)                      mono_substance_drug(aspirin)
severity(lever_damage,80)                   mono_substance_drug(ratio_paracetamol)
severity(kidney_damage,80)                  mono_substance_drug(novalgin)
severity(reduction_of_white_blood_corpuscles,60)   mono_substance_drug(ben_u_ron)
severity(nausea,8)                          multi_substance_drug(thomapirin_n)
dose(asa,aspirin,500)                       multi_substance_drug(arantil)
dose(paracetamol,ratio_paracetamol,350)     multi_substance_drug(aspirin_plus))
dose(aminophenazon,inalgon,475)             multi_substance_drug(inalgon)
dose(metamizol,novalgin,800)
substance_side_effect(asa,3000,nausea)
substance_side_effect(paracetamol,800,
                      stomache_ache)
substance_side_effect(metamizol,200,
          reduction_of_white_blood_corpuscles)
```

theory_3

```
x elem all_except(metamizol_drug):: multi_substance_drug(x)
          --> causes_harmless_side_effect(x)
x :: mono_substance_drug(x)
          --> not(causes_harmless_side_effect(x))
causes_harmless_side_effect(thomapirin_n)
causes_harmless_side_effect(aspirin_plus)
causes_harmless_side_effects(inalgon)
causes_harmless_side_effect(arantil)
not(causes_harmless_side_effect(novalgin))
not(causes_harmless_side_effect(ratio_paracetamol))
not(causes_harmless_side_effect(ben_u_ron))
metamizol_drug(novalgin)
metamizol_drug(arantil)
```

noisy_data(theory_3)

```
causes_harmless_side_effect(
    ratio_paracetamol)
causes_harmless_side_effect(
    aspirin)
not(
  causes_harmless_side_effect(
    thomapirin_n))
```

theory_4

```
x:: mono_substance_drug(x)
          --> causes_harmless_side_effect(x)
x:: contains_mutually_reinforcing_substances(x)
          --> not(causes_harmless_side_effects(x))
x:: mono_substance_drug(x)
          --> not(contains_mutually_reinforcing_substances(x))
causes_harmless_side_effect(aspirin)
causes_harmless_side_effect(ben_u_ron)
causes_harmless_side_effect(ratio_paracetamol)
not(causes_harmless_side_effect(arantil))
not(causes_harmless_side_effect(inalgon))
not(causes_harmless_side_effect(thomapirin_n))
causes_harmless_side_effect(novalgin) --- ep: [1000,1000]
contains_mutually_reinforcing_substances(arantil)
contains_mutually_reinforcing_substances(inalgon)
```

noisy_data(theory_4)

```
causes_harmless_side_effect(
    arantil)
```

Figure 12: An example of competing theories

pain-killers says that all multi-substance drugs (except metamizol drugs) only cause harmless side-effects whereas mono-substance drugs are not causing harmless side-effects. In contrast, the second theory describes mono-substance drugs to cause only harmless side-effects. This theory is based on a concept of "drugs which contain mutually reinforcing substances". Only drugs of this type are assumed to cause harmful side-effects. Since mono-substance-drugs cannot contain mutually reinforcing substances, they cause only harmless side-effects.

It is not very surprisingly that the assertional knowledge of both theories differs considerably. The drug 'thomapirin_n' has been classified as a drug with harmless side-effects by theory-3 as opposed to being classified with harmful side-effects by theory-4. Theory-3 has lead to the rejection of two inputs describing mono-substance drugs as harmless and one input describing a multi-substance as not harmless. In contrast, theory-4 has lead to the rejection of an input describing the multi-substance drug 'arantil' as a drug with only harmless side-effects.

The reader may still ask why it is necessary to store a set of theories instead of selecting just the best one and improving it by all means available. The answer to this question is that just such a competition between theories is able to facilitate the improvement of theories, as is the case with competing theories in science. A competing theory may give hints in what directions a theory can be improved, or it may point to weak spots in and invalid assumptions of the prevailing theory. In the following, an example is given as how to a competing theory might influence the handling of noisy data and force a learning program to reconsider the rejection of particular input data.

An input telling that the drug 'novalgin' does not cause harmless side-effects has been accepted by theory-4, although the contrary has been deduced using the inference rules and the background knowledge. The input has been accepted and led to a contradictory assertion because theory-4 was notified that theory-3 is able to "explain" (i.e. can be used to deduce) this input. The knowledge revision triggered by this contradiction may lead to an improvement of theory-4. For example, the formation and introduction of a concept describing substances which are able to cause severe side-effects independent of the existence of other substances would bring theory-4 closer to reality [24]. force the improvement of theories. Note that the (incorrect) input about 'arantil' did not cause a contradiction and has been classified as "noisy" because this input is not "explained" by theory-3.

Nevertheless, it is possible to prevent theories from being hastily changed if they worked well in the past. Theory-4 "explains" that 'aspirin' and 'ratio_paracetamol' cause only harmless side-effects. Nevertheless, corresponding inputs were rejected as "noisy data" of theory-3 because more conservative heuristics (than those used for theory-4) are used to maintain the consistency of this theory. An input which will cause a contradiction is not accepted by theory-3 "only because" a competing theory is able to explain the input data.

5 Discussion and final remarks

In this paper, we have shown that the extent of the learning task can create requirements for the knowledge representation formalism used in the learning program. Some requirements which closed-

---

[24] Substances like 'metamizol' or 'phenacetin' cause harmful side-effects whether they are combined with other substances or not.

loop learning brings about were described in detail, and the knowledge representation made available by the inference engine IM-2 fulfilling these requirements was presented. In the last section, the usefulness of the organization of knowledge in "worlds" learning was described in more detail.

The worlds concept as it is made availible IM-2 allows the learning program to organize its knowledge, to separate knowledge of different generality, and to separate declarative knowledge from more procedural knowledge. Even more important, "worlds" enable a learning system to represent competing models about a domain. Having access to more than one model the learning program is able to run a contest between them and to use the result for further improvements, thus enhancing its effectiveness.

We dealt with the problem of representing the epistemological states of learning programs. In this sense, the work reported here is closely related to the work of Pavel Brazdil, who has been concerned with the representation of the epistemological states which occur if a learning system works together with a teaching system ([Brazdil 86a], [Brazdil 86b], [Brazdil 87]). The difference, however, is that Brazdil is dealing with a kind of 'learning-by-being-told' scenario, in which the teaching system must increase the learner's competence in problem solving, e.g. to sort numbers. As an example of one subtask, the teaching system is required to be able to locate gaps in the knowledge of the learning system. Brazdil has adopted a meta-level programming language for the representation of the epistemological states of the teaching and learning systems, an approach which seems to be well-suited for these kinds of tasks related to questions about capabilities of theories. In contrast, the intended application of IM-2 is a closed-loop learning system, for which a pure horn-clause representation is not sufficient, as described in section 2. This also has to be considered if a logic programming language is used as the basis for a representation language of concepts as is advocated by C. Sammut ([Sammut 88]).

The inference engine IM-2 is implemented in PROLOG. It runs on a SYMBOLICS LISP machine (using SYMBOLICS PROLOG) and on an IBM 4381 (using MPROLOG).

6 Acknowledgements

Thanks to Pavel Brazdil, who asked me two years ago if meta-level PROLOG representations of multiple theories are useful in non-cumulative learning. I am grateful to Christopher Habel and Claus-Rainer Rollinger for explaining the secrets of SRL, and to Kai von Luck, Bernhard Nebel, and my colleagues of the KIT-LERNER project for helpful discussions and comments. Thanks also to Jay Tucker for correcting my English.

7 References

Adams, D. (88): "Dirk Gently's Holistic Detective Agency"; Pan Books, London, 1988

Attardi, G./ Simi, M. (84): "Metalanguage and Reasoning about Viewpoints"; Proc. European Conference on Artificial Intelligence, 1984

Belnap, N.D. (76): "How a Computer Should Think"; In: G. Reyle (ed.): Contemporary Aspects of Philosophy, Oriente Press, 1976

Bentrup, J.A./ Mehler, G.J./ Riedesel, J.D. (87): "INDUCE 4: A Program for Incrementally Learning Structural Descriptions from Examples"; ISG Report 87-2, University of Illinois at Urbana-Champaign, 1987

Bowen, K.A. (85): "Meta-Level Programming and Knowledge Representation"; New Generation Computing, Vol. 3, 1985, pp. 359-383

Brazdil, P.B. (86a): "Transfer of Knowledge between Systems: Use of Meta-Knowledge in Debugging"; To appear in: Y. Kodratoff, A. Hutchinson (eds.): Machine and Human Learning, Horwood Pub.

Brazdil, P.B. (86b): "Transfer of Knowledge between Systems: A Common Approach to Teaching and Learning"; In Proc. ECAI-86, Brighton, 1986, pp. 73-78 (Volume II)

Brazdil, P.B. (87): "Knowledge States and Meta-Knowledge Maintenance"; In: I. Bratko, N. Lavrac (eds.): Progress in Machine Learning - Proceedings of the EWSL-87, Bled, Yugoslavia, Sigma Press, Wilmslow, 1987, pp. 138-146

Brebner, P.C. (85): "Paradigm Directed Computer Learning"; Master's Thesis, Computer Science Department, University of Waikato, Hamilton, New Zealand, 1985

Collins, A.M./ Quillian, M.R. (72): "Experiments on Semantic Memory and Language Comprehesion"; In: L.W. Gregg (ed.): Cognition in Learning and Memory, 1972

Dietterich, T.G./ London, B./ Clarkson, K./ Dromey, G.(82): "Learning and Inductive Inference"; In: P.R.Cohen/E.A.Feigenbaum (eds.): The Handbook of Artificial Intelligence, Chapter XIV, Volume 3, Kaufmann, Los Altos, 1982, pp.325-605

Dietterich, T.G./ Michalski, R.S. (83): "Inductive Learning of Structural Descriptions: Evaluation Criteria and Comparative Review of Selected Methods"; In: R.S. Michalski/ J.G. Carbonell/ T.M. Mitchell (eds.): Machine Learning, Tioga, Palo Alto, 1983, pp. 41-81

Emde, W. (86): "Big Flood in the Blocks World (or Non-Cumulative Learning)"; In: B. Boulay, D. Hogg, L. Steels (eds.) : Advances in Artificial Intelligence II (7th ECAI-86, Brighton, England, 1986), Elsevier Pub. (North Holland), Amsterdam, 1987, pp. 103-109

Emde, W. (87): "Non-Cumulative Learning in METAXA.3"; KIT-Report 56, Fachbereich Informatik, Technische Universität Berlin, 1987, a short version appeared in: Proc. IJCAI-87, Milan, Italy, 1987, pp. 208-210

Emde, W./ Habel, Ch./ Rollinger, C.-R. (83): "The Discovery of the Equator (or Concept Driven Learning)"; In: Proc. IJCAI-83, Karlsruhe, F.R.G, 1983, pp. 569-575

Emde, W./ Morik, K. (86): "Consultation Independent Learning"; To appear in: Y.Kodratoff/ A. Hutchinson (eds.): Human and Machine Learning, Horwood Pub.

Emde, W./ Rollinger, C.-R. (87): "Wissensrepräsentation und Maschinelles Lernen"; In: G. Rahmsdorf (ed.): Wissensrepräsentation in Expertensystemen, Springer, Berlin, 1988, pp. 172-189

Emde, W./ Schmiedel, A. (83): "Aspekte der Verarbeitung unsicheren Wissens"; KIT-Report 6, Fachbereich Informatik, Technische Universität Berlin, 1983

Fisher, D.H. (87): "Knowledge Acquisition Via Incremental Conceptual Clustering"; In: Machine Learning 2(2), 1987, pp. 139-172

Flann, N.S./ Dietterich, T.G. (86): "Selecting Appropriate Representations for Learning from Examples"; In: Proc. AAAI-86, Phil., PA, 1986, pp. 460-466

Haase, K.W. (86): "Discovery Systems"; In: B. Boulay, D. Hogg, L. Steels (eds.) : Advances in Artificial Intelligence II (7th ECAI-86, Brighton, England, 1986), Elsevier Pub. (North Holland), Amsterdam, 1987, pp. 111-120

Habel, Ch. (82): "Inferences - The Base of Semantics?"; In: R.Bäuerle, C.Schwarze, A.v.Stechow (eds.): Meaning, Use and Interpretation of Language, deGruyter, Berlin, 1983

Habel, Ch. (86): "Prinzipien der Referentialität - Untersuchungen zur propositionalen Struktur von Wissen"; Informatik-Fachbericht 122, Springer, Berlin, 1986

Habel, Ch./ Rollinger, C.-R. (82): "The Machine as Concept Learner"; In: Proc. of the ECAI-82, Orsay, Frankreich, 1982

Holte, R.C. (86): "Alternative Information Structures in Incremental Learning Systems; To appear in: Y. Kodratoff, A. Hutchinson (eds.): Machine and Human Learning, Horwood Pub.

Hayes-Roth, F. (83): "Using Proofs and Refutations to Learn from Experience"; In: R.S. Michalski/ J.G. Carbonell/ T.M. Mitchell (eds.): Machine Learning, Tioga, Palo Alto, 1983, pp. 221-240

Kauffman, H./ Grumbach, A. (86): "MULTILOG: Multiple Worlds in Logic Programming"; In: B. Boulay, D. Hogg, L. Steels (eds.) : Advances in Artificial Intelligence II (7th ECAI-86, Brighton, England, 1986), Elsevier Pub. (North Holland), Amsterdam, 1987, pp. 233-247

Langley, P./ Gennari, J.H./ Iba, W. (87): "Hill-Climbing Theories of Learning"; In: Proceedings of the Fourth International Workshop on Machine Learning, Irvine, California, Morgan Kaufmann, Los Altos, CA, 1987, pp. 312-323

Lebowitz, M. (87): "Experiments with Incremental Concept Formation: UNIMEM"; In: Machine Learning 2(2), 1987, pp. 103-138

Lenat, D.B. (82): "AM: Discovery in Mathematics as Heuristic Search"; In: R.Davis/D.G.Lenat: Knowledge Based Systems in Artificial Intelligence"; McGraw Hill, New York, 1982

Lenat, D. (83): "The Role of Heuristics in Learning by Discovery: Three Case Studies"; In: R.S. Michalski/J.G. Carbonell/T.M. Mitchell (eds.): Machine Learning, Tioga, 1983, pp. 243-306

McAllester, D.A. (82): "Reasoning Utility Package - User's Manual"; MIT, Memo 667, 1982

McDermott, D. (83): "Contexts and Data Dependencies: A Synthesis"; In: IEEE Transactions of Pattern Analysis and Machine Intelligence, Vol. PAMI-5, No. 3, May, 1983, pp. 237-246

Michalski, R.S./ Winston, P.H. (86): "Variable Precision Logic"; Artificial Intelligence, Vol. 29, 1986, pp. 121-146

Mitchell, T.M./ Utgoff, P.E./ Banerji, R. (83): "Learning by Experimentation: Acquiring and Refining Problem-Solving Heuristics"; In: R.S. Michalski/ J. Carbonell/ T.M. Mitchell (eds.): Machine Learning; Tioga Press, Palo Alto, CA, 1983, pp. 163-190

Morik, K. (87): "Acquiring Domain Models"; In: International Journal of Man-Machine Studies, 26, 1987, pp. 93-104

Morik, K. (88): "Sloppy Modeling"; In this volume

Morik, K./ Rollinger, C.-R. (85): "The Real Estate Agent - Modeling Users by Uncertain Reasoning"; In: The AI Magazine, Summer 1985; pp. 44-52

Neches, R./ Swartout, W.R./ Moore, J. (85): "Explainable (and Maintainable) Expert Systems"; In: Proceedings IJCAI-85, Los-Angeles, CA, 1985, pp. 382-389

Reinke, R.E./ Michalski, R.S. (85): "Incremental Learning of Concept Descriptions: A Method and Experimental Results"; In: Michie, D. (Ed.): Machine Intelligence XI, 1986.

Reiter, R. (80): "A Logic for Default Reasoning"; In: Artificial Intelligence 13(1,2), 1980, pp. 81-132

Rendell, L. (85): "Utility Patterns as Criteria for Efficient Generalization Learning"; Report UIUCDCS-R-85-1209, Department of Computer Science, University of Illinois at Urbana-Champaign, April 1985

Rollinger, C.-R. (83): "How to Represent Evidence - Aspects of Uncertain Reasoning"; In: Proc. IJCAI-83, Karlsruhe, 1983

Rollinger, C.-R. (84): "Die Repräsentation natürlichsprachlich formulierten Wissens - Behandlung der Aspekte Unsicherheit und Satzverknüpfung"; Dissertation, Fachbereich Informatik, Technische Universität Berlin, 1984

Rose, D./ Langley, P. (87): "Chemical Discovery as Belief Revision"; Machine Learning, Volume 1, 1986, pp. 423-451

Russell, S.E. (85): "The Complete Guide to MRS"; Report No. KSL-85-12, Stanford University, CA, 1985

Sammut, C. (88): "Logic Programs as a Basis for Machine Learning"; In: P. Brazdil (ed.): Proceedings of the Workshop on Machine Learning, Meta reasoning and Logics (Sesimbra, Portugal, 1988)

Schlimmer, J.C./ Granger, R.H. (86): Machine Learning, 1(3), 1986, pp. 317-354

Someren, M. W. van (88): "Using Dependencies between Attributes for Rule Learning"; In this volume

Thieme, S. (88): "The Acquisition of Model-Knowledge for a Model-Driven Machine Learning Approach"; In this volume

Wrobel, S. (87a): "Design Goals for Sloppy Modeling Systems"; To appear in: International Journal of Man-Machine Studies

Wrobel, S. (87b): "Higher-order Concepts in a Tractable Knowledge Representation"; In: Procs. 11th German Workshop on Artificial Intelligence 87, Springer, Berlin 1987

Wrobel, S. (88): "Demand-Driven Concept Formation"; In this volume

The Acquisition of Model-Knowledge for a Model-Driven Machine Learning Approach

Sabine Thieme *

Technical University of Berlin

Project-Group KIT

Abstract

Knowledge acquisition systems with a model-driven learning mechanism require the representation of that model in the system. The model which guides the learning mechanism must be distinguished from the knowledge (domain model) which is to be learned with the learning mechanism; only the former is the concern of this paper. If the model for guiding the learning mechanism is to be enlarged and improved while working with such a system, the acquisition and representation of new parts of this model must be supported. In addition to the insertion of new parts into the existing model, it is very important to consider redundancy, integrity and completion, because the quality of the model influences the quality of the learning capabilities of the knowledge acquisition system.

In this paper, we present the acquisition facilities for meta-knowledge in the knowledge acquisition system BLIP. The meta-knowledge represents the model used by the learning mechanism in BLIP. It mainly consists of ruleschemes, which describe sets of possible rules in different domains concerning the structure of these rules. The chief task is to acquire new ruleschemes.

Introduction

The number of model-driven learning systems is much lower than the number of data-driven learning systems. In the literature only a few approaches for model-driven learning systems can be found (Dietterich, Michalski 83).

The META-DENDRAL system (Buchanan, Mitchell 78) has a domain-oriented learning mechanism and acquires knowledge in the context of a practical problem. The knowledge, which guides the learning mechanism, is a domain model consisting of a very simple theory of mass spectrometry. The model contains constraints about possible fragmentations and atom migrations in molecular structures and is used for proposing hypotheses about rules. For learning rules in a different domain, a different theory is necessary, but the learning algorithm could be the same.

In SPARC/G (Dietterich, Michalski 87) three different basic models are used for learning predictive, sequence-generating rules. With these rules a special sequence of events should be predictable. The learning algorithm was tested with, among other things, the card game Eleusis. These models consist of a set of constraints that the model places on the form of a special description and can be parameterized. A parameterized model forms a more specific model. The models used in SPARC/G thus can be modified and manipulated, but only by choosing parameters. One example of such model is the decomposition model, which constrains the description to be a set of implications. The other two models concern a periodic description and a description of disjunctive normal forms. The three basic

----

* This work was partially supported by the German Ministry for Research and Technology (BMFT) under contract ITW8501B1 (project LERNER). Industrial partners are Nixdorf Computer AG and Stollmann GmbH.

description models can be combined to describe more complex rules.

In TEIRESIAS (Davis 79) domain-dependent rule-models are used, which describe prototypes of a subset of rules in a domain. These rule models are used for knowledge refinement and interpretation and not for guiding a learning algorithm. They contain examples of rules and pointers to more general or specific rule models. Although it has been argued that the models the system TEIRESIAS employs can be generated and continually revised as a by-product of its experience in interacting with the expert, how this can be achieved is not described.

For none of these systems it is described in detail *how* the model knowledge can be entered, modified or enlarged in the system. As a result, these model-driven machine learning systems are unable to profit from experiences with their model knowledge automatically. The main way of improving their performance is by hand-coding new parts of model knowledge.

In the system BLIP, which also incorporates a model-driven machine learning approach, there exist facilities for acquiring model knowledge (besides the facilities for acquiring domain knowledge). Providing the possibility of augmenting model knowledge, the system needs to check redundancy and integrity because the quality of the model knowledge must be conserved. This paper descibes first the kind of model knowledge used in BLIP and then the acquisition of new model knowledge, which is illustrated by an example. In the last paragraph some features of this approach are summarized and unsolved problems are mentioned.

The Model In BLIP

BLIP is a system for supporting the knowledge acquisition process for the construction of a domain theory. It concentrates on a view of both system and user modeling a domain rather than transferring a complete model of a domain to a computer system. We call this view of the knowledge acquisition process "sloppy modeling" (see Morik, in this volume). BLIP's knowledge representation is based on a sorted logic with selected higher-order concepts (for details see Wrobel 87). The knowledge about objects and their properties and relations between objects can be expressed in predicates and facts. A fact is a predicate with arguments, for example

    can_fly(tweety)

and a predicate definition lays down the argument sort mask, in this example

    can_fly(<bird>).

Also, the user can express relations between properties and relations of objects in rules, for example,

    can_fly(X) & is_a(Y,X) --> can_fly(Y).

One main task of the system is the automatic induction of rule knowledge in a domain. This induction process is based on factual knowledge of the domain on the one hand and on models of possible rule knowledge in any domain on the other hand. The rule-model knowledge in the BLIP system is called *meta-knowledge* and the acquisition of meta-knowledge is the topic of this paper.

The meta-knowledge in BLIP consists of definitions for ruleschemes on two different levels, the metalevel and the metametalevel (note that predicate-definitions, facts and rules belong to the domain-level). On the metalevel ruleschemes for predicates are expressed as *metapredicate-definitions*, on the metametalevel ruleschemes for metapredicates are expressed as *metametapredicate-definitions* (examples will follow). As in the BLIP system facts exist for a predicate, there exist metafacts (which can be transformed into rules) for metapredicates and *metametafacts* (which can be transformed into metarules) for metametapredicates. (Meta(meta))facts are the actually instances of definitions. Metapredicates, metametapredicates and metametafacts build the meta-knowledge of the system BLIP. Metafacts, however, are the result of the learning algorithm and thus not part of the rule-model knowledge but part of the domain model in the BLIP system (see figure 1).

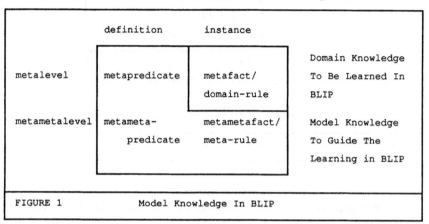

The rule-model knowledge in BLIP is domain-independent and describes possible schemes of rules (metapredicates and metametapredicates) and structural dependencies between those schemes (metametafacts/metarules). In figure 2 one example is given to illustrate the kind of model knowledge in BLIP [1]. The metapredicate "opposite" in figure 2 defines a rulescheme reflecting an inferential relation between two facts in the sense that if the premise is part of the knowledge base and holds true, the conclusion is not true and the negated fact can be added to the knowledge base by deduction [2]. The metametafact in the example describes that "opposite defines an inferential relation in both directions".

With ruleschemes on the meta- and metametalevel and with metametafacts, the search space for learnable rules (metafacts) in BLIP is stretched. The quality of this search space ("what kind of rules is the system looking for") and hence the quality of the meta-knowledge influences the quality of the learning algorithm's results and thus of a major part of the BLIP system.

---

[1] BLIP incorporates today 52 metapredicates, 42 metametapredicates and 84 metametafacts.

[2] Besides a rulescheme a metapredicate definition has some applicability constraints, which will be not described in this paper.

	definition	instance

metalevel	`all p,q opposite(p,q):`
	`(all x: p(x) --> ¬q(x))`
		`opposite(big,small):`
		`(all x:big(x)-->¬small(x)),`
		and deduced by the
		metametafact,
		`opposite(small,big):`
		`(all x:small(x)-->¬big(x))`

metameta-
level
	`all a symmetrical(a):`
	`(all p,q: a(p,q)-->a(q,p))`
		`symmetrical(opposite):`
		`(all p,q:opposite(p,q) -->`
		`opposite(q,p))`

FIGURE 2   Example Of Model Knowledge In BLIP

Three possibilities exist to incorporate all this meta-knowledge into the system. One possibility is that the user of the system enters metapredicate-definitions, metametapredicate-definitions and metametafacts. This is possible with the BLIP system. The user is supported by the system with menus and an input parser. Meta-knowledge cannot only be entered but also deleted and modified in the BLIP system.

Another possibility to get the meta-knowledge is the systematic generation of metapredicates, metametapredicates and metametafacts by the same process [3]. However this would not only be inefficient, it is also undesirable. For example, with two predicates with arity two, at maximum one premise in a rulescheme, the possible negation of a proposition and with sorted arguments, 64 ruleschemes can be built systematical. Here are only some examples out of 64, which can be generated:

```
p(x,y) --> q(x,y)      p(x,y) --> q(y,x)      p(x,y) --> p(x,y)
¬p(x,y) --> q(x,y)     p(y,x) --> q(x,y)      q(x,y) --> q(x,y)
p(x,y) -->¬q(x,y)      p(y,x) --> q(y,x)      q(x,y) --> p(x,y)
¬p(x,y) -->¬q(x,y)
```

The search space for learning rules resulting by a systematical generation of meta-knowledge would be enormous. No methods are known for adaquately handling such a large search space for the learning algorithm in BLIP, and indeed it would no longer be a model-based learning component.

The third possibility to get useful rule structures is the acquisition by an example rule. Examples of rules given by the user are also a base for acquiring meta-knowledge in the BLIP system. This

---

[3] Metapredicates and Metametapredicates differ in the syntax in one point not described here. In general the ruleschemes are the same independent of the level.

possibility is described in the following.

Acquiring Meta-Knowledge

While the strategy of the learning algorithm is in part a top down one, searching with a generalization for an instance, the strategy of the meta-knowledge acquisition process is a *bottom up* one, creating from an instance a generalization (see figure 3).

```
                    RS=G           Lexicon**  RS=G

strategy of          ↑               ↓↙  Top Down    strategy of

meta-knowledge       R               R               learning

acquisition          ↑               ↓ ↘             algorithm

process              I               I'  I"

                Bottom Up


FIGURE 3 with RS as a rulescheme, R as a rule and I as an Inference
```

The results of the meta-knowledge acquisition process are mainly ruleschemes, which cannot be either true or false. Therefore no problem of over-generalizing can occur, so one inference is sufficient. Techniques used in Mitchells version-space search algorithm (Mitchell 83) or in explanation-based generalization approaches like in LEAP (Mitchell 85) are not necessary.

After the brief introduction to the meta-knowledge acquisition process in BLIP we will now describe the acquisition of each part of the meta-knowledge seperately.

Acquiring Metapredicates

The base technique for the acquisition of metapredicates is generalization. The starting-point is a domain-rule given by the user. The goal of the generalization is the abstraction from the content of the rule. This is done in two *"turning constants to variables"* steps by first turning argument constants into variables and second turning predicate constants into variables (see figure 4). The first generalization rule is like one of the generalization rules used in the INDUCE system (Michalski 83, page 107). The same generalization process is called enumerative generalization in (Russel 1986). The same generalization rule is also used in DISCIPLE (Kodratoff 87, page 101) in one first step to generate an explanation of a rule. DISCIPLE is an interactive Learning Apprentice System, in which an example of a rule is also interpreted as an example of a general rule, where the constant arguments have changed into variables.

In BLIP the following two generalization rules transform the input of the user into a general rule in a first step and to a rulescheme in a second step. The resulting rulescheme specifies the syntactic form of a set of rules.

** The lexicon is a knowledge source containing possible predicates of the domain which can be used for building a hypothesis about a rule. The hypothesis building is not described here.

```
        one or more        f(a)      |
        statements         f(b)      |
                            "         |   all x: f(x)
                            "         |
                            f(n)      |

        with constants a,b,....,n and variable x
```

FIGURE 4a Turning Argument-Constants to Variables Generalization Rule

```
        one or more    all x:  f(x)     |
        statements     all x:  g(x)     |
                          "      "      |   all p: (all x: p(x))
                          "      "      |
                       all x:  z(x)     |

        with constants f,g,....,z and variables p and x
```

FIGURE 4b Turning Predicate-Constants to Variables Generalization Rule

These two generalization rules are used to generate a rulescheme based not on a set of statements (as they are called facts in BLIP), but rather on a single inferential relation between statements given by the user. The following example should illustrate the use of the two generalization rules.

Example Of Rulescheme Acquisition

Suppose the user enters the following inference:

     (1) can_fly(bird) & is_a(tweety,bird) --> can_fly(tweety).

This kind of relation characterizes a class to instance inheritance. With the "turning argument-constants to variables" generalization rule this relation can be generalized to a rule:

     (2) all x,y : can_fly(x) & is_a(y,x) --> can_fly(y)

     with constant bird turned into variable x and constant tweety turned into variable y.

This rule is more general than the inferential relation entered by the user. For example the following inferential relation is covered by the same rule (2):

     (3) can_fly(plane) & is_a(boeing,plane) --> can_fly(boeing).

In a second generalization step this rule can be generalized into a rulescheme, which has no truth value. In addition a name for the rulescheme can be given by the user, reflecting the kind of this relation, in this example:

     (4) all p,q *inheritance* (p,q) : (all x,y: p(x) & q(y,x) --> p(y)).

     with turning constant can_fly into variable p and constant is_a into variable q.

This name is used to express the metafact corresponding to the rule (2):

     (5) inheritance(can_fly,is_a).

While the process of rulescheme acquisition, with the example rule given by the user, a new metafact (5) is entered to the system. Although the generalized rulescheme would cover the corresponding rule (2), the rule or metafact need not be correct in respect to the domain model. For example the following rule is also covered by (4):

can_fly(x) & is_smaller(y,x) --> can_fly(y)

with the corresponding metafact

inheritance(can_fly,is_smaller),

but the rule will probably be incorrect. So the example rule of the user is not only used to form a rulescheme but also to provide a hypothesis for the learning component. The learning component is divided into two major parts: into the generation part of hypotheses and into the testing part of hypotheses. With the acquisition process of metapredicates one way of generating hypotheses is given; these hypotheses can be proved with the testing part of the learning component.

The example has shown that with an input (1) by the user, a metafact (5) and the corresponding rule (2) as a hypothesis can be generated, and at the same time a rulescheme (4) in a metapredicate-definition can be acquired. With (4) the model knowledge of BLIP is enlarged and the learning algorithm can search for new instances as hypotheses in the current and any other knowledge base.

In the BLIP system one exception for each generalization rule exists. They increase the expressive power for rules in domains where arithmetical operations are needed. For the "argument-constants to variables" generalization rule, specially marked constants are not to be generalized, but themselves become part of the metafact. For the "predicate-constants to variables" generalization rule, some arithmetical predicates like "greater_than (gt)" or "equal" are excluded. One example of the result of the generalization process concerning the exceptions is the metapredicate definition

all p,q,c threshold(p,q,c): (all x,y: p(x,y) & gt(y,c) --> q(x))

generalized based on a given rule like

temperature(sabine,38) & gt(38,37) --> fever(sabine)

and the resulting hypothesis is

threshold(temperature,fever,37).

Checking Redundancy

Before a new metapredicate is defined, it must be checked whether the rule entered by the user cannot be expressed by one or more already existing metapredicates. This prevents redundant metapredicate-definitions. In the BLIP system one algorithm tries to instantiate the known ruleschemes with the entered rule and offers the user the possibility of choosing between metafacts resulting from the matching process. The chosen metafact will be tested then as a hypothesis.

Completion

With metapredicates the syntactical structure of rules is acquired. By getting a more complete model of possible rules, the relations between generalized ruleschemes, expressible on the metametalevel, should also be acquired. On the metametalevel, properties of metapredicates and relations between metapredicates can be expressed. The task can be divided into two parts: the acquisition of new metametapredicates (which kinds of properties and relations for metapredicates can be expressed) and the acquisition of metametafacts (which properties concern the newly acquired metapredicates).

Acquiring Metametapredicates

The acquisition of metametapredicates can be done in the same way as the acquisition of metapredicates. The necessary input of the user must be on a higher level, i.e., an example of an inference on the metalevel, called metarule. The generalization rules used to acquire a metametapredicate are, in general, the same as on the metalevel, with the difference that the constants represent predicates and metapredicates instead of objects and predicates.

In general, the generalization rules can be used to acquire meta-(meta-.....)predicates on each meta-(meta-...)level. In all cases, the user must enter a relation between concepts of the level directly below.

One difference exists in handling the input by the user, which on the metalevel is a metafact and on the metametalevel is a metametafact: while a metafact is handled as a hypothesis, a metametafact is not. The reason is that metafacts are domain-dependent and the result of the learning algorithm, but metametafacts are used to guide the process of learning metafacts. Therefore metametafacts are not to be learned, although they could be learned in principle with the same learning algorithm. How metametafacts guide the learning process is described in the section below.

Integrity

Metametafacts represent possible structural dependencies between ruleschemes. They have two functions in the BLIP system: first, to detect some contradictions in the knowledge base, and second, to reduce the search space for the learning algorithm. Therefore metametafacts are made available to the system BLIP.

Two types of metametafacts can be distinguished, *constructive* ones and *restrictive* ones. Restrictive metametafacts restrict the search space for generating hypotheses. Metarules corresponding to restrictive metametafacts conclude metafacts, which should be not generated and tested by the learning component, because if they would be added to the knowledge base, they would cause contradictions. An example of a restrictive metametafact is that based on the same premises, a property p and ¬p cannot be inferred by two rules simultaneously. So if one rule like

      big_object(x) -> ¬can_swim(x)

is part of the knowledge base, one may not add to the knowledge base the rule

      big_object(x) -> can_swim(x).

The first rule can be expressed by the metapredicate 'opposite':

      opposite(big_object,can_swim)

      with the metapredicate definition

      all p,q opposite(p,q): (all x: p(x) --> ¬q(x)).

The second rule can be expressed with the metapredicate 'inclusive':

      inclusive(big_object,can_swim)

      with the metapredicate-definition

all p,q inclusive(p,q): (all x: p(x) --> q(x)).

The inferential relation on the metalevel, which expresses that not both rules can be part of the knowledge base is:

opposite(big_object,can_swim) --> ¬inclusive(big_object,can_swim).

The metarule is

(6) all p,q opposite(p,q)--> ¬inclusive(p,q).

This metarule is expressed by the metametafact

(7) m_opposite(opposite,inclusive)

[4] with the metametapredicate-definition

all mp,mq m_opposite(mp,mq): (all p,q: mp(p,q) --> ¬mq(p,q)).

So instantiations of the metametapredicate m_opposite are always restrictive metametafacts.

Constructive metametafacts restrict the search space for generating hypotheses in the sense that the conclusions (rules) of the corresponding metarules can be inferred based on known rules and can be added to the knowledge base without testing them. An example of a constructive metametafact is the following: If a relation holds true between two predicates p and q and the same relation holds true between two predicates q and r, then the relation properly holds true also between the two predicates p and r. One such relation is "inclusive" with the metapredicate definition

all p,q inclusive(p,q): (all x: p(x) --> q(x)).

For example if inclusive(woman,human) and inclusive(human,living_thing) is part of the knowledge base, inclusive(woman,living_thing) can also be added to the knowledge base. The metarule is

all p,q,r: inclusive(p,q) & inclusive(q,r) --> inclusive(p,r),

the metametafact is

m_transitive(inclusive)

and the metametapredicate-definition of m_transitive is

all mp m_transitive(mp): (all p,q: mp(p,q) & mp(q,r) --> mp(p,r)).

Correctness Of Metametafacts

To guarantee the correctness of metametafacts on the one hand, and the possiblity for the user to enter new metametafacts on the other hand causes a serious problem. Experience with the BLIP system has shown that entering metametafacts is a very difficult task for the user, because such a metametafact is a very abstract representation of a complex piece of knowledge. Indeed after testing our original set of metametafacts with a theorem prover [5] it turned out that only 32 out of 84 (38%) metametafacts were *provable* (although the rest were plausible).

The testing of metametafacts with a theorem prover is possible, because metametafacts can be considered as a logical implication from a conjunction of well-formed formulas into one well-formed formula. So one rulescheme is considered as a well-formed formula (in detail, see Wrobel 87).

---

[4] With (7) it becomes clear, that a relation between predicates (opposite) can also be a relation between metapredicates (m_opposite).

[5] The theorem prover "CG5", which was developed by Mark E.Stickel, was used.

One example of a provable metametafact is the following:

(8) m_inclusive(symmetrical,symmetrical_neg)

with the definition of the metametapredicate m_inclusive:

all mp,mq m_inclusive(mp,mq): (all p: mp(p) --> mp(q))

and the definitions of the metapredicates:

all p symmetrical(p): (all x,y: p(x,y) --> p(y,x))

all p symmetrical_neg(p): (all x,y: ¬p(x,y) --> ¬p(y,x))

The equivalent metarule for metametafact (8) is:

(9) all p: symmetrical(p) --> symmetrical_neg(p)

and to make a metarule/metametafact much more clearer it really is:

all p:[all x,y: p(x,y) --> p(y,x)]-->[all x,y: ¬p(x,y) --> ¬p(y,x)]

To prove (8) or (9), it must be shown that the rulescheme of symmetrical_neg follows from the rulescheme of symmetrical. Writing this in logical formulas results in

A: all x,y: p(x,y) -> p(y,x)

B: all x,y: ¬p(x,y) -> ¬p(y,x)

Prove: A -> B or ¬A v B

B follows from A if the negation of the formula, A & ¬B, is unsatisfiable, which can be checked by resolution (see figure 5).

```
all x,y: p(x,y)-> p(y,x)          ¬(all x,y: ¬p(x,y) -> ¬p(y,x))

all x,y: ¬p(x,y) v p(y,x)         ¬(all x,y: p(x,y) v ¬p(y,x))

                |                   exist xs,ys: ¬(p(xs,ys) v ¬p(ys,xs))

                |          ____     exist xs,ys: ¬p(xs,ys)

        y=xs,   |    /                       exist xs,ys: p(ys,xs)

        x=ys    |  /                                  |

                |/                                    |

          ¬p(ys,xs)                                   |

                 \                                    |

                  \                                   |

                   \ ____     FALSUM _____|
```

FIGURE 5   Resolution

Thus the metametafacts which can be proven by a theorem prover are tautologies. One example of a predicate p which is symmetrical is "sibling". The rule in the knowledge base for the metafact 'symmetrical(sibling)' would be:

all x,y: sibling(x,y) --> sibling(y,x).

In the BLIP system the following rule would be added to the knowledge base automatically because of the provable metametafact (8):

all x,y: ¬sibling(x,y) --> ¬sibling(y,x).

All known metametafacts which have been proven by a theorem prover are constructive ones. But not all constructive metametafacts can be proven.

The set of metametafacts which are not provable by a theorem prover but plausible, can be divided into four subsets: consistency-maintaining metametafacts, defining metametafacts, metametafacts which concern ordered predicates and metametafacts which prevent the system from adding reflexive metafacts. In the following paragraphs an example for each subset is given.

Consistency-Maintaining Metametafacts

One example of a consistency-maintaining metametafact is (7) with the corresponding metarule (6), see above. This metametafact prevents the knowledge base from incorporating two rules which have the same premise (that would cause the application of both rules) but contradictory conclusions. These kinds of metametafacts in the BLIP system are useful for detecting contradictions among rules while modeling a domain. If the user can not dissolve such a contradiction, one possibility to handle such a contradiction by the system is to develop alternative domain theories, whereby one theory uses the first rule and a second theory the second rule. This approach is under development by (Emde, this volume).

Defining Metametafacts

Examples of defining metametafacts are

(10) m_inclusive(equivalent,inclusive2)

with the corresponding metarule

all p,q: equivalent(p,q) --> inclusive2(p,q)

and

(11) m_inclusive_x(equivalent,inclusive2)

with the corresponding metarule

all p,q: equivalent(p,q) --> inclusive2(q,p)

and with the metapredicate definitions

all p,q equivalent(p,q): (all x,y: p(x,y) --> q(x,y))

all p,q inclusive2(p,q): (all x,y: p(x,y) --> q(x,y)).

This metametafact is necessary, because the metapredicate definitions of equivalent and inclusive2 are identical, which is caused by the fact that "<=>" (logical equivalence) is not part of the knowledge representation formalism (see Wrobel 87). Thus the difference of inclusiveness (one direction) and equivalence (both directions) must be expressed on the metametalevel by (10) and (11). This must be done by the user during the task of defining a new metapredicate.

Metametafacts Concerning Ordered Predicates

One example of a metametafact, which concerns an ordered predicate, is

m_w_reductive_f_s(equivalent,transitive)

with the corresponding metarule

all p,q: equivalent(p,q) & transitive(p) --> transitive(q)

and with the metapredicate definition (the definition for equivalent see above)

all p transitive(p): (all x,y,z: p(x,y) & p(y,z) --> p(x,z)).

If the predicate p is transitive and therefore ordered and equivalent to another predicate q, then q must also be transitive. One example of p and q might be "greater_than" and "bigger_than". Ordered predicates are very important in modeling a domain, because they express an important part of the structure of the domain. Today it is still not clear how the acquisition of metametafacts about ordered predicates can be supported.

Metametafacts Preventing Reflexive Metafacts

Two examples of metametafacts, which prevent the adding of a reflexive metafact are

      m_irreflexive1(opposite)

      with the corresponding metarule

      all p,q : opposite(p,q) --> ¬ opposite(p,p)

and

      m_irreflexive2(opposite)

      with the corresponding metarule

      all p,q : opposite(p,q) --> ¬ opposite(q,q).

These kind of metametafacts prevent rules like

      all x: p(x) --> ¬p(x)

from being added to the knowledge base, which would cause contradictions. It also makes it possible to prevent rules like

      all x: p(x) --> p(x)

with the same kind of metametafacts because these rules are undesired. These kinds of metametafacts could become unnecessary if irreflexiveness of metafacts as a fundamental principle would be integrated in the inference strategy.

Acquiring Metametafacts

The examples above have illustrated that a lot of metametafacts exist which cannot be tested with a theorem prover. One reason for this is that all known metametafacts, which were entered over time during sessions with BLIP, had been taken under consideration. A discussion about metametafacts pointed out, that the task of entering metametafacts into the BLIP system can be considered as the task of designing the representation language. With the metametafacts the inferential behavior of the system can be influenced (for more details about this view see Morik, this volume). The metametafacts can be subdivided into sets and each set can influence the system in a different way. Thus, it is the task of the user to guarantee in one sense "correctness" by entering a set of metametafacts.

Today the user is supported by the system in generating only some syntactical possible metametafacts. When the user enters a rule and a new metapredicate is defined by the system, the system tries to instantiate known metametapredicate-definitions with the new metapredicate for generating metametafacts or metarules. The resulting metametafacts are shown to the user, who must then decide which of them fit in her or his design of the representation language or not.

The following figure illustrates an example.

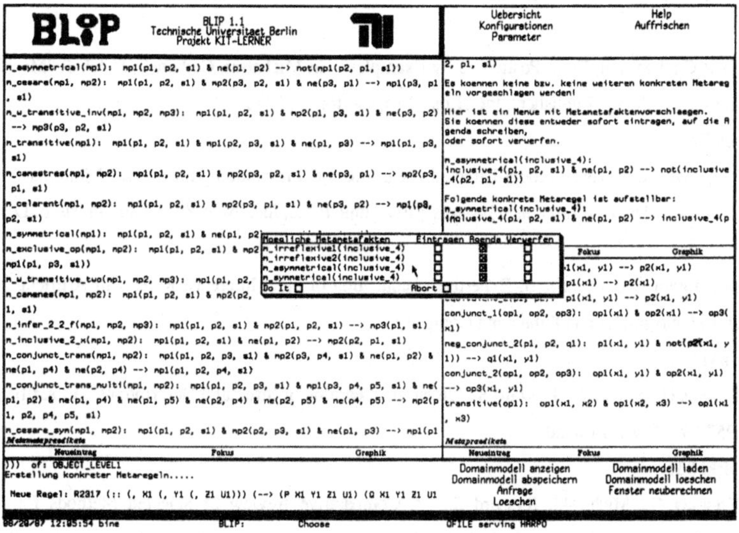

FIGURE 6   The Acquisition of Metametafacts

In this example the metapredicate inclusive_4 has just been acquired and four instantiations of metametapredicate-definitions resulting in four metametafacts or metarules are shown to the user. Of course, the user can enter additionally metametafacts.

Conclusion

The kind of generalization used in the BLIP system for acquiring metapredicates, metametapredicates and metametafacts has shown the use of generalization for acquiring model-knowledge instead of domain-knowledge. With this acquisition facility the system can profit from its experience with domain modeling by learning of new rulestructures from the user of the system. Important features are that a single instance is sufficient for the generalization process and that the process is domain independent.

One task for the future is to get more experience with the influence of different sets of model-knowledge on the learning behaviour and inferential behaviour of the system and thus on the modeling process with the system.

References

[Balzer 85]

Balzer, Robert:"Automated Enhancement of Knowledge Representations". In Proceedings IJCAI 1985, Los Angeles, p.203-207 Distributed by Morgan Kaufmann Publishers, Inc., Los Altos, California

[Berwick 86]

Berwick, Robert C.:"Learning From Positive-Only Examples". In Michalski, Carbonell, Mitchell:"Machine Learning", Volume II,Morgan Kaufmann Publishers, Inc., Los Altos, California, 1986

[Buchanan, Mitchell 78]

Buchanan, B.G; Mitchell, T.M.:"Model-Directed Learning of Production Rules". In Waterman, D.A.; Hayes-Roth,F.(eds.): "Pattern-Directed Inference Systems"; Academic Press, Inc., New York, San Fransisco, London 1978

[Davis 79]

Davis, Randall:"Interactive Transfer of Expertise: Acquisition of New Inference Rules". In Artificial Intelligence 12 (1979), p.121-157, North-Holland Publishing Company

[Dietterich, Michalski 81]

Dietterich, Thomas G.; Michalski, Ryszard S.: "Inductive Learning of Structural Descriptions". In Artificial Intelligence 16(1981), p.257-294, North-Holland

[Dietterich, Michalski 83]

Dietterich, Thomas G.; Michalski, Ryszard S.: "A Comparative Review of Selected Methods for Learning from Examples". In Michalski, Carbonell, Mitchell:"Machine Learning", Togia Publishing Company, Palo Alto, California, 1983

[Dietterich, Michalski 85a]

Dietterich, Thomas G.; Michalski, Ryszard S.: "Discovering Patterns in Sequences of Events". In Artificial Intelligence 25 (1985), p.187-232, North-Holland Publishing Company

[Dietterich, Michalski 85b]

Dietterich, Thomas G.; Michalski, Ryszard S.: "Learning to Predict Sequences". In Michalski, Carbonell, Mitchell:"Machine Learning", Volume II,Morgan Kaufmann Publishers, Inc., Los Altos, California, 1986

[Emde 87]

Emde, W.:"An Inference Engine for Multiple Theories", in this volume

[Kodratoff 87]

Kodratoff,Ives :"Is AI a Sub-Field of Computer Science - or is AI the Science of Explanations". In Bratko; Lavrac: Progress in Machine Learning (EWSL 87, Bled, Yugoslawia), Sigma Press, Wilmslow, England, 1987

[Michalski 83]

Michalski, Ryszard S.:"A Theory and Methodology of Inductive Learning". In Michalski, Carbonell, Mitchell:"Machine Learning", Togia Publishing Company, Palo Alto, California, 1983

[Michalski, Ko, Chen 87]

Michalski,R.; Ko,H.; Chen,K.:"Qualitative Predication: The SPARC/G Methodology for Inductively Describing and Predicting Discrete Processes". Intelligent Systems Group, Department of Computer Science, University of Illinois at Urbana-Champaign, 1987

[Mitchell 83]

Mitchell, Tom M.:"Learning and Problem Solving". In Proceedings IJCAI 1983, Karlsruhe, Germany. Distributed by William Kaufmann, Inc., Los Altos, California, 1983

[Mitchell 85]

Mitchell, Tom M.:"LEAP: A Learning Apprentice for VLSI Design". In Proceedings IJCAI 1985, Los Angeles. Distributed by Morgan Kaufmann Publishers, Inc., Los Altos, California

[Morik 87]

Morik,K.:"Sloppy Modeling", in this volume

[O'Rorke 84]

O'Rorke, Paul:"Generalization for Explanation-Based Schema Acquisition". In Proceedings AAAI 1984, Austin, Texas. Distributed by William Kaufmann, Inc., Los Altos, California, 1984

[Russell 86]

Russell,Stuart J.:"Preliminary Steps Toward The Automation Of Induction". In Proceedings AAAI 1986, Philadelphia Distributed by Morgan Kaufmann Publishers, Inc., Los Altos, California

[Sowa 84]

Sowa, J.F.:"Conceptual Structures". The Systems Programming Series, Addison-Wesley Publishing Company, 1984

[Wrobel 87]

Wrobel, Stefan:"Higher-Order Concepts In A Tractable Knowledge Representation". In Proceedings GWAI 1987, Geseke, Germany. Informatik Fachberichte, Springer-Verlag Berlin Heidelberg New York Tokyo

USING ATTRIBUTE DEPENDENCIES FOR RULE LEARNING

Maarten W. van Someren

Department of Social Science Informatics
University of Amsterdam
Herengracht 196
1016 BS Amsterdam
The Netherlands

ABSTRACT

The attributes that are used in a rule learning task may depend on each other in several ways. Three examples are: two attributes may be associated, the availability of the value of an attribute may depend on another attribute or an attribute may affect the relation between another attribute and the class that is learned. If such dependencies exist, they need a rule language that can express rules dealing with missing values. Also, due to these dependencies there are classes of examples that will not appear as classified training examples and the learning algorithm should be able to handle that. If these dependencies are explicitly known to the system, they can be used to construct an intermediate description language that simplifies and reduces the learning task.

1. Introduction

A very common task for learning systems is learning classification rules from classified examples. The examples are presented to the system as descriptions in terms of observable attributes with a class label. (The language used to describe the objects is called "object description language".) The classification rules assign a class to an object on the basis of the attributes. (The language in which the rule is stated is called "rule language".) Some techniques (such as Explanation Based Learning) also use a theory about the relation between observable attributes and classes to derive a generalization from the theory, Here I shall call these "analytical" learning techniques, as opposed to "empirical learning techniques", that use only examples.

In practise, learning processes occur in a rather rich context. In that case, It is not always clear from the beginning which attributes of objects must be used in the learning process, how they are to be incorporated into classification rules, what knowledge about the domain will be available to support induction and how this knowledge can be represented and used in the learning process. Because of this, techniques that allow **incremental** construction of their components are an important topic for research.

Dimensions:

* examples can be entered one by one

* the theory (if a theory is used) can be changed incrementally (either directly by the user or by inference)

* the object description language can be modified during learning

* the rule language can be modified during learning (as in "bias adjustment", Utgoff, 1985)

Until recently, research in machine learning addressed simplified versions of this task, by making several simplifying assumptions:

- The language in which the rule will be stated must contain an adequate rule and the process by which rules are selected or constructed must be able to produce this rule. Eg. if the rule language is limited to conjunctions of disjunctions of values on attributes, then it is not possible to learn the rule *(colour: red and shape: square) or (colour: blue and shape: triangle)*, because that rule is not in the rule language.

- The examples that are presented to the system during learning must allow the technique to reach the correct rule. Depending on the technique, certain examples may be critical to learn a correct or optimal rule.

- Practical applications are likely to cause problems with the administration of large sets of candidate hypotheses. Therefore heuristics or "bias" will be needed to direct the construction or selection of the rule. There are several kinds of bias. One kind of bias consists of a preference order on possible rules, that allow the technique to make a (provisional) choice between different possible generalisations. (A backtracking scheme may be added, to recover from faulty generalisations.)

Another kind of 'bias' is in the descriptive terms that are used to describe an example. The way in which an example is presented to the learning system is often tailored to meet the assumptions mentioned above. Attributes that are unlikely to be relevant are left out and others are grouped or structured, such that they do not overlap and interact. It is the latter kind of 'bias' that we address here.

In this paper I want to show several ways in which domain knowledge can be implicit in the description language. I shall also show why this knowledge is important and how it can be presented to the learning system in a natural form and then "brought into" the description language, assuming only that the object description language is given.

2. Dependent descriptors

In many domains, the attributes that are used to describe objects and that appear in the rule, are related to each other. Some examples are:

* In the blocks world as used in Winstons ARCH program, some of the attributes that are used to describe block structures are related, eg. the relations "next to(X, Y)" and "supports(X, Y)" are related, because objects don't support other objects that are next to them and vice versa. (In Winstons representation this is implicit, because "negative" attributes (ie. attributes that are not true of an object) are left out of the representation and the matching predicate uses negation by failure: if a rule demands that an attribute be absent, then it is enough if the description of the object does not mention that attribute.)

* In a medical domain, a patient can be described as (1) having had a certain symptom before, (2) having taken pills at that time, (3) having taken the same pills this time, but (4) without effect. Note that these attributes all depend on each other: if the patient had not had this before, the other attributes are meaningless. In fact (1) - (4) refer to one or two underlying attributes: if the patient has had these symptoms before, than the old diagnosis is a good candidate for the new symptoms. However, if the same therapy if not effective this time, it either something different or more severe. Note that an "attribute" as (2) by itself is rather meaningless and has no predictive value.

* Often diagnostic practise incorporates laboratory tests. These are expensive and are avoided if possible. Therefore, for many examples the attribute(s) that are measured by these tests will not be available.

* In the same domain, two symptoms that suggest one particular diagnosis are "recent physical exercise" and "sweating", however physical exercise may cause sweating would results in the following (simplified) examples:

sweating & no physical exercise   *positive*

no sweating & no physical exercise *negative*

sweating & physical exercise   *negative*

no sweating & physical exercise   *negative*

Here sweating in itself does not predict class membership (at least not very well), but combined with "no physical exercise" it does.

More in general, we find at least three different types of dependencies:

(a) **associations between attributes**, ie. two or more attributes may be related by a common cause, co-occurrence, etc.. This association may take many forms in terms of the observable attributes. Important types are covariation, entailment, exclusion (ie. a value of attribute A excludes values from attribute B), also they may be deterministic or probabilistic. Some examples of attribute dependencies that I shall consider in this paper are

* *one to one attribute mapping*: the values of an attribute map onto the values of another attribute. Two attributes may be synonyms, or a mapping may exist for some other reason, as between "support" and "next to".

* *attribute entailment*: many to one mapping between attributes. An example is when one attribute is the cause of another.

* *mutual exclusion*: a value on one attribute excludes one or more values on another and vice versa.

(b) **associations between "availability" of attribute values**, ie. if a value is known of an example may depend on the value of another attribute, as in the medical domain above. These associations can be due to the structure of the dialogue in which attribute values are collected. Eg. in the medical domain that we illustrated above, questions are asked in a series of steps. This is part of a strategy to improve communication with the patient who must provide the data and has nothing to do with the actual classification. As a result, questions that appear later in a sequence, are only applicable for certain cases. In other cases, they make no sense. Alternatively, "missing" data may be due to the diagnostic strategy that was in effect when the data were collected. Eg. a lab test may not have been necessary for the diagnosis and therefore no such data may be available.

(c) **interactions in predictive value**, the relation between an attribute and a class may depend on (the value of) one or more other attributes. There are many examples of such interactions and they are often seen as a source of difficulty. In medical domains patients with multiple diseases are often difficult to diagnose, when the symptoms of one affect the symptoms of the other.

Dependencies in predictive value can take many forms. Here I shall discuss only a simple type:

* *simple interaction*: the predictive value of an attribute depends on the value(s) of a single other attribute.

In the next section we shall consider the effect that such dependencies have on rule learning. Here we assume a situation where the learning system is passive. Examples of object descriptions with their classes are collected and presented to the system, which tries to learn the best classificaton rule.

3. The effect of dependencies on learning

The effect of dependencies on rule learning depends on the object description language, the rule language and the learning algorithm. If the rule language cannot represent certain concepts, then the system will not be able to learn the rule, so the first question is: can rule languages express the concepts that must be learned ? There is no structured set of "rule languages", so we only discuss some common rule languages.

3.1. Rule description languages and dependencies between attributes

Some rule learning systems, such as *AQ15* (Michalski, 1986), the *version space* method (Mitchell, 1979) and *EBG* (Mitchell et.al. 1986) don't commit themselves to a specific rule language. The language can be selected as parameter of the technique.

ID3/C4 (Quinlan, 1987) employs a rule language that has the form of a decision tree. The nodes represent the attributes and the branches correspond to the values. Decision trees are very well suited to represent interactions in predictive value. Dependencies between attributes also do not cause any problems here. ID3 had no facility to handle values that were unavailable during classification. Quinlan describes an extension of ID3, that is partial solution for this problem in the case of probablistic trees. The idea is to descend all branches of the tree and compute the plausibility of the answer from the plausibilities of the labels that are reached in this way. However, this solution is not very elegant when availability is systematic, and does not express well what should have been learned.

If it happened that attributes with "unavailable values" would only appear in subtrees that are dominated by the attribute on whcih they depend, there would be no problem if the tree were traversed in the standard top down direction. However, ID3 cannot guarantee that the tree that results from learning is indeed the optimal tree.

Focussing (Bundy et.al., 1986) is used with two possible representation languages: in the first a (partial) concept is represented as a collection of trees with markers at the nodes. Normally a tree corresponds to the values of an attribute. This representation corresponds to rules that are conjunctions of disjunction of values, where values may be true/false or other values. This representation cannot express interacting attributes. However Bundy et.al. describe an extended rule language, where a rule may consist of a collection of rules in the basic (tree) form. A collection of rules is interpreted as a disjunction and this resolves the limitations of the rule language.

To deal with missing attribute values the "match" predicate for a rule and an example must be adjusted. In practise (eg. Winston, 1975), this is done by a "closed world" assumption, which says that an attribute that is not mentioned is false of the example. As for ID3, this is not quite satisfactory, when there is a conceptual distinction between unapplicable or meaningless attributes and predicates that are false of an object.

3.2. Learning algorithms

I shall first consider the effect of the three types of dependencies on performance of a few empirical techniques and then the effect on EBL.

Focussing

Associations between attributes may cause difficulties with the focussing technique (Bundy et.al. 1986) if the program learns from real examples. Eg. suppose that there is an association between the (relational) attributes "supports" and "next to", because if an object supports another, then it cannot be next to it and vice versa. Now, if the program is learning the concept "arch" it will obviously never encounter an object with two parts that violate this association. If a "support" attribute is a counterindication for the classification (ie. for an object to be an instance of a class, two of its parts may not have the support relation), then it will be necessary for the program to meet a "near miss" that differs in only a single attribute from previous positive examples. However, due to the association between "support" and "next to" this will never happen: these objects don't exist. As a consequence, learning will not terminate (van Someren, 1986).

If values of attributes may be unknown, then the focussing technique must be adapted. There is no obvious adaptation that could deal with this.

ID3/C4

ID3 and its successor C4 (Quinlan, 1987) build decision trees from a large collection of examples. An attempt is made to construct a simple tree by selective introduction of new attributes into the tree. The attribute with the most predictive power is selected to create new branches.

Associations between attributes cause no problems with these techniques: the criterion for selecting the next attribute will do its job correctly.

Association with availability causes two kinds of problems. The first is, that the program may construct a decision tree that not easily be used and the second is, that the statistic used to select the next attribute is not adequate. (These problems are related.) The following example illustrates the first problem. An initial analysis, with a small data set, of the medical domain that we discussed above, showed that the most predictive attribute was "is the pain at the same place as last time". However, if this attribute is the first in the decision tree, then the dialogue that is generated by the tree becomes awkward, since many patients have not had this pain before, or have no pain at all.

If attributes interact in their relation with the class, then ID3 again may happen to take a suboptimal solution. Consider the following (artificial) example, where examples have value 1 or 2 on three attributes and a class label ('+' or '-'):

Example	Att1	Att2	Att3	Class
1	1	1	1	+
2	1	2	2	-
3	1	1	1	+
4	1	2	2	-
5	1	2	2	-
6	2	1	1	-
7	2	2	1	+
8	2	1	2	-
9	2	2	2	+

Here Att3 is the attribute that gives the best split of thee examples and ID3 will prefer it over Att1 and Att2. However, applying first Att1 and then Att2 will give a perfect tree of depth four, which cannot be achieved after Att3 is selected. ID3 could detect this, if it would have a 'lookahead' of two rather than one in its search procedure, however, that would make it much more expensive.

3.3. Explanation Based Learning

The EBL techniques that are described by Mitchell et.al. (1986) and DeJong et.al. (1986) use a domain theory to select relevant attributes. An explanation is constructed that shows how the conclusion in the right hand side of the rule can be inferred from the description of the object (using a domain theory). This explanation is then generalized and used to derive a (partial) general rule in terms of observable attributes.

In domains where attributes are associated, there will often be several possible explanations. As a simple illustration, consider the following example, adapted from Mitchell et.al. (1986). The concept in which we are interested is "safe to stack". The theory says:

volume(p1, v1) & density(p1, d1) --> weight(p1, v1 * d1)
weight(p1, w1) & weight(p2, w2) & less(w1, w2) --> lighter(p1, p2)

isa(p1, endtable) --> weight(p1, 5) (default)
isa(p1, endtable) --> colour(p1, blue)
colour(p1, blue) --> weight(p1, 5)
less(.1, 5)

...

The concept is defined as:

'safe to stack(x, y)' <--> (not(fragile(y)) or lighter(x, y))

and "operational" attributes are 'volume', 'density', 'isa', 'material' and
possibly more.

Now if we see some positive example of objects that are stacked on an iron
table, there are several possible explanations of why this is safe to
stack. EBG will generate some of these, but not all, because the rules that
are derived by EBG can be used to classify new objects, without constructing
a new explanation. However, the order in which explanations are generated is
not specified, so EBG does not detect that a new explanation may
be equivalent to another. Eg. from the theory above there are several ways
to explain why a certain object can be stacked on a blue endtable. These
explanations are closely related, but this remains invisible to EBG, because
it does not 'see' that endtables are blue.

It would be better, if EBG would find out that these explanations are related
and can be merged to a single explanation.

4. An analysis of the problem and a partial solution

There is are several ways to look at the problems described in the previous section. In each
case, search for the rules can be difficult under non-optimal conditions, such as incomplete object
descriptions or interrelated attributes. There are several ways to deal with these problems:

(1) In many cases the problems can be avoided by careful formulation of the descriptive attributes.
Eg. when learning a concept like "arch" in the blocks world, instead of the descriptors "next-to(X,
Y)" and "next-to(Y, X)" we could use a different attribute, such as the closure under symmetry
of "next-to": next-to-each-other(X, Y). This would resolve the problem for our example. Two
attributes that affect each others relation with the criterion can be represented as a single attribute,
eg. the attributes "sweating" and "high heart rate" could be replaced by "high physical arousal",

the criterion. However, this solution in some sense begs the problem, because here knowledge about the way in which these attributes are related to each other is used to structure the representation in advance.

(2) We could add knowledge about the meaning of attributes such as "next-to" and "sweating" and "heart rate" and modify the learning technique such that it tries to infer the classification rule from this background knowledge. This knowledge can be provided by the user/domain expert in a declarative form, or alternatively it could be induced from a set of examples (cf. Bundy, 1982). In the latter case, this would amount to a form of explanation based learning. For the former case, modification of the learning techniques is an open issue, that is worth exploring.

(3) A third way to approach the problem, is to add a kind of standardization step to the learning process. This combines the ideas of (1) and (2) by using knowledge about the domain to restructure the object description language. The reduced description language is used during classification as follows:

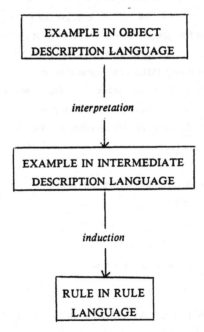

Figure 1: Structure of the system

The main purpose of constructing an intermediate representation language, is to achieve that the description language will have certain desirable properties, such as

* minimal number of descriptors

* minimal number of "unavailable" attributes ie. attributes that have no value for some objects

* conjunctive rule language (ie. rules are conjunctions of attribute/value ranges)

This can be achieved by restructuring the descriptive terms using general facts about the attributes and their relation to the class. At this stage we have no method to achieve this for the general case, but only for dependencies that occur frequently in classification rules.

The object description language consists of attributes and values. Some attributes represent relations, but these are treated in the same way as simple (propositional) attributes. Since the description language uses no variables, matching a description to a rule requires no structural matching. Consider for example the relation "the location of the current pain is below the location of the previous pain". Since the location of current and previous pain are both explicitly known, matching is straightforward.

Rules are conjunctive expressions, where each conjunct is a value range (ie. a subset of values) of an attribute or a relation. The dependencies that the system currently deals with are expressed in terms of the object description language and can be characterised as follows: *

(A) **Attribute dependencies:**

Two or more attributes may be interdependent in two ways: availability dependencies and associations:

(A1) **Availability dependencies:** if the value of an attribute or relation is available depends on another attribute or relation. Some examples:

"location of pain" **only available if** "has pain" **has value** "yes"

"equal(location of pain, previous location of pain) **only available if** "had this pain before" has value "yes"

(A2) **Associations**

Attributes and relations can be associated. Associations are indicated by the user in a simple language as given below.

- *Equivalence* (eg. synonyms): there exists a one-to-one mapping between the values of the attributes
- *Entailment*: there exists a more complex mapping between the values of two attributes

---

* Note that the intermediate attributes that are derived by the system, as described below, are not used in the interaction with the user.

Other types of associations are designed, but not used in the current system, because they apply to a richer description language. An example is

- *Symmetry*: a special type of equivalence, that only applies attributes representing binary relations. This can mean that a relation is symmetrical with itself, as in *connected* or with another relation, as in *above/below*.

(B) Interacting attributes:

The relation between an attribute or a relation and the class cannot be described by a simple (conjunctive) rule language, because two or more attributes or relations affect each others relation with the class. The language in which this is given to the system is the following:

Between attributes:

- Attribute 1 **interacts** with attribute 2: combining attributes 1 and 2 in a conjunctive rule does not result in an optimal relation with the class. A better prediction can be obtained by considering combinations of values.

- Attribute1 **hides** attribute 2: a special kind of interaction, if attribute 1 has value V1, then A2 is not related to the class (ie. a generalization can be made over attribute 2).

5. Constructing intermediate descriptors

Here we describe how intermediate descriptive terms are constructed from object attributes and relations, using various kinds of dependencies.

5.1. Attribute dependencies

(a) Attribute 1 **only available if** attribute 2 **has value** V: a new attribute is constructed from attribute 1 and attribute 2, with as its values only the possible combinations of values of the component attributes 1 and 2. Eg. if the user indicates that "location of pain" **only applies if** "has pain" has value "yes", a new attribute is constructed with as its values the possible combinations of values of attribute 1 and 2, thus we get:

```
value 1:  pain=no
value 2:  pain=yes & location=left arm
value 3:  pain=yes & location=left chest
etc.
```

Another example: "equal(location of pain, previous location of pain) **only available if** "had this pain before" has value "yes" results in an intermediate attribute defined as follows:

value 1: had this pain before=no
value 2: had this pain before=yes & equal(location, previous location)=yes
value 3: had this pain before=yes & equal(location, previous location)=no

The system builds tree structures from nested *only available if* relations.

5.2. Attribute dependencies

Attribute dependencies are treated in a way that is similar to what we described above. A new attribute is constructed that has only the combinations of values that are possible on the basis of the dependency.

- Equivalent attributes: a new attribute is constructed with as its values the coresponding values of the equivalent attributes

- Entailment: there exists a more complex mapping between the values of two attributes, eg.

- Symmetry: this is treated as equivalence. For a symmetric relation this results in the closure under symmetry.

5.3. Complex relations

Sofar we only indicated how simple relations between pairs of attributes, an attribute and a relation or two relations are handled. The method for dealing with more complex dependencies is basically the same as for simple dependencies: a compound attribute is constructed from basic attributes, such that only relevant combinations of values remain in the composed attribute. However, some complex relations allow more efficient representations. Eg. *only available if* relations are represented in tree structures and equivalent attributes are collected in set like representations.

6. An example

The scenario in which the system should operate is an expert who instructs the program using training examples and entering facts as indicated above. A particularly interesting scenario is one where the system generates the examples from an object description language that is given by the expert/user. In that case, examples are likely to elicit general facts from the user. Eg. if the user has given the system a standard medical anamnetic questionnaire as object description language, the system will generate all sorts of odd examples, such as a patient who besides a number of other characteristics, *has no pain, had the same pain the previous time* and *has had pain for over 15 minutes.* This will probably make the user enter the appropriate generalisations, especially since the system will begin to produce a whole series of (imaginary) patients that are equally implausible.

To illustrate the systems behaviour, we show a complete example of the system in operation. The example is taken from a medical domain. The attributes were given by a domain expert. They were taken from the interviews that normally take place with incoming patients and augmented with other attributes that might possibly be relevant in this domain (taken from the literature). The program now presents example patients to the expert and asks the expert to classify them by their diagnosis. The examples are generated by combining attributes and relations following a simple scheme, that need not concern us here. The user can select one of three possible actions: let the system generate an example for classification, enter a (classified) example or enter a domain fact.

Here we show only some fragments from the dialogue, with partial representations of the examples. The attributes used here are:

- blood pressure
- age
- transpires
- uses insulin
- nature of complaint (multiple answers with open category)
- location of pain (multiple answers with open category)
- relative location of previous pain (below, above, left of, right of, same-as previous pain)
- duration of pain
- respiration rate
- activity at start (rest / physical exercise / sleeping / other)

The systems takes the initative:

What do you want to do next: (a) classify an automatically generated example, (b) enter a classified example or (c) enter a domain fact ?

USER: **(a)**

blood pressure	high
age:	55
transpires:	yes
uses insulin:	no
nature of complaint:	pain
location of pain:	left arm, left chest
had pain before:	yes
relative location of previous pain:	below
duration of pain:	10
respiration rate:	normal
activity at onset:	physical exercise

Indicate class:

USER: **not acute**

Comment: a standard example

OK - What do you want to do next: (a) classify an automatically generated example, (b) enter a classified example or (c) enter a domain fact ?

USER: **(c)**

Fact: entails: physical exercise / transpiration

USER:

Mapping: **"physical exercise: yes" --> "sweating: yes"**
      "physical exercise: no" --> "sweating: yes OR no"

Comment: User realises that "transpiration" can be viewed as an indication of heart malfunction, but in this case transpiration can be explained from physical exercise. This information leads the system to construct a new attribute, defined in terms of "physical exercise" and "transpiration", with values:

- physical exercise: yes & transpiration: yes
- physical exercise: no & transpiration: yes
- physical exercise:no & transpiration: no

In the induction technique, this new attribute replaces its two components.

OK - What do you want to do next: (a) classify an automatically generated example, (b) enter a classified example or (c) enter a domain fact ?

USER: **(a)**

blood pressure	high
age:	55
transpires:	yes
uses insulin:	no
nature of complaint:	pain
location of pain:	left arm, left chest
had pain before:	no
relative location of previous pain:	??
duration of pain:	10
respiration rate:	normal
activity at onset:	physical exercise

Indicate class:

USER: **not acute**

Comment: The next example makes no sense: the relative location of pain is not available if the patient has no pain now. The user enters a kind of explanation for this, by entering an "only available if" fact. The system uses this fact by constructing a new attribute from the components "has pain" and "location of previous pain", with as its values only the "available situations:

- has pain: no
- has pain: yes & location of pain: above
- has pain: yes & location of pain: below
- has pain : yes & location of pain: next-to
- has pain: yes & location of pain: elsewhere

OK - What do you want to do next: (a) classify an automatically generated example, (b) enter a classified example or (c) enter a domain fact ?

USER: **(c)**

"location of previous pain" only available if "had pain before = yes"

OK - What do you want to do next: (a) classify an automatically generated example, (b) enter a classified example or (c) enter a domain fact ?

USER: **(b)**

```
blood pressure:        ??
age:                   35
transpires:            yes
uses insulin:          no
nature of complaint:   throws up
location of pain:      chest
had pain before:       no
duration of pain:      10
respiration rate:      fast
activity at onset:     physical exercise
```

Indicate class:

USER: **not acute**

Comment: note that in this example the relative location of the previous pain is left out.

USER: **(c)**

USER: **equivalent: vomits / throws up**

Equivalent;
Mapping: **"vomits: yes"** = **"throws up: yes"**
　　　　　"vomits: no" = **"throws up: no"**

Comment: The user entered an example and realised that non-standard but common terminology was used. He indicates that the terms "vomits" and "throws up" are equivalent. The system uses this to construct a new attribute, defined in terms of "vomits" and "throws up", after asking how exactly the values of these attributes map onto each other.

Now suppose that a more complex relation exists, eg. between "duration of pain", "transpiration" and "physical exercise": pain that lasts longer than 5 minutes and physical exercise can both lead to transpiration. The user now enters the second part of this statement:

USER: **entails: duration of pain / transpiration**
Mapping:

```
*  duration of pain: 0-5      -->  transpiration: yes OR transpiration: no
*  duration of pain: 5-15     -->  transpiration: yes
*  duration of pain: 15-30    -->  transpiration: yes
*  duration of pain: over 30  -->  transpiration: yes
```

The system now constructs a complex intermediate attribute that consists of three components: duration of pain, transpiration and physical exercise, defining as its values only the value combinations of the components that are possible according to the facts entered by the user.

7. The effect of reduction on learning

Note the effect that the construction of intermediate descriptors has on the learning process. The effect of collapsing two attributes is that of removing one attribute. This cuts the space of possible examples and possible rules in half ! Introducing a tree from an availablity fact about two binary attributes gives a reduction of 25 percent, since 4 possible combinations of values are now reduced to 3.

8. Discussion

Although we do not yet have practical experience with this system, it is clear that it will meet some of the objectives:

(1) The method is not particular to any learning technique. It can be added as a separate module to any learning system.

(2) It can be used incrementally to handle incoming new statements about the relation between descriptive terms.

(3) It has the effect of reducing the search space for the learning process. Since dependencies like those that we mentioned here are very common in practise, this is likely to be a useful extension of the available techniques.

(4) The resulting representation nicely separates two different types of knowledge (relations between attributes and relations between attributes and class), but yet allows them to collaborate.

At the "knowledge level" we can characterize the technique presented here as using knowledge of relations between descriptive terms to reduce the search space for learning by constructing a minimal representation.

Possible extensions are:

* a richer language for rules, objects and dependencies.

* automated induction from examples of the dependencies that are now entered by the user

One of the problems with this technique are, that the constructed descriptors can become very involved and complex. This makes them difficult to understand for a user, which is a potential problem.

Another point is, that a conjunctive generalisation language cannot be assumed from the start. If a dependencies is entered, it may be necessary to revise an earlier generalisation. At the moment, no explicit revision is undertaken, but learning simply continues with the new intermediate representation (a kind of hill climbing).

Also, we don't yet have experience with user interaction. It is not clear how easy it will be for humans to enter correct statements of the form that our system can handle.

9. Related work

Holte (1986) pointed out that learning programs show a wide range of information structures and that some of these are better for performance and others better for learning. The effect of introducing intermediate descriptions results in a structure that allows efficient processing for the learning task, but not for classification, the performance task of the system. In fact, we showed a general fact about the different types of information structures that are required for learning as opposed to performance: since classification will only involve objects that actually exist, the information structures for learning should emphasize properties that distinguish between existing objects, hiding properties that are properties that are universal among existing objects (distinguishing them from non-existing objects. Thus, learning to answer true-false questions about a domain will require different information structures than learning to classify actual objects.

In BLIP (Morik et.al. 1987; see also this volume) domain theory is used in a different way to construct rules from examples. In BLIP metalevel descriptions of domain facts are used to guide induction.

Kodratoff and Ganascia (1985) follow a different approach: they use the domain theory in matching a concept to a rule. Also, they have elaborated their technique to deal with full predicate calculus theories. However, this technique requires a considerable amount of inference, each time an instance is matched to a rule during learning.

Rollinger (1986) describes an extension to the version space method that addresses the problems caused by dependencies between the descriptors (in the case of the version space method: no convergence to a single rule) by learning from "impossible examples". The fact that impossible examples will not be an instance of any concept, is used by treating them as negative examples of all concepts and as postive examples of an "impossible concept".

Rendell (1985, 1986) shows how relations between descriptive attributes can be detected empirically and used to define bias for the learning process. The effect of this technique is similar to my method, but introduces as preference for certain rules, instead of constructing new descriptive terms.

210

References:

Bundy, A., Silver, B. and Plummer, D. (1985) An anlytical comparison of some rule-learning programs, **Artificial Intelligence, 27**, p.137-181.

Bundy, A. (1982) The indispensibility of inference in focussing, Internal note Department of Artificial Intelligence, University of Edinburgh.

DeJong, G. and Mooney, A. (1986) Explanation Based Learning: an alternative view, **Machine Learning,** vol.1, p.145-176.

Flann, N.F. and Dietterich, T. G. (1986) Selecting appropriate representations for learning from examples, Procs. AAAI-86, p. 460-466.

Holte, R.C. (1986) Alternative information structures in incremental learning systems, in: Y. Kodratoff (ed): Procs. EWSL.

Michalski, R.S. (1983) A theory and methodology of inductive learning, in: Michalski e.a. (1983).

Michalski, R.S., Carbonell, J. and Mitchell, T.M. (eds) (1983) **Machine learning: an AI approach,** Tioga Press.

Mitchell, T.M., (1982), Generalization as search, **Artificial Intelligence, 18**, p.203-226.

Mitchell, T.M., Keller, R. and Kedar-Cabelli, S.T. (1986) Explanantion based generalization, **Machine learning,** vol. 1, p.47-80.

Quinlan, J.R. (1987) Decision trees as probabilistic classifiers, in: Procs. 4th IWML, p.31-37.

Rendell, L. (1985) Substantial constructive induction using layered information compression: tractable feature formation in search, in: Proceedings IJCAI-85, Los Angeles.

Rendell, L. (1986) A general framework for induction and a study of selective induction, **Machine Learning,** vol.1, p.177-226.

van Someren, M.W. (1986) Reducing the description space for rule learning, Procs. ECAI 1986.

Winston, P.H. (1975) Learning structural descriptions from examples, in: Winston, P.H. (ed), **The psychology of computer vision,** McGraw-Hill.

LEARNING DISJUNCTIVE CONCEPTS[*]

Michel MANAGO

Inference and Learning Group
LRI (U.A. 410 du CNRS)
Bât 490, Université de Paris-sud
91405, ORSAY Cedex, France

Jim BLYTHE

GEC-Research
West Hanningfiled Road,
Great Baddow, Chelmsford
United Kingdom, CM2H8N

1. INTRODUCTION

As shown in [Mitchell, 1982], *concept learning* may be viewed as a search process in a hypothesis space that is defined by the *language of description*. The goal is to find plausible versions of the target concept, called *version space*, given positive and negative training examples of that concept. The items inside the version space are partially ordered by generality. Using this property, the version space can be efficiently represented by its sets of lower and upper bounds respectively called S and G sets. Mitchell defines the S and G sets as follows [Mitchell, 1982, pp 210-212] :

S = {*s* / *s* is a generalization that is consistent with the observed instances, and there is no generalization which is both more specific than *s*, and consistent with the observed instances}

G= {*g* / *g* is a generalization that is consistent with the observed instances, and there is no generalization which is both more general than *g*, and consistent with the instances}

In these definitions, Mitchell uses the terminology "the generalization is consistent with the observed instances" to mean that it covers all the observed positive examples and rejects all the observed negative examples. Given these definitions, it is assumed that a conjunctive description of the target concept exists. Otherwise, if disjunctions were allowed, the S set would always be reduced to a trivial set containing a single element: the disjunction of the positive examples.

[*] Fundings for this research has been provided by the European Economic Community under ESPRIT contract P1063, the INSTIL project. The partners of INSTIL are GEC research (UK), LRI (F), and Cognitech (F). LRI's research has also been supported by the GRECO and PRC "Intelligence Artificielle" and by Intellisoft.

However, with real life concepts this assumption does not always hold. Consider the following example:

Let E_1, E_2, E_3 be three positive examples of a concept and CE a negative one.

  $E_1(+)$: [x: <color red> <size very-big> <texture soft>]
  $E_2(+)$: [x: <color green> <size big> <texture hard>]
  $E_3(+)$: [x: <color green> <size very-big> <texture hard>]
  CE(-): [x: <color red> <size big> <texture hard>]

Let G be any conjunctive generalization that covers E_1, E_2 and E_3. The attribute values of color, size and texture in G must be more general than respectively (red,green), (big, very-big) and (soft, hard) otherwise G would not be more general than all three positive examples. Therefore, they will be more general than the corresponding attribute values in CE and since these are the only *discriminant attribute values*[1], G has to be more general than CE. Hence, there is no conjunctive generalization that covers all the positive examples and rejects CE.

Note that this is not a problem of shifting biases by introducing intermediary terms in the vocabulary as done in [Utgoff, 1986; Fu & Buchanan, 1985]. Given the descriptors color, size and texture, one would neverbe able to describe the examples so as to obtain a consistent conjunctive generalization. We will not consider the case where the language of description is drastically altered as done, for instance, in *tree hacking* [Wielemaker & Bundy, 1985]. The main drawback of this approach is that the vocabulary can become totally meaningless for the human being.

In this paper, we present a learning tool that is able to find a *characteristic* (most specific version of the concept) and *discriminant* (most general version of the concept) disjunctive generalizations of examples that belong to several classes. The system treats all the data at once doing so-called revolutionary learning [Michalski, 1983] and performs a heuristic, hill-climbing, top-down search of the space of possible hypothesis. Let us first briefly review the state of the art and describe what kind of disjunctive concept we are looking for.

---

[1] A discriminant attribute value is defined as an attribute value which prevents negative examples from being covered by positive ones

2. LEARNING DISJUNCTIVE CONCEPTS

2.1. STATE OF THE ART REVIEW

The original version space strategy has been extended to learn disjunctive concepts [Mitchell 1978, p 127]. The algorithm is stated as follows: "At each step, select the version space consistent with all negative instances and the largest possible number of positive instances". By requiring that the version space be consistent with the *largest* number of positive instances, Mitchell informally introduces a notion of "quality" of the disjuncts. Before discussing this notion in more detail, let us first criticize the method.

Firstly, this extended candidate elimination algorithm fails to produce a target concept for the example we have shown previously when the training data is presented in the order E_1, E_2, E_3, CE. When CE is encountered, the algorithm has already produced a S set that is overly general (all the items in S cover CE). To find a consistent generalization, the S set must be specialized (this is what has been called the *inconsistency condition* in [Murray, 1987]). If the examples previously encountered are forgotten ([Mitchell, 1978, p. 24]), on does not know which S set will produce a version space consistent with the largest number of positive instances. The algorithm would therefore fail to find a solution.

Secondly, the process of generating the disjuncts is totally data-driven. At the moment the S set becomes too general (or the G set becomes too specific), disjunctions are introduced in S and/or G. One can show that due to this, the algorithm lacks the ability to obtain results independently of the order in which the training instances are presented (the original candidate elimination algorithm was able to do so [Mitchell, 1978, p 24]).

Another improved candidate elimination algorithm, called multiple convergence [Murray, 1987], can learn any disjunctive concept. As done in [Iba, 1979], each positive example is memorized and is indexed by the items in G that cover it (if G contains disjunctive generalizations, then the disjuncts that cover the example are used as an index). When over-generalization occurs, the items in S that cover the negative example are "minimally" specialized by introducing disjunctions. This specialization is done in all possible directions and all the disjuncts are retained even when they do not cover any positive examples.

There are several advantages to multiple convergence. It can always produce a concept consistent with the training data, the incrementality of the candidate elimination algorithm is more or less preserved (depending on the definition of incrementality, one might consider that the algorithm is not incremental since the positive instances are memorized) and, according to the author, the final concept is independent of the order in which the training instances are presented to the system. However, the method is computationally expensive (the complexity is exponential) and the generation of the disjuncts is data-driven. The latest implies that when the data is not perfect, the algorithm produces concepts with too many disjuncts and that pre-pruning based on statistical significance cannot take place. Furthermore, for the example discussed in the last section, multiple convergence does not find one of the optimal consistent generalizations (with two disjuncts): $Gen(E_2,E_3) \lor E_1$ and $Gen(E_1,E_3) \lor E_2$. Instead, it finds a generalization with three disjuncts where each disjunct is simpler than the ones in $E_1 \lor E_2 \lor E_3$).

There are other learning systems, which will not be reviewed in here, that can learn disjunctive concepts (see for instance [Michalski, 1983; Quinlan, 1983; Iba, 1979]). Let us now describe the kind of disjunctive concepts we are interested in.

2.2. "QUALITY" OF THE DISJUNCTIONS.

As we have mentioned, if we want to learn characteristic versions of a disjunctive concept, we must add constraints on the kind of generalizations that are desirable.

The lower and upper bounds of the entire version space of complete and consistent disjunctive concepts are :

$S = S_1 \cup S_2 \cup ... \cup S_n$

$G = G_1 \cup G_2 \cup ... \cup G_n$

Where S_i ($1 \le i \le n$) is the set of most specific complete and consistent generalizations with exactly i disjuncts, G_i the set of most general complete and consistent generalizations with i disjuncts and n is the number of positive training examples. (Note that if there is no complete and consistent generalizations with i disjuncts, S_i is empty.). S_n is a singleton that contains the disjunction of the positive examples and G_n contains each positive example *generalized against* [Michalski, 1983] the negative examples in all possible ways.

Let us assume we are interested in minimally disjunctive generalizations. Then, the learning task can be stated as finding S_i and G_i such that $\forall j$, $1 \le j < i$, $S_j = \emptyset$. Note that whenever there is a non empty set S_j, then G_j is also non empty and vice-versa. Otherwise, if G_j was empty, it would mean that there is no complete and consistent generalizations with j disjuncts and therefore S_j would also be empty. The modified definition of S and G for minimally disjunctive concepts can be stated the following way:

S = {s / s is a generalization that is complete and consistent, there is no complete and consistent generalization containing fewer disjuncts than s, and there is no complete and consistent generalization containing the same number of disjuncts that is more specific than s}

G = {g / g is a generalization that is complete and consistent, there is no complete and consistent generalization which contains fewer disjunct than g, and there is no complete and consistent generalization containing the same number of disjuncts that is more general than g}

In these definitions, the terminology *is consistent* means that the generalization must reject all the negative example, and "is complete" means that it must cover all the positive examples. Given these definitions, it is clear that if there exists a conjunctive description of the target concept (a "one disjunct" solution), then we obtain the same S and G sets as in Mitchell's definitions.

However, we are not always interested in minimally disjunctive concepts. (These will minimize the total number of recognition rules since disjunctive rules of the form "A ∨ B ⟹ C" are interpreted as the two recognition rules "A ⟹ C" and "B ⟹ C".) We could prefer, for instance, a generalization which contains more disjuncts but where the disjuncts are smaller on the average. (This will minimize the average size of the recognition rules.) We could also prefer concepts that are more reliable and resilient to noise during consultation [Manago & Kodratoff, 1987]. In our previous example, we would favor concepts that do not rely on the difference between big and very-big to be identified. These two low level concepts are polymorphic [Manago & Kodratoff, 1987] and are a potential source of error during consultation. We might also prefer concepts that are "cheaper" to identify in some sense. For example, in the medical domain, we would like to minimize pain inflicted to a patient, or the actual cost of performing the tests etc. Intuitively, in our applications we are interested in finding generalizations with a fixed number of disjuncts that meet all the criteria mentioned previously. (There is usually a trade-off between these and we aim to reach the appropriate equilibrium.) We will not attempt giving a more formal definition of S and G for the following reason:

When learning disjunctive concepts, the search space cannot be constrained as in the candidate elimination algorithm. The complexity of the search being exponential (we can view the space as a directed graph where nodes are concepts descriptions and arcs are features to be tested), if the algorithm is to be used on real life, large scale applications, it must heuristically search that graph using an evaluation function that estimates the path to the optimal node, whatever the corresponding definition is. In the still experimental stage of our research, we feel that it would be vain to carefully define formally what the optimal number of disjuncts i is (which yield the "best" S_i and G_i) since we will only get an estimation of these anyway. Instead, we prefer empirically judging the quality of S_i and G_i using real life data (i.e. learn the concept using part of the example base and test it using another unseen part of the example base)

To conclude this section, let us note that we do not even aim at finding the entire S and G sets given a fixed number of disjuncts. We are only interested in finding a single element of these, that will be chosen according to the heuristic evaluation function. In the case of disjunctive concepts, even the size of S and G quickly becomes intracktable. Roughly, the order of magnitude of the cardinal of S and G is roughly n^p where n is the average number of conjunctive generalizations for each disjunct and p is the total number of disjuncts.

3. THE INSTIL LEARNING SYSTEM

The INSTIL project aims at integrating several learning systems and several approaches to Machine Learning. We will briefly describe each of the systems and explain why and how they are combined.

3.1. NEDDIE

NEDDIE is a descendant of ID_3 [Quinlan, 1983] that has been developed at GEC-research. Given a set of examples that may belong to a number of different classes, it outputs a decision tree that efficiently separates the classes. In terms of search strategies, NEDDIE performs a general-to-specific, hill-climbing search using information gain [Quinlan, 1983] as its heuristic evaluation function.

As we will see later, NEDDIE is able to find one of the elements in G (in fact, NEDDIE can transform a decision tree into a set of production rules [Corlett, 1983] that can be viewed as the disjuncts of an item in G) The tree can be terminated at any point if its overall reliability, based on a chi-square test, falls below a certain value called min-branch-safety. Thus the conclusions of the tree can be "fuzzy" since it may terminate before reaching an exact classification.

3.2. MAGGY

MAGGY is a generalizer, developed at LRI, that outputs conjunctive characteristic generalizations of the positive examples. It can be used to :

• find all the possible conjunctive generalizations (given a fixed background knowledge)

- select a generalization based on the amount of information contained in the original examples that is lost during the process.

Consider the following examples:

E$_1$: [x <isa mold> <color brown>] [y <isa spot> <color yellow>]
E$_2$: [x <isa mold> <color yellow>] [y <isa spot> <color brown>]

MAGGY ends up finding the generalization "there is a yellow symptom and a brown symptom" rather than "there is a mold and a spot" if asked to output a single generalization. This is motivated by the fact that more information is lost to obtain the second generalization (two attributes are dropped). In MAGGY, there is a pre-processing stage which heuristically decides which combinations of objects will be used before actually performing the generalization. The heuristics attempt to estimate quantities such as "how many objects would be dropped during generalization", "how many relational attributes would be dropped", "how many attributes would be dropped", "how high in the taxonomy would it climb" etc.

As demonstrated in the above example, domain specific heuristic information (given by the expert) and general information of the kind "the isa attribute is more important than the color attribute" ought to be taken into account. This would enable choices based on the quality of the information lost as well as on the quantity. Another "qualitative measure" would be "how well does this attribute discriminates from the negative examples" or in other words "how great is information gain". This show one possible way MAGGY can benefit from NEDDIE. We are currently working toward implementing this in the integrated system.

MAGGY returns the generalization (s) and a measure of how much information was lost during the process. To represent the examples, MAGGY uses a language based on first order logic (with conjunctions, negations and internal disjunctions [Manago & Blythe, 1988]). It is able to handle objects, variables. Universal quantifiers are handled using the negation of an existential one (i.e. all the elephants are gray would be represented as there is no elephant which is not gray). The generalizer is efficient and uses object oriented like expressions which are based on first order logic [Nilsson, 1980, section 9.1]. Each individual object is from a certain type and the complexity of the method is a function of how many objects have a compatible type. For instance, it would not make any sense to match a red spot with a red fruit! We only want to match symptoms with other symptoms and so on.

MAGGY also uses an object layer (*schemas* or *frames*) to efficiently represent background knowledge [Manago & Blythe, 1988]. Schemas are used to represent structural knowledge (ex: [spot (a-kind-of ($VALUE symptom))] , [leaves (part-of ($VALUE plant))]), rules (using $IF-NEEDED daemons attached to the appropriate slots in the frames), default information (ex:

[leaves (color ($DEFAULT green))]]) and constraints (ex: [tomato-fruit (color ($RANGE red green yellow orange))]]). Daemons are Lisp procedures. For example, the following daemon would be fired when accessing the color attribute of the TOMATO-FRUIT frame:

```
(Defdaemon ()
;;;; This daemon will return green if the fruit is young, red if it is ripe

    (CASE    (gol:send-message $self-example $self-object :stage)

                ;; $Self-example and $Self-object are system variables provided by
                ;; MAGGY. They are bound to the example and the object to which the
                ;; message was sent originally.

                (:ripe :red)
                (:young :green)
                (t nil)))
```

MAGGY can handle multiple inheritance and has an open architecture. For example, the variables *generalization-paths* and *inheritance-paths* can be different and are defined by the user using a simple grammar. The way the search is done is also a parameter ($breadth-first or $depth-first) etc. Although our goal was not to design "yet another object-oriented language", we found that none of the ones currently available were flexible enough for Machine Learning. The schema layer evolved into a language well suited for generalization of objects as well as for inheritance of properties.

3.3.   DEFICIENCIES OF THE LEARNING SYSTEMS

Like ID3, NEDDIE uses feature vectors (attribute-value pairs) to represent the examples. It is a form of propositional calculus that does not use any background knowledge such as taxonomies (testing the information gain of an intermediary attribute values such as *light-color* could yield very interesting results), rules which allow to deduce an attribute value from another (for instance, if there is a multitude of spots on a leaf, their size is small) and that cannot handle composite objects. The latest can be a source of problems. For instance, it is irrelevant to consider the information gain of the attribtue color-of-the-spot before knowing that there is a spot! We also wanted to be able to deal with an arbitrary number of objects (there could be several different spots on the leaf). Extensions were made to NEDDIE in order to handle composite objects (analogous to Part-of hierarchies) but it turned out that this representation formalism was not flexible enough and not rich enough in the context of our applications.

MAGGY cannot learn disjunctive concepts and cannot learn generalizations in the G set efficiently. When there is no consistent conjunctive description, MAGGY outputs a description that is complete and inconsistent. MAGGY is data-driven and works incrementally. Thus, it cannot decide to avoid generalizing an attribute based on the weakness of the statistical evidence (when the different color is supported by only 0.0001% of the examples). Note that in Meta-

Dendral [Mitchell, 1978], some of the motivation for merging the data-driven algorithm Update-S and the model-driven algorithm Rulegen were close to ours.

4. THE INSTIL LEARNING SYSTEM

The first step was to test how the two learning systems could be merged using a switchbox approach. The two programs were first ported in the same programming language (Common Lisp) but were kept separate. They communicated by exchanging information when appropriate.

This approach is far from being optimal, let it be because the two algorithms use two different representations of the training examples (attempts were made to automatically transform feature vectors into objects but the limit of what could be done was quickly reached). The important point is that using this switchbox mechanism to undertake experiments, we were able to identify the main features of each program that ought to be preserved in the final learning system. It also improved our understanding of the problems involved in merging the systems in a more satisfactory manner. After analyzing the experiment, we made several design choices for the fully integrated learning system.

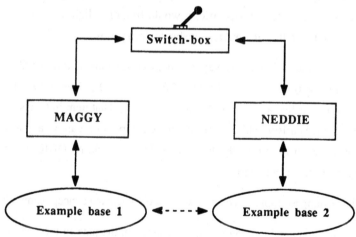

Fig. 1 A switchbox integration of MAGGY and NEDDIE

4.1. FINDING A DISCRIMINANT GENERALIZATION OF A DISJUNCTIVE CONCEPT

We can take the decision tree that is generated by NEDDIE and separates it into its component rules. These are conjunctions of tests along with their conclusions. Due to the structure of the decision tree, these production rules can be re-generalized [Corlett, 1983;

Quinlan 1987]: each test in the conjunct is experimentally dropped from right to left (from the leaves toward the root, or in other words from specific-to-general). If the new conclusion based on the examples that satisfy the modified rule is weaker than the original one, the test is put back in. Otherwise it is dropped permanently (all tests in a rule that were originally in the tree but not directly associated with that rule's conclusion are dropped).

After this procedure, if one applies the *dropping condition rule* to any conjunct in this production rule, the resulting description will cover at least one negative training instance. However, this is not enough to conclude that the description is a member of the G set since there are other generalization rules beside the dropping condition rule. When the two programs were kept separated without making any drastic changes in them and due to the fact that NEDDIE was unable to deal with structural knowledge, we could not go any further. However, we were able to make several design choices for the fully integrated system.

The search for the concept had to be general-to-specific and post-pruning of the production rule had to be specific-to-general. For example, if the test <color yellow> is required to appear before the test <color light-color> in the decision tree, post-pruning from the leaves toward the root will generate the most general version of the concept (assuming that yellow was not necessary but that light-color was, it would drop yellow and keep light-color). Otherwise, if pruning was done from general-to-specific, it would first drop light-color (at that stage, it is considered redundant) and then it would be unable to drop yellow.

Each production rule obtained this way is a disjunct of an element in the G set. Taking the disjunction of all these rules will produce one of the items in the G set. (in the litterature, each disjunct has also been called a *complex* [Michalski, 1983].) That item in G has been estimated best according to our heuristic which is to maximize information gain in a general-to-specific search. It is not necessarily minimally-disjunctive. In this work, NEDDIE is not viewed as a decision tree grower, but as a tool to:

- cluster the training examples (decide how many disjuncts the concept should have)

- compute a most general version of each cluster from the path in the tree by applying the dropping rule and testing for inconsistencies starting from the leaves and working our way up toward the root

As we have just described, the discriminant disjunctive generalization of the positive examples is computed by taking the disjunction of all the discriminant conjunctive generalization of each cluster.

4.2. FINDING A CHARACTERISTIC GENERALIZATION OF A DISJUNCTIVE CONCEPT

Once we have clustered the space of examples using NEDDIE, one way to generate the characteristic generalization is to run MAGGY on each cluster. However, instead of choosing one of the generalizations found by MAGGY in the usual manner (based on how much information is lost during generalization), we add the constraint that the characteristic generalization must be more specific than the corresponding G generalization computed as we have shown in the previous section. Since MAGGY can find all the characteristic generalizations, at least one of them will be more specific than the one in G (Otherwise, it would either mean that MAGGY does not do its job or that there is something wrong with our definitions of S and G.) We are then insured of finding a characteristic generalization s of the cluster that is consistent since there is a generalization g that is more general than s and that is consistent. By taking the disjunction of each of characteristic conjunctive description of the clusters, we obtain (heuristically) a characteristic description of the disjunctive target concept.

We can take the decision tree that is generated by NEDDIE and extract descriptions of the target concepts that are in S or G. NEDDIE builds the disjuncts and, using different methods, we compute the appropriate descriptions of these disjuncts. In the switchbox implementation, this could not really be done since we were unable to compare the generalization g produced by NEDDIE and the generalizations in S produced by MAGGY to pick an element of S that was more specific than g (they used two different Knowledge Representation formalisms). NEDDIE could tell MAGGY what to generalize, but MAGGY did not know what generalization to keep.

Further improvements required a more complete integration of the two systems so that they could talk the same language and work on the same database of examples.

4.3. MERGING THE TWO SYSTEMS INTO ONE

The first step toward complete integration was to develop a uniform Knowledge Representation formalism and a common pattern matcher for NEDDIE and MAGGY. Both systems were upgraded according to a common Knowledge Representation framework. For the sake of simplicity, we have presented in section III.B., the new INSTIL Knowledge Representation formalism. It is a more powerful superset of what was originally found in MAGGY but there are a lot of similarities between the old MAGGY and the new INSTIL formalisms. In this paper, we decided to present only one Knowledge Representation formalism in order to avoid confusions in the reader's minds.

The next problem to be solved was how to generate the tests to compute information gain. In a feature vector language, all possible hypothesis are known from the language of description (i.e. you can compute information gain of knowing the value of attribute1, attribute2 etc.). In our object-based language this simple approach could not be used. For example, when you want to say that there are no spots on a leaf, spots on the leaf is not part of the description of the example. The question is then how does the system know that it should consider computing information gain of [x: <isa spot> <on y>] [y: <isa leaf>]?

To date, we have used two methods to generate plausible tests to compute information gain using the INSTIL representation. There are other possibilities which we are currently investigating, but just those two are described here. Before describing these, let us first consider for a moment the implications of the object based representation on a system like NEDDIE because it leads us to extend the notion of the decision tree somewhat.

As mentioned before, we prefer to think of objects in an example in terms of their types that enable us not to match, for instance, a red spot with a red leaf. An example, however, may have any number of objects of a given type. That means that if we were to replace a simple feature, like color, with color-of-spot, the question that naturally arise is "which spot ?" (there can be more than one spot in the example that have a color!). It is more natural and useful in this representation language to replace the color-of-spot idea with a series of tests "Is there a red spot?", "Is there a yellow spot?" and so on. If one of these simpler tests is succesfully passed, we then have explicit bindings in the example we are looking at. We can propagate these bindings in the tree and later ask questions such as "Is the red spot on a leaf ?" to specialize the object.

In order to adjust NEDDIE to behave in a more natural way with its new representation language, the decision tree representation has been adjusted in the following ways. Rather than a node of the tree consisting of a single feature, and branches from that node representing all possible values of the feature, a node contains a set of tests, each with a branch attached should the test be true. This has several implications such as the ability to grow a decision lattice instead of a decision tree. Secondly, each individual test may be a conjunction of attributes. For instance, in our representation the test "Is there a red spot ?" is a conjunction of two tests of the form [x: <isa spot> <color red>]. Let us see how tests can be generated using this representation in order to compute the heuristic evaluation fonction.

The first method for generating the tests aims to be as close as possible to the system when it used the feature-value representation, where all possible tests were tried. Extensions were added to cope with a variable number of objects of a given type, as well as with relations between objects. This is done with the following simple heuristics:

- A node will ask questions about only one attribute

- We prefer to specialize existing objects rather than introduce new ones

- New objects are introduced by type (isa attribute) and one other attribute

- Relations are considered to be attributes that also introduce new objects

With this simple method, NEDDIE can be generalized to handle more complex domains. In many cases, however, the number of possible tests to evaluate, based on the rules above, quickly becomes very large as new objects are introduced. We would also like to consider longer conjunctions in our tests since many features are only interesting in tandem and considering them piece-meal, as NEDDIE does, will fail to discover the most interesting tests. It is clear that this would increase the search space intolerably however. So our next step is to find a good way to constrain this.

The second method we have used to generate the tests for NEDDIE is based on Michalski's star algorithm [Michalski, 1983]. Using a randomly selected seed example, the systems start to grow a partial star (using the usual Michalski's preference criteria). However, the system first builds conjunctions of length one (*partial stars*) and pass these to NEDDIE. If information gain is above a threshold, it uses the partial star with highest information gain to grow the decision tree. Otherwise, if it is not sufficient, the program tries conjunctions with more conjuncts (specialize the partial stars) and iterates the process .

In the annex, we have included the results of the two methods of building the tests for the Michalski's train problem [Medin et al, 1987].In the description we have given, the first car is the actual car train and not the engine and that we did not actually describe all the information in the example (we ignored the color of the wheels for instance). In the decision lattice, CAR1 CAR2 etc.. are names of dummy variables that carry no semantic meaning.

Considering that in this problem, there were a lot more descriptors than examples, it is not surprising that the second method produced much better results than the first one (a tree with 9 nodes instead of 26). However, the reader should not draw any premature conclusions from this quick experiment. We are currently in the process of testing all of these on larger sets of examples (for instance, diseased tomato plants). We are also implementing other methods for building the tests based on structural matching [Kodratoff & Ganascia, 1986].

Thanks to Ross Quinlan who has kindly made available the 3000 examples of hypothyroid cancer he has used with C_4 [Quinlan, 1986], we will also try to apply INSTIL on this domain. The main difficulty to overcome for this last application is that the example base was formated for C_4 which uses no background knowledge at all. Since INSTIL can use background knowledge, we prefer to first seek taxonomies, rules, constraints and other information about the domain which we do not know at this point before starting the experiment (so that INSTIL is able demonstrate its power as a Knowledge Intensive "empirical" learning system).

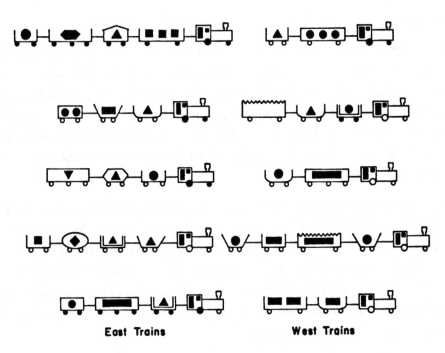

Fig. 2 East-Bound and West-Bound Trains.

5. CONCLUSION

We have presented in this paper a learning system that is able to produce characteristic and discriminant versions of disjunctive target concepts. The algorithm is able to process all classes at once. It integrates several inductive learning methods : An ID3-based system (with several important improvements over the original ID3) and a generalization engine. The first way we approached integration was to use a switchbox mecanism that enabled us to quickly identify strong and weak points of each learning systems. The switchbox integration was also used to test plausible ways of fully merging the systems. When the limit of what could possibly be done was reached, we then went on integrating totally the learning systems. This required major changes in the systems themselves and was achieved by designing a powerful object-based representation formalism and implementing a common pattern-matcher. Following this work, several problems remained to be solved and lead us to experiment with other learning systems such as the star algorithm. The integrated system can use domain knowledge and is being applied on large scale problems.

Acknowledgments:

We wish to thank Dr Yves Kodratoff (M. Manago's thesis advisor) who initiated most of the work presented in this paper, and Rob Corlett who originally developed NEDDIE and who has contributed a great deal to this work. We also would also like to thank the people who have provided a large scale real life application for this project: Christine Piaton and Noel Conruyt, two students in agronomy, who patiently collected and described hundreds of diseased tomatos. Special thanks to Bruce Buchanan and to the Helix group at Stanford University, to Dave Neeham at GEC-research, and to Celine Rouveirol and Alexandre Parodi at LRI-IA for the useful comments and feedback that they provided on this work. MAGGY has been developed on a TI-EXPLORER 1 Lisp machine, NEDDIE on a SUN3/160 workstation. The kernel of the systems is written in pure COMMON LISP.

REFERENCES

[Corlett 1983] Corlett, R.
"Explaining induced decision trees," *Proc. Expert Systems Conference,* pp. 136-142, 1983.

[Fu & Buchanan, 1985] Fu, L. M. & Buchanan, B. G.
"Learning Intermediate Concepts in Constructing a Hierarchical Knowledge Base," in *Proc. of the ninth International Joint Conference in Artificial Intelligence,* Vol 1., pp. 659-666, Joshi, A. ed, Morgan-Kaufmann, Los Altos (CA), 1985.

[Iba, 1979] Iba, G.
Learning Disjunctive Concepts From Examples, A.I. Memo 548, MIT AI Lab, 1979.

[Kodratoff & Ganascia, 1986]   Kodratoff, Y. & Ganascia J. G.
"Improving the Generalization Step in Learning," in Machine Learning : An artificial Intelligence Approach, Vol. 2 pp. 215-244, Michalski R. S., Carbonell J. G., Mitchell T. M. eds, Morgan Kaufmann, Los Altos (CA),1986.

[Manago & Kodratoff, 1987] Manago, M. & Kodratoff, Y.
"Noise and Knowledge Aquisition", *Proc. IJCAI 1987,.*Vol 1, pp. 348 - 354, McDermott, J. ed., Morgan Kaufmann, Los Altos (CA), 1987.

[Manago & Blythe, 1988] Manago, M. & Blythe, J.
"The INSTIL Knowledge Representation Reference Manual," ESPRIT Deliverable, *to be published in march 1988.*

[Medin et al, 1987] Medin, D. L. & Wattenmaker, D. & Michalski, R.S.
"Constraints and Preferences in Inductive Learning : An experimental Study of Human and Machine Performance," *Cognitive Science,* Vol 11-3, pp. 299-349, Ablex Pub., Norwood, July 1987.

[Michalski, 1983] Michalski, R.S.
"Theory and Methodology of Inductive Learning," in Machine Learning: an Artificial Intelligence Approach, Vol 1, pp.83-134, Michalski R.S., Carbonell J.G., Mitchell T.M. eds, Morgan Kaufmann, Los Altos (CA), 1983.

[Mitchell, 1978] Mitchell, T.M.
"Version Space: An Approach to Concept Learning", Ph.D. Thesis, Stanford CS Rept. STAN-CS-78-711, HPP-79-2, Stanford University, December 1978.

[Mitchell, 1982] Mitchell, T.M.
"Generalization as Search," *Artificial Intelligence,,* Vol 18-2, pp.203-226, North Holland, Amsterdam, 1982

[Murray, 1987] Murray, K.
"Multiple Convergence: An approach to Disjunctive Concept Acquisition," *Proc. IJCAI 1987,* Vol 1, pp. 297 - 300, McDermott, J. ed., Morgan Kaufmann, Los Altos 1987.

[Nilsson, 1980] Nilsson, N.
"Principles of Artificial Intelligence," Morgan Kaufmann, Los Altos, 1980.

[Quinlan, 1983] Quinlan, J. R.
"Learning efficient classification procedures and their application to chess end games," in Machine Learning 1: An Artificial Intelligence Approach, pp.463-482, Michalski R. S., Carbonell J. G., Mitchell T. M. eds, Morgan Kaufmann, Los Altos 1983.

[Quinlan, 1986] Quinlan, J. R.
"Simplifying Decision Trees," *Proc. of the first AAAI workshop on Knowledge Acquissition for Knowledge Based Systems*, pp. 36.0 - 36.15, Banff, Oct. 1986.

[Quinlan, 1987] Quinlan, J. R.
"Generating Production Rules from Decison Trees," *Proc. IJCAI 1987*, Vol 1, pp. 304-307,.McDermott, J. ed., Morgan Kaufmann, Los Altos 1987.

[Utgoff, 1986] Utgoff, P.
"Shift of Bias for Inductive Concept Learning," in Machine Learning 1: An Artificial Intelligence Approach, Michalski R. S., Carbonell J. G., Mitchell T. M. eds, pp. 107-148, Morgan Kaufmann, Los Altos 1983.

[Wielemaker & Bundy, 1985] Wielemaker, J. & Bundy, A.
"Altering the Description Space for Focussing," in *Proc.of the fifth technical conference of the british computer society specialist group on expert systems*, Merry, M. ed, pp. 287-298, Cambridge University Press, London, 1985.

APPENDIX A: SAMPLE OUTPUT FROM THE INSTIL LEARNING SYSTEM USING THE TRAIN DATA

> (eget :ex1)
(EX1 (EXAMPLE (ISA EXAMPLE) (NO-OF-CARS 4))
  (C1 (ISA CAR) (LENGTH LONG) (CAR-SHAPE OPEN-RECT) (LOAD-SHAPE SQUARE)
    (IN-FRONT C2) (NO-PTS-LOAD 3) (NO-WHEELS 2))
  (C2 (ISA CAR) (LENGTH SHORT) (CAR-SHAPE HOUSE) (LOAD-SHAPE TRIANGLE)
    (IN-FRONT C3) (NO-PTS-LOAD 1) (NO-WHEELS 2))
  (C3 (ISA CAR) (LENGTH LONG) (CAR-SHAPE OPEN-RECT) (LOAD-SHAPE
HEXAGON)
    (IN-FRONT C4) (NO-PTS-LOAD 1) (NO-WHEELS 3))
  (C4 (ISA CAR) (LENGTH SHORT) (CAR-SHAPE OPEN-RECT) (LOAD-SHAPE CIRCLE)
    (NO-PTS-LOAD 1) (NO-WHEELS 2)))

> *desired-node-builder*
NEDDIE_STANDARD
> ;;; now we will grow a decision lattice using a "Quinlan like" approach

(induce)
GENERATING...
If NO-OF-CARS >= 3 then
 If there is a CAR (CAR4) with CAR-SHAPE = POLYGON then
  If CAR4 has LENGTH = LONG then
   If CAR4 has NO-WHEELS >= 3 then
   class is POS with probability 1.00
   If CAR4 has NO-WHEELS < 3 then
   class is NEG with probability 1.00
  If CAR4 has LENGTH = SHORT then
   If CAR4 has LOAD-SHAPE = POLYGON then
   class is POS with probability 1.00
   If CAR4 has LOAD-SHAPE = OVAL then
    If CAR4 has NO-PTS-LOAD >= 2 then
    class is POS with probability 1.00
    If CAR4 has NO-PTS-LOAD < 2 then
    class is POS with probability 0.50
    class is NEG with probability 0.50
   If CAR4 has LOAD-SHAPE = HOUSE then
   If CAR4 has LOAD-SHAPE = DISH then
 If there is a CAR (CAR4) with CAR-SHAPE = OVAL then
 class is POS with probability 1.00
 If there is a CAR (CAR4) with CAR-SHAPE = HOUSE then
 class is POS with probability 1.00
 If there is a CAR (CAR4) with CAR-SHAPE = DISH then
  If there is a CAR (CAR5) with CAR-SHAPE = POLYGON then
   If CAR5 has LENGTH = LONG then
    If CAR5 has NO-WHEELS >= 3 then
    class is POS with probability 1.00
    If CAR5 has NO-WHEELS < 3 then
    class is NEG with probability 1.00
   If CAR5 has LENGTH = SHORT then
    If CAR5 has LOAD-SHAPE = POLYGON then
    class is POS with probability 1.00
    If CAR5 has LOAD-SHAPE = OVAL then

If CAR5 has NO-PTS-LOAD >= 2 then
  class is POS with probability 1.00
If CAR5 has NO-PTS-LOAD < 2 then
  class is NEG with probability 1.00
 If CAR5 has LOAD-SHAPE = HOUSE then
 If CAR5 has LOAD-SHAPE = DISH then
 If there is a CAR (CAR5) with CAR-SHAPE = OVAL then
  class is POS with probability 1.00
 If there is a CAR (CAR5) with CAR-SHAPE = HOUSE then
  class is POS with probability 1.00
 If there is a CAR (CAR5) with CAR-SHAPE = DISH then
That would have been an infinite loop
If NO-OF-CARS < 3 then
 class is NEG with probability 1.00
The lattice is complete, containing twenty-six nodes.

> (setq *desired-node-builder* 'star_creation)
STAR_CREATION
> ;we will now build the decision lattice using the star algorithm to construct the
; test, but using entropy to pick which star we will use

(induce)
GENERATING...
5 positive & 5 negative examples
The seed chosen is EX6

Trying conjunctions of length one
Trying conjunctions of length two

If NO-OF-CARS = 2 then
 class is NEG with probability 1.00
If there is no EXAMPLE with NO-OF-CARS = 2 then

5 positive & 2 negative examples
The seed chosen is EX3

Trying conjunctions of length one

 If there is a CAR (C2) with LOAD-SHAPE = TRIANGLE then

5 positive & 1 negative examples
The seed chosen is EX1

Trying conjunctions of length one

  If there is a CAR (C4) with CAR-SHAPE = OPEN-RECT then
   class is POS with probability 1.00
  If there is no CAR with CAR-SHAPE = OPEN-RECT then

2 positive & 1 negative examples
The seed chosen is EX2

Trying conjunctions of length one
Trying conjunctions of length two

If C2 has LOAD-SHAPE = RECT then
   class is POS with probability 1.00
If there is no CAR with LOAD-SHAPE = RECT then
   class is NEG with probability 1.00
If there is no CAR with LOAD-SHAPE = TRIANGLE then
   class is NEG with probability 1.00
The lattice is complete, containing nine nodes.

The Use of Analogy in Incremental SBL

Christel Vrain, Yves Kodratoff
Equipe Inférence et Apprentissage, Bat. 490
Laboratoire de Recherche en Informatique, UA 410 CNRS
Université de Paris Sud, 91405 Orsay Cedex, France

Summary:

Analogy is clearly one of the key issues of Learning, since it constitutes a major tool for constructing new concepts, or new rules or new strategies. Our view of analogy is that it must take into account not only the resemblances within a set of different datas but also the **differences** among them. We describe how to apply this view of the analogical process to incremental similarity-based learning.

Keywords: Analogy, causal relation, similarity, dissimilarity, Concept Learning from sets of examples, incremental learning.

1. Introduction

From the point of view of the strategies they use, one tends now to put Machine Learning under several headings: Deductive Learning which includes EBL and EBG systems (Mitchell 86, DeJong 86), Inductive Learning, as developed by Michalski (Michalski 83) or by Kodratoff (Kodratoff 83), Analogy (Carbonell 83, Chouraqui 82), ...

This paper illustrates our point of view about Analogy and shows how relationships between background knowledge enable to use Analogy in the domain of concepts formation from a set of examples.

1.1. Classical definition of analogical situations

Analogy theory relies on causal reasoning. This kind of reasoning may use three different forms of inference:

- the classical formal inference,
- the uncertain or possible inference,
- the "causal" inference where we only suggest that a fact is linked to some causes.

For instance, when we say that the climate of a town is linked to its geographical position and to its latitude, we only express a causality relation without expliciting the nature of the concerned causality.

In this paper, we start from the classical paradigm of Analogy (Chouraqui 82):

A' is analogous to B' in the same way as A is analogous to B.

which can be illustrated by the following diagram:

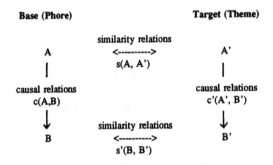

Notations:

Given two situations S_1 and S_2,

we denote $s(S_1, S_2)$ a set of similarities between S_1 and S_2,

we denote $c(S_1, S_2)$ a set of causality relations between S_1 and S_2, which enables to infer S_2 from S_1.

In this diagram, we suppose that we have two pairs of situations {A, B} and {A', B'}. Moreover, we suppose that between A and B, there is a set of causality relations, called c(A, B), which enables to infer B from A and we suppose also that between A' and B', there is a set of causality relations, denoted by c'(A', B').

Definition: analogous situations

We say that the pairs {A, B} and {A', B'} are analogous if we can compute similarities between A and A', similarities between B and B' and if {A, B} and {A', B'} have identical causality relations.

It is impossible to define more precisely this notion, since it first depends on the definition of similarity and it depends also on our goals during the learning process. These two criteria to define analogous situations are contradictory: the similarity between two situations is all the greater as it tends toward the identity relation, but, if two situations S_1 and S_2 are completely identical, we learn nothing more about S_2 from the antecedent S_1.

In order to insist on the fact that the falsity/truth of an analogy does not rely on the falsity/truth of its output, we shall illustrate our definition by two examples. The first example will illustrate our definitions rather than the analogical process itself. The second one will illustrate the importance of different relations.

First example:

We suppose that in the base, we have:
A = Earth has an atmosphere of 1013 mb containing oxygen.
B = Earth is inhabited by humans.

We suppose that in the target, we have:
A' = Mars has an atmosphere of 5mb containing oxygen.
B' = Mars is inhabited by algae.

This example relative to the presence of algae on Mars is totally imaginary.

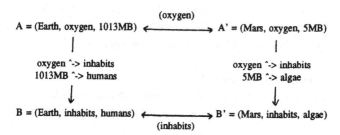

We have similarities between A and A': their atmospheres contain oxygen, which can be expressed by:

$$s(A, A') = oxygen,$$

we have similarities between B and B': they are both "inhabited",

$$s(B, B') = inhabits$$

and we have a common causality relation between A and B on the one hand, and between A' and B' on the other hand: an atmosphere containing oxygen is a "cause" for life,

$$oxygen \hat{} ->inhabits.$$

Therefore, we can say that {A', B'} is analogous to {A, B}.

But, we can notice that they are also partially different since there is the following causality relation between A and B: 1013mb pressure "causes" human beings, and since between A' and B' there is the relation: 5mb pressure "causes" algae life but not human life.

Second example:

Let us suppose now that we would like to apply techniques of Analogy to translate sentences from French to English. Recall that our aim is the illustration of Analogy, not the proposal of a new French-English translator.
We may have the following diagram:

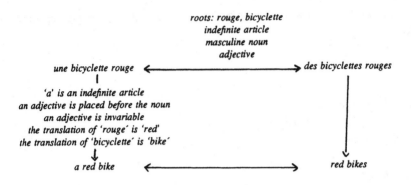

roots: rouge, bicyclette
indefinite article
masculine noun
adjective

une bicyclette rouge ⟵————————⟶ *des bicyclettes rouges*

'a' is an indefinite article
an adjective is placed before the noun
an adjective is invariable
the translation of 'rouge' is 'red'
the translation of 'bicyclette' is 'bike'

a red bike ⟵————————⟶ *red bikes*

A = une bicyclette rouge, which can be described by:
(composed-by une bicyclette rouge) & (article une) & (indefinite une) & (noun bicyclette) & (feminine bicyclette) & (singular bicyclette) & (adjective rouge) & (root bicyclette bicyclette).
This conjunction expresses that the sentence is composed of at least *three words: 'une', 'bicyclette' and 'rouge', that the word 'une' is an indefinite article, the word 'bicyclette' is a feminine and singular noun whose root is 'bicyclette' and that the word 'rouge' is an adjective.*

A' = des bicyclettes rouges, which can be described by:
(composed-by des bicyclettes rouges) & (article des) & (indefinite des) & (noun bicyclettes) & (feminine bicyclettes) & (plural bicyclettes) & (root bicyclettes bicyclette) & (adjective rouges) & (root rouges rouge).

B = a red bike, which can be described by the conjunction:
(composed-by a red bike) & (article a) & (indefinite a) & (noun bike) & (neuter bike) & (singular bike) & (root bike bike) & (adjective red)

B' = red bikes
(composed-by red bikes) & (noun bikes) & (neuter bikes) & (plural bikes) & (root bikes bike) & (adjective red).

We can compute the similarity between A and A':the two sentences A and A' are made of three words, named x, y and z, x is an indefinite article, y is a feminine noun and z is an adjective. It can be expressed by the following conjunction of atoms:
s(A, A') = (composed-by x y z) & (article x) & (indefinite x) & (noun y) & (feminine y) & (adjective z).

We can also compute the similarity between B and B': the two sentences B and B' are made of at least two words, one is an adjective and the other is a neuter noun.
s'(B, B') = (composed-by x y) & (adjective x) & (noun y) & (neuter y).

We can define some causality relations between A and B, c(A, B), which explain why B is the English translation of A:

c_1: "in English, 'a' is an indefinite article",

c_2: "in English, an adjective, used as an attribute is placed before the noun",

c_3: "in English, an adjective is invariable",

c_4: "the word 'red' is the translation of the word 'rouge'",

c_5: "the word 'bike' is the translation of the word 'bicyclette'".

A possible set of causality relations between A' and B', $c'(A', B')$, is composed of c_2, c_3, c_4, c_5 and of:

c_6: "in English, there are no plural and indefinite article",

c_7: "the plural noun 'bikes' is obtained by adding an 's' to the translation of the word 'bicyclette'".

1.2. Analogical reasoning

Referring to the general scheme given in the previous section, the pairs of situations {A, B} is called the **phore** or the **base**: it is the information that bears the analogy, it therefore describes the situation one starts from. The pairs of situations {A', B'} is called the **theme** or the **target**: it is the result of the analogy, it contains the information that has been completed by analogy.

Analogical reasoning:

If we know A, B, c(A, B) and A' and if we are able to compute the similarities s(A, A') between A and A', then we know causality relations between A' and B', we can deduce similarities between B and B' and partially infer B'.

First example:

Let us consider again the first example of the previous section. Let us suppose that we only know A, B, c(A, B) and A':

A = Earth has an atmosphere of 1013 mb containing oxygen,

B = Earth is inhabited by humans,

A' = Mars has an atmosphere of 5mb containing oxygen,

c(A, B) = {oxygen ^-> inhabits, 1013mb ^-> humans}

We can compute similarities between A and A': they have both an atmosphere containing oxygen. We know that the oxygen of A is a 'cause' for life, we can apply this causality relation to B to infer that Mars is inhabited. So, we get:

B' = Mars is inhabited.

Second example:

Let us consider now the second example about the translation of expressions from French to English. Let us suppose that we only know A, B, c(A, B) and A':

A = une bicyclette rouge,

B = a red bike,

A' = des bicyclettes rouges,

We know some causality relations between A and B:

c_1: "in English, 'a' is an indefinite article",

c_2: "in English, an adjective, used as an attribute is placed before the noun",

c_3: "in English, an adjective is invariable",

c_4: "the word 'red' is the translation of the word 'rouge'",

c_5: "the word 'bike' is the translation of the word 'bicyclette'".

We can easily compute the similarity between $s(A, A')$: the two expressions A and A' have three common features: an indefinite article, a feminine noun and an adjective.

We are interested in the causality relations between A and B, the preconditions of which contain some of these common features. In our example, this last condition is satisfied by all the causality relations c_1, c_2, c_3, c_4 and c_5. We can apply these relations to A' and we can infer for B' that it is possible to use the indefinite article 'a', that the adjective 'red' is placed before the noun 'bike' and we get:

B' = a red bike.

This translation of A' is not correct and this example shows that the analogical reasoning can be correct and its result may not be valid.

Now, if we take into account the dissimilarities between A and A', we notice that the expression A is a singular one whereas the expression A' is a plural one. We can verify if the causality relations which use common features do not use discriminant features too and we can also search for new causality relations, based on these discriminant features. In our example, the causality relation c_1 is correct only for a singular expression and we need the causality relations c_6 and c_7 to infer correctly B'. This point is developed in the next section.

2. Analogy and dissimilarities

We have seen in the previous example the importance of the dissimilarities in the process of analogy.

We still suppose that we have a base {A, B} and a target {A', B'} but now we also take into account the dissimilarities between A and A' and between B and B'.

Let us denote sd(A, A') = $[s_A \mid d_A \longleftarrow d_{A'}]$ the similarity and dissimilarity relations between A and A'. Here, s_A represents the similarities between A and A' and '$d_A \longleftarrow d_{A'}$' means that d_A is an element of A and that it must be replaced by $d_{A'}$ to obtain the corresponding element of A', it therefore represents the dissimilarities between A and A'.

The diagram of the section 1.1. becomes:

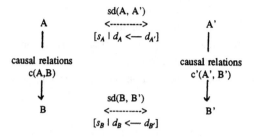

where:

- sd(A, A') is the similarity and dissimilarity relation between A and A', it is given by:
$$sd(A, A') = [s_A \mid d_A \longleftarrow d_{A'}],$$
- sd(B, B') is the similarity and dissimilarity relation between B and B', it is given by:
$$sd(B, B') = [s_B \mid d_B \longleftarrow d_{B'}]$$

Let us consider again the first example of the section 1.1.

A = Earth has an atmosphere of 1013 mb containing oxygen.
B = Earth is inhabited by humans.
A' = Mars has an atmosphere of 5mb containing oxygen.
B' = Mars is inhabited by humans.

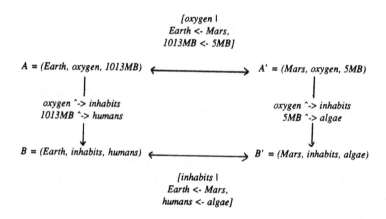

We can compute the similarity and dissimilarity relation between A and A': they both have an atmo-sphere containing oxygen but A is about Earth whereas A' is about Mars and the pressure of A is 1013mB whereas the pression of A' is 5mB:
sd(A, A') = [oxygen | Earth <- Mars, 1013mB <- 5mB]
We can also compute the similarity and dissimilarity relation between B and B':
sd(B, B') = [inhabits | Earth <- Mars, humans <- algae].

We have still causality relations which enable to infer B from A:
c(A, B) = {oxygen ^-> inhabits, 1013mB ^-> humans}.
We can notice that we have now two kinds of causality relations between A and B:

- the causality relations based on similarities between A and A', as for instance:

$$oxygen \text{ } \hat{} \text{-> } inhabits,$$

- the causality relations based on dissimilarities between A and A', as for instance:

$$1013mB \text{ } \hat{} \text{-> } humans.$$

This last kind of causality relations **should not be used** during an analogical reasoning to infer B' from A'.

We have also causality relations which enable to infer B' from A':
$$c'(A', B') = \{oxygen \text{ } \hat{} \text{-> } inhabits, 5mB \text{ } \hat{} \text{-> } algae\}.$$

Let us notice that we have also two kinds of causality relations between A' and B':
- the causality relations based on similarities between A and A', as for instance:

$$oxygen \text{ } \hat{} \text{-> } inhabits,$$

- the causality relations based on dissimilarities between A and A', as for instance:

$$5mB \text{ } \hat{} \text{-> } algae.$$

This last kind of causality relations **must be found** during an analogical reasoning to infer more correctly B' from B.

Analogical reasoning based on similarities and dissimilarities:

Let us now suppose that it is possible to find the following causality relations.

$$R1 \text{ between } s_A \text{ and } s_B,$$
$$R2 \text{ between } d_A \text{ and } d_B,$$
$$R3 \text{ between } d_{A'} \text{ and } d_{B'}.$$

We then suggest the following analogy paradigm:

Knowing A, B, A', s_A, d_A and $d_{A'}$ and being able to compute R1, R2 and R3 from some general knowledge, one is then able to infer s_B, d_B and $d_{B'}$, therefore to invent B', which is a new concept or a new rule, learned by analogy.

Let us consider the second example of the section 1.2. and let us suppose that we know A, B, A', sd(A, A') and the causality relations c_1, c_2, c_3, c_4, c_5, c_6 and c_7 and that we want to find the English translation of the expression A':
A = une bicyclette rouge,
B = a red bike,
A' = des bicyclettes rouges.

We can compute the similarity and dissimilarity relation between A and A': the two expressions A and A' are made of three words, named x, y and z, x being an indefinite article, y being a feminine noun and z being an adjective, but in A, the noun y is singular and in A' it is a plural one, it can be expressed by:
sd(A, A') = [(composed-by x y z) & (article x) & (indefinite x) & (noun y) & (feminine y) & (adjective z) | (singular y) <— (plural y)]
The causality relations between A and B are the same as in the section 1.2.:

c_1: "*in English, 'a' is an indefinite article*",

c_2: "*in English, an adjective, used as an attribute is placed before the noun*",

c_3: "*in English, an adjective is invariable*",

c_4: "*the word 'red' is the translation of the word 'rouge'*",

c_5: "*the word 'bike' is the translation of the word 'bicyclette'*".

We have the following diagram:

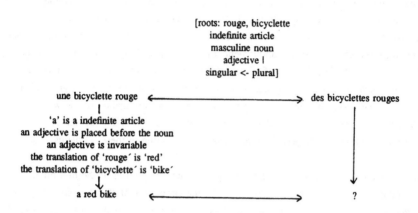

Moreover, we suppose that we know the following causality relations:

c_6: "*in English, there are no plural and indefinite article*",

c_7: "*the plural noun 'bikes' is obtained by adding an 's' to the translation of the word 'bicyclette'*".

We have two causality relations based on the notion of indefinite article: c_1 and c_6. To choose among them, we can notice that in the second one, c_6, we have the notion of "plural and indefinite article" and the property 'plural' is a difference between A and A'. We may wonder whether c_1 is still true for a plural and indefinite article. The article 'a' is not a plural and indefinite article. Therefore, we can only apply c_6.

We can use the other causality relations between A and B. We can also apply the causality relations c_7 based on the notion of 'plural'.

We can now infer the expression of B':
B' = red bikes.

In fact, in this example, we can infer the correct expression of B'. To take into account the differences between A and A' is not always sufficient to infer correctly B', but it leads to a better result than by using only the resemblances between A and A'.

Our definition contains the classical one which is restricted to the analogy between s_A and s_B. It also defines an analogy between the dissimilarities $[d_A \longleftarrow d_{A'}]$ and $[d_B \longleftarrow d_{B'}]$.

3. A simple application to incremental learning of concepts

3.1. Incremental learning

We are interested in the problem of learning incrementally a concept from some examples of this concept, because we have developed a system which learns a recognition function of a concept from a set of its examples but which is not incremental. This system is called OGUST, from the French: un Outil de Généralisation Utilisant Systématiquement les Théorèmes (Vrain 87) and it is based on the principle of Structural Matching (Kodratoff 83, 86). This system is not incremental: if we learn a new example after we have obtained a generalization, we are not able to improve our generalization to take into account the new example and we have to start again a generalization of the whole set of examples including the new one. Moreover, if we have a great number of examples, the combinatory problems are very important, and incremental learning may be a solution to these problems.

The representation of the examples and of the knowledge is based on a subset of the first order logic, containing only predicates of any arity and constants. All the properties of the domain are used in order to learn a generalization of a given set of examples. The justification that an example is really an instance of the obtained generalization may be very complicated and may use a number of theorems.

Given a concept C and a set of its examples, we can learn a recognition function of C by generalizing the examples. But, we can have two problems:
- the set of examples can be too large and we would like to generalize only a subset of these examples; then we have to test for each other examples if they are truly instances of the obtained generalization and otherwise, we have to modify the learned recognition function so that it covers the examples.
- we can get a new example of the concept C afterwards, and then we still have to check if it is an instance of the generalization and possibly have to modify the generalization.

These two problems can be summed up into the following one:

Definition of the problem to solve

We have learned by a process P, a generalization G of a set E of examples, $E = \{E_1, ..., E_p\}$, we get a new example E_{p+1} and we would like to find a generalization of $E_1, ..., E_p$ and E_{p+1}, without using the whole generalization process P on the new set of examples, $E \cup \{E_{p+1}\}$.

Therefore, we have:
- to check if E_{p+1} is an instance of G,
- otherwise to modify G so that E_{p+1} will be an instance of G.
A first means to solve this second point is to generalize G and E_{p+1}. We shall not discuss in this pa-

per the advantages and the drawbacks of this method. Our aim is just to show how analogy can provide us with a new means of solving some problems of the incrementality.

3.2. Analogy and incremental learning

Let us give two very simple examples in order to illustrate this point.

3.2.1. The use of analogy to test if an example is an instance of a generalization

First example:

Let us suppose that we have the two following examples:
E_1 = *(rectangle A) & (red A),*
E_2 = *(circle B) & (red B).*

A generalization of these two examples is:
G = *(convex x) & (red x).*
To get this generalization, we have used on the one hand, the property that a rectangle is a convex object and on the other hand, the property that a circle is a convex object.

We can say that G is more general than E_1 because of the relations:
$$\forall x, (rectangle \ x) \Rightarrow (convex \ x)$$
$$\forall x, (red \ x) \Rightarrow (red \ x).$$
In terms of causal reasonings, it means that we have causality relations between E_1 and G:
$c(E_1, G)$ = { *(rectangle A) ^-> (convex x), (red A) ^-> (red x)*}.
In the same way, we have causality relations between E_2 and G:
$c(E_2, G)$ = { *(circle B) ^-> (convex x), (red B) ^-> (red x)* }.

Now, let us suppose that we get a new example E_3:
E_3 = *(rhombus C) & (red C).*

We have first to check if E_3 is an instance of G. In order to do this, let us use an analogical process and let us try to find analogies between E_1 and E_3.

We can compute a similarity and dissimilarity relation between E_1 and E_3, since the two examples are composed of a single object, called 'A' in E_1 and 'C' in E_3, 'A' and 'C' are red in both examples but 'A' is a rectangle whereas 'C' is a rhombus.
$sd(E_1, E_3)$ = [*red | A <- C, rectangle <- rhombus*]

(We could also compute a similarity and dissimilarity relation between E_2 and E_3: $sd(E_2, E_3) = [$ red |
B <- C, circle <- rhombus], the choice of the best example among E_1, ..., E_p to which the new exam-
ple E_{p+1} should be compared is a very important and not trivial problem.)

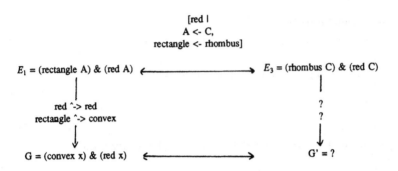

[red |
A <- C,
rectangle <- rhombus]

E_1 = (rectangle A) & (red A) ⟵————————⟶ E_3 = (rhombus C) & (red C)

red ^-> red
rectangle ^-> convex

?
?

G = (convex x) & (red x) ⟵————————⟶ G' = ?

To test if E_3 is an instance of G, we can consider the reasons why E_1 is an instance of G and see if
they are still available for E_3:

- E_1 is an instance of G, because 'A' is red and '(red A) ^-> (red x)'. The object 'C' in E_3 is also red
and if we substitute 'A' to 'C' in the previous causality relation, as suggested by the similarity and
dissimilarity relation between E_1 and E_3, we find (red C) ^-> (red x).
- E_1 is an instance of G, because 'A' is a rectangle and '(rectangle A) ^-> (convex x)'. The object 'C'
is not a rectangle but a rhombus. We see that the causality relation:

(rhombus C) ^-> (convex x)

obtained by substituting 'A' by 'C' and 'rectangle' by 'rhombus' in the previous causality relation is
available, due to the property that a rhombus is a convex object.

The example E_3 is an instance of G, because of the following causality relations:

(red C) ^-> (red x)
(rhombus C) ^-> (convex x).

In a general case, with this kind of representation, to check that a new example E_{p+1} is an instance of
G, we have to find which objects of G and of E_{p+1} have to be matched together. The use of analogy
helps us in this choice; let us suppose that we find analogies between E_{p+1} and an old example E_i, i ∈
{1, ..., p}, for each object O_{p+1}^t of E_{p+1}, we know the object O_i^t of E_i which is the most similar to O_{p+1}^t,
we know also the variable of G, called x, which corresponds to this object O_i^t and this variable x is
the variable of G which should also correspond to the object O_{p+1}^t of E_{p+1}.

In our previous example, this choice is trivial since we have only an object in each example and an
object in the generalization G. But, let us use this example to illustrate the last point. The similarity
and dissimilarity relation between E_1 and E_3 shows us that the corresponding element of 'A' in E_3 is
'C', in the generalization G, the variable 'x' corresponds to the constant 'A' of E_1, therefore it should
correspond to the constant 'C' of E_3.

3.2.2. The use of analogy to improve a generalization

Second example:

Let us suppose that we have the two following examples:
E_1 = *(rectangle A) & (red A),*
E_2 = *(rhombus B) & (red B).*

A generalization of these two examples is:
G = *(parallelogram x) & (red x).*
To get this generalization, we have used on the one hand, the property that a rectangle is a kind of parallelogram and on the other hand, the property that a rhombus is also a kind of parallelogram.

We can say that G is more general than E_1 because of the relations:
$$\forall x, (rectangle\ x) \Longrightarrow (parallelogram\ x)$$
$$\forall x, (red\ x) \Longrightarrow (red\ x).$$
In terms of causal reasonings, it means that we have causality relations between E_1 and G:
$c(E_1, G)$ = { *(rectangle A) ^-> (parallelogram x), (red A) ^-> (red x)*}.
In the same way, we have causality relations between E_2 and G:
$c(E_2, G)$ = { *(rhombus B) ^-> (parallelogram x), (red B) ^-> (red x)* }.

Now, let us suppose that we get a new example E_3:
E_3 = *(circle C) & (red C).*

We have first to check if E_3 is an instance of G. In order to do this, let us use an analogical process and let us try to find analogies between E_1 and E_3.

```
                              [red |
                               A <- C,
                           rectangle <- circle]

E₁ = (rectangle A) & (red A) ⟵————————————————⟶ E₃ = (circle C) & (red C)
            |                                            |
      red ^-> red                                        ?
rectangle ^-> parallelogram                              ?
            ↓                                            ↓
G = (parallelogram x) & (red x)  ⟵————————⟶        G' = ?
```

We can compute a similarity and dissimilarity relation between E_1 and E_3: the two examples are composed of a single object, called 'A' in E_1 and 'C' in E_3, 'A' and 'C' are red in both examples but 'A' is a rectangle whereas 'C' is a circle.
$sd(E_1, E_3)$ = [*red | A <- C, rectangle <- circle*]

To test if E_3 is an instance of G, we can consider the reasons why E_1 is an instance of G and see if they are still available for E_3:

- E_1 is an instance of G, because 'A' is red and '(red A) ^-> (red x)'. The object 'C' in E_3 is also red and if we substitute 'A' to 'C' in the previous causality relation, as suggested by the similarity and dissimilarity relation between E_1 and E_3, we find (red C) ^-> (red x).

- E_1 is an instance of G, because 'A' is a rectangle and '(rectangle A) ^-> (parallelogram x)'. The object 'C' is not a rectangle but a circle. We see that the causality relation:

$$(circle\ C)\ \hat{}\text{->}\ (parallelogram\ x)$$

obtained by substituting 'A' by 'C' and 'rectangle' by 'circle' in the previous causality relation is not available.

Therefore, the example E_3 is not an instance of G and we have to improve G in order to cover this new example.

We have located the problem, we know now that we have to find a common generalization of '(circle C)' and '(parallelogram x)'. If we know that in our domain that a parallelogram and a circle are convex objects, we get a generalization G' of E_1, E_2 and E_3:

G' = (convex x) & (red x).

The two examples given in this section 3.2.2. and in the previous section 3.2.1. are quite trivial but their aim is only to illustrate how we can use analogy to do incremental learning.

We see that Analogy enables to take into account the work which has already been done during the generalization process of E_1, ..., E_p and to locate the place where we have to improve the generalization and the way it must be done.

4. Conclusion

In this paper, we have shown the importance of dissimilarities in the process of Analogy. We are interested in the problem of incremental inductive learning by Analogy. There are still a lot of problems to solve and solving them will make precise the limits of this approach.

We see three main problems for this approach of incremental learning:

1. Given a new example, find those it must be compared to in order to draw the most useful analogies:

This problem includes several subproblems:

1.1. How to compute the similarity and dissimilarity relation between two examples?

1.2. How important is the choice of the example E_i, i∈ {1, ..., p}, to which E_{p+1} must be compared?, i.e. does the choice of E_i rather than E_j, j ∈ {1, ...,p}, j≠ i, influence the final genralization or is it only important to increase the efficiency of the process?

The answer to this problem depends on the kind of representation of the example, on the background knowledge and on the way the generalization is improved to cover the new example.

For instance, if the examples are represented by pairs (attribute, value) and if we only know taxonomies of generality between values, then the final generalization of the whole set of examples {E_1, ..., E_p} $\cup$ {E_{p+1}} does not depend on the choice of the example to which E_{p+1} is compared.

But, if the examples are expressed in first order logic and if we use also background knowledge expressed as theorems, as in the system OGUST (Vrain 87), then the result of the analogical process is strongly dependant on the choice of the example.

2. How to improve the generalization G to cover the new example?

It can still be decomposed into several subproblems:

2.1. How to use the causality relations between the example E_i to which is compared E_{p+1} and the generalization G of this example? Do we only use those based on the similarities between E_i and E_{p+1} or can the other causality relations (based on dissimilarities between E_i and E_{p+1}) guide us to find the "interesting" or "useful" background knowledge.

2.2. What is our aim: do we want to find the best generalization of E_1, ..., E_p, E_{p+1} or do we want only a generalization of these examples? In the first case, we must be more careful about the use of the analogical process.

3. When can we use an analogical process to do incremental learning? Can we find some criteria to determine when the obtained generalization will be too general?

Incremental inductive learning by Analogy is a very difficult problem which is far from being completely solved.

Bibliography

(Carbonell 82)
> Carbonell J.G.: " Experiential Learning in Analogical Problem Solving",
> *Proc. of the Second Meeting of the American Association for AI, Pittsburg, PA, 1982.*

(Chouraqui 82)
> Chouraqui E.: "Construction of a model for reasoning by analogy",
> *Proceedings of the European Conference on Artificial Intelligence, pp. 48-53, Orsay, France.*

(DeJong 86)
> DeJong G., Mooney R. "Explanation Based Learning: an Alternative View",
> *Machine Learning Journal, Volume 1, Number 2, 1986, pp 145-176.*

(Kodratoff 83)
> Kodratoff Y.: "Generalizing and Particularizing as the techniques of Learning",
> *Computers and Artificial Intelligence 2, pp.417-441, 1983.*

(Kodratoff 86)
> Kodratoff Y., Ganascia J.G.: "Improving the Generalization Step in Learning",
> *Machine Learning, an Artificial Intelligence Approach, vol. II, eds. Michalski R.S., Carbonell J.G., Mitchell T.M; Morgan Kaufmann Publishers, pp 215-244.*

(Michalski 83)
> Michalski R.S., "A theory and Methodology of Inductive Learning",
> *Machine Learning, an Artificial Intelligence Approach, Michalski R.S., Carbonell J.G., Mitchell T.M. eds, Tioga Publishing Company 1983, pp. 83-129.*

(Mitchell 86)
>Mitchell T.M., Keller R., Kedar-Cabelli S., "Explanation Based Generalisation: An Unifying View."
>*Machine Learning Journal, Volume 1, Number 1 , 1986, pp 47-80.*

(Vrain 87)
>Vrain C.: "Un Outil de Généralisation Utilisant Systématiquement les théorèmes: le système OGUST",
>*Thèse de troisième cycle soutenue le 25 Février 1987, Université Paris Sud, Orsay.*

Knowledge Base Refinement
Using Apprenticeship Learning Techniques

David C. Wilkins

Dept. of Computer Science
University of Illinois
Urbana, Illinois 61801 U.S.A.

Abstract

This paper describes how apprenticeship learning techniques can be used to refine the knowledge base of an expert system for heuristic classification problems. The described method is an alternative to the long-standing practice of creating such knowledge bases via induction from examples. The form of apprenticeship learning discussed in this paper is a form of learning by watching, in which learning occurs by completing failed explanations of human problem-solving actions. An apprenticeship is the most powerful method that human experts use to refine their expertise in knowledge-intensive domains such as medicine; this motivates giving such capabilities to an expert system. A major accomplishment in this work is showing how an explicit representation of the strategy knowledge to solve a general problem class, such as diagnosis, can provide a basis for learning the knowledge that is specific to a particular domain, such as medicine.

1 Introduction

Traditional methods for semi-automatic refinement of the knowledge base of an expert system for heuristic classification problems (Clancey, 1985) have centered around induction over a case library of examples. Well-known systems that demonstrate this approach include ID3 [Quinlan, 1983], INDUCE [Michalski, 1983], SEEK [Politakis and Weiss, 1984; Ginsberg et al., 1985], and RL [Fu and Buchanan, 1985]. Over the last five years, we have been investigating a different approach to knowledge base refinement, called apprenticeship learning. This paper provides an overview of how the ODYSSEUS apprenticeship program improves an expert system by watching an expert.[1]

In induction from examples, a training instance consists of an unordered set of feature-value pairs for an entire diagnostic session and the correct diagnosis. In contrast, a training instance in apprenticeship learning is a single feature-value pair given within the context of a problem-solving session. This training instance is hence more fine-grained, can exploit the information implicit in the order in which the diagnostician collects information, and allows obtaining many training instances from a single diagnostic session. Our apprenticeship learning program attempts

---

[1] ODYSSEUS can also improve an expert system by watching the expert system solve problems. This is another important form of apprenticeship learning, which is usually referred to as learning by doing, but is beyond the scope of this paper. The reader interested in further details is referred to (Wilkins, 1987).

to construct an explanation of each training instance; an explanation failure occurs if none is found. The apprenticeship program then conjectures and tests modifications to the knowledge base that allow an explanation to be constructed. If an acceptable modification is found, the knowledge base is altered accordingly. This is a form of learning by completing failed explanations.

Apprenticeship learning involves the construction of explanations, but is different from explanation based learning as formulated in EBG (Mitchell et al., 1986) and EBL (DeJong, 1986); it is also different from explanation based learning in LEAP (Mitchell et al., 1985), even though LEAP also focuses on the problem of improving a knowledge-based expert system. In EBG, EBL, and LEAP, the domain theory is capable of explaining a training instance and learning occurs by generalizing an explanation of the training instance. In contrast, in our apprenticeship research, a learning opportunity occurs when the domain theory, which is the domain knowledge base, is incapable of producing an explanation of a training instance. The domain theory is incomplete or erroneous, and all learning occurs by making an improvement to this domain theory.

2   Heracles Expert System Shell

ODYSSEUS is designed to improve any knowledge base crafted for HERACLES, an expert system shell that was created by removing the medical domain knowledge from the NEOMYCIN expert system (Clancey, 1984). HERACLES uses a problem-solving method called *heuristic classification*, which is the process of selecting a solution out of a pre-enumerated solution set, using heuristic techniques (Clancey, 1985). Our experiments used the NEOMYCIN medical knowledge base for diagnosis of neurological disorders. In a HERACLES-based system, there are three types of knowledge: domain knowledge, problem state knowledge, and strategy knowledge.[2]

Domain knowledge consists of Mycin-like rules and simple frame knowledge (Buchanan and Shortliffe, 1984). An example of rule knowledge is finding(photophobia, yes) ⟶ conclude(migraine-headache yes .5), meaning 'if the patient has photophobia, then conclude the patient has a migraine headache with a certainty factor of .5'. A typical example of frame knowledge is subsumed-by(viral-meningitis meningitis), meaning 'hypothesis viral meningitis is subsumed by the hypothesis meningitis'.

Problem state knowledge is knowledge generated while running the expert system. For example, rule-applied(rule163) says that Rule 163 has been applied during this consultation. Another example is differential(migraine-headache tension-headache), which says that the expert system's active hypotheses are migraine headache and tension headache.

Strategy knowledge is contained in the HERACLES shell. The strategy knowledge approximates a cognitive model of heuristic classification problem solving. The different problem-solving strategies that can be employed during problem solving are explicitly represented. This facilitates using the model to follow the the line-of-reasoning of a human problem solver. The strategy knowledge determines what domain knowledge is relevant at any given time, and what additional information is needed to solve a particular problem case.

The strategy knowledge needs to access the domain and problem state knowledge. To

---

[2]In this paper, the term *meta-level knowledge* refers to strategy knowledge; and the term *object-level knowledge* refers to domain and problem state knowledge.

achieve this, the domain and problem state knowledge is represented as tuples. Even rules are translated into tuples. For example, if Rule 160 is `finding(diplopia yes)` $\wedge$ `finding(aphasia yes)` $\longrightarrow$ `conclude(hemorrhage yes .5)`, it would be translated into the following four tuples: `evidence.for(diplopia hemorrhage rule160 .5)`, `evidence.for(aphasia hemorrhage rule160 .5)`, `antecedent(diplopia rule160)`, `antecedent(aphasia, rule160)`. Strategy metarules are quantified over the tuples. Figure 3 presents four strategy metarules in Horn clause form; the tuples in the body of the clause quantify over the domain and problem state knowledge. The rightmost metarule in Figure 3 encodes the strategy to find out about a symptom by finding out about a symptom that subsumes it. The metarule applies when the goal is to find out symptom P1, and there is a symptom P2 that is subsumed by P1, and P2 takes boolean values, and it is currently unknown, and P2 should be asked about instead of being derived from first principles. This is one of eight strategies in HERACLES for finding out the value of a symptom; this particular strategy of asking a more general question has the advantage of cognitive economy: a 'no' answer provides the answer to a potentially large number of questions, including the subsumed question.

3 Odysseus' Apprenticeship Learning Method

The solution approach of the ODYSSEUS apprenticeship program in a learning by watching scenario is illustrated in Figure 1. As Figure 1 shows, the learning process involves three distinct steps: detect knowledge base (KB) deficiency, suggest KB repair, and evaluate KB repair. This section defines the concept of an explanation and then describes the three learning steps.

The main observable problem-solving activity in a diagnostic session is finding out features-values of the artifact to be diagnosed; we refer to this activity as asking *findout questions*. An *explanation* in ODYSSEUS is a proof that demonstrates how an expert's findout question is a logical consequence of the current problem state, the domain and strategy knowledge, and one of the current high-level strategy goals. An explanation is created by backchaining the meta-level strategy metarules; Figure 3 provides examples of these metarules represented in Horn clause form. The backchaining starts with the findout metarule, and continues until a metarule is reached whose head represents a high-level problem-solving goal. To backchain a metarule requires unification of the body of the Horn clause with domain and problem state knowledge. Examples of high-level goals are to test a hypothesis, to differentiate between several plausible hypotheses, to ask a clarifying question, and to ask a general question.

The first stage of learning involves the detection of a knowledge base deficiency. An expert's problem solving is observed and explanations are constructed for each of the observed problem-solving actions. An example will be used to illustrate our description of the three stages of learning, based on the NEOMYCIN knowledge base for diagnosing neurology problems. The input to ODYSSEUS is the problem-solving behavior of a physician, John Sotos, as shown in Figure 2. In our terminology, Dr. Sotos asks findout questions and concludes with a final diagnosis. For each of his actions, ODYSSEUS generates one or more explanations of his behavior.

When ODYSSEUS observes the expert asking a findout question, such as asking if the patient has visual problems, it finds all explanations for this action. When none can be found, an explanation failure occurs. This failure suggests that there is a difference between the knowledge of

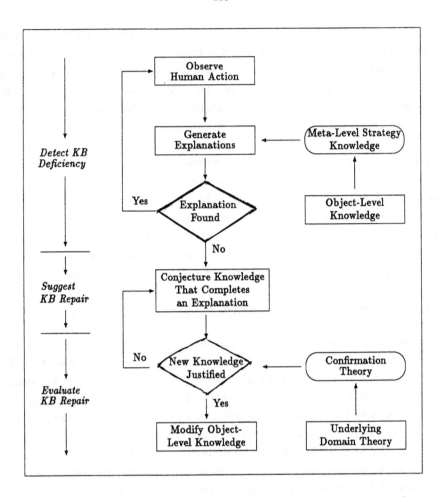

Figure 1: Overview of ODYSSEUS' method in a learning by watching apprentice situation. This paper describes techniques that permit automation of each of the three stages of learning shown on the left edge of the figure. An explanation is a proof that shows how the expert's action achieves a problem-solving goal.

the expert and the expert system and it provides a learning opportunity. The knowledge difference may lie in any of the three types of knowledge that we have described: strategy knowledge, domain knowledge, or problem state knowledge. Currently, ODYSSEUS assumes that the cause of the explanation failure is that the domain knowledge is deficient. In the current example, no explanation can be found for findout question number 7, asking about visual problems, and an explanation failure occurs.

The second step of apprenticeship learning is to conjecture a knowledge base repair. A confirmation theory (which will be described in the discussion of the third stage of learning) can judge whether an arbitrary tuple of domain knowledge is erroneous, independently from the other knowledge in the knowledge base. A preprocessing stage allows the problem of erroneous knowledge to be corrected before the three stages of apprenticeship learning commences. The preprocessing stage also removes unsuitable knowledge. Knowledge is unsuitable if it is correct in isolation, but does not interact well with other knowledge in the knowledge base due to sociopathic interactions

---

Patient's Complaint and Volunteered Information:
  1. Alice Ecila, a 41 year old black female.
  2. Chief complaint is a headache.
Physician's Data Requests:
  3. Headache duration?
     focus=tension headache. 7 days.
  4. Headache episodic?
     focus=tension headache. No.
  5. Headache severity?
     focus=tension headache. 4 on 0-4 scale.
  6. Visual problems?
     focus=subarachnoid hemorrhage. Yes.
  7. Double vision?
     focus=subarachnoid hemorrhage, tumor. Yes.
  8. Temperature?
     focus=infectious process. 98.7 Fahrenheit.
     ......
Physician's Final Diagnosis:
  25. Migraine Headache.

Figure 2: An example of what the ODYSSEUS apprentice learner sees. The data requests in this problem-solving protocol were made by John Sotos, M.D. The physician also provides information on the focus of the data requests. The answers to the data requests were obtained from an actual patient file from the Stanford University Hospital, extracted by Edward Herskovits, M.D.

(Wilkins and Buchanan, 1986). Hence, when a KB deficiency is detected during apprenticeship learning, we assume the problem is missing knowledge.

The search for the missing knowledge begins with the single fault assumption.[3] Conceptually, the missing knowledge could be eventually identified by adding a random domain knowledge tuple to the knowledge base and seeing whether an explanation of the expert's findout request can be constructed. How can a promising piece of such knowledge be effectively found? Our approach is to apply backward chaining to the findout question metarule, trying to construct a proof that explains why it was asked. When the proof fails, it is because a tuple of domain or problem state knowledge needed for the proof is not in the knowledge base. If the proof fails because of problem state knowledge, we look for a different proof of the findout question. If the proof fails because of a missing piece of domain knowledge, we temporarily add this tuple to the domain knowledge base. If the proof then goes through, the temporary piece of knowledge is our conjecture of how to refine the knowledge base.

Figure 3 illustrates the set of failed explanations that ODYSSEUS examines in connection with the unexplained action findout(visual problems) — the right most node of the graph.

---

[3]The missing knowledge is conceptually a single fault, but because of the way the knowledge is encoded, we can learn more than one tuple when we learn rule knowledge. For ease of presentation, this feature is not shown in the following examples.

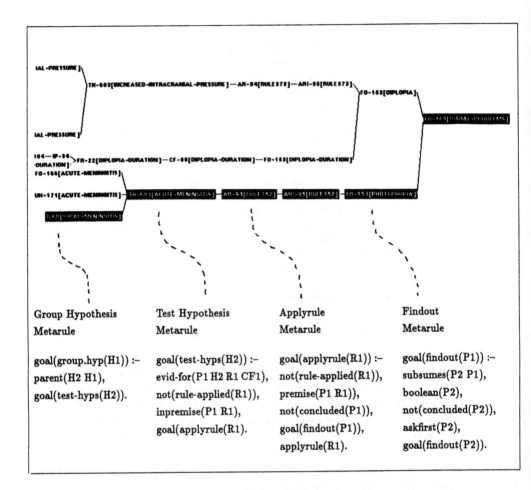

Figure 3: Learning by completing failed explanations. Each path in the graph is a failed explanation proof of attempts to connect a findout question about visual problems to a high-level problem solving goal; the nodes in the graph are metarules. The highlighted path is currently being examined during the second stage of learning, in which Odysseus tries to add knowledge to the domain knowledge base to complete the failed highlighted explanation. Four of the metarules in this highlighted path are illustrated in Horn clause form.

Each path in the graph is a potential explanation and each node in a path is a strategy metarule. The failed explanation that ODYSSEUS is examining is highlighted, and the associated metarules are shown below the graph. For a metarule to be used in a proof, its variables must be instantiated with domain or problem state tuples that are present in the knowledge base. In this example, the evidence.for tuple is responsible for the highlighted chain not forming a proof. It forms an acceptable proof if the tuple evidence.for(photophobia acute.meningitis $rule $cf) or evidence.for(diplopia acute.meningitis $rule $cf) is added to the knowledge base. During this step that generates repairs, neither the form of the left hand side of the rule (e.g., number of conjuncts) or the strength is known. In the step to evaluate repairs, the exact form of the rule is produced in the process of evaluation of the worth of the tuple.

The task of the third step of apprenticeship learning is to evaluate the proposed repair. To do this, we use a confirmation theory containing a decision procedure for each type of domain knowledge that tells us whether a given tuple is acceptable. There are different types of tuples in HERACLES' language. We only implemented a confirmation theory for three of the thirty-three different types of tuples in HERACLES's language: `evidence.for, clarifying.question, and ask.general.question` tuples.

`Evidence.for` tuples were generated in the visual problems example. In order to confirm the first candidate tuple, ODYSSEUS uses an induction system that generates and evaluates rules that have photophobia in their premise and acute meningitis in their conclusion. A rule is found that passes the rule 'goodness' measures, and is automatically added to the object-level knowledge base. All the tuples that are associated with the rule are also added to the knowledge base. This completes our example.

The confirmation theory also validates frame-like knowledge. An example of how this is accomplished will be described for clarify question tuples, such as `clarify.questions(head-ache-duration headache)`. This tuple means that if the physician discovers that the patient has a headache, she should always ask how long the headache has lasted. The confirmation theory must determine whether headache-duration is a good clarifying question for the 'headache' symptom. To achieve this, ODYSSEUS first checks to see if the question to be clarified is related to many hypotheses (the ODYSSEUS explanation generator allows it to determine this), and then tests whether the clarifying question can potentially eliminate a high percentage of these hypotheses. If these two criteria are met, then the clarify questions tuple is accepted.

4 Experimental Results

Our knowledge acquisition experiments centered on improving the knowledge base of the NEOMYCIN expert system for diagnosing neurology problems. The knowledge base of NEOMYCIN was constructed manually over a seven year period and had never been tested on a library of test cases. The NEOMYCIN vocabulary includes sixty diseases; our physician, Dr. John Sotos, determined that the existing data request vocabulary of 350 manifestations only allowed diagnosis of ten of these diseases. Another physician, Dr. Edward Herskovits, constructed a case library of 115 cases for these ten diseases from actual patient cases from the Stanford Medical Hospital, to be used for testing ODYSSEUS. The validation set consisted of 112 of these cases. The most recent version of NEOMYCIN, version 2.3, initially diagnosed 31% of these cases correctly.

For use as a training set, problem-solving protocols were collected of Dr. Sotos solving two cases, consisting of approximately thirty questions each.   ODYSSEUS discovered ten pieces of knowledge by watching these two cases being solved; eight of these were domain rule knowledge. These eight pieces of information were added to the NEOMYCIN knowledge base of 152 rules, along with two pieces of frame knowledge that classified two symptoms as 'general questions'; these are questions that should be asked of every patient.

The set of 112 cases was rerun, and NEOMYCIN solved 44% of the cases correctly, a 42%

Disease	Number Cases	True Positives	False Positives	False Negatives
Brain Abscess	7	0	0	7
Bacterial Meningitis	16	16	47	0
Viral Meningitis	11	4	5	7
Fungal Meningitis	8	0	0	8
TB Meningitis	4	1	0	3
Cluster Headache	10	0	0	10
Tension Headache	9	9	20	0
Migraine Headache	10	1	1	9
Brain Tumor	16	0	0	16
Subarachnoid Hemorrhage	21	4	0	17
None	0	0	4	0
Totals	112	35	77	77

Table 1: Performance of Neomycin before apprenticeship learning. There were 112 cases used in the validation set to test Neomcyin's performance. A misdiagnosis produces a false positive and a false negative.

improvement in performance. The performance of NEOMYCIN before and after learning is shown in Tables 1 and 2. All of this new knowledge was judged by Dr. Sotos as plausible medical knowledge, except for a domain rule linking aphasia to brain abscess. Importantly, the new knowledge was judged by our physicians to be of much higher quality than when straight induction was used to expand the knowledge base, without the use of explanation based learning.

The expected diagnostic performance that would be obtained by randomly guessing diagnoses is 10%, and the performance expected by always choosing the most common disease is 18%. NEOMYCIN initially diagnosed 31% of the cases correctly, which is 3.44 standard deviations better than always selecting the disease that is *a priori* the most likely. On a student-t test, this is significant at a t=.001 level of significance. Thus we can conclude that NEOMYCIN's initial diagnostic performance is significantly better than guessing.

After the apprenticeship learning session, NEOMYCIN correctly diagnosed 44% of the cases. Compared to NEOMYCIN's original performance, the performance of NEOMYCIN after improvement by ODYSSEUS is 2.86 standard deviations better. On a student-t test, this is significant for $t = .006$. One would expect the improved NEOMYCIN to perform better than the original NEOMYCIN in better than 99 out of 100 sample sets.

It is important to note that the improvement occurred despite the physician only diagnosing one of the two cases correctly. The physician correctly diagnosed a cluster headache case and misdiagnosed a bacterial meningitis case. As is evident from examining Tables 1 and 2, the improvement was over a wide range of cases. And the accuracy of diagnosing bacterial meningitis cases actually decreased. These counterintuitive results confirm our hypothesis that the power of our learning

Disease	Number Cases	True Positives	False Positives	False Negatives
Brain Abscess	7	1	2	6
Bacterial Meningitis	16	12	31	4
Viral Meningitis	11	4	5	7
Fungal Meningitis	8	0	1	8
TB Meningitis	4	1	0	3
Cluster Headache	10	6	0	4
Tension Headache	9	9	11	0
Migraine Headache	10	2	0	8
Brain Tumor	16	5	3	11
Subarachnoid Hemorrhage	21	9	1	12
None	0	0	9	0
Totals	112	49	63	63

Table 2: Performance of NEOMYCIN after apprenticeship learning. This shows the results of NEOMYCIN after a learning by watching session using ODYSSEUS that involved watching a physician solve two medical cases.

method derives from following the line of reasoning of a physician on individual findout questions, and is not sensitive to the final diagnosis as is the case when learning via induction from examples.

5   Conclusions

Apprenticeship is the most effective means for human problem solvers to learn domain-specific problem-solving knowledge in knowledge-intensive domains. This observation provides motivation to give apprenticeship learning abilities to knowledge-based expert systems. The paradigmatic example of an apprenticeship period is medical training. Our research investigated apprenticeship in a medical domain.

The described research illustrates how an explicit representation of the strategy knowledge for a general problem class, such as diagnosis, provides a basis for learning the domain-level knowledge that is specific to a particular domain, such as medicine, in an apprenticeship setting. Our approach uses a given body of strategy knowledge that is assumed to be complete and correct, and the goal is to learn domain-specific knowledge. This contrasts with learning programs such as LEX and LP where the domain-specific knowledge (e.g., integration formulas) is completely given at the start, and the goal is to learn strategy knowledge (e.g., preconditions of operators) [Mitchell, et al., 1983]. Two sources of power of the ODYSSEUS approach are the method of completing failed explanations and the use of a confirmation theory to evaluate domain-knowledge changes.

Our approach is also in contrast to the traditional induction from examples method of refining a knowledge base for an expert system for heuristic classification problems. With respect to learning certain types of heuristic rule knowledge, induction over examples plays a significant role in our work. In these cases, an apprenticeship approach can be viewed as a new method of biasing selection of which knowledge is learned by induction.

An apprenticeship learning approach, such as described in this paper, is perhaps the best possible bias for automatic creation of large 'use-independent' knowledge bases for expert systems. We desire to create knowledge bases that will support the multifaceted dimensions of expertise exhibited by some human experts, dimensions such as diagnosis, design, teaching, learning, explanation, and critiquing the behavior of another expert.

6 Acknowledgments

Many people have greatly contributed to the evolution of the ideas presented in this paper. I would especially like to thank Bruce Buchanan, Bill Clancey, Tom Dietterich, Haym Hirsh, John Holland, John Laird, Pat Langley, Bob Lindsay, John McDermott, Ryszard Michalski, Roy Rada, Tom Mitchell, Paul Rosenbloom, Ted Shortliffe, Paul Scott, Devika Subramanian, Marianne Winslett, the members of the Grail learning group, and the Guidon tutoring group. Marianne Winslett provided invaluable comments on draft versions of this paper. Larry Rendell also provided helpful comments. This work would have not been possible without the help of physicians Eddy Herskovits, Kurt Kapsner, and John Sotos. This research was principally supported by NSF grant MCS-83-12148, and ONR grants N00014-79C-0302 and N00014-88K0124.

References

Buchanan, B. G. and Shortliffe, E. H. (1984). *Rule-Based Expert Systems: The MYCIN Experiments of the Stanford Heuristic Programming Project.* Reading, Mass.: Addison-Wesley.

Clancey, W. J. (1984). NEOMYCIN: reconfiguring a rule-based system with application to teaching. In Clancey, W. J. and Shortliffe, E. H., editors, *Readings in Medical Artificial Intelligence*, chapter 15, pages 361–381, Reading, Mass.: Addison-Wesley.

Clancey, W. J. (1985). Heuristic classification. *Artificial Intelligence*, 27:289–350.

DeJong, G. (1986). An approach to learning from observation. In Michalski, R. S., Carbonell, J. G., and Mitchell, T. M., editors, *Machine Learning, Volume II*, chapter 19, pages 571–590, Los Altos: Morgan Kaufmann.

Fu, L. and Buchanan, B. G. (1985). *Inductive knowledge acquisition for rule based expert systems.* Knowledge Systems Laboratory Report KSL-85-42, Stanford University, Stanford, CA.

Ginsberg, A., Weiss, S., and Politakis, P. (1985). SEEK2: a generalized approach to automatic knowledge base refinement. In *Proceedings of the 1985 IJCAI*, pages 367–374, Los Angeles, CA.

Michalski, R. S. (1983). A theory and methodology of inductive inference. In Michalski, R. S., Carbonell, J. G., and Mitchell, T. M., editors, *Machine Learning: An Artificial Intelligence Approach*, chapter 4, pages 83–134, Palo Alto: Tioga Press.

Mitchell, T., Utgoff, P. E., and Banerji, R. S. (1983). Learning by experimentation: acquiring and refining problem-solving heuristics. In Michalski, T. M., Carbonell, J. G., and Mitchell, T. M., editors, *Machine Learning: An Artificial Intelligence Approach*, pages 163–190, Palo Alto: Tioga Press.

Mitchell, T. M., Keller, R. M., and Kedar-Cabelli, S. T. (1986). Explanation-based generalization: a unifying view. *Machine Learning*, 1(1):47–80.

Mitchell, T. M., Mahadevan, S., and Steinberg, L. I. (1985). LEAP: a learning apprentice for VLSI design. In *Proceedings of the 1985 IJCAI*, pages 573–580, Los Angeles, CA.

Politakis, P. and Weiss, S. M. (1984). Using empirical analysis to refine expert system knowledge bases. *Artificial Intelligence*, 22(1):23–48.

Quinlan, J. R. (1983). Learning efficient classification procedures and their application to chess end games. In Michalski, R. S., Carbonell, J. G., and Mitchell, T. M., editors, *Machine Learning*, chapter 15, pages 463–482, Palo Alto: Tioga Press.

Smith, R. G., Winston, H. A., Mitchell, T. M., and Buchanan, B. G. (1985). Representation and use of explicit justifications for knowledge base refinement. In *Proceedings of the 1985 IJCAI*, pages 673–680, Los Angeles, CA.

Wilkins, D. C. (1987). *Apprenticeship Learning Techniques For Knowledge Based Systems*. PhD thesis, University of Michigan. Also, Knowledge Systems Lab Report KSL-88-14, Dept. of Computer Science, Stanford University, 1988, 153pp.

Wilkins, D. C. and Buchanan, B. G. (1986). On debugging rule sets when reasoning under uncertainty. In *Proceedings of the 1986 National Conference on Artificial Intelligence*, pages 448–454, Philadelphia, PA.

Creating High Level Knowledge Structures
from Simple Elements

Michael Pazzani
UCLA Artificial Intelligence Laboratory
3531 Boelter Hall
Los Angeles, CA 90024
USA
pazzani@CS.UCLA.EDU

> *One of the most curious features of the history of economic sanctions has been the extent to which the experience of past cases has been overlooked or ignored.* [Renwick, pg. 1]

1. Introduction

Understanding the cause of an event enables the understander to explain, to predict, and perhaps to control the event. Therefore, learning causal relationships is a crucial task in understanding and mastering the environment. An additional benefit of learning causal relationships is that the future learning can be constrained by ignoring those possibilities that are inconsistent with existing causal knowledge.

I present a theory of learning to predict and explain the outcome of events. This theory is implemented in a computer program called OCCAM. OCCAM is able to learn to predict and explain possible outcomes in a variety of domains from simple physical causality (breaking glass and inflating balloons) to more complex events (kidnapping and economic sanctions). Two sources of information are utilized by OCCAM:
- Correlational information which reveals perceived regularities in events.
- Prior causal and intentional theories which explain regularities in events.

In machine learning, these sources of knowledge have been explored individually (similarity-based learning and explanation-based learning, respectively). I advocate the strategy of relying first on prior theories to attempt to explain and generalize events. When the current theories cannot produce an explanation, new causal or intentional theories are induced from correlational information. This strategy was influenced by a number of studies which indicate that for people prior causal knowledge is more influential than correlational information for attributing causality (see [26, 27]). This approach is illustrated in Figure 1-1.

The primary benefit of this approach is that the knowledge necessary to perform explanation-based learning can be acquired by the learning system. In OCCAM, explanation-based learning is preferred, but if there is not enough knowledge to produce an explanation, similarity-based techniques are used. For example, by similarity-based techniques OCCAM learns that parents have a goal of preserving the health of their children. This social knowledge provided an explanation for a parent paying the ransom in kidnapping, which enables OCCAM to create a kidnapping schema by explanation-based learning techniques. It is important to realize that OCCAM is much more than a switch which decides when to run

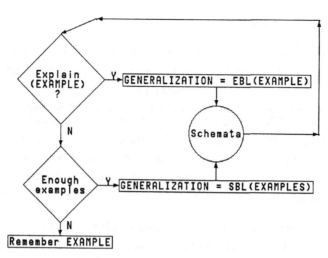

Figure 1-1: **Preferring explanation-based to similarity-based learning. Schemata are formed by similarity-based or explanation-based learning and serve as background knowledge for explanation-based learning.**

each type of learning program. The separate parts of OCCAM cooperate by utilizing the same memory to store the results of learning and to retrieve domain knowledge for explanation. Michalski calls this type of system "closed-loop" learning [20].

One issue that OCCAM addresses is the re-representation of complex input configurations into a high-level representation. These high-level representations can be decomposed back into more primitive elements when required for some processing. For example, the **coercion** schema can be constructed from primitive elements representing **asking, goal failure, goal conflict,** and **goal dominance.** The **coercion** schemata contains a number of roles (e.g., the actor and the target of the coercion) and a sequence of events (e.g., the demand, the threat, and the response). Some tasks, such as comparing the threat of two different episodes are best done in the high-level coerce representation. Other tasks, such as explaining why a particular threat was not effective are best done at the more primitive goal representation.

1.1. Background: Generalization-based Memory

In this section, I briefly review the concept of utilizing a hierarchy of schemata to represent the knowledge needed to infer, predict and explain.

It has long been claimed in artificial intelligence (e.g., [31, 7, 9, 3, 25]) and cognitive psychology (e.g., [4, 11, 1]) that when understanding a story, answering questions, or planning a course of action a memory structure commonly called a schema is accessed which aids in making predictions and inferences. Schemata represent previous experiences abstractly, removing irrelevant details. The type of schemata I consider in this paper are more properly called *explanatory schemata* because they provide explanations and predictions for outcome of events. Other types of schemata have also been proposed. For example, frames [21, 29, 5] can represent default information about objects (such as the color of elephants or typical organization of a room).

To be useful, an explanatory schemata must represent causal information which can assist the understander to make predictions and inferences. For example, consider the following kidnapping story:

Kidnapping-1

John Doe who was abducted on his way to school Monday morning was released today after his father left $50,000 in a trash can in a men's room at the bus station.

This short story leaves many things unstated. For example, it does not state why the father put money in a trash can nor why John Doe was abducted or released. However, a typical adult reading this story has no difficulty answering these questions. General knowledge about kidnapping including the motives of a kidnapper and the goals of a parent must be used to infer the missing information.

There is a dilemma concerning the level of generality of schemata that should be represented in memory. A very abstract representation will apply to many future events. However, a more specific representation will provide more detailed predictions and inferences to facilitate the understanding process.

Consider the complexity of the inferences a person would need to make to understand Kidnapping-1 if there were an abstract schema describing coercion instead of a kidnapping schema in memory. Neither Kidnapping-1 nor the coercion schema state that the kidnapper's goal is to possess money. Instead, the understander must infer this from other knowledge. For example, a person reading this story could infer that the kidnapper might threaten to harm John unless his father helps the kidnapper achieve his goal. From this, and the fact that John is not harmed after his father puts the money in the trash can, a reader might infer that the kidnapper's goal is achieved by retrieving the money from the trash can. Of course, when there is only a coercion schema the search for an explanation must explore alternative explanations such as the kidnapper wanted John Doe's father to throw out money.

In contrast, understanding Kidnapping-1 is much easier if a kidnapping schema has been learned. The task of explaining why the father puts money in a trash can is much easier: an understander can utilize an expectation from the kidnapping schema (that the father might pay a ransom to achieve his goal of preserving the health of his child) to interpret this otherwise unusual action. Similarly, identifying the kidnapper's goal is trivial since the goal of obtaining money is part of the kidnapping schema. The advantage that a kidnapping schema has over the coercion schema for understanding this story is that explanation is already associated with the kidnapping schema. In contrast, even if Kidnapping-1 is recognized as an instance of coercion, the explanation for the kidnapper's actions must be constructed from different information.

Although understanding kidnapping stories is much easier with a kidnapping schema, it is still possible to understand stories about kidnapping with a coercion schema. The coercion schema provides very general predictions while the kidnapping schema provides more specialized predictions. For example, the coercion schema indicates that the threat could be any action; the kidnapping schema indicates that the threat will be to harm a relative of the person threatened. Kidnapping is called a *specialization* of coercion. There is an important advantage a general schema has over a more specific schema: A general schema is applicable in a wider variety of situations. Consider, the following situations:

General-Hospital-1

Leo, the tall dark masseur at the Avalon heath Spa, secretly filmed Amanda, a wealthy middle aged woman, while he seduced her. Then, he told Amanda that unless she paid him $10,000, he would show her husband the pictures of her being unfaithful.

Economic-Sanction-1

In 1983, Australia refused to sell uranium to France, unless France ceased nuclear testing in the South Pacific. France paid a higher price to buy uranium from South Africa.

Playground-1

John told the other kids at the playground that if they didn't let him pitch, he was going to take his ball and go home.

All of these examples can be understood as instances of coercion. The specialized kidnapping schema would be of little use for inferring the goals and plans of the participants of these examples. In fact, the kidnapping schema may provide the wrong inferences in many cases. For example, in kidnapping the anonymity of the kidnapper is important while in blackmail (e.g., General-Hospital-1) it is not essential that the identity of the blackmailer be unknown to the victim. The more general coercion schema contains no information about the anonymity of the perpetrator. However, the coercion schema still provides a general framework for understanding General-Hospital-1. Of course, this story would be easier to understand if a specialization of the coercion schema for blackmail had been formed. Similarly, Economic-Sanction-1 would be easier to understand if there were a schema for economic sanctions. Very general schema such as coercion provide the opportunity for learning across domains. If the coercion schema were learned from kidnapping stories, it could be used to understand blackmail stories. Of course, in small children, it is more likely that they learn about coercion from arguments with their parents and other children (e.g., Playground-1) and then later specialize it for kidnapping and blackmail.

The solution to the dilemma is to have both abstract and more specialized schemata in a memory [16, 18]. A schema can be specialized by further specifying any of its features. A specialized schema is indexed in memory under a more general one by the features which elaborate on the more general schema. Such a memory organization allows memory to be traversed so that the most specific schema which applies to a situation can be easily found and recognized. Once found the schema can aid the processes of inference, prediction, and explanation.

In OCCAM, a schema includes a generalized event representation and an optional sequence of events. The sequence of events is a network of more primitive goals, plans or events connected by temporal, causal, or intentional links [9]. These links include the following:

- RESULT- a physical event can result in a state.
- ENABLE- a state can enable a physical event to occur.
- ACHIEVES- an event can result in the satisfaction of a goal.
- THWARTS- an event can cause the failure of a goal.

- MOTIVATES- an event can cause the creation of a goal.
- REALIZED- a plan can be realized by an event.
- INTENDS- a plan can be a means for accomplishing a goal.

In the remainder of this paper, I discuss the similarity-based and explanation-based learning mechanisms in OCCAM. These mechanisms produce schema consisting of a generalized event and a sequence of events. Finally, I demonstrate how the knowledge acquired supports answering question about the outcome of economic sanctions incidents.

2. Similarity-based learning in OCCAM

The first step in the similarity-based learning is to detect a regularity between the outcome of a new event and the outcome of previously encountered similar events. OCCAM aggregates events into clusters which have similar plans (see [28] for details). Once a set of events has been identified as a useful cluster, the second step is to construct a general description of the class of events. OCCAM takes a conservative approach to constructing this general description. The most specific description which is consistent with the examples is selected. If the general description of a cluster of events is sufficiently complex, OCCAM will change the representation to facilitate future matching and specialization.

The conservative generalization strategy acknowledges that the initial concept description is bound to be wrong. By initially choosing the most specific consistent description, the revision process is simplified considerably. The only type of revision necessary is to delete parts of the concept description which do not describe later examples. Finally, when adding a new event to memory, the impact of this new data must be accessed. If the new event confirms a prediction of an existing schema, the support for that schema is increased. On the other hand, if the event contradicts a prediction of an existing schema, the support for that schema is decreased. The idea here is that the confirmation process should be able to tolerate some noise in the data. For example, when a glass is dropped from about the height of a kitchen table onto a tile floor, it typically breaks. Although there are exceptions to this rule, it is true often enough that most parents do not give small child glass dinnerware.

An example will help to make this process a little more concrete. Assume that the new event describes the situation where Lynn wants some Play Doh so she asks her father Mike to give her some, and her goal succeeds. The Conceptual Dependency (CD) [31] representation of this event is in Figure 2-1. For the remainder of this example, I will refer to this event as play-doh-1. Rather than repeating all of the features of Lynn, Mike, and the Play Doh in the representation of play-doh-1 in this figure, a shorthand notation is used. The first time each concept is listed a unique-id is given as one of the features. The remaining times that the same concept appears, the only feature listed is the unique-id. In addition to the representation of this goal and its resolution, OCCAM is also given representations of subordinate goals and actions which are related to the main goal by intentional links. Figure 2-2 shows the network of the related concepts. To conserve space, the action, plans, and goals are given in English rather than CD.

In this example, assume that the following events are in OCCAM's memory when play-doh-1 is

```
GOAL actor HUMAN name LYNN
                 age KID
                 hair BLOND
                 eyes BLUE
                 unique-id lynn
      goal STATE type POSS-BY
                 actor HUMAN unique-id lynn
                 value YES
                 object P-OBJ type TOY
                             stype PLAY-DOH
                             unique-id play-doh.1
      plan ACT type MTRANS
                 actor HUMAN unique-id lynn
                 to HUMAN name MIKE
                          relation IPT type FAMILY-REL
                                       stype FATHER
                                       of HUMAN unique-id lynn
                          age GROWN-UP
                          hair BROWN
                          eyes GREEN
                          unique-id mike
                 object ACT type ATRANS
                          actor HUMAN unique-id mike
                          object P-OBJ unique-id play-doh.1
                          to HUMAN unique-id lynn
      outcome GOAL-OUTCOME type SUCCESS
                          actor HUMAN unique-id lynn
                          goal STATE type POSS-BY
                                       actor HUMAN unique-id lynn
                                       value YES
                                       object P-OBJ unique-id play-doh.1
```

Figure 2-1: `play-doh-1` **Lynn wants some Play Doh. She asks Mike to give her some, and her goal succeeds.**

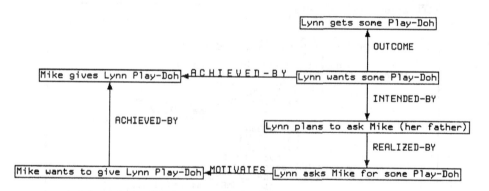

Figure 2-2: The relationship between `play-doh-1` (i.e., Lynn wants some Play-Doh) and other actions, plans, and goals is represented by intentional links.

encountered:

1. `zoo-1`: Karen wants to go to the zoo. She asks Mike to take her to the zoo. Her goal succeeds.

2. `refrigerator-1`: Karen wants to open the refrigerator. She pulls on the door, but it doesn't open.

3. `pizza-1`: Karen has a goal of possessing a slice of pizza. Her plan is to ask Mike for a slice of pizza. Her goal succeeds.

These examples are stored in memory, indexed under the `goal` schema. The aggregation process identifies `pizza-1`, `zoo-1`, and `play-doh-1` as a useful cluster for generalization with similarity-based learning. The strategy for similarity-based learning in OCCAM is to find all features which a cluster of events have in common. This is similar to the wholist strategy proposed by Bruner [6]. The primary difference is that Bruner's strategy is entirely incremental. It assumes the general description to be learned is initially the first positive example, and removes features from the general description which are not present in new positive examples. In contrast, the strategy implemented in OCCAM waits until a small number of examples are encountered and the general description is all features which these examples have in common. The reason for the difference is that OCCAM does not have a teacher to categorize examples for it. Rather, it waits until several events share a number of features, determines that these events should form a cluster and creates a new schema by generalizing the events. The idea here is that a few initial events are formed into a new schema which will be further refined as more events are added to memory.

In the current example, the aggregation process has found a cluster of events (**zoo-1 play-doh-1** and **pizza-1**) to be generalized. Figure 2-3 illustrates the result of finding all common features of these events. This generalization indicates that when a child with blue eyes and blond hair wants something and asks her father Mike who has brown hair and green eyes, the child's goal will succeed. Obviously, this generalization is not accurate, but it is a reasonable starting point. This generalization is refined by removing information such as the hair and eye color of the people involved that does not apply in future cases.

```
GOAL actor HUMAN age KID
                hair BLOND
                eyes BLUE
                unique-id p.1
        goal STATE actor HUMAN unique-id p.1
                value YES
                object P-OBJ unique-id obj.1
        plan ACT type MTRANS
                actor HUMAN unique-id p.1
                to HUMAN name MIKE
                        relation IPT type FAMILY-REL
                                stype FATHER
                                of HUMAN unique-id p.1
                        age GROWN-UP
                        hair BROWN
                        eyes GREEN
                        unique-id p.2
                object ACT actor HUMAN unique-id p.2
        outcome GOAL-OUTCOME type SUCCESS
                actor HUMAN unique-id p.1
                goal STATE actor HUMAN unique-id p.1
                        value YES
                        object P-OBJ unique-id obj.1
```

Figure 2-3: **A generalized event formed by finding all the features in common between zoo-1, play-doh-1 and pizza-1.**

In addition to extracting the common features of the main concepts, the common features of the concepts related to the main concept by identical intentional links are also found. It is in this manner, that not only is a goal generalized, but also the means of accomplishing that goal. If there are a number of related concepts[1] connected by intentional links, then a **macro-schema** is created. In OCCAM, there are two types of schemata: simple schemata and macro-schema.

---

[1]This is a parameter in OCCAM. Its value in the current version of OCCAM is four.

A simple schema contains a generalized event which may be connected by means of intentional links to a small number of other generalized events. In addition, a simple schema also contains indices to other events and other schemata, as well as support information which indicates how the schema was created and how accurate the predictions of the schema have been.

A macro-schema is high-level knowledge structure which can be thought of as a shorthand notation for a useful network of concepts. The idea here is that instead of reasoning at the level of goals (e.g., obtaining an object), and actions (e.g., asking for an object), it is possible to reason at a higher level, treating the interactions between goals and actions as a single unit. In addition to the components of a simple schema, a macro-schema contains a <u>sequence of events</u>. When constructing a macro-schema the sequence of events is constructed from the network of generalized events connected by intentional links. The generalized event for a macro-schema summarizes the objects which play a role in the sequence of events.

The macro-schema serves as much more than a notational shortcut. There are a number of reasons for creating chunks of higher level knowledge:

- Storage economy- Typically, there will be a sequence of events in a schema involving a number of different actors and objects. However, often the actors or objects of several different actions will be the same. By creating a macro-schema, the attributes of these entities need to be represented only once as attributes of the roles of the schemata.

- Ease of memory indexing- New examples are indexed under the high level knowledge structure in memory rather than recording them with the primitive components. This facilitates easier recall and recognition of known schemata.

The macro-schema in OCCAM at first may appear to be similar to the mega-concepts which Swartout advises against [32]. After all, there is really no difference between a concept called KIDNAP and a hyphenated concept such as THREATEN-TO-KILL-A-CHILD-SO-PARENT-MEETS-DEMAND. The fact "kidnap" is an English word does not make a concept any more or less complex. The primary difference between a macro-schema and a mega-concept is that a macro-schema can be decomposed into simpler units.

2.1. Creating a Macro-schema- an example

The creation of a macro-schema is a relatively straightforward process. I will illustrate the process by continuing the example of the previous section. In this example, the events zoo-1, pizza-1, and play-doh-1 have been identified as a useful set to generalize. The following steps are followed to create a macro-schema:

1. A new simple schema is constructed. The generalized event of this schema is formed from the features common to the main concept of all the instances. The simple schema is integrated into memory under the goal schema which was the most specific schema in memory for play-doh-1.

   The impact of creating the new specialized goal schema on the organization of memory is shown in Figure 2-4. The event refrigerator-1 and the specialized goal schema are indexed under goal. The events zoo-1, play-doh-1 and pizza-1 are indexed under the new schema. This organization allows the new schema to be located as the most specific schema when appropriate during future memory searches. In addition, the events indexed under the new schema can be found to specialize this schema even further.

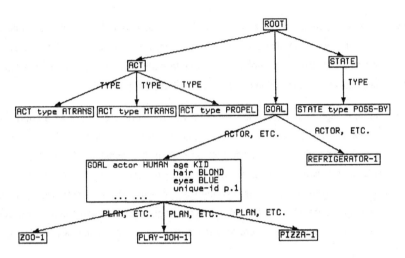

Figure 2-4: A picture of OCCAM's memory after the goal schema is specialized by extracting the common features of zoo-1, play-doh-1 and pizza-1.

2. The intentional links of the main goal concept of each example are traversed. When all examples have the same intentional link, a generalized event is constructed from the related concepts. For example, the goal of **pizza-1** is achieved by Mike giving Karen pizza, the goal of **zoo-1** is achieved by Mike taking Karen to the zoo, and the goal of **play-doh-1** is achieved by Mike giving Lynn some Play-Doh. The generalized event contains the common features of all of these actions (i.e., Mike doing something). The process of finding the common features continues recursively until all intentional links in common have been traversed. A network of generalized events is created. The result of this process for the current example is shown in Figure 2-5.

3. A generalized event is created for the macro-schema. This is constructed by finding objects which play a role in the description of more than one of the events in the network of generalized events. These objects may be thought of as the roles of the schema. A unique name is given to each of the roles. In this example, there are three objects which are repeated. The actor of the main goal concept is called the **the-actor**. The actor of the action which achieves the goal is called the **the-helper** and the object of the goal state is called the **the-obj**[2]. In addition, a unique name is selected for each of events in the network of generalized events. These events may be thought of as the scenes of the schema. In the current example, the main concept is called the **the-goal**, the action which achieves the goal is called the **the-sub-act**. A unique name is also generated for the generalized event of the macro-schema. In the current example, the macro-schema is called **DELTA-AGENCY**. The names of roles and the scenes become the feature names of the generalized event. The values of these features are constructed by replacing any occurrence of a role or a scene by a role token which represents that role. For example, instead of the actor of the **the-sub-act** being a human named Mike with brown hair, the actor of the **the-sub-act** is the **the-helper**. It is in this manner that the creation of a macro-schema results in economical storage, since the attributes of the roles need not be repeated. Furthermore, it facilitates finding similarities among the scenes to specialize the macro-schema. Rather than noticing say a person with brown hair doing a particular action under certain circumstances for a person with blond hair, OCCAM can notice when the **the-helper** does something for the **the-actor**. Figure 2-6 illustrates the generalized event for the macro-schema of the current example.   The notation **=THE-ACTOR** indicates a role token for the **the-actor**.

4. The next two steps are performed to create the sequence of events. The general idea is

---

[2]OCCAM operates in two modes. In unattended mode, OCCAM generates names for these roles (e.g., **ROLE-17**). In interactive mode, it asks the user to provide a meaningful name for the roles.

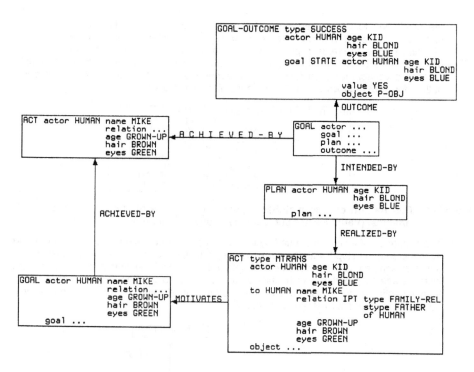

Figure 2-5: The result of finding the common features of concepts related to the main concept of `zoo-1`, `refrigerator-1` and `pizza-1`.

```
DELTA-AGENCY the-outcome GOAL-OUTCOME type SUCCESS
                                       actor =THE-ACTOR
                                       goal STATE actor =THE-ACTOR
                                                  value YES
                                                  object =THE-OBJ
             the-sub-goal GOAL actor =THE-HELPER
                               goal ACT actor =THE-HELPER
             the-plan PLAN actor =THE-ACTOR
                           plan =THE-MTRANS
             the-sub-act ACT actor =THE-HELPER
             the-goal GOAL actor =THE-ACTOR
                           goal STATE actor =THE-ACTOR
                                      value YES
                                      object =THE-OBJ
                           plan =THE-MTRANS
                           outcome GOAL-OUTCOME type SUCCESS
                                                actor =THE-ACTOR
                                                goal STATE actor =THE-ACTOR
                                                           value YES
                                                           object =THE-OBJ
             the-mtrans ACT type MTRANS
                            actor =THE-ACTOR
                            to =THE-HELPER
                            object ACT actor =THE-HELPER
             the-helper HUMAN name MIKE
                              relation IPT type FAMILY-REL
                                           stype FATHER
                                           of =THE-ACTOR
                              age GROWN-UP
                              hair BROWN
                              eyes GREEN
             the-actor HUMAN age KID
                             hair BLOND
                             eyes BLUE
             the-obj P-OBJ
```

Figure 2-6: The generalized event of a macro-schema. DELTA-AGENCY represents a plan for achieving a goal by asking someone to perform an action which achieves the goal.

that some reasoning can be done by treating the macro-schema as a black box. Typically, the macro-schema can predict what may occur. Other reasoning tasks require

268

the black box to be opened up. The macro-schema can be decomposed into the sequence of events. The sequence of events indicates why a prediction can be made. The first step is to create a pattern which can be matched against an instance of the macro-schema binding variables to the roles and scenes. This is accomplished by simply creating a variable for each feature of the generalized event. Figure 2-7 illustrates the pattern for **DELTA-AGENCY**. In this figure variables are preceded by a question mark.

```
DELTA-AGENCY the-goal ?V-17163
             the-mtrans ?THE-MTRANS
             the-helper ?THE-HELPER
             the-actor ?THE-ACTOR
             the-obj ?THE-OBJ
             the-sub-act ?THE-SUB-ACT
             the-plan ?THE-PLAN
             the-sub-goal ?THE-SUB-GOAL
             the-outcome ?THE-OUTCOME
```

Figure 2-7: **This pattern can be matched against an instance of** **DELTA-AGENCY** **binding the variables. (Variables are preceded by a question mark.)**

5. The sequence of events is created by replacing each event in the network of generalized events created in step 2 with the corresponding variable created in step 4. An instance of a macro-schema can be decomposed into more primitive elements by matching the instance against a pattern which binds a number of variables. The sequence of events is then instantiated by replacing each variable by its bound value. The sequence of events for **DELTA-AGENCY** is illustrated in Figure 2-8.

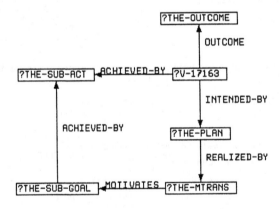

Figure 2-8: **The sequence of events for** **DELTA-AGENCY.**

6. The final step is necessary to recognize new examples as instances of a macro-schema. What is needed is a means of transforming one representation into another. For example, **DELTA-AGENCY** is a particular configuration which represents the interaction between a goal and a means of accomplishing that goal (i.e., by asking). When a new example has the same configuration of goals, plans, and actions, it is recognized as example of **DELTA-AGENCY** and the representation is changed. This representation change is accomplished by matching the instance against a pattern in the old representation and instantiating a pattern in the new representation. The generalized event of the simple schema created in step 1 serves as a template for the old representation and the generalized event of the macro-schema serves as a template for the new representation. Two patterns are created by replacing the corresponding components in the two representations by variables. Figure 2-9 illustrates the pattern in the original goal representation for **DELTA-AGENCY** and Figure 2-10 displays the pattern for the new representation. When a variable is followed by a CD structure in these figures (e.g., **?THE-MTRANS**) it indicates that the binding of the variable is permitted only if the corresponding component of the example matches the CD structure (which may bind other variables). These two patterns are called representational transfers and are associated with the simple schema. The macro-schema is indexed from the root of

memory (see Figure 2-11).

```
?V-17163 GOAL actor ?THE-ACTOR
             goal STATE actor ?THE-ACTOR
                        value YES
                        object ?THE-OBJ
             plan ?THE-MTRANS ACT type MTRANS
                             actor ?THE-ACTOR
                             to ?THE-HELPER
                             object ACT actor ?THE-HELPER
             outcome GOAL-OUTCOME type SUCCESS
                             actor ?THE-ACTOR
                             goal STATE actor ?THE-ACTOR
                                        value YES
                                        object ?THE-OBJ
```

Figure 2-9: The pattern for recognizing a particular configuration of goals and plans as an instance of DELTA-AGENCY.

```
DELTA-AGENCY the-outcome GOAL-OUTCOME type SUCCESS
                             actor ?THE-ACTOR
                             goal STATE actor ?THE-ACTOR
                                        value YES
                                        object ?THE-OBJ
             the-sub-goal GOAL actor ?THE-HELPER
                               goal ACT actor ?THE-HELPER
             the-plan PLAN actor ?THE-ACTOR
                           plan ?THE-MTRANS
             the-sub-act ACT actor ?THE-HELPER
             the-goal ?V-17163 GOAL actor ?THE-ACTOR
                                goal STATE actor ?THE-ACTOR
                                           value YES
                                           object ?THE-OBJ
                                plan ?THE-MTRANS
                                outcome GOAL-OUTCOME type SUCCESS
                                           actor ?THE-ACTOR
                                           goal STATE actor ?THE-ACTOR
                                                      value YES
                                                      object ?THE-OBJ
             the-mtrans ?THE-MTRANS
             the-helper ?THE-HELPER
             the-actor ?THE-ACTOR
             the-obj ?THE-OBJ
```

Figure 2-10: The pattern for creating an instance of DELTA-AGENCY once a configuration of goals and plans has been recognized as an instance of DELTA-AGENCY.

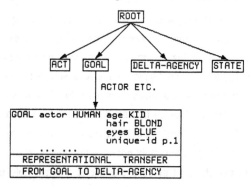

Figure 2-11: The location of the DELTA-AGENCY schema in memory. The simple schema indexed under goal contains a representational transfer pattern which recognizes DELTA-AGENCY.

This algorithm creates a macro-schema and a means of recognizing new events as instances of the macro-schema. When searching memory for the most specific schema which accounts for a new episode, if a simple schema is encountered which has representational transfers, then the representation of the new episode is transformed to the higher-level representation. This is accomplished by determining that the schema and the new episode have the same structure of intentional links and then matching the new episode against the pattern in the old representation. The pattern in the new representation is then instantiated and the role tokens are inserted in the resulting new representation (as in step 3). Further memory search, as well as indexing and specialization is done in the high-level representation.

2.2. Refining schemata created by similarity-based learning.

There is a serious problem with making generalizations by comparing the similarities and differences of a number of examples. The problem is even more severe if, as in OCCAM, the set of examples is small. The problem is that some of the generalizations are bound to be incorrect. Apparent regularities may, in fact, turn out to be mere coincidences. OCCAM contains a mechanism to deal with this problem. Although generalizations are not required to be 100% accurate, it is desirable that they make correct predictions often enough to be useful. Therefore, it is important to evaluate a generalization when more data is available. OCCAM's revision strategy is similar to the one implemented in UNIMEM [19].

When a sufficient number of examples contradict a feature predicted by a generalization, then the generalized event is modified. In UNIMEM, the generalized event is modified by deleting the feature entirely. This makes sense in UNIMEM because the feature values are atomic. In contrast, in OCCAM the feature values can be composite objects which have their own features. Instead of deleting an erroneously predicted feature, the feature is generalized by retaining those features which the predicted feature and the corresponding feature in a new example have in common. For example, the predicted feature value may be "a parent with brown hair" and the new example may have the feature value "a sister with blond hair". Therefore, the feature would be revised to "a relative".

After a number of examples, both the simple schema and **DELTA-AGENCY** are revised to eliminate feature values which are too specific. As more examples are encountered, the **DELTA-AGENCY** schema becomes more accurate. It finally contains only the restriction that the helper must be related to the the actor. This reflects the fact that a small child typically interacts with family members. Of course, there are many instances when a member of one's family does not help to achieve a goal. In [28], I show how OCCAM deals with these. OCCAM first tries to find an explanation for why a prediction does not hold before refining a schema in the manner outlined in this section. There are many reasons that a parent might not give a child something: the parent might not have the desired object, or the parent might think the desired object will harm the child. If these explanations are available then these contradictions should not be treated as noise in the data. Rather, there is much that can be learned from these counterexamples.

2.3. Learning about coercion

OCCAM's primary domain is economic sanctions. OCCAM acquires a coercion schema by similarity-based learning which is then specialized with explanation-based learning in these domains. The process that OCCAM goes through to learn about coercion is identical to the process that OCCAM goes through to learn **delta-agency**. The only differences are the complexity of the domain and the variety of the examples. The **coerce** domain is more complex than **delta-agency** because more goals and participants are involved. For example, **apple-1** is an instance of **delta-agency** while **broccoli-1** is an instance of **coerce**.

- **apple-1**: Karen wants an apple. She asks her mother Chris for one and Chris gives her one.

- **broccoli-1**: Chris wants Karen to eat her broccoli. Chris tells Karen that if Karen eats her broccoli, then Chris will let Karen have some soda to drink. Otherwise, Chris will give Karen water. Karen has a goal conflict between avoiding a food she doesn't like and not eating a food she does like. Karen decides to eat her broccoli and Chris gives Karen some soda.

I choose to describe the similarity-based learning and the creation of a macro-schema with **delta-agency** for two reasons. First, it is less complex so that figures of the intermediate stages are not cluttered with too many details to fit on a page. Second, it provides support for my claim that the learning mechanisms in OCCAM are general since they have been successfully applied in several domains.

The second difference between learning **delta-agency** and learning **coerce** is the greater variety of the **coerce** examples. In **delta-agency**, all of the initial examples were examples of goal success. Some of the **coerce** examples illustrate failures as well as successes. For example, one example presented to OCCAM is the following event:

- **ball-1**: Mat and Sam are playing football. Mat tells Sam that if he doesn't allow Sam to kick the ball, Sam will take his ball and go home. Mat decides that he does not want to play with Sam, and that he will go buy a frisbee. Mat goes to the store, but finds that he does not have enough money to buy a frisbee. Both Sam's and Mat's goals fail.

The greater variety of examples results in a more general **coerce** schema which does not predict the outcome of a coercion incident. Instead, specializations allow the outcome to be predicted. The final version of the coercion schema is illustrated in Figure 2-12.

The coerce schema contains a number of different roles:

- **the-actor**: the person who has a goal and who plans to make a threat to achieve the goal.
- **the-bene**: the person who benefits if the goal of the actor is achieved. Typically, this is the actor, however in **broccoli-1**, it is Karen who benefits since Chris has a goal of making sure Karen eats a healthy meal.
- **the-target**: the person who the actor threatens.
- **demand-obj**: The object involved in the demand.
- **threat-obj**: The object involved in the threat.
- **the-alt-obj**: The object involved in the alternative which the actor offers if the demand is met.
- **response-obj**: The object involved in the response to the actor's demand.

The generalized event contains abstract goals, plans and events in addition to the people and objects which participate in coercion. In the **coerce** generalized event in Figure 2-12 these roles are:

- **goal**: The goal which the actor wishes to achieve.
- **goal-state**: The state which would be true if the actor achieves his goal.

```
COERCE goal GOAL outcome =OUTCOME
              plan =PLAN
              goal =GOAL-STATE
              actor =THE-ACTOR
      goal-state STATE actor =THE-BENE
      outcome GOAL-OUTCOME goal GOAL goal =GOAL-STATE
                                     actor =THE-ACTOR
                        actor =THE-ACTOR
      plan PLAN plan =THE-ASK
              actor =THE-ACTOR
      the-ask ACT type MTRANS
              actor =THE-ACTOR
              object COND if =THE-DEMAND
                         then =THE-ALTERNATIVE
                         else =THE-THREAT
                    to =THE-TARGET
      the-prep ACT actor =THE-ACTOR
      the-demand ACT actor =THE-TARGET
                     object =DEMAND-OBJ
      the-threat ACT actor =THE-ACTOR
                     object =THREAT-OBJ
                     to =THE-TARGET
      the-alternative ACT actor =THE-ACTOR
                          object =THE-ALT-OBJ
                          to =THE-TARGET
      the-sub-goal GOAL-CONFLICT actor =THE-TARGET
                          goal1 GOAL-OUTCOME-LINK goal-b GOAL actor =THE-TARGET
                                                  goal-a GOAL actor =THE-TARGET
                          goal2 GOAL-OUTCOME-LINK goal-b GOAL actor =THE-TARGET
                                                  goal-a GOAL actor =THE-TARGET
      the-sub-plan PLAN plan =THE-TARGET-RESPONSE
                        actor =THE-TARGET
      the-target-response ACT object =RESPONSE-OBJ
                              actor =THE-TARGET
      the-actor-response ACT actor =THE-ACTOR
      the-target-outcome GOAL-OUTCOME actor =THE-TARGET
```

Figure 2-12: The final version of the generalized event for the coerce schema.

- **outcome**: The outcome of the actor's goal.
- **plan**: The plan the actor has to achieve his goal. In **coerce** the plan is to tell a target that if he meets a demand then the actor will do **the-alternative**, otherwise the actor will do **the-threat**.
- **the-ask**: The actual act of asking the target to do the demand.
- **the-prep**: The preparation which is necessary for the actor to carry out the plan.
- **the-demand**: The act the actor wants the target to perform. This act will achieve the actor's goal.
- **the-threat**: The act the actor will do if the the target meets the demand.
- **the-alternative**: The event which will occur if the target does not meets the demand. The alternative is sometimes that the actor will not perform the threat (as in **ball-1**) but it can also be that the actor will do something else (as in **broccoli-1**).
- **the-sub-goal**: A goal of the target which is motivated by the actor making the demand. In **coerce**, this goal is a goal conflict for the target caused by the actor linking the outcome of the demand, to the outcome of the threat.
- **the-sub-plan**: the plan the target pursues to resolve the **the-sub-goal**.
- **the-target-response**: The action the target performs which realizes the **the-sub-plan**. This response may be meeting the demand, ignoring the demand, or pursuing some plan which mitigates the effect of the threat.
- **the-actor-response**: The action which the actor performs in response to the **the-target-response**.
- **the-target-outcome**: The outcome of the target's goal.

When OCCAM forms a macro-schema such as **coerce**, it also constructs a sequence of events which indicate the temporal, causal, or intentional relationships between the various components of the event. In Figure 2-13 the sequence of events for the **coerce** schema is illustrated.

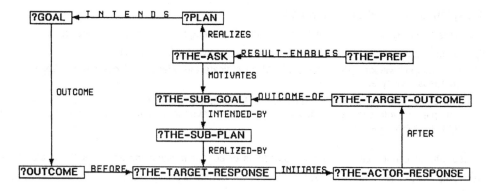

Figure 2-13: The sequence of events for the coercion schema.

3. Explanation-based Learning in OCCAM

The information encoded in schemata can be accessed to make predictions about future events. Therefore, a schema should only contain features when an understander has a justification for believing that these features will appear in future events. One justification for believing that features will appear in future events is that they have always appeared in previous events. In Section 2, I discussed the process of similarity-based learning which utilizes this justification when building generalizations by retaining all features which are common to a number of examples. In this section, I discuss explanation-based learning which relies on another justification for believing that features which appeared in previous events will also appear in future events. The justification is to demonstrate deductively that a set of features are sufficient to produce the predicted outcome. Explanation-based learning creates a schema by retaining only those features which were necessary to explain why an event occurred. The explanation indicates that when a particular class of events occurs, a particular effect will result. This causal knowledge is associated with the schema and serves as the justification for predicting the consequences of future events.

The idea behind explanation-based learning is quite simple. It is easier to learn that **A** results in **C**, if you already know that **A** results in **B**, and **B** results in **C**. Instead of correlating over a number of examples of **A** and **C** to arrive at this conclusion, only one example is needed. Note however, that explanation-based learning does not add to the knowledge of the learner [8]. The new schema makes it easier to solve a particular class of problems in the future. Instead of an inference process to chain together a number of facts, explanation in the future will be a memory search to recognize that a new problem is an instance of a known schema. Because of the advantage that explanation-based learning has over other forms of learning, it is attempted first in OCCAM.

3.1. Explanation-based Generalization

OCCAM is provided with a large amount of domain knowledge represented as inference rules which help it to learn about economic sanction incidents. This knowledge is of two sorts:

- economic knowledge: inference rules which indicate the effects of decreases in supply, increases in price etc.

- political knowledge: inference rules which indicate the goals of political entities. For example, one inference rule indicates that countries have the goal of reducing the influence of their adversaries.

These inference rules can explain the outcomes of economic situations and infer the goals of the participants. With this knowledge, explanation-based learning is possible and OCCAM does not need to rely on correlation. For example, consider the following two events:

Economic-Sanction-1

In 1983, Australia refused to sell uranium to France, unless France ceased nuclear testing in the South Pacific. France paid a higher price to buy uranium from South Africa and continued nuclear testing.

Economic-Sanction-2

In 1980, the US refused to sell grain to the Soviet Union unless the Soviet Union withdrew troops from Afghanistan. The Soviet Union paid a higher price to buy grain from Argentina and did not withdraw from Afghanistan.

If a schema were formed encoding all of the similarities between these two events it would indicate that when a democracy which imports oil threatens a country in the Northern Hemisphere which has a strong economic health and exports weapons, then the sanctions will fail because a country in the Southern Hemisphere will sell the product. Explanation-based learning solves both the problem of selecting the relevant features. With explanation-based learning, OCCAM constructs a schema which indicates that if a country that exports a commodity tries to coerce a wealthy country which imports the commodity by refusing to sell them the commodity, then a response might be to bid the price of the commodity higher until another country which exports the product is willing to sell the product.

OCCAM chains together inference rules to explain the outcome of an event such as an economic sanctions incident. When OCCAM has constructed an explanation for an unexpected outcome, it also keeps track of the inference rules which were accessed to produce the explanation. This information is needed to generalize the explanation. The idea is to find the class of outcomes for which the exact same explanation structure will apply. Each inference rule which helped produce the explanation has a number of constraints which specify the conditions under which the inference rule is applicable.

There have been a number of different algorithms presented for generalizing an explanation structure. For example, Kedar-Cabelli [14] and Hirsh [12] present algorithms based on resolution theory proving and logic programming. Mooney [23] presents an algorithm (EGGS) based on unification which improves upon the unification-based algorithm used by STRIPS [10]. Finally, Mitchell et. al. [22] present an algorithm based upon goal regression [33]. The approach to explanation-based generalization in OCCAM follows closely the intuitive idea of what explanation-based learning should accomplish. A generalized explanation should contain only those features which are required to produce the explanation. The algorithm in OCCAM simply marks a feature name and feature value in the input concept when it has been matched against a feature of an inference rule. The marking process is performed after the explanation is complete, rather than marking during the explanation. Otherwise, if backtracking were required to find the explanation, the features of the inference rules on failed paths would also be marked. Once the marking has determined which features are relevant, the explanation is generalized by removing all features which were not marked. The approach to determining the relevant information is similar to an approach used by SOAR [17, 30].

Explanation-based learning can be viewed as a mechanism for operationalizing concept definitions [24, 15]. The idea here is that the a learner already has a means of constructing an explanation, but does not have an efficient mechanism to recognize when the explanation applies. For example, when learning about economic sanctions OCCAM already has enough domain knowledge to explain the outcome of an event. The first time it explains an outcome, it must search for an explanation by a brute force technique: trying various combinations of inference rules. This search for an explanation can be viewed as an inefficient mechanism for recognizing instances of concepts such as "Those economic sanctions incidents which will fail to achieve the desired goal because the target will buy the commodity elsewhere". What explanation-based learning does in OCCAM is to operationalize concepts by creating an efficient means of recognition. Operationalizing a concept in OCCAM consists of finding a description of the concept in terms of easily observable features. In OCCAM, the "observable" features are those features which are used to represent the input examples. For example, the generalization of the Economic-Sanction-1 in OCCAM operationalizes the implicit concept "Those economic sanctions incidents which will fail to achieve the desired goal because the target will buy the commodity elsewhere". This generalization only references features which were present in the input example to indicate that if a country that exports a commodity tries to coerce a wealthy country which imports the commodity by refusing to sell them the commodity, then a response might be to bid the price of the commodity higher until another country which exports the product is willing to sell the product.

In OCCAM, the operationality criteria are rather strict, requiring that the feature be present in input examples rather than derivable from the feature of the input example. For example, the generalization that OCCAM learns contains the threat that a country refuse to sell a product. This threat is directly represented in OCCAM's input. A more general feature might indicate the threat to be any action which results in an increased demand for a commodity. However, this feature is not easily observable and is not included in the representation of an input concept. If a feature such as this were included in a generalization, then an inference process would be needed to traverse memory and recognized when saved explanations apply. There is a trade-off in selecting the operationality criteria. A more specific description of a feature is easy to recognize, but it may also be less generally applicable. For example, if OCCAM did indeed represent the threat in an economic sanction schema as an action which results in an increased demand for a commodity, then the schema would apply to more examples, such as increasing demand by destruction of the targets supply, or a naval blockade, or even a natural disaster such as a drought. This feature is harder to recognize, but applies to more cases. Because of its operationality criteria OCCAM requires a separate schema to handle each method of increasing demand. The benefit that OCCAM derives from its strategy is that it does not require inference to recognize when a saved explanation applies. In addition, there is a potential problem with representing the features more abstractly. The particular instantiation of increasing demand in OCCAM's schema (refusing to sell a product) does not interact with the target's plan to obtain the commodity through other means. Another instantiation of increasing demand such as restricting supply with a blockade might interact with other parts of the explanation such as the ability of another country to supply the commodity. By having a more strict operationality criterion, OCCAM avoids a potential problem which can arise if there is an unforeseen interaction.

3.2. Economic Sanctions

When OCCAM learns about economic sanction incidents, it utilizes the coercion schema in two ways. First, the input representation to OCCAM is in the high-level language of coercion rather than the language of goals and plans. A practical benefit obtained by utilizing the high level representation for OCCAM's input is that `coerce` representation is considerably more compact than the goal representation and is easier to read and write. The second way that OCCAM uses the coercion schema is that the sequence of events of the coercion schema provides the general structure of the explanation of the outcome of a sanction incident.

In the domain of economic sanctions, OCCAM was presented with examples in the twentieth century in which economic sanctions were not accompanied by covert or overt military operations. In total, 26 incidents were presented to OCCAM. However, because many of the sanctions incidents had identical explanation structures, OCCAM did not acquire 26 different schemata with explanation-based learning. For example, once OCCAM acquired a schema from Economic-Sanction-1, it merely recognized that Economic-Sanction-2 was an instance of that same schema.

3.2.1. A detailed explanation-based learning example

In this section, I provide a detailed example of OCCAM acquiring an economic sanction schema with explanation-based learning. In Section 3.2.2 I sketch the generalizations that OCCAM builds from a number of other examples. The detailed example I present is Economic-Sanction-3:

Economic-Sanction-3

In 1948, the Soviet Union threatened to stop granting economic aid to Yugoslavia if Yugoslavia continued its attempts at political independence from the Soviet Union. The United States offered $35 million in economic aid to Yugoslavia which continued to distance itself from the Soviet Union.

Figure 3-1 contains the representation of the input to OCCAM for the objects and countries which participate in this episode. Figure 3-2 continues the representation of Economic-Sanction-3 by illustrating the events. Note that these two figures do not contain all of the features of the coercion schema. There are two reasons for this. First, some of the features take their values from the general coercion schema. For example, the `plan` in Economic-Sanction-3 is the same as the general coercion `plan`: to make a demand of the target. Second, some of the feature values are unknown. In particular, Economic-Sanction-3 does not indicate the reason that the United States helped out or why Yugoslavia

```
COERCE the-actor POLITY type COUNTRY
                       name USSR
                       ideology COMMUNIST
                       language RUSSIAN
                                SLAVIC
                       location NORTHERN-HEMISPHERE
                       continent ASIA
                       economic-health STRONG
                       political-relationships ANTAGONISTIC with =RESPONSE-OBJ
                       ...
                       business-relationship =THE-TARGET
                                             =RESPONSE-OBJ
                                             POLITY type COUNTRY
                                                    name FINLAND
                                 ...
                       exports COMMODITY type MANUFACTURED-GOODS
                               COMMODITY type GAS
                               ...
                       imports COMMODITY type FOOD
                               COMMODITY type CONSUMER-GOODS
                       life-expectancy *SEVENTIES*
                       literacy *NINTIES*
                       religions RUSSIAN-ORTHODOX
                                 MUSLIM
              the-bene =THE-ACTOR
              the-target POLITY type COUNTRY
                                name YUGOSLAVIA
                                economic-health WEAK
                                business-relationship =THE-ACTOR
                                strategic-importance HIGH
                       ...  ....
              threat-obj MONEY dollars 35000000
              the-alt-obj =THREAT-OBJ
              response-obj POLITY type COUNTRY
                                  name US
                                  economic-health STRONG
                                  location NORTHERN-HEMISPHERE
                       ...  ...
```

Figure 3-1: The countries and objects which participate in Economic-Sanction-3.

adopted this plan. The features `the-sub-goal` and `the-sub-plan` are not specified for this reason. These features are also inherited from the `coerce` schema, but the values of the features are too abstract to be useful. For example, the value of the `the-sub-plan` in `coerce` is that the target has a plan which leads to the `outcome`.

```
COERCE the-threat ACT type ATRANS
                      actor =THE-ACTOR
                      object =THREAT-OBJ
                      to =THE-TARGET
                      mode NO
             the-alternative ACT type ATRANS
                                 actor =THE-ACTOR
                                 object =THE-ALT-OBJ
                                 to =THE-TARGET
                                 mode YES
             the-demand ACT type CHANGE-RELATIONSHIP
                            actor =THE-TARGET
                            to DOMINATED with =THE-ACTOR
             the-target-response ACT type AGREEMENT
                                     actor =THE-TARGET
                                     object =RESPONSE-OBJ
                                     agreement ACT type ATRANS
                                                   actor =RESPONSE-OBJ
                                                   object =THREAT-OBJ
                                                   to =THE-TARGET
                                                   mode YES
             goal-state STATE type RELATIONSHIP
                            actor =THE-BENE
                            object DOMINANT with =THE-TARGET
             outcome GOAL-OUTCOME type FAILURE
                         actor =THE-ACTOR
                         goal GOAL actor =THE-ACTOR
                                   goal =GOAL-STATE
             the-actor-response ACT type ATRANS
                                    actor =THE-ACTOR
                                    object =THREAT-OBJ
                                    to =THE-TARGET
                                    mode NO
```

Figure 3-2: The events which occur in Economic-Sanction-3.

When Economic-Sanction-3 is added to OCCAM's memory, it must determine if it can account for the outcome of the new event. OCCAM finds that the coercion schema is the most specific schema in memory for this event. However, it does not account for the events outcome: a goal failure for the Soviet Union.

Since, the coercion schema does not predict the outcome of this event, OCCAM must search for an explanation by identifying the circumstances which led up to this goal failure. OCCAM constructs the following chain of events to explain the outcome:

1. When the Soviet Union issues the threat to halt the economic aid to Yugoslavia, this motivates conflicting goals for Yugoslavia. In effect, the threat of the Soviet Union has linked together the outcome of two goals. Either (a) the goal of maintaining economic health will fail and the goal of achieving political freedom will succeed, or (b) the goal of maintaining economic health will succeed and the goal of achieving political freedom will fail.

2. Yugoslavia has a plan to undo the linkage between the two conflicting goals. Its plan is to find another means of maintaining economic health and to continue on the path toward political freedom.

3. Since the United States is an adversary of the Soviet Union, it has a goal of reducing the political influence of the Soviet Union.

4. Providing economic assistance to Yugoslavia will reduce the influence of the Soviet Union.

5. Since the United States has a strong economy, it can afford to give economic aid to Yugoslavia.

6. When United States gave aid to Yugoslavia, Yugoslavia's goal of economic health was achieved.

7. Since Yugoslavia's goal of economic health was achieved by the United States, the Soviet threat will not cause a goal failure.

8. When Yugoslavia continued to distance itself from the Soviets, the Soviet goal of dominating Yugoslavia was thwarted.

```
COERCE the-actor POLITY political-relationships ANTAGONISTIC with =RESPONSE-OBJ
       the-target POLITY economic-health WEAK
                         strategic-importance HIGH
       the-threat ACT type ATRANS
                      actor =THE-ACTOR
                      object =THREAT-OBJ
                      to =THE-TARGET
                      mode NO
       response-obj POLITY economic-health STRONG
       the-target-response ACT type AGREEMENT
                               actor =THE-TARGET
                               object =RESPONSE-OBJ
                               agreement ACT type ATRANS·
                                             actor =RESPONSE-OBJ
                                             object =THREAT-OBJ
                                             to =THE-TARGET
                                             mode YES
       outcome GOAL-OUTCOME type FAILURE
                            actor =THE-ACTOR
                            goal GOAL actor =THE-ACTOR
                                      goal =GOAL-STATE
```

Figure 3-3: The generalization which OCCAM acquires from Economic-Sanction-3.

Once OCCAM has constructed the explanation, it can create a schema by deleting those features of the example, which were not needed to explain the failure of the Soviet Union's goal. The generalized event which OCCAM constructs for this situation is displayed in Figures 3-3 and 3-4. Figure 3-3 contains abstract descriptions of the participants and events. This is the most general description of the episode for which the explanation found by OCCAM is applicable. The following constraints are placed on the coercion structure so that this explanation applies:

- the **the-actor** must have an adversarial relationship with the **response-obj**. This feature is required for the **response-obj** to have a goal of reducing the influence of the **the-actor**.

```
COERCE the-sub-goal GOAL-CONFLICT actor =THE-TARGET
                    goal1 GOAL-OUTCOME-LINK goal-b GOAL actor =THE-TARGET
                                                   goal STATE type POSS-BY
                                                             actor =THE-TARGET
                                                             object =THREAT-OBJ
                                                             value YES
                                            outcome-b SUCCESS
                    goal2 GOAL-OUTCOME-LINK goal-b GOAL actor =THE-TARGET
                                                   goal STATE type POSS-BY
                                                             actor =THE-TARGET
                                                             object =THREAT-OBJ
                                                             value YES
                                            outcome-b FAILURE
      the-sub-plan PLAN actor =THE-TARGET
                   plantype UNDO-GOAL-LINKAGE goal GOAL actor =THE-TARGET
                                                   goal STATE type POSS-BY
                                                             actor =THE-TARGET
                                                             object =THREAT-OBJ
                                                             value YES
               plan =THE-TARGET-RESPONSE
               intends GOAL actor =RESPONSE-OBJ
                            goal STATE type RELATIONSHIP
                                       actor =THE-ACTOR
                                       object DOMINANT with =THE-TARGET
                                       value NO
                        actor =RESPONSE-OBJ
```

Figure 3-4: The generalized goal and plan of the target in an economic sanction schema.

- the **the-target** must have a weak economy. This is required so that the threat will harm the **the-target**. In addition, the **the-target** must have high strategic importance so that it is worthwhile for the **response-obj** to intervene.
- the **response-obj** must have a strong economy so that it can afford to intervene.
- the **the-threat** is that the **the-actor** will not give the **the-target** the **threat-obj**.
- the **the-target-response** is for the **the-target** to make an agreement with the **response-obj** for the **response-obj** to give **the-target** the **threat-obj**
- the **outcome** is that the goal of the **the-actor** will fail.

In the process of constructing the explanation, OCCAM also infers the goal of Yugoslavia and the plan Yugoslavia was undertaking in pursuit of its goal. Since the goal and plan are features of the coercion schema, they are also included in the generalized event for the economic sanction schema. The **the-sub-goal** and **the-sub-plan** are illustrated in Figure 3-4. The generalized goal indicates that the target has a conflict between some unspecified goal and the goal of obtaining the **threat-obj**. The plan that the target took to resolve this conflict was to find a different means of obtaining the **threat-obj**.

When OCCAM creates a specialized version of a macro-schema such as **coerce** it also updates the sequence of events for the schema. For example, the coercion schema indicates that the outcome of the actor's goal comes after the target's response (see Figure 2-13). In this type of economic sanction incident, the sequence of events is specialized to indicated that the target's response thwarts the actor's goal so the outcome is a failure. Figure 3-5 shows the modified sequence of events for this economic sanction schema.

The schema acquired from explanation-based learning on Economic-Sanction-3 accounts for a number of other incidents. For example, consider the following two episodes:

Economic-Sanction-4

In 1948, the Soviet Union threatened to block the import of goods into West Berlin to prevent the formation of a West German government. The United States agreed to airlift

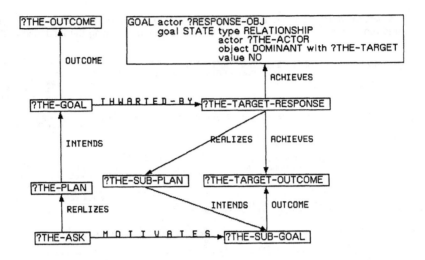

Figure 3-5: **The sequence of events of an economic sanction schema. This elaborates on the relationships specified in the coercion schema.**

supplies to West Berlin.

Economic-Sanction-5

In 1960, the United States cut of all exports to Cuba in retaliation for the nationalizing of oil refineries. The Soviet Union ships goods and extends credit to Cuba.

Both of these incidents fit the same general pattern as Economic-Sanctions-3. When OCCAM encounters these examples, it can already predict their outcomes and there is nothing for OCCAM to learn. Furthermore, OCCAM can easily infer the goals of the target countries and the motivation of the supporting country by simply instantiating the explanation saved with the schema. The schema does not account for the following economic sanction incident, however:

Economic-Sanction-6

In 1983, South Africa threatened to eliminate rail service (the means of import) to Lesotho (a small country completely surrounded by South Africa) if Lesotho did not expel members of the African National Congress. Twenty-two members of the African National Congress left within two weeks of the implementation of the blockade.

There are several reasons the schema acquired from the Soviet threat to Yugoslavia does not fit this pattern. First, South Africa does not have a wealthy adversary who would gain politically by helping Lesotho. Second, the strategic importance of Lesotho is minimal. It's location is of no military importance and it has little mineral reserves. This example does demonstrate that in the proper circumstances, economic sanctions can be effective. In the words of Lesothoan Foreign Minister Evaristus Sekhonyana in the *Washington Post* on 12 August 1983:

But unless some kind of pressure can be brought to bear on South Africa there is nothing we can do. We have to comply with the demands. We have no other options.

From this example, OCCAM acquires another economic sanction schema that indicates when a country is of low strategic importance, poor economic health, and the actor does not have a wealthy adversary, then a threat to cut off imports will produce the desired effect.

3.2.2. Summary of economic sanction schemata

OCCAM acquires a total of eleven economic sanction schemata. In this section, I summarize a few of the economic sanctions incidents and the lessons that OCCAM learned from the incidents.

In addition to the Lesotho example, economic sanctions have been effective in two other types of circumstances in the examples that OCCAM has encountered. First, in the 1960's there were a number of incidents of the nationalization of American companies. The following example is typical:

Economic-Sanction-7

In 1962, Brazil expropriated the national telephone company, a subsidiary of the ITT corporation valued at $7 million dollars. The United States threatened to cut off foreign aid totaling $173 million and Brazil agreed to reimburse ITT.

From this example, OCCAM acquires a schema which indicates that if a threat to cut off aid is for an amount which is greater than a demanded payment, the target country will agree to the demand. OCCAM comes up with the schema due a rather simple cost-benefit analysis of choosing between two goals. Once acquired, this schema applies to a number of cases, such as Ceylon's expropriation of oil companies in 1961, and Peru's nationalization of oil and sugar companies in 1968. In response to a number of similar incidents the US Congress approved the Hickenlooper amendment which requires a termination of US aid to countries that do not settle expropriation disputes. This amendment was quite successful in producing favorable settlements [13].

Another example of a economic sanction incident which achieved the desired goal is also the first example in modern times. It is also noteworthy because it is an example of stopping a military aggression with economic warfare:

Economic-Sanction-8

In 1921, the League of Nations voted to stop all exports including food supplies to Yugoslavia in retaliation for an invasion of Albania. Yugoslavia yielded to threat before sanctions were implemented.

The schema that OCCAM acquires in this case indicates that if the withheld commodity is essential and not manufactured internally, and the target economy is weak (to prevent the country from bidding up the price of the product until it finds a supplier), then the goal will be successful. This same schema also applies to another threat by the League of Nations which stopped Greece from invading Bulgaria in 1925.

Despite the best intentions, not all League of Nations sanctions incidents were successful:

Economic-Sanction-9

In 1935, Italy invaded Abyssinia (Ethiopia). The League of Nations refused to sell Italy weapons if it continued its conquest. Italy, which had the capability of manufacturing its own weapons, ignored the threat and quickly occupied Abyssinia.

From this example, OCCAM learns that if a threat is made to refuse to sell a country a commodity which is manufactured by that country, the threat will be ignored.

There is a common theme in OCCAM's mastery of the domain of economic sanctions. The understanding of a novel episode requires a great deal of search to explain the outcome of an episode.

Once this work is performed, the result of the search is saved as a schema. The schema serves as a quick efficient method of recognizing when a general explanation applies. Once a set of economic sanction schema are acquired, OCCAM can function as an economic sanction expert system.

What does explanation-based learning accomplish for OCCAM? In one example, OCCAM starts with knowledge of coercion and some simple economic knowledge of supply and demand. It finds a useful interaction between coercion and the economic knowledge and saves this as a schema. Answering questions about future economic sanction incidents that fit this pattern will be simple since there is an appropriate schema in memory. All that needs to be done is a memory traversal to find the appropriate schema, recognize the new instance as an example of the schema, and instantiate the explanation. In essence, OCCAM is a general problem solving system with domain knowledge of coercion and supply and demand, and after a number of experiences, it evolves into an efficient specialized expert on economic sanctions. With some different examples, OCCAM could become expert in a different domain. For example, OCCAM's knowledge of supply and demand might be useful to create a financial expert. For example, if an emerging technology needs a particular commodity, then the demand for that commodity may increase in the future. OCCAM's knowledge of supply and demand would predict that the price of the commodity would increase. Therefore, given an example of an investment in yttrium which is a component of many superconductors, OCCAM could create a schema which indicates that an investment in companies that produce materials required by an emerging technology is likely to profitable.

4. Question answering

In this section, I discuss the question answering component of OCCAM which illustrates the use of a macro-schema and the re-representation of a user query.

OCCAM demonstrates its knowledge of economic sanctions by answering questions about hypothetical economic sanctions incidents. OCCAM answers questions about the effectiveness of applying economic sanctions in hypothetical circumstances. It is not intended to predict whether or not a nation will implement a program of economic sanctions. Indeed, this would be a much more difficult problem because it appears that economic sanctions are often attempted when there is no hope of success.[3] The process of question answering has a number of steps involved. First, OCCAM must parse the user's question to represent the meaning of the question in terms of CD goal, plans, and events. OCCAM has a simple expectation-based parser based on CA [2] and DYPAR [9]. Next, OCCAM must search memory to attempt to recognize the question as referring to the instance of a known schema. The process of searching memory can re-represent the meaning of the question by creating a high-level representation. There are three possible results of the memory search:

1. OCCAM does not have any schemata which can help answer the question. In this case, OCCAM simply replies that it does not know the answer to the question. One could think of extending OCCAM so that it searches for an explanation when it cannot find an appropriate

---

[3]One reason that economic sanctions are proposed when they cannot bring about the desired goal becomes apparent when one considers the alternatives: doing nothing or military retaliation.

schema in the same manner that it searches for an explanation to acquire schemata with explanation-based learning. However, the search from question answering would be more difficult. Examples presented to OCCAM contains an problem statement and a resolution, and OCCAM must explain the resolution in terms of information in the problem statement. In question answering, however, an explanation also requires a search to find the solution. Since it is easier to verify that a plan achieves a goal than to find a plan to achieve a goal, searching for an answer to question would be computationally more expensive. However, if OCCAM were capable of this task, it would raise the interesting issue of learning when answering a question.

2. There is exactly one schema in memory which accounts for the situation. In this case, OCCAM instantiates the sequence of events of the schema with information from the question. This instantiation process provides an answer to the question and OCCAM's justification for the answer.

3. There is more than one applicable schema in memory. In this case, OCCAM cannot decide on a correct answer to the question. For example, if the United States were to try to threaten Kuwait by refusing to sell a commodity, there are two schemata that apply: Kuwait might be willing to pay a higher price for the commodity and ignore the threat, or Kuwait might approach an adversary of the United States such as the Soviet Union for assistance. OCCAM cannot decide among these explanations and offers both.

When OCCAM finds an answer and a justification, these are represented in Conceptual Dependency. OCCAM must select some of this information to tell the user and generates a response in English. This is accomplished by simple recursive application of patterns which transform CD representations into English.

An example will help to illustrate this process of question answering. For example, OCCAM is presented with the following question:

Question: What would happen if the US refused to sell computers to South Korea unless South Korea stopped exporting automobiles to Canada?

The results of parsing this question is shown in Figure 4-1. The representation indicates that the US has a goal and the outcome of the goal is in question. The plan the US is pursuing to achieve the goal is to tell South Korea that the US will not sell computers to South Korea unless it stops the exporting of automobiles to Canada.

Once the question has been parsed, the next step is to traverse memory to find a schema which can answer the question. In the current example, the memory traversal starts at the top of the goal hierarchy. Following an index of the plan feature, OCCAM arrives at a simple schema which represents those goals whose plan is to issue a threat. This schema has no specializations, but it contains a representational transfer which can convert the **goal** representation to a **coerce** representation. The question is re-represented in a high-level representation (see Figure 4-2). This representation indicates that the **the-actor** is the US, the **the-target** is South Korea, the **the-threat** is to refuse to sell computers and **the-demand** is to stop selling cars to Canada. The **outcome** of the **goal** is the focus of the question. OCCAM continues memory traversal with the new representation, following indices from the general coercion schema formed by similarity-based learning. There are a number of schemata indexed under the coerce schema, including kidnapping schema which are not appropriate since the threat is not to kill someone, and a number of economic sanction schemata. Only one economic

284

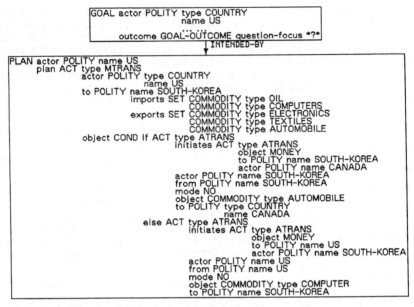

```
GOAL actor POLITY type COUNTRY
          name US

     outcome GOAL-OUTCOME question-focus *?*
                   INTENDED-BY

PLAN actor POLITY name US
     plan ACT type MTRANS
          actor POLITY type COUNTRY
                name US
     to POLITY name SOUTH-KOREA
          imports SET COMMODITY type OIL
                      COMMODITY type COMPUTERS
          exports SET COMMODITY type ELECTRONICS
                      COMMODITY type TEXTILES
                      COMMODITY type AUTOMOBILE
     object COND If ACT type ATRANS
               initiates ACT type ATRANS
                            object MONEY
                            to POLITY name SOUTH-KOREA
                            actor POLITY name CANADA
                  actor POLITY name SOUTH-KOREA
                  from POLITY name SOUTH-KOREA
                  mode NO
                  object COMMODITY type AUTOMOBILE
                  to POLITY type COUNTRY
                        name CANADA
               else ACT type ATRANS
                  initiates ACT type ATRANS
                            object MONEY
                            to POLITY name US
                            actor POLITY name SOUTH-KOREA
                  actor POLITY name US
                  from POLITY name US
                  mode NO
                  object COMMODITY type COMPUTER
                  to POLITY name SOUTH-KOREA
```

Figure 4-1: The result of parsing the question "What would happen if the US refused to sell computers to South Korea unless South Korea stopped exporting automobiles to Canada?". Many features of the countries are not shown to conserve space.

sanction schema is appropriate. This schema (which is displayed in Figure 4-3) indicates that since the **the-target** has a strong economy, its response would be to buy the commodity at a higher price from another country which exports the commodity. Notice that the schema in Figure 4-3 contains a general description of the target's response, the target's plan (**the-sub-plan**) and the goal outcome. This description will be specialized with information from the question to form an answer.

Once a schema with a general explanation has been found, the next step in the process of question answering is to specialize the general explanation so it applies to the particular circumstances described by the question. This involves matching the input event against a pattern, binding a number of variables. Typically, there is one variable for each feature of the macro-schema. The values of these variables are substituted into the general explanation to produce a particular explanation which applies in the current situation.

The explanation in the current example (which is partially illustrated in Figure 4-4) indicates that the threat motivated a goal conflict in the South Koreans by linking together the success of their goal to export automobiles and the failure of their goal to possess computers. A plan to resolve the conflict is to find another means of possessing computers. The schema suggests that importing computers from another country is one such plan. This will result in the failure of the US goal.

Once OCCAM has found the CD representation of the answer, it must generate the answer in English. Although quite simple, OCCAM's generation capabilities are sufficient to generate understandable English replies for questions in this restricted domain. The following is OCCAM's answer to the question:

```
COERCE the-actor POLITY type COUNTRY
                       name US
                       imports COMMODITY type OIL
                                COMMODITY type ELECTRONICS
                       exports =THREAT-OBJ
                                COMMODITY type WEAPONS
                                COMMODITY type ELECTRONICS
                                COMMODITY type MANUFACTURED-GOODS
            the-target POLITY type COUNTRY
                       name SOUTH-KOREA
                       exports COMMODITY type ELECTRONICS
                                COMMODITY type TEXTILES
                                =DEMAND-OBJ
                       imports COMMODITY type OIL
                                =THREAT-OBJ
                       continent ASIA
                       economic-health STRONG
            threat-obj COMMODITY type COMPUTER
            demand-obj COMMODITY type AUTOMOBILE
            the-threat ACT type ATRANS
                       actor =THE-ACTOR
                       object =THREAT-OBJ
                       to =THE-TARGET
                       from =THE-ACTOR
                       mode NO
                       initiates ACT actor =THE-TARGET
                                     to =THE-ACTOR
                                     object MONEY
                                     type ATRANS
            the-demand ACT type ATRANS
                       actor =THE-TARGET
                       object =DEMAND-OBJ
                       from =THE-TARGET
                       to POLITY type COUNTRY
                             name CANADA
                       mode NO
                       initiates ACT actor POLITY type COUNTRY
                                                  name CANADA
                                     to =THE-TARGET
                                     object MONEY
                                     type ATRANS
            goal GOAL actor =THE-ACTOR
                       outcome GOAL-OUTCOME question-focus *?*
```

Figure 4-2: The new representation for the question created during memory traversal.

```
COERCE the-actor POLITY exports =THREAT-OBJ
       the-target POLITY economic-health STRONG
                         imports =THREAT-OBJ
       threat-obj COMMODITY
       the-threat ACT type ATRANS
                  actor =THE-ACTOR
                  to =THE-TARGET
                  object =THREAT-OBJ
                  from =THE-ACTOR
                  mode NO
       the-demand ACT actor =THE-TARGET
                  mode NO
       the-target-response ACT initiates ACT type AGREEMENT
                                           actor =THE-TARGET
                                           object POLITY business-relationship =THE-TARGET
                                                        exports =THREAT-OBJ
                                           agreement ACT type ATRANS
                                                      initiates ACT type ATRANS
                                                                from =THE-TARGET
                                                                object MONEY value >MARKET
                                                                actor =THE-TARGET
                                           object =THREAT-OBJ
                                           to =THE-TARGET
                               mode YES
       outcome GOAL-OUTCOME type FAILURE
                            actor =THE-ACTOR
                            goal GOAL actor =THE-ACTOR
                                      goal =GOAL-STATE
       the-sub-goal GOAL-CONFLICT actor =THE-TARGET

       the-sub-plan PLAN actor =THE-TARGET
                    plantype UNDO-GOAL-LINKAGE goal GOAL actor =THE-TARGET
                                                         goal STATE type POSS-BY
                                                                    actor =THE-TARGET
                                                                    object =THREAT-OBJ
                                                                    value YES
                    plan =THE-TARGET-RESPONSE
```

Figure 4-3: The schema which provides a general explanation to answer the question "What would happen if the US refused to sell computers to South Korea unless South Korea stopped exporting automobiles to Canada?". This schema indicates that if a country that exports a commodity tries to coerce a country which imports the commodity by refusing to sell them the commodity, then a response might be to buy the commodity at a higher price from another country.

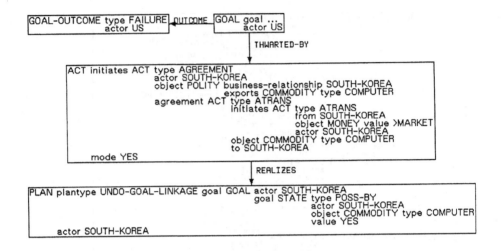

Figure 4-4: Part of the explanation which indicates why the US goal will fail.

Question: What would happen if the US refused to sell computers to South Korea unless South Korea stopped exporting automobiles to Canada?

OCCAM: The goal of the United States that South Korea not sell automobiles to Canada will fail and South Korea will agree to purchase computers from a country which exports computers.

There are a number of possible extensions, to the question answering capabilities of OCCAM. For example, OCCAM finds an abstract specification of the country which would sell computers to South Korea: "a country which exports computers". A simple scheme to find such a country could be implemented so that OCCAM might be able to generate "some country, such as Japan, which exports computers" for this concept. In addition, since the schema which produces is the answer is already located, it should be simple to retrieve an example to help make the point:

OCCAM+: The goal of the United States that South Korea not sell automobiles to Canada will fail and South Korea will agree to purchase computers from a country such as Japan which exports computers in the same manner as the Soviets purchased grain from Argentina during the US grain embargo.

Finally, a more elaborate question answering capability might provide for a more interactive dialogue. OCCAM currently cannot adjust the level of detail it includes in an answer. Although the instantiated explanation for the question contains information about supply and demand, OCCAM currently has no means of articulating this information. For example, the answer which OCCAM finds for this question is similar to the answer provided by a expert political analyst with the Rand Corporation:

Question: What would happen if the US refused to sell computers to South Korea unless South Korea stopped exporting automobiles to Canada?

Answer: S. Korea will probably buy computer equipment from some other country.

Although, OCCAM has the necessary information, it is not able to continue the dialogue in the same manner as the political analyst:

Question: Why?

Answer: If the US restricts S. Korea's supply of computers, they would be willing to pay a higher price for the computers and some other country would move in.

5. Conclusion

In spite of the limitations of OCCAM's language capabilities, I believe that the approach outlined in this paper is a promising means of creating knowledge-based systems to perform useful functions. The approach consists of using similarity-based learning to acquire general schemata which represent plans for achieving goals. These schemata are specialized with explanation-based learning to create a memory which indicates the conditions under which the plans for achieving goals have proved successful. Explanation-based learning in OCCAM makes use of the representation for complex plans which is created by the similarity-based learning process. The schemata formed by explanation-based learning serve as efficient means of recognizing the class of situations which would have the same explanation as a training example.

References

1. Bartlett, F.. *Remembering: A study in experimental and social psychology.* Cambridge University Press, New York, 1932.

2. Birnbaum, L. & Selfridge, M. Conceptual analysis of natural language. In *Inside computer understanding: Five programs plus miniatures*, Schank, R., & Riesbeck, C., Ed., Lawrence Erlbaum Associates, Hillsdale, NJ., 1981, pp. 318-354.

3. Bobrow, D.G., Kaplan, R., Kay, M., Norman, D., Thompson, H.S., & Winograd, T. GUS, A frame-driven dialog system. *Artificial Intelligence 8*, 1 (1977), 155-173.

4. Bower, G., Black, J. & Turner, T. Scripts in Memory for Text. *Cognitive Psychology 11* (1979), 171-216.

5. Brachman, R., & Schmolze, J. An overview of the KL-ONE knowledge Representation System. *Cognitive Science 9*, 2 (1985), 171-216.

6. Bruner, J.S., Goodnow, J.J., & Austin, G.A.. *A Study of Thinking.* Wiley, New York, 1956.

7. Cullingford, R. E. Script Application: Computer Understanding of Newspaper Stories. Computer Science Research Report 116, Yale University, 1976.

8. Diettrich, T. Learning at the knowledge level. *Machine Learning 1*, 3 (1986), 287-315.

9. Dyer, M.. *In Depth Understanding.* MIT Press, 1983.

10. Fikes, R., Hart, R., & Nilsson, N. Learning and executing generalized robot plans. *Artificial Intelligence 3* (1972), 251-288.

11. Graesser, A., Gordon, S., and Sawyer, J. Recognition Memory for typical and atypical actions in scriptal activities: Tests of a script pointer + tag hypothesis. *Journal of Verbal Learning and Verbal Behavior 18* (1979), 319-332.

12. Hirsh, H. Explanation-based learning in a logic programming environment. *Proceedings of the Tenth International Joint Conference on Artificial Intelligence*, Milan, Italy, 1987, pp. 221-227.

13. Hufbauer, G. & Schott, J.. *Economic Sanctions Reconsidered: History and Current Policy.* Institute For International Economics, Washington, D.C., 1985.

14. Kedar-Cabelli, S. Explanation-based generalization as resolution theorem proving. *Proceedings of the Fourth International Machine Learning Workshop*, Irvine, CA, 1987, pp. 383-387.

15. Keller, R. Defining operationality for explanation-based learning. *Proceedings of the National Conference on Artificial Intelligence*, Seattle, WA., 1987, pp. 482-487.

16. Kolodner, J. *Retrieval and organizational strategies in conceptual memory: A computer model.* Lawrence Erlbaum Associates, Hillsdale, NJ., 1984.

17. Laird, J., Rosenbloom, P., and Newell, A. Chunking in Soar: The anatomy of a general learning mechanism. *Machine Learning 1*, 1 (1986), 11-46.

18. Lebowitz, M. Generalization and memory in an integrated understanding system. Computer Science Research Report 186, Yale University, 1980.

19. Lebowitz, M. Correcting erroneous generalizations. *Cognition and Brain Theory 5*, 4 (1982), 367-381.

20. Michalski, R. & Ko, H. On the nature of explanation or Why did the wine bottle shatter. *Proceedings of the AAAI Symposium on Explanation-Based Learning*, Geseke, Germany, 1988, pp. 12-17.

21. Minsky, M. A Framework for Representing Knowledge. In *The Psychology of Computer Vision*, Winston, P.H., Ed., McGraw-Hill, New York, NY, 1975, pp. 211-277.

22. Mitchell, T., Kedar-Cabelli, S. & Keller, R. Explanation-based learning: A unifying view. *Machine Learning 1*, 1 (1986), 47-80.

23. Mooney, R. & Bennett, S. A domain independent explanation-based generalizer. *Proceedings of the Ninth International Joint Conference on Artificial Intelligence*, Los Angeles, CA, 1985, pp. 551-560.

24. Mostow, J. Searching for operational concept descriptions in BAR, MetaLex, and EBG. *Proceedings of the Fourth International Machine Learning Workshop*, Irvine, CA, 1987, pp. 376-382.

25. Pazzani, M. Interactive Script Instantiation. *Proceedings of the National Conference on Artificial Intelligence*, Washington, D.C., 1983, pp. 320-326.

26. Pazzani, M., Dyer, M. & Flowers, M. The role of prior causal theories in generalization. *Proceedings of the National Conference on Artificial Intelligence*, American Association for Artificial Intelligence, 1986, pp. 545-550.

27. Pazzani, M. Inducing causal and social theories: A prerequisite for explanation-based learning. *Proceedings of the Fourth International Machine Learning Workshop*, Irvine, CA, 1987, pp. 230-241.

28. Pazzani, M. J. *Learning causal relationships: An integration of empirical and explanation-based learning methods.* Ph.D. Th., University of California, Los Angeles, 1988.

29. Roberts, R. & Goldstein, I. The FRL Manual. MIT AI Lab. Memo 409, MIT, 1977.

30. Rosenbloom, P. & Laird, J. Mapping explanation-based generalization onto Soar. *Proceedings of the National Conference on Artificial Intelligence*, American Association for Artificial Intelligence, 1986, pp. 561-567.

31. Schank, R. & Abelson, R.. *Scripts, plans, goals, and understanding.* Lawrence Erlbaum Associates, Hillsdale, NJ., 1977.

32. Swartout, W. Explanation: A source of guidance for knowledge representation. *This volume*, 1988.

33. Waldinger, R. Achieving several goals simultaneously. *Machine Intelligence 8* (1977), 94-130.

Demand-driven Concept Formation

Stefan Wrobel

Technische Universität Berlin,
FR 5-12, Franklinstr. 28/29,
1000 Berlin 10, West Germany

E-mail: wrobel@db0tui11.bitnet

Abstract

Most existing work on concept formation (e.g., *conceptual clustering*) has focused on the formation of concepts for classification purposes, resulting in an emphasis on producing sets of concepts that are complete, i.e., cover all observed instances. In this research, we are primarily concerned with concept formation as a solution to the *new term problem*, which results in a new set of requirements on concept formation: concept formation must be triggered in a demand-driven fashion by the shortcomings of the existing representation, and a concept's quality must be evaluated in terms of its contribution to the representation. The approach to demand-driven concept formation that we present in this paper is part of an integrated learning system called the MODELER, the learning component of the knowledge acquisition system BLIP, and is capable of forming concepts incorporating both disjunctions and relational information. Much of the power of the approach stems from its close integration with the other components of the learning system, namely, rule discovery and knowledge revision, which are also presented in this paper.

Keywords:

concept formation, new-term problem, closed-loop learning, knowledge acquisition, rule discovery, knowledge revision

1. Introduction

For quite a long time, research on the acquisition of concepts in the field of machine learning has concentrated almost exclusively on the task of learning from examples, i.e., given a number of entities pre-labeled as positive or negative instances of one or several classes, the learner is to produce generalized descriptions (concepts) for each of those classes. The results of research on this problem (referred to as concept learning, concept acquisition, or concept identification) have been impressive [Dietterich Michalski 83]; nonetheless, the need to move towards more realistic assumptions about the learning task has become increasingly more obvious [Langley 87]. Consequently, in work on *concept formation* (concept discovery), the assumption that there must always be some oracle to provide pre-classified examples to the learner is abandoned in favor of a view of learning as observation and discovery: given a set of entities, not pre-separated into classes, the learner is to identify (one or more) interesting collections (aggregates) of entities and produce generalized descriptions (concepts) of those collections.

As expressed by this definition, concept formation consists of two essential steps, namely, finding interesting collections of entities and forming a generalized description of that collection. In a model of concept formation proposed in [Easterlin Langley 85], the step of finding interesting collections is called *aggregation*, and the step of forming a generalized description is referred to as *characterization*. The model also includes a third step called *utilization*, defined as monitoring both the use and the usefulness of the new concept in subsequent processing and modifying or discarding the concept, if necessary.

Most existing work on concept formation has been in the area of *conceptual clustering* [Michalski 83]. The basic learning task in conceptual clustering is the same as in concept formation, but since the learning result is intended to serve as a basis for classification, the task is typically augmented with the additional requirement of coming up with an exhaustive set of concepts that is structured hierarchically, i.e., each domain entity must be covered by exactly one leaf node. Numerous conceptual clustering systems have been developed, including the series of CLUSTER programs [Stepp Michalski 86], OPUS [Nordhausen 86], UNIMEM [Lebowitz 87], and COBWEB [Fisher 87], to name only a few (see [Fisher Langley 85] and [Stepp 87] for insightful discussions of conceptual clustering and its relation to concept learning and concept formation, and a more complete overview of existing programs).

In contrast to the above systems, the primary concern of this research is not with concept formation for classification purposes, but concept formation as a way to partially solve the *new-term problem* of machine learning. The representation language initially provided to a learning system immediately implies a strong bias on the part of the system: things that cannot be represented cannot possibly be learned. It is the task of the system developer to make sure that the bias he or she puts into the representation includes the desired target concepts [Utgoff 86]. This, however, is a non-trivial task sometimes requiring a considerable amount of effort (e.g., the chess endgame terms designed in [Quinlan 83]), which makes the need for an automated solution of the new-term problem, or the representation selection problem in general, very evident.

In the domain of learning from examples, some approaches to this problem have been taken, including the work on constructive induction by Michalski [Michalski Stepp 83], Utgoff's STABB [Utgoff 86], the VBMS system [Rendell et al. 87], and Schlimmer's STAGGER [Schlimmer 87].

In the domain of learning from observation, we have to mention the BACON system [Langley et al. 86], which creates new numerical terms and intrinsic properties of objects, and the AM system [Lenat 82], which forms new classes of objects and new relations. Other discovery systems are compared and evaluated in [Langley Nordhausen 86].

Returning to concept formation, it is clear that, in a sense, every concept formation or conceptual clustering program is an answer to the new term problem because whenever we have formed a new concept, we can give it a name and include that name in the representation language, thus making the language richer. Employing concept formation for this purpose, and not mainly for classification, has some immediate implications on the general requirements and assumptions one must make, however:

- Concept formation must be triggered not only by observed similarities of objects, but also by shortcomings of the current representation.
- Evaluation of a concept's quality must be based not only on its internal coherence, but also on how much it adds to the representation.
- There is no need to maintain an exhaustive hierarchy of concepts at all times; concept formation can be demand-driven.

In this paper, we will present the MODELER, the learning component of the knowledge acquisition system BLIP, as an example of a concept formation approach in an integrated, closed-loop[1] system that addresses the above issues:

- In BLIP, concept formation is *demand-driven* by the needs of the system: whenever the existing set of concepts is insufficient to express a target set of objects (the *support sets* generated during *knowledge revision*, see 3.2.2), a concept formation attempt is triggered.
- The system keeps only those concepts that have both a coherent characterization *and* are used elsewhere in the system (in the future, we plan to use (a *concept garbage collector* to keep track of this over time, see 5.1.5).
- Finally, concept descriptions are rich enough to be interesting - they can include both relational information and disjunctions.

There is one additional point that we should emphasize before proceeding further, namely, the important consequences of building an integrated learning system such as BLIP. The field of machine learning as a whole has been moving towards a study of integrated systems [Langley 86], and rightly so: the study of isolated, stand-alone algorithms can only go so far - the proper study of intelligent behavior will have to take an integrated view because the interaction effects, synergistic or detrimental, between the various components imply an entirely different set of design and evaluation criteria not present otherwise. What is good engineering for stand-alone systems needn't be good engineering in integrated systems (and vice versa); what appears to be a non-optimal method when looked at alone may turn out to be a natural part of an integrated system because it nicely exploits the other parts. Maximizing those synergistic effects was an important goal in designing BLIP, and we will briefly discuss its impact at the end of the paper (5.2).

A Reader's Guide. The rest of this paper is divided into 4 parts (sections 2 through 5). Section 2 presents a general overview of the BLIP system, and presents an introductory example of what the system is capable of learning, illustrating the system's processing without technical detail. Along the way, BLIP's knowledge representation is introduced. Sections 3 and 4 describe the components of the MODELER at a detailed technical level, and will frequently refer back to the example presented in section 2.2 for clarification. Section 3 describes those parts of the MODELER that concept formation was built upon, namely, rule discovery (3.1) and knowledge revision (3.2). In section 4, we then describe the concept formation approach and show how it integrates with the other system parts. In section 5, we conclude with a discussion of the strengths and weaknesses of the approach and point out some future research directions.

---

[1] By a *closed-loop* system, we refer to a learning system in which the results of one learning step are "looped back" in such a way that they can be used as the basis for further learning in subsequent steps (either by the component which produced the result, or by others).

2. The BLIP System

2.1. Overview

BLIP is a knowledge acquisition system in a paradigm that we have called *sloppy modeling* [Morik, this volume]. The central idea behind that paradigm is that knowledge acquisition is a modeling activity, i.e., in the head of the expert there usually is no model that could simply be transferred to the machine, so the model is (at least partially) *created during knowledge acquisition*. A sloppy modeling system supports that process in two ways: first of all, it provides a knowledge acquisition environment that the expert uses to enter knowledge into the machine, work with that knowledge, and revise it at will [Wrobel 87a]. Second, a sloppy modeling system provides additional feedback to the user about the structure of the knowledge being entered by using machine learning techniques (see BLIP's system architecture in Figure 1). A new rule that has been discovered by the system, for example, tells the user a great deal about the facts s/he has entered.

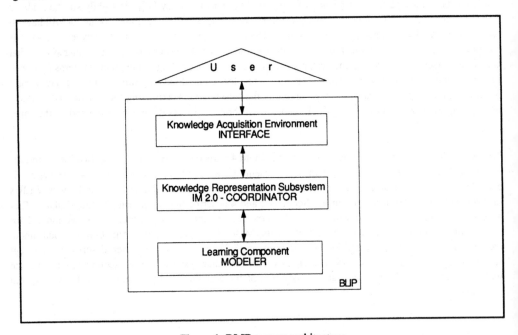

Figure 1: BLIP system architecture

The crucial point about the learning task of the MODELER is that the user never needs to explicitly invoke or control the learning component, e.g., by preparing special examples for it, running it, and deciding what to do with the results. Instead, the learning component *observes* the knowledge being entered by the user and independently tries to discover new properties of that knowledge and add them to the knowledge base, thus making them known to the user. Therefore, BLIP's learning component can be best understood as an *observational discovery* system.

Figure 2 shows the architecture of the MODELER in more detail. The MODELER consists of three integrated subcomponents, namely, rule discovery (RDISC), knowledge revision (KREV), and concept

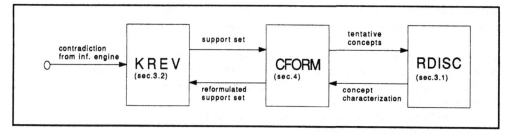

Figure 2: MODELER architecture in more detail

formation (CFORM), which interact in a multitude of ways as represented by the arrows between the components. In what follows, we will explain in detail what each of those components does and what the interactions are; first, however, we will take you through an introductory example that illustrates the system's processing, presenting BLIP's knowledge representation along the way.

2.2. An introductory example

In this section, we will describe a sample domain used to illustrate the system's processing throughout the paper, and show what kind of learning behavior the system is capable of. While doing that, we will also get to know BLIP's knowledge representation.

2.2.1. The traffic law domain

The domain used might be roughly identified as "German traffic laws". No attempt was made to represent the complex legal reasoning that can go into a court decision on such matters; instead, the domain represents the kind of knowledge you might need to take a driver's license test, i.e., knowledge about where to park and where not to park, knowledge about speed limits, traffic safety, violations and fines. The basis of the domain is the list of the various traffic violations committed by members of our project plus some made-up cases to make the knowledge base large enough. Each case is described by featural and relational information expressed in *facts*. Here is BLIP's representation for the author's own "towing event" (Figure 3):

```
vehicle_involved(event1,b_au_6773)
parks(b_au_6773,place1)
buslane(place1)
owner(sw,b_au_6773)
towed(b_au_6773)
responsible(sw,event1)
fine(event1,20)
pays_fine(sw,20)
not(appeals(sw,event1))
not(court_citation(sw))
not(tvr_points_p(event1))
not(additional_points_p(sw))
```

Figure 3: An event described with BLIP facts

Basically, the above information tells you that one day, I was unfortunate enough to park my car (license number B-AU 6773) in a bus lane, from which it promptly got towed away. I own the car, and I was the person to be held responsible for this traffic violation (which we have called "event1"). The fine for the violation was 20 DM (ignoring the towing charges), which I paid. I did not have to go to court, I did not appeal the fine, and, fortunately, did not get any points on my traffic violation record (TVR)[2].

To prevent the entry of nonsensical facts (an important function of a knowledge acquisition environment), the user defines an *argument sort mask* (ASM) for each predicate. Based on these ASMs, all terms are assigned to a sort when they are used for the first time; resulting in a (sub-) sort hierarchy. In the traffic-law domain, we have defined

> involved_vehicle(<event>,<vehicle>), and
> parks(<vehicle>,<place>),

etc., so when entering

> involved_vehicle(event1,car1), and
> parks(place1,car1)

(with accidentally reversed arguments), the system can warn us that **car1** is already a member of the sort **car** and thus conflicts with **place** (since neither one is a subsort of the other). (Sorts play a similar role in restricting the space of rule hypotheses to semantically sensible rules; see section 3.1).

Figure 4 shows BLIP's representation of some inferential relationships that are valid in our traffic-law domain:

```
time(event,time) & dark(time) --> lights_necessary(event)
road_edge(place) --> not(second_row(place))

second_row(place) --> no_parking(place)
sidewalk(place) --> no_parking(place)
bus_lane(place) --> no_parking(place)
fire_hydrant(place) --> no_parking(place)
level_crossing(place) --> no_parking(place)

road_edge(place) & not(no_parking_sign(place))
                        --> parking_allowed(place)

parks(car,place) & no_parking(place)
                        --> illegal_parking(car,place)
parks(car,place) & parking_allowed(place)
                        --> not(illegal_parking(car,place))

involved_vehicle(event,car) & illegal_parking(car,place)
                        --> parking_violation(event)
involved_vehicle(event,car) & worn_tires(car)
                        --> unsafe_vehicle_violation(car)
```

Figure 4: Basic rules of the traffic-law domain

The rules in figure 4 are to be interpreted as implicitly all-quantified and state things such as one needs to drive with the lights turned on when it is dark, or a parking spot at the curb will not qualify as second-row parking. There are several rules expressing knowledge about where one may not park (in bus and bike lanes, on the sidewalk, next to a fire hydrant, or too close to a railroad crossing). The final group of

---

[2] The traffic violation record (*Flensburger Punktekartei*) is a central database recording major traffic violations, each of which has a certain point value. (Needless to say, if you accumulate too many points, you lose your license.)

rules defines more abstract attributes of events, such as parking violations or violations due to safety problems with the car. The graphical representation in Figure 5 nicely reveals the structure of the rules in Figure 4[3].

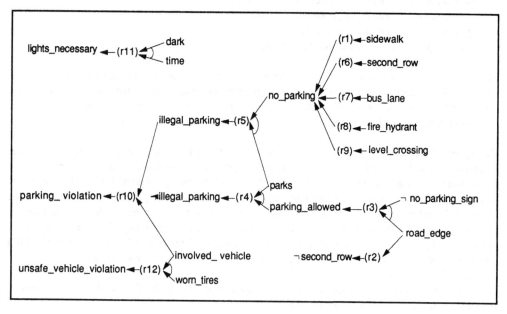

Figure 5: Graph of rules in figure 4

Rules like those shown in figure 4 can either be entered by the user upon which they become background knowledge for learning, or they can themselves be discovered by the system from an appropriate fact base. This constitutes a very flexible way of incorporating background knowledge into the learning system - the user can provide as many or as few rules as he or she wants. As we will see in section 3.1, the system automatically uses all available rules (input or system discovered) for further learning.

2.2.2. Metaknowledge

The rules shown in figure 4 above are only half the story about the representation of inferential knowledge in BLIP. Inferential knowledge is represented internally not only in the rule form shown above, but also in a factual form as *metafacts*. To that end, the system is equipped with a set of *metapredicates* (as part of its domain-independent knowledge), each of which can be used to express one particular inferential relation between predicates[4]. A metapredicate definition uses a *rule schema* [Habel Rollinger 82] to describe how a metafact with that metapredicate is to be translated into a domain

---

[3] In this and subsequent similar figures, rules are shown with the antecedents to the left, and the consequents to the right of the node labeled with the rule number. Only the predicate names are shown, the arguments have been left out to avoid cluttering the figure. The antecedents are to be read as connected with a logical *and* (indicated by the arcs connecting the arrows).

[4] Even though metaknowledge in BLIP is higher-order knowledge in the sense of logic, it is still possible to provide a fact-complete set of inferences in polynomial time (see [Wrobel 87b]).

level rule. Here's an example: The metapredicate definition

opposite_1(p,q): p(x) --> not(q(x))

states that the metafact **opposite_1(p,q)** (where **p** and **q** are predicate variables) is to be translated into the domain level rule **p(x) --> not(q(x))**. Thus, the metafact

opposite_1(road_edge,second_row)

corresponds to the second rule in figure 4:

road_edge(x) --> not(second_row(x)).

The important thing to remember is that there is a one-to-one correspondence between rules and metafacts: for each rule, there is exactly one corresponding metafact in the system. Facts and rules at the domain and meta levels are stored in BLIP's inference engine (IM2, [Emde, this volume]), which also carries out inferences and performs the necessary reason maintenance operations.

During knowledge acquisition, a user never needs to work with metaknowledge directly, because the system automatically transforms input rules into the appropriate metafacts, defining new metapredicates if necessary [Thieme, this volume]. The appendix shows the metapredicates used in the traffic law domain; many of them have been generated automatically. The advantage of re-representing rules as metafacts is that one can now easily have *rules about rules* that can be used to infer more rules, or prevent the entry of other, inconsistent rules. In keeping with the philosophy, those *metarules* are of course also represented by *metametafacts*. Metametafacts, just like metapredicates, are part of BLIP's domain-independent background knowledge (see [Thieme, this volume] for more detail).

As we will see in section 3.1, metapredicates also play a central role in BLIP's rule discovery algorithm: they define the algorithm's hypothesis space.

2.2.3. Learning results

Given the background rules shown in figure 4, and a set of facts describing traffic violation cases similar to **event1** above, the system was able to discover several rules about when a violation results in additional points on the traffic violation record, and about when a person receives a court citation for a violation (see section 3.1 for how those rules can be learned). Figure 6 shows the rules that were discovered:

```
parking_violation(x1)  --> not(tvr_points_p(x1))
parking_violation(x1) & appeals(x2, x1) --> court_citation(x2)
involved_vehicle(x1,y1) & not(buckled_up(z1,y1))
                                    --> not(tvr_points_p(x1))
unsafe_vehicle_violation(x1) & appeals(x2,x1) --> court_citation(x2)
lights_necessary(x1) & involved_vehicle(x1, y1)
                & not(headlights_on(y1) --> not(tvr_points_p(x1))

involved_vehicle(x1, y1) & owner(z1, y1) --> responsible(z1, x1)
```

Figure 6: Rules discovered in traffic law domain

What the system has discovered is essentially that for vehicle safety violations, parking violations, driving without proper light, and not being buckled up, you don't go to court unless you appeal, and you don't get any points on your record.

The system has also discovered that the owner of a car is always responsible for violations in which that car was involved. Unfortunately, that rule is only partially correct: in Germany, the owner is responsible for all minor violations regardless of who the driver was. For major violations, however, the driver is responsible. Since all members of the KIT project were safe drivers, the cases the program had seen did not include any major violations, which is why that rule was learned.

When we then gave the program some cases where the owner was not responsible, the system derived contradictions between its knowledge and what was input, and adjusted the rule by excluding the cases that had led to contradictions (see section 3.2 for how knowledge revision arrives at these so-called *support set restrictions*).

When the set of exceptions finally became unplausibly large, the concept formation routines were triggered to search for a reformulation of the now too-large support set. After unsuccessfully trying to characterize the set of owners and the set of cars for which the "responsibility" rule might be valid, the system tried to redescribe the set of events. Since the representation used for cases did *not* include a predicate that characterized the events, the system hypothetically defined a new predicate and searched for rules characterizing it, finally succeeding (section 4 tells you how). The resulting concept description is shown in figure 7; we have already renamed the gensym the system had introduced for the concept to **minor_violation**, since that is what the concept is: minor violations include parking violations, vehicle safety violations, driving with improper lights, and without one's seatbelts fastened. For minor violations, you don't get points on your traffic violation record, and you go to court when you appeal.

```
(Sufficient conditions)

parking_violation(x1) --> minor_violation(x1)
involved_vehicle(x1, y1) & not(buckled_up(z1, y1)
                                        --> minor_violation(x1)
lights_necessary(x1) & involved_vehicle(x1, y1)
              & not(headlights_on(y1)) --> minor_violation(x1)
unsafe_vehicle_violation(x1) --> minor_violation(x1)

(Necessary conditions)

minor_violation(x1) --> not(tvr_points_p(x1))
minor_violation(x1) & appeals(x2, x1) --> court_citation(x2)
```

Figure 7: Rules describing the new concept **minor_violation**

There are two interesting aspects of this concept description that we should point out[5]: First, /minor_violation/ is a *polymorphic* concept, i.e., there is no set of features shared by all its members that sufficiently characterizes the concept; the set of necessary conditions above is not jointly sufficient[6], and the set of sufficient conditions is disjunctive. Second, the definition of **minor_violation** uses relational information in several places, e.g., an event is of a certain kind if the vehicle that was involved

---

[5] See 4.1 for a detailed definition of what we mean by a *concept*.

[6] Consider the case of murdering somebody, which meets the necessary conditions of minor_violation (for example, you do not get points on your traffic violation record), but which definitely is not a minor violation.

has certain properties.

Note also that the system has used the new concept to reorganize the rules it had discovered before; the rules in figure 6 have been replaced by the rules describing `minor_violation` in figure 7. Figure 8 shows a graphical representation of that part of the domain before and after the introduction of `minor_violation`.

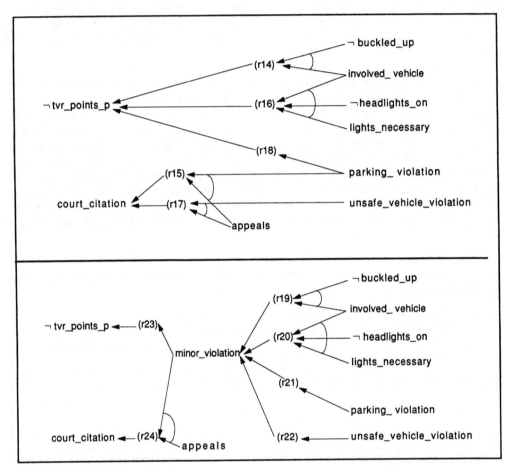

Figure 8: Rule set before (top) and after (bottom) introduction of **minor_violation**

3. Rule Discovery and Knowledge Revision

After reading section 2, you now have a pretty good idea of *what* BLIP's learning routines do. It is the task of this section and section 4 to explain in detail *how* the processing described in section 2.2.3 was done. In particular, in this section, we will describe the two components of the modeler which served as the basis for the construction of the concept formation component, namely, the rule discovery algorithm (RDISC) and the knowledge revision routines (KREV).

3.1. Discovering Rules

The rule discovery algorithm used in BLIP is based on a model-driven, two-step empirical learning approach originally inspired by the series of METAXA learning programs [Emde et al. 82]. In step 1 (HGEN), the system uses its model of possible rules to generate one or more hypotheses about rules that might hold over the given data (i.e., there is not just one, but many rules to be learned). In step 2 (HTEST), those hypotheses are then empirically tested against the knowledge base, and entered into the knowledge base if they are confirmed. The system then returns to the hypothesis generation step, and the cycle recommences (Figure 9).

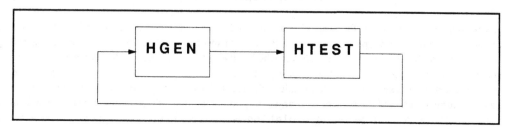

Figure 9: Rule discovery learning steps

The questions to be asked about such a learning approach are of course,

- What is the rule model, i.e., what does the hypothesis space look like?
- How does the system focus its search of the hypothesis space? Which hypothesis from the space does it generate at a given point?
- How are hypotheses empirically tested?

3.1.1. The rule model

In BLIP, the set of available metapredicates constitutes the rule model. The hypothesis space can be generated by instantiating all metapredicates with all syntactically compatible (domain) predicates found in the knowledge base (Figure 10).

In other words, a hypothesis in BLIP is a metafact, which corresponds to a domain-level rule, such as
     opposite_1(road_edge,second_row),
which corresponds to the rule
     road_edge(x1) --> not(second_row(x)).

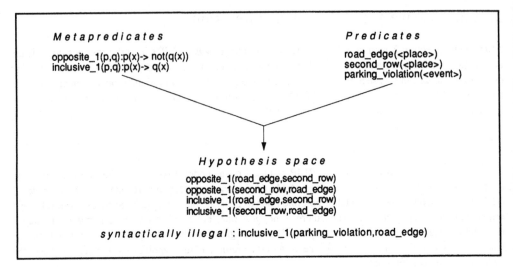

Figure 10: Hypothesis space example

As mentioned in section 2.2, the sorts play an important role in excluding semantically non-sensical hypotheses: the hypothesis space is not the entire cartesian space of combinations of metapredicates and predicates, because the system always checks whether the arities and sorts of all predicates match the rulescheme of the metapredicate in the hypothesis. Thus, the instantiation of **p** with **road_edge**, and **q** with **second_row** is syntactically compatible with the rulescheme for **opposite_1**, because **p** and **q** have the correct arity, and the sorts of their arguments do not conflict. We could not, however, come up with the hypothesis that a **parking_violation** is the opposite of a **road_edge**, because the former predicate is defined on the sort **event**, while the latter is defined on the sort **place**.

3.1.2. Focusing hypothesis generation

For any reasonably-sized domain, the hypothesis space described above is enormous: Given the default set of about 40 metapredicates with an average arity of two, and 50 domain predicates, the space of cartesian combinations of metapredicates and predicates contains 100.000 elements (50**2 for each of the 40 metapredicates). Even though the syntactic restrictions described above considerably reduce the size of this space, it is obviously still much too large for a generate-and-test search, since empirically testing a hypothesis can be expensive if the knowledge base is large. Therefore, some way of focusing the search is needed. Unfortunately, since we do not assume that the user points the program to explicit examples of a possible rule[7], we have to look for some other information that we can exploit.

We have identified three general heuristics that can guide the hypothesis generation process:

---

[7] Nonetheless the user can of course input rules or provide explicit examples of suspected rules to the system. Those are then generalized by turning constants into variables and immediately become high-priority hypotheses.

- The learning routines should be working on the same parts of the domain as the user, because that makes it easier for the user to understand the learning results.
- One should avoid forming hypotheses about parts of the knowledge base where only few facts have been input, because it is likely that there will be no conclusive evidence for or against such a hypothesis.
- A knowledge acquisition system should prefer breadth of knowledge over depth of knowledge, because this avoids creating unbalanced domain models.

In BLIP, these general heuristics are translated into predicate selection criteria as follows:

- Prefer generating hypotheses about predicates that have been used in recent user inputs.
- Prefer generating hypotheses involving predicates that have been used in a large number of facts.
- Prefer generating hypotheses about predicates about which few rules are known.

Those rules are expressed by numerical measures which are combined by weighted addition to select a predicate[8], which is then paired with a metapredicate (progressing from simpler to more complicated ruleschemes), and possibly other predicates, to form a complete hypothesis. The weights are parameters of the rule discovery algorithm; we are still experimenting to find out what the optimal values are.

We should again emphasize that, just as the entire learning module, hypothesis generation works in an incremental fashion: on each iteration of the basic rule discovery cycle, the system generates a group of hypotheses (currently, always one) and passes them on to hypothesis testing. On the next iteration of this cycle, all internal tables are updated to reflect a potentially changed state of the knowledge base, and the generation of the next group of hypotheses is based on the then-current state of the indicators. Book-keeping routines ensure that the space of hypotheses is searched in a systematic manner.

Another source of control for the hypothesis generation step comes from the metametafacts/metarules in the system. Based on existing metafacts, they derive new positive or negative metafacts which influence hypothesis generation, because if we derive that a certain metafact is true or false, there is no need to propose it as a hypothesis any more. The following is an example of such a metarule:

> `opposite_1(p,q) --> not(inclusive_1(p,q))`

which becomes obvious once we regard the rulescheme of the involved metapredicates:

> `inclusive_1(p,q): p(x) --> q(x)`
> `opposite_1(p,q): p(x) --> not(q(x))`

More detail about the functions of metametafacts can be found in [Thieme, this volume].

3.1.3. Hypothesis testing

After the hypothesis generation module has suggested one or more possible rules that might hold over the current set of facts, it is the job of the hypothesis testing module to verify each of those hypotheses.

Testing a hypothesis against the knowledge base is a conceptually very simple step: all we need to do is count the number of positive and negative instances of the rule, and then decide if we have sufficient

---

[8] score(p) = $w_1 \cdot$recency(p) + $w_2 \cdot$facts(p) + $w_3 \cdot$rules(p)   where   recency(p) = 1 / input-stack-position(p), facts(p) = no-of-facts-with(p) / average-no-of-facts,   rules(p) = 1 - (no-of-rules-with(p) / average-no-of-rules).   Predicates with no-of-facts-with(p) below a threshold are not considered.

evidence to either accept or reject the rule. This search is performed with two search patterns called *characteristic situations*, one matching the positive instances of the rule, the other matching the negative instances of a rule. Characteristic situations are very simple: for the rule

```
involved_vehicle(event,car) & owner(person,car)
                     --> responsible(person,event)
```

the characteristic situations are

```
PosCS: involved_vehicle(event,car) & owner(person,car)
                          & responsible(person,event)
NegCS: involved_vehicle(event,car) & owner(person,car)
                          & not(responsible(person,event))
```

Before they are applied, those search patterns are reordered in such a way that clauses which have less facts are matched first. One important fact that we should point out is that in BLIP (as in any learning system), we cannot in general make a *closed-world assumption*, i.e., assume that everything not known to be true is false, because that obviously is not the case in an incremental knowledge acquisition system. Thus, the **not** in the negative search pattern above is not to be interpreted as negation by failure. Instead, we require the negated facts to be explicitly present in the knowledge base.

The testing step automatically takes previous rule knowledge into account when trying to prove or disprove a hypothesis: during the search for characteristic situations, we do not distinguish between input facts and inferred facts, so that all inferences made with existing rules, no matter whether they are user-input or system discovered, can be used to prove a new rule. This is a very simple and effective way of incorporating existing knowledge into further learning steps.

For deciding whether to accept or reject a hypothesis, we currently use a simple threshold rule that accepts only perfect hypotheses with sufficient support, i.e., rules that don't have any exceptions and have enough positive instances in the knowledge base. If there are negative instances, the rule is rejected. If there is neither enough positive evidence, nor negative evidence, the system does not make a decision on the rule, and it can be reproposed later.

If a hypothesis is confirmed, the corresponding rule is entered into the knowledge base, and is used to infer additional facts: the system always performs all possible forward inferences with the facts and rules it possesses. In the next iteration of the learning cycle, those facts can then be used to confirm some other hypothesis, as described above. Thus, the rule discovery algorithm alone can already be regarded as a closed-loop learning system.

3.2. Knowledge Revision

From the point of view of a learning system in a knowledge acquisition setting, the world is far from perfect:

- the user enters information incrementally in a piece-meal fashion
- the information entered may not be representative of what is going on in the world (selection bias),
- and finally, information may turn out to be false, and is retracted by the user.

In the sample acquisition session in the traffic law domain (section 2.2), we already saw an example of how those factors can result in the discovery of erroneous rules by the system. There, the problem was due to a non-representative example selection bias[9] on our part: we had inadvertently given the system only cases where the owner of the vehicle involved in a violation was reponsible for the violation, so the rule that was learned,

```
involved_vehicle(event,car) & owner(person,car)
                        --> responsible(person,event)
```

looked perfectly valid to the system. When we then gave it some information to the contrary, the system noticed that there was a contradiction (user input prefixed with ">"):[10]

```
> involved_vehicle(tv_event,cab1).
New EP: involved_vehicle(tv_event, cab1) - (1000,0)[11]
> driver(mr_t, cab1).
New EP: driver(mr_t, cab1) - (1000,0)
> owner(ace_cab_co, cab1).
New EP: owner(ace_cab_co, cab1) - (1000,0)
New EP: responsible(ace_cab_co, tv_event) - (1000,0)
> not(responsible(ace_cab_co,tv_event).
Classified as noisy: responsible(ace_cab_co, tv_event) - (0,1000)
Please repeat your input if you are sure that it is correct.
> not(responsible(ace_cab_co,tv_event).
Classification "noisy" rejected.
New EP: responsible(ace_cab_co, tv_event) - (1000,1000)
*** Beginning knowledge revision ...
```

Whenever such a contradiction occurs, it is the task of the *knowledge revision* component (KREV) to appropriately adjust the system's knowledge to the new facts by selecting a set of rules and/or facts to be changed or deleted.

3.2.1. Selecting Where to Change

The first step in selecting where to change the existing knowledge is to determine which parts of that knowledge are responsible for producing the incorrect conclusion (blame assignment). Since in BLIP, the inference engine maintains a record of which knowledge base elements were used in a derivation, this step is simple - the inference engine provides a complete derivation tree for a contradiction. To remove the contradiction, it then suffices to "cut" one of the branches of the derivation tree.

The basic strategy for selecting where to cut is to select those changes that have the least consequences for the knowledge base ([Salzberg 85] calls this the *conservatism* heuristic). This behavior is consistent with what people do when faced with new knowledge that contradicts their existing beliefs: rather than making far-reaching changes, a small incremental fix is made if possible. The advantages of this strategy are that it requires relatively little effort as compared to restructuring the entire model, and it allows the system to preserve most of what it knows.

To avoid a combinatorial explosion in the application of this strategy, BLIP does not perform an exhaustive global comparison of all possible changes, but instead uses a fixed sequence of local decision steps. Even though it is not guaranteed to find the optimal change, this simplified approach performs

---

[9] [Rissland 87] discusses the example selection problem in the context of learning-from-examples systems.

[10] All output is shown in interface presentation format, which is easier to read than the internal format of inference engine trace messages.

[11] EP stands for *evidence point*. BLIP's inference engine represents the truth value of each statement by a two-dimensional evidence measure, where (1000,0) corresponds to *true*, (0 1000) to *false*, (1000 1000) to *contradictory*, and (0 0) to *unknown* (see [Emde, this volume]). Only those four cornerpoints are actually used by BLIP.

reasonably well. To decide where to make a modification, the system first selects whether to keep the positive or negative conclusion by checking which one is supported more strongly, keeping the user input, or the fact derived by more rules. This eliminates one half of the derivation tree from consideration. To actually select a rule in the derivation that is to be deleted for modification, the system examines which changes each modification would cause on the *metalevel*[12] using this as an estimate of the expected changes to the entire knowledge base. Following the conservatism heuristic, it then selects the rule modification with the least consequences.

Going back to the contradiction we saw above, we see that the choice in this case is very easy. There is an input fact contradicted by an induced rule, so the system chooses to modify that rule.

```
Resolving conflict in favor of input fact ...
Need to modify rule
involved_vehicle(x1, y1) & owner(z1, y1)
                         --> responsible(z1, x1)
```

3.2.2. Modifying a rule: support sets

The simplest way of preventing a rule from contributing to a contradictory derivation is by deleting the rule entirely. This achieves the desired effect of removing the contradiction, but it isn't very smart: a rule that has proven useful in many cases should not be abandoned because of one or a few exceptions. Consequently, the method of choice for rule modification in BLIP is what Hayes-Roth has called the *exclusion method* [Hayes-Roth 83]. The rule is prevented from applying in the case that produced the contradiction by excluding that case from the rule's domain of applicability.

To that end, each rule in BLIP has an associated *support set* [Habel Rollinger 82] specifying the allowed instantiations of the rule's variables. The maximal, unrestricted support set of a rule allows each variable to range over all known terms. The maximal support set for the rule

involved_vehicle(x1, y1) & owner(z1, y1)
--> responsible(z1, x1),

for example, is

(x1, y1, z1) elem ALL x ALL x ALL

The inference engine makes sure that a rule is applied only if the proposed variable bindings are in the rule's current support set, which creates an effect similar to Winston's *censored production rules* [Michalski Winston 86].

The general form of a support set is shown in figure 11. Each support set is the cartesian product of the allowed *domains* for its variables, minus a set of explictly listed exception tuples (*global exceptions*). Each variable's domain is specified by a BLIP concept (see section 4.1), optionally minus a set of explicitly listed exception terms.

Preventing a rule from applying in a case which produced a contradiction can thus be done simply by including the current variable bindings in the support set's global exception list[13]. For the rule we saw above, this is how processing the contradiction will result in a new support set:

---

[12]   The inference engine keeps a record of all derivations, so it is easy to find the metafacts derived from the metafact that is to be changed.

[13]   The more complex forms of support sets are produced during the support set reformulation step (see 4.3, and Figure 14 for some examples).

General form of a support set:

$(x_1, ..., x_n) \in D_1 \times ... \times D_n \setminus \{T_1, ..., T_j\}$

where:

$x_1, ..., x_n$: variables in the rule
$D_1, ..., D_n$: allowed domains of those variables
$T_1, ..., T_j$: exceptions (n-tuples of terms) (*global exceptions*)

General form of a domain D_i:

$D_i = C$, *or* $D_i = C \setminus \{t_1, ..., t_k\}$

where C is a BLIP concept (see 4.1), and $t_1, ..., t_k$ are terms (objects) excluded from the domain.

Figure 11: General form of a support set

```
Trying support set restriction, support set was:
(x1,y1,z1) elem ALL x ALL x ALL
New support set:
(x1,y1,z1) elem ALL x ALL x ALL
                    \ {(tv_event, cab1, ace_cab_co)})
Judged acceptable.
*** End knowledge revision.
```

3.2.3. The plausibility criterion

The rationale for using the exclusion method to modify rules that produced erroneous conclusions is that a good rule should not be abandoned because of a few exceptions. This rationale, however, also indicates the limits of the exclusion method: if the set of exceptions from a support sets becomes too large, we are in danger of keeping a rule that has more exceptions than successful applications. Therefore, when proposing a support set restriction, the knowledge revision module checks to see whether the number of exceptions from the rule is still plausibly small in relation to the successful applications of the rule, both for the global exceptions and the exceptions from different variable domains. If one of those exception sets has grown too large, the support set cannot be accepted in its present form any more.

Thus, if we continue telling the system about more and more cases where the owner of a car was not responsible for violations committed with that car, the system will sooner or later find the list of accumulated exceptions too long, and this (finally) is where the *concept formation* module comes in. Its task is to reformulate the support set in such a way that the explicit list of exceptions can be replaced by a general description of the rule's domain of applicability, i.e., replace an extensional description of the support set with an intensional one, either by using an existing concept, or by forming a new concept. If that cannot be done, the rule needs to be deleted.

4. Concept formation

In the preceding section, we have described the operational need for a concept formation capability in the MODELER: whenever a rule's support set has acquired an implausibly large list of exceptions as a result of knowledge revision activities, that support set must be reformulated. Otherwise, we need to delete the rule. From this perspective, the concept formation module is performing an important service function for the knowledge revision component.

From the point of view of concept formation, however, the situation looks quite different. As pointed out in section 1, an important and difficult part of concept formation is *aggregation*, i.e., finding an interesting collection of entities to examine. The list of accumulated rule exceptions, however, is just such an interesting collection of entities. By being exceptions from one and the same rule, all members of that list must have something interesting in common that might be uncovered during concept formation. From this point of view, it is thus the knowledge revision component that is performing an important service for concept formation, because it provides an interesting aggregate of entities upon which the characterization part of concept formation can focus.

In this section, we will describe concept formation from both of the above perspectives. After explaining how concepts are represented in BLIP (section 4.1), section 4.3 will describe the reformulation steps that are applied to the supports sets provided by the knowledge revision module to achieve a more plausible support set. Those reformulation steps, in turn, may ultimately lead to the formation of a new concept based on the given support set exceptions (section 4.4).

4.1. Representation of concepts in BLIP

In the design of the concept representation for BLIP, there are two important groups of constraints to consider. The first (and obvious) set of constraints stems from the desired functionality of concept descriptions: the concept must provide a generalized, summary description of a class of entities useful for inference, and its description language must be powerful enough to add interesting new terms to the representation. Furthermore, it must be possible to organize the system's concepts in multiple hierarchical levels to realize the benefits of inheritance and storage economy. The second set of constraints may not be so obvious for the reader accustomed to thinking in terms of stand-alone algorithms: the concept representation employed should integrate well with the other components of the learning system and should use the existing representation formalism as well as possible.

The representation that was chosen achieves both of the above sets of requirements by employing BLIP facts and rules *for concept representation*, i.e., without requiring the introduction of new special-purpose constructs for concepts:

- concept membership is represented by *facts* using the concept's name as a predicate
- sufficient and necessary conditions on concept membership are represented by *rules* (Figure 12).

Sufficient conditions. Every rule that has the concept predicate in its conclusion states a sufficient condition on concept membership. Whenever the premises of the rule are true, the rule deduces concept membership. Thus, if we know that **p1** holds for an object, we know that it must be a member of **concept1**. On the other hand, from knowing that an object belongs to that class, we cannot deduce **p1** -

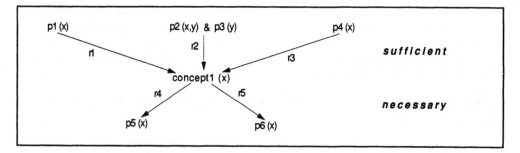

Figure 12: Necessary and sufficient conditions

concept membership may be due to some other known or unknown sufficient condition[14]. Thus, those conditions are sufficient, but not necessary.

Necessary conditions. Conversely, each rule that uses the concept predicate is a necessary condition, because if we know that the conclusion is false, we can deduce non-membership: if **p5** were known not to hold for an object, the object could not possibly be a member of **concept1** (because then **p5** would need to hold). On the other hand, knowing that the conclusions of rules **r4** and **r5** are true tells us nothing about the truth of their premise (i.e., concept membership), so those rules express necessary, but not sufficient conditions.

Note that by representing concepts by unary predicates, the notions of unary predicate and concept are virtually identified in BLIP: every unary predicate corresponds to a concept (the set of all terms for which the predicate holds), and each concept corresponds to a unary predicate (its membership predicate).

4.2. Properties of the concept representation

BLIP's concept representation does quite well on both sets of requirements mentioned at the beginning of section 4.1. From the functional point of view, the important characteristics are

- the use of relational information,
- the inclusion of disjunctive concepts,
- and the organization of concepts in hierarchies.

Relational information. By using BLIP rules to represent necessary and sufficient conditions, it is possible to base a concept definition on relational information. **r2**, for example, states that an object **x** is a member of **concept1** if it is **p2**-related to an object **y**, and if **y** has property **p3**. This greatly increases the range of concepts that can be expressed as compared to a featural representation[15].

---

[14] Inferring **p1** would be an (unsafe) abductive inference, which could be guaranteed to hold only if we were to make a closed-world assumption on the concept definition, and if **p1** were the only sufficient condition for **concept1**.

[15] It is sometimes pointed out that every relational concept can be compiled into a feature, so that **involved_vehicle(x,y)** & **owner(z,y)** becomes **owner-of-involved-vehicle(z,x)**. That is besides the point, however, because all such features must be predefined, and their values input by the user of the learning system, so that those systems effectively do *not* use relational information. Even if we assume that a learning system ultimately compiles all its concept descriptions into a featural form once they have been learned, the system will still require rules that can derive those compiled features - and those rules will have to use relational information.

Disjunctive concepts. Furthermore, since several independent rules can make inferences about concept membership, concept descriptions can include *non-necessary* conditions and allow *disjunctive, poly-morphic* concepts to be expressed. In figure 12, there are three non-necessary (but sufficient) conditions, namely, **r1, r2,** and **r3,** that are disjunctively combined to form a sufficient condition for **concept1.** In addition, **concept1** has two necessary features (**r4** and **r5**) shared by all its members.

Building hierarchies. The third important aspect of our representation is that it allows hierarchies to be represented easily (Figure 13).

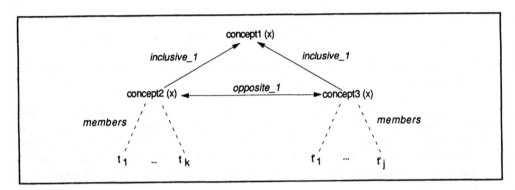

Figure 13: Concept hierarchy

The hierarchical subsumption relation (*isa*) maps to rules of the form
        concept2(x) --> concept1(x)
        concept3(x) --> concept1(x)
which correspond to **inclusive_1** metafacts. In addition to those inclusion relationships, rules that correspond to **opposite_1** metafacts, such as
        concept2(x) --> not(concept3(x))
can express that two concepts at one level of the hierarchy are the opposite of each other.

From the point of view of integration, the concept representation described above has an equally impor-tant set of advantages. Since the facts and rules used to represent concepts are in no way different from other facts and rules in the system, the functionality of all existing components of BLIP applies to con-cepts as well:

- concept membership is maintained automatically by the inference engine,
- hierarchical relationships are discovered automatically by the existing rule discovery algorithm,
- and inferences with hierarchical relationships are performed automatically by the infer-ence engine.

The most important advantage from this point of view, however, is that when using rules to represent the concept description, the *characterization* part of concept formation can be handled by the already exist-ing rule discovery algorithm as well - but see section 4.4 about that.

4.3. Support set reformulation

After this discussion of concept representation in BLIP, let us return to the problem that originally motivated the introduction of concepts in the first place: the reformulation of implausible support sets that come from the knowledge revision module. Such an implausible support set is characterized by an overly large number of explicitly listed exceptions. Figure 14 shows the rule (with associated support set) that gets passed from knowledge revision to concept formation after we have input too many cases contradicting the rule. Also shown are a number of possible, more plausible reformulations of the original support set. How can we arrive at those more "plausible" reformulations?

```
involved_vehicle(x1,y1) & owner(z1,y1)
--> responsible(z1,x1)
support set:
(x1, y1, z1) ∈ ALL x ALL x ALL
               \ {(tv_event, cab1, ace_cab_co),
                  (loan_event, b_xs_400, sw),
                  (stolen_event, b_cd_1234, michel), ...}
```
Examples of possible reformulations:

```
(x1, y1, z1) ∈ MINOR_VIOLATION x ALL x ALL
```

"If the event is a minor violation, then the owner of the involved vehicle is responsible." (This is the correct support set actually discovered by BLIP after forming the concept minor_violation.*)*

```
(x1, y1, z1) ∈ ALL x (BUSINESS \ {car1, car2}) x ALL
```

"If the vehicle involved in an event is used for business purposes, then the owner is responsible, except for car1 *and* car2. *" (A legal support set, but not the correct one for our example.)*

Figure 14: Examples of support set reformulations

The notion of plausibility essentially refers to the degree of generality of a rule: as long as a rule can be stated in general terms, as opposed to explicitly listing all the cases where it applies and does not apply, we will find that rule plausible. Consequently, the goal of support set reformulation must be to transform the *extensional* description used in the implausible support set into an *intensional* description characterizing the support set more generally (cf. [Emde et al. 83]). Reformulation thus always involves *generalization*. Figure 15 shows the reformulation steps that the concept formation module applies to an implausible support set.

The key idea is to simplify the support set by turning global exceptions into local (domain) exceptions on single variables, and to redescribe these local exceptions intensionally by using BLIP concepts. Therefore, reformulation begins by collecting all instances and exceptions for each variable (step 1). The set of exceptions is the union of the variable's values in all global exception tuples with the local exceptions the variable might have had from previous reformulations. The set of instance values cannot be extracted from the support set, it needs to be collected from the successful applications of the rule in the knowledge base. In our example, the resulting sets are

> (1) collect all instances **I(v)** and exceptions **E(v)** of all variables **v** in the support set
>
> (2) for each variable **v** with disjoint sets **I(v)** and **E(v)** (and where **E(v)** is non-empty)
>
>   (3) check if there is an existing concept that
>   (3a) covers all the instances **I(v)** and only plausibly few of the exceptions **E(v)**
>   (3b) or one that covers all the exceptions **E(v)** and only plausibly few of the instances **I(v)**.
>
>   (4) If no such concept exists, call *concept formation*
>   (4a) with the instances **I(v)** as positive examples of the concept to be formed, and **E(v)** as negative examples
>   (4b) with the exceptions **E(v)** as positive examples of the concept to be formed, and **I(v)** as negative examples.
>
> (5) compare the reformulations for the single domains thus generated, and select the one that leaves the fewest exceptions
>
> (6) change the corresponding variable's domain **D** in the support set accordingly:
>   (6a) if you found a concept C covering the instances, replace D with C.
>   (6b) if you found a concept C_{neg} covering the exceptions, define a new concept C such that **opposite_1(C,C_{neg})**, and replace D with C.

Figure 15: Support set reformulation steps

I(x1) = {event1, event2, event3, event4, event5, ...}
E(x1) = {tv_event, loan_event, stolen_event, ...}

I(y1) = {b_au_6773, hh_dc_1978, b_dc_238, b_xy_007, ...}
E(y1) = {cab1, b_xs_400, b_cd_1234, ...}

I(z1) = {st, md, sw, mo, cp, ...}
E(z1) = {ace_cab_co, sw, michel, ...}

The real reformulation work gets done in the iteration beginning with step 2, where for each variable **v** with disjoint instance and exception sets **I(v)** and **E(v)**, we try to find an intensional characterization of either instances or exceptions. Obviously, if the variable takes on common values in successful (instances) and unsuccessful applications of the rule (exceptions), we cannot possibly find a concept that separates the two. Thus, in the example, BLIP does not consider the set of owners (variable **z1**) as a candidate for reformulation, because the owner **sw** appeared both in cases where he was responsible for the violation and in cases where he was not.

For the remaining variables (**x1**, events, and **y1**, vehicles), we first look for existing concepts that could get the job done (step 3). In our particular example, it so happens that all of the violations that the owner was responsible for involved sedans (as opposed to sportscars, taxicabs, etc.,), so the concept **sedan** covers **I(y1)**. Unfortunately, it also covers one of the exceptions: **b_cd_1234** is known to be a sedan as well. So, if we were to reformulate the support based on which cars were involved, the corresponding domain specification would be

D(y1) = SEDAN \ {b_cd_1234}

which would be acceptable, so it is remembered for the comparative evaluation that happens in step (5).

Since no existing concepts cover the instances or exceptions of **x1** (events), the system proceeds to step 4: trying to form new concepts that would help to reformulate the domain. As we will see in the next section (4.4), this attempt will indeed be successful, and the system will introduce the new concept **minor_violation**, that covers all the instances **I(x1)** of events, and excludes all exceptions **E(x1)**.

In the comparative evaluation step (5), the system applies a few simple criteria to select among possible reformulations (in the following order):

(1) select the reformulation that leaves the fewest explicit exceptions
(2) prefer existing concepts over new concepts
(3) break remaining ties by choosing the variable with the largest instance set.

In our example, the choice is simple, since a reformulation on **y1** (vehicle) would leave one exception, so in step (6), the system produces the new support set

   (x1, y1, z1) elem MINOR_VIOLATION x ALL x ALL.

4.4. Characterizing a new concept

After a long journey through the other modules of the MODELER, rule discovery, knowledge revision, and support set reformulation, we have finally returned to what was our original point of departure, namely, concept formation. By now, it should be clear that the modules we have described in the preceding sections are in no way subroutines of the concept formation process that were constructed just to make concept formation possible. Rather, rule discovery and knowledge revision are necessary parts of the normal operation of an incremental learning system that need to be present with or without concept formation.

The power in the approach presented here consequently lies in how those existing components work together to achieve a new functionality, namely, concept formation. Section 4.1 has already presented the key to achieving this cooperation: BLIP's concept representation. By using facts to represent concept membership, and rules to represent necessary and sufficient conditions, the full power of all existing components, especially inference engine and rule discovery can be brought to bear on the concept formation task. Furthermore, the preceding section has shown how knowledge revision and support set reformulation provide concept formation with a set of objects that concept formation can focus on: the instance and exception lists.

With the *aggregation* step of concept formation thus already performed, the task of concept formation is to find a *characterization* of the aggregate provided to it, and that is where the rule discovery algorithm comes in: by hypothetically asserting membership facts for the proposed aggregate, we can let rule discovery search for a characterization of those objects for us. Figure 16 shows the precise steps that are necessary to do that.

The characterization process starts up by first creating a new subworld **W** in the inference engine (step 1). **W** is set up in such a way that it inherits from the main world (the knowledge base). After creating a new predicate for the hypothetical new concept (a gensym beginning with "**concept**", step 2), we can then go ahead and enter the membership facts into the new subworld. All positive examples of the concepts become positive facts, and all negative examples become negated facts (step 3). This is already all the preparation we need for running the rule discovery algorithm to characterize the new concept (step 4). Since at this point, we are only interested in rules about our new concept, we restrict the hypothesis generation module to hypotheses with the new concept. Just like the membership facts, the rules discovered in this step are entered into the hypothetical subworld created in step 1.

---

(1) Create a new hypothetical subworld **W** in the inference engine

(2) Create a (gensym) predicate **p** for the new concept

(3) For every object o⁺ in the aggregate under consideration, enter a membership fact **p(o⁺)** into the subworld **W**, for every negative example o⁻, enter **not(p(o⁻))**.

(4) Call *rule discovery* to search for rules expressing necessary and sufficient conditions on the new concept by
    (4a) restricting hypothesis generation (HGEN) to hypotheses with the concept predicate **p**
    (4b) entering confirmed rules into the hypothetical subworld **W**.

(5) Evaluate the concept description found in step (4) for whether it makes a contribution to the representation
    (5a) If yes, give the user a chance to rename the concept, and incorporate **W** into main knowledge base (reorganizing existing rules, if possible)
    (5b) If no, discard the hypothetical subworld **W**.

Figure 16: Concept characterization steps

After the rule discovery algorithm has explored all hypotheses with the new concept, we need to decide whether the concept we have introduced is really worth keeping. That decision is based on two criteria: we require that the concept

    (a) can be recognized, and
    (b) that it has predictive power.

In other words, we are not interested in concepts defined only by membership facts in the knowledge base, because there would not be any way for new objects to ever become members of that concept (unless the user would directly use the new concept predicate). Second, we are not interested in concept membership for its own sake - knowing that an object is a member of a class should tell us something about that object. This is what we mean by *predictive power*.

The above requirements translate into two simple checks on the concept characterization in step 5: it must

    (a) have at least one rule representing a sufficient condition on concept membership
    (b) have at least one rule representing a necessary condition, i.e., a condition predictable from concept membership.

The advantage of using a separate hypothetical subworld to enter facts and rules about the new concept is that we can simply discard the entire subworld whenever a concept does not pass the interestingness test in step 5. If we do judge the concept to be interesting, the user is given a chance to provide a symbolic name for the concept, and the information about the renamed concept is incorporated into the main knowledge base in a step we sometimes call *post concept formation cleanup*: In this step, the system tries to use the new concept and the rules that characterize it to express existing rules in a better way, or replace them entirely (see the example below)[16].

---

[16] Note that whether the concept is kept is based only on its interestingness, and does not depend on whether the concept is actually used in the support set reformulation that originally triggered the concept formation attempt.

In our traffic-law example, recall that support set reformulation had triggered two concept formation attempts, one on the involved vehicles, another on events. The first attempt fails, because there is no information about cars other than whether they are sedans or sports cars in the knowledge base. As you already know from section 2.2.3, the second attempt does a lot better:

```
*** Beginning concept characterization ...
Creating new IM subworld ...
Positive examples: [event1, event2, event3, event4,
                    event5, event6, event7, event8]
Negative examples: [tv_event, loan_event, stolen_event,
                    event12, event13, event14]
Hypothetical concept is: concept1
Entering membership facts ...
New EP: concept1(event1) - (1000,0)
(...)
New EP: concept1(event14) - (0, 1000)
Triggering hypothesis generation ... Done.
Hypothesis testing ... Done.
--- Sufficient conditions found:
parking_violation(x1) --> concept1(x1)
involved_vehicle(x1, y1) & not(buckled_up(z1, y1) --> concept1(x1)
lights_necessary(x1) & involved_vehicle(x1, y1)
                      & not(headlights_on(y1)) --> concept1(x1)
unsafe_vehicle_violation(x1) --> concept1(x1)
--- Necessary conditions found:
concept1(x1) --> not(tvr_points_p(x1))
concept1(x1) & appeals(x2, x1) --> court_citation(x2)
--- concept1 has 4 sufficient conditions, 2 necessary conditions.
Judged acceptable. Do you want to rename concept1?
> minor_violation.
Incorporating minor_violation into object_level1 ...
Replaced 5 existing rules: r14 r16 r18 r15 r17.
*** End concept characterization
```

5. Discussion and Future Research

In the preceding sections, we have presented the components of the modeler in detail at a technical level. In this section, we will step back again and see what we have achieved with the learning modules discussed above, and what is left to do.

5.1. The new term problem

The discussion in section 4 has presented concept formation mainly in the context of the support set reformulation problem, and we have seen that indeed concept formation can help us solve that problem. As pointed out in the introduction, however, the real interesting issue for concept formation in an integrated learning system is whether it provides an answer to the *new-term* problem. How, then, does the system benefit from the introduction of **minor_violation** into the representation? Besides the improved support set representation discussed above, the new term has helped in

- improving the structure of the rule set
- moving the *learnability cliff*.

5.1.1. Improving the rule set structure

Whenever there is a key concept missing in a knowledge representation, the knowledge about that concept will have to be incorporated implicitly into several different knowledge structures that would otherwise simply refer back to the concept description. As a result, all those knowledge structures become considerably more complex than the underlying domain knowledge they are intended to represent. In our traffic law example, we have seen an example of how this phenomenon is manifest in BLIP (Figure 8, top): the information about the missing concept **minor_violation**, namely that it does not result in points on the traffic violation record and that you don't go to court unless you appeal, is (incompletely) distributed across 5 different rules. Essentially, the distributivity of the logical disjunction has been used to "factor out" the missing concept. Since **minor_violation** consists of 4 disjuncts, a total of 8 rules would have been needed to completely represent the information contained in the concept (see 5.1.2 for why the system has only discovered five).

Consequently, there is a large potential for improving the structure of a rule set through the introduction of a suitable new term/concept. In BLIP, this potential is exploited by the post-concept-formation cleanup step, where the existing rules are inspected to see whether they can be reexpressed or replaced by using the new concept. In our example, this has led to the replacement of the five existing rules, because their information is already contained in the concept definition, resulting in the rule structure shown at the bottom of figure 8.

5.1.2. Moving the learnability cliff

You might have wondered why the system was only able to discover only five of the eight rules mentioned above. For two of those rules, the reason is simply that there weren't enough data to confirm them, for the third one however, the reason is of more general interest: this rule fell off the *learnability cliff*, and could therefore not be learned. This is the rule in question:

   lights_necessary(x1) & involved_vehicle(x1,y1) & not(headlights_on(y1)) & appeals(x1,y1)
   --> court_citation(x2)

If you carefully inspect the set of metapredicates shown in figure &metapreds., you will notice that there is no metapredicate that can express this rule - all metapredicate ruleschemes have three or fewer premises. Therefore, this rule could not possibly be learned, independent of the fact base, because the system cannot produce it as a hypothesis. So this is what we mean by the learnability cliff: by making a rule slightly more complex, it suddenly falls out of the range of things that can be learned. Of course we could simply add another metapredicate, but that would not get us around the fundamental problem which is even more general than BLIP: any learning system will have to be biased with respect to the complexity of expressions it wants to consider for learning.

Fortunately, the ability to form new concepts can help us get around the strict representational bias imposed by the set of available metapredicates: After the introduction of **minor_violation**, the above rule is expressible with only two premises:

   minor_violation(x1) & appeals(x2,x1) --> court_citation(x2)

and can thus be learned[17]. Therefore, the introduction of the new concept has effectively *moved* the learnability cliff, allowing the system to discover rules it could not have discovered before.

---

[17]   Actually, since the condition replaced by **minor_violation** is only one disjunct (of four) in that concept's definition, the rule shown here is more general, but that does not affect our argument: It would have matched exactly if **minor_violation** had only one sufficient condition (**lights_necessary(x1) & involved_vehicle(x1,y1) & not(headlights_on(y1))**).

5.1.3. Future research: New concept formation triggers

The concept formation trigger employed in the BLIP system (support set exceptions provided by the knowledge revision module) has proven very effective in focusing the efforts of the concept formation module: a concept formation attempt is made only if the existing set of terms fails to express what we want to express: *failure-driven lazy concept formation*. In future research, it might nonetheless be interesting to think about other triggers for concept formation, since the observations made above about the usefulness of concept formation for rule set restructuring also suggest a good reason for triggering concept formation. Currently, BLIP does not recognize when a rule set has become overly complex and might benefit from restructuring with a new concept. To do that, it would be necessary to notice that a set of rules can be seen as the factorization of a hypothetical concepts. Unfortunately, that would require giving up on the laziness of concept formation and switching to an "eager" approach because finding those rule sets would invariably involve search.

Another potential concept formation trigger that does not require search comes from the system's sort hierarchy. BLIP dynamically collects all terms used in a particular argument position of a predicate into the corresponding sort; those sets could then be used as aggregates for concept formation. GLAUBER [Langley, Zytkow, Simon, Bradshaw 86] uses a similar strategy to define new classes (it defines them extensionally by grouping together all objects appearing in the same argument position of facts that share at least one argument).

5.1.4. Future research: forming new relations

Besides forming new concepts (sets of objects), the approach discovered here has the potential to also discover new relations. Currently, a support set reformulation attempt immediately tries to reexpress the support by coming up with conditions on single variables (concepts). If, however, the system were to examine the set of instance and exception *tuples*, it could use the same approach that is used for concept formation to form new relations: by hypothetically asserting the tuples (or a projection of those tuples) in the knowledge base, we could again let rule discovery search for rules about the new relation.

5.1.5. Future research: the concept garbage collector

At present, all concepts ever introduced in BLIP remain part of the representation forever (unless the user chooses to remove them). Consequently, the concept formation module is very careful about introducing a new concept and requires it to be characterizable and to have predictive power. Nonetheless, since we have to deal with a changing knowledge base (including deletions), a once useful concept may become less useful in the future. In such a situation, it would be nice to have a "concept garbage collector" periodically check the usefulness of each concept in BLIP, deleting those that are not used anywhere any more. This would also allow the concept formation routines to be somewhat more generous. Concepts could be introduced even if they don't meet the stringent criteria in effect right now, to see if maybe an interesting characterization can be found at some later point, letting the concept garbage collector remove the concept if that is not the case.

5.2. The integration perspective

In the introduction, we mentioned a very important issue that has influenced very many of the design decisions made in the MODELER, and in BLIP as a whole: when building an integrated learning system, it must be a high priority to fully exploit the potential synergistic effects in the cooperation of the various modules.

5.2.1. Synergistic effects

Reexamining what we have said about the MODELER under that perspective, it seems that in BLIP, we have exploited many, but not all of those effects. Here are those that are indeed exploited:

- *Synergistic effect #1*: Knowledge revision is exploited to focus concept formation through the set of support set exceptions.

- *Synergistic effect #2*: By choosing a proper concept representation, the reason mainte-nance and inference services of the inference engine can be used to maintain concept membership and perform hierarchical inferences.

- *Synergistic effect #3*: A concept hierarchy is automatically built during the normal opera-tion of the rule discovery module.

- *Synergistic effect #4*: Concept formation uses rule discovery to perform the concept char-acterization step.

There are at least two other such beneficial interactions that are not used in BLIP yet:

- *Potential synergistic effect #5*: As described in section 5.1.3, besides basing concept for-mation on support set exceptions, the system could exploit sort intersections for that pur-pose.

- *Potential synergistic effect #6*: Right now, hypothesis testing is an all-or-none affair: either the hypothesis we have holds for all the data, or we regard it as disconfirmed. With the availability of concepts, a more sophisticated approach is possible. If the knowledge base does not support the hypothesis in its most general form, we can try to find a con-cept that excludes the observed exceptions, and use it to restrict the support set of the rule right when it is first discovered.

5.2.2. Closed-loop learning

A second aspect of integration in BLIP is what above we have called *closed-loop learning*. In a closed-loop learning system, the results of one learning step are fed back into the system in such a way that they can be used as the basis for further learning in subsequent steps, either by the component which pro-duced the result, or by others. Clearly, by its very design, BLIP is such a closed-loop learning system with regard to both the rules it discovers and the concepts it forms. Every rule discovered by the system (or input by the user) is used to infer additional facts that can then be employed to verify yet another rule. Thus, a learned rule effectively becomes background knowledge for further rule discovery. Simi-larly, every new concept is fully used by in rule discovery - as we have seen in section 5.1.2, it can even move the learnability cliff.

5.3. The MODELER as an empirical discovery system

To conclude this discussion, let us go back and look at the overall behavior of the MODELER as a learning system. From this perspective, the MODELER can be interpreted as an empirical discovery system whose task it is to observe the facts being entered into the knowledge base by the user, discovering rules, forming concepts, and revising its knowledge whenever it contradicts the evidence that is available. Thus, the MODELER's task can be seen as a combination of two searches, namely, searching for rules in the data and searching for concepts. Only the first of those searches is actually performed however: the system's rule discovery module searches the space of possible hypotheses, guided by certain focus heuristics. Concept formation is failure-driven and "lazy", and thus does not involve search.

As a whole, the MODELER may be characterized as a hill-climbing learning system [Langley et al. 87]: the system never keeps more than one current theory about the world around. If that theory turns out to be insufficient, it is adjusted incrementally through the knowledge revision procedures. Thus, the quality of knowledge revision is critically important for the system to be able to recover from bad generalizations. The governing principle for knowledge revision in BLIP is conservatism, i.e., making the minimal changes to the existing theory. Despite its simplicity, this method has severe limitations: it might get stuck in self-stabilizing local maximum states. Even though in a knowledge acquisition system, we can rely on the user to help us out of such a situation, we have developed approaches that allow a learning system to leave such a state by making a *non-cumulative* learning step called a *paradigm shift* [Emde 87].

Another problem with the current knowledge revision approach that will require some attention in the future is the exclusive concentration on removing contradictions between the system's theory and the incoming facts. While this is successful in producing a theory that is consistent with the world, it may ultimately do that by sacrificing all predictive power of the theory: once a rule has been learned, the system only restricts it, and never checks to see if the world (or its knowledge of the world) has changed in a way that would allow generalizing the rule again.

Finally, the view on the MODELER as an empirical discovery system points to some interesting avenues for further research already being considered in work on empirical discovery, namely, experiment generation. Right now, the MODELER is restricted to observing the facts that come in and cannot search for data itself. There is no reason, however, why it should not take on a more active role, proposing experiments to test out its hypotheses. An "experiment", in a knowledge acquisition setting, is of course a simple question to the user. Nonetheless, care must be taken not to ask too many questions, so one will have to make do with a few questions at strategically important points. Furthermore, not all "experiments" are possible: questions that are not phrased in the user's terms will not be answerable for the user.

Acknowledgements

I am grateful to the other members of the KIT-LERNER project for their ideas, comments and criticism which made this paper possible. Sabine Thieme also implemented the hypothesis generation and testing steps.

The KIT-LERNER project is partially supported by the German Federal Ministry of Research and Technology under grant no. ITW8501B1. Industrial partners are Nixdorf Computer AG and Stollmann GmbH.

Appendix

Metapredicates used in the **traffic_law** domain:

```
inclusive_1(p1, q1): p1(x1) --> q1(x1)
opposite_1(op1, op2):  op1(x1) --> not(op2(x1))
conjunct_2_1(op1, op2, op3): op1(x1, y1) & op2(y1) --> op3(x1)
conjunct_neg(op1, op2, op3):  op1(x1) & not(op2(x1)) --> op3(x1)
m3(op1, op2, op3):  op1(x1, y1) & not(op2(z1, y1)) --> not(op3(x1))
m5(op1, op2, op3, op4): op1(x1) & op2(x1, z1) & not(op3(z1)) --> not(op4(x1))
m14(op1, op2, op3):  op1(x1, y1) & op2(y1) --> not(op3(x1, y1))
m15(op1, op2, op3):  op1(x1, y1) & op2(y1) --> op3(x1, y1)
w_trans_red(op1, op2, op3):  op1(x1, y1) & op2(y1, z1) --> op3(x1)
m31(op1, op2, op3, c1, c2): op1(x1, c1) & not(op2(z1, c1)) --> op3(x1)
m32(op1, op2, op3, op4): op1(x1) & op2(x1, y1) & not(op3(y1)) --> op4(x1)
w_trans_2(op1, op2, op3):  op1(x1, y1) & op2(z1, y1) --> op3(z1, x1)
inherit_3(op1, op2, op3):  op1(x1) & op2(x2, x1) --> op3(x2)
```

References

Dietterich, T. G. and Michalski, R. S., "A Comparative Review of Selected Methods for Learning from Examples", in *Machine Learning - An Artificial Intelligence Approach*, Vol. I, pp. 41 - 82, Morgan Kaufman, Los Altos, CA, 1983.

Easterlin, J. Daniel and Langley, Pat, "A Framework for Concept Formation", Proc. *Seventh Annual Conference of the Cognitive Science Society*, pp. 267 - 271, Irvine, CA, August 1985.

Emde, Werner, Habel, Christopher, and Rollinger, Claus-Rainer, "Automatische Akquisition von inferentiellem Wissen", Proc. *GWAI-82, 6th German Workshop on Artificial Intelligence*, pp. 72 - 81, Springer-Verlag, Berlin, West Germany, September 1982.

Emde, Werner, Habel, Christopher U., and Rollinger, Claus-Rainer, "The Discovery of the Equator or Concept Driven Learning", Proc. *IJCAI-83*, pp. 455 - 458, Morgan Kaufman, Los Altos, CA, 1983.

Emde, Werner, "Non-Cumulative Learning in METAXA.3", Proc. *IJCAI-87*, Morgan Kaufman, Los Altos, CA, August 1987.

Emde, Werner, "An Inference Engine for Representing Multiple Theories", this volume.

Fisher, Douglas and Langley, Pat, "Approaches to Conceptual Clustering", Proc. *IJCAI-85*, pp. 691 - 697, Los Angeles, CA, August 1985.

Fisher, Douglas H., "Knowledge Acquisition Via Incremental Conceptual Clustering", *Machine Learning*, Vol. 2, pp. 139 - 172, Kluwer, Boston, September 1987.

Habel, C.U. and Rollinger, C.-R., "The Machine as Concept Learner", Proc. *ECAI-82*, pp. 158 - 159, Orsay, France, 1982.

Hayes-Roth, Frederick, "Using Proof and Refutations to Learn From Experience", in *Machine Learning - An Artificial Intelligence Approach*, ed. R.S. Michalski, J.G. Carbonell, T.M. Mitchell, pp. 221 - 240, Tioga, Palo Alto, CA, 1983.

Kolodner, Janet L., "Reconstructive Memory: A computer model", *Cognitive Science*, Vol. 7, pp. 281 - 328, 1983.

Langley, Pat, Zytkow, Jan M., Simon, Herbert A., and Bradshaw, Gary L., "The Search for Regularity: Four Aspects of Scientific Discovery", in *Machine Learning Volume II*, ed. R.S. Michalski, J.G. Carbonell, T.M. Mitchell, pp. 425 - 469, Morgan Kaufman, Los Altos, CA, USA, 1986.

Langley, Pat and Nordhausen, Bernd, "A Framework for Empirical Discovery", Proc. *International Meeting on Advances in Learning*, Les Arcs, France, 1986.

Langley, Pat, "Editorial: On Machine Learning", *Machine Learning*, Vol. 1, pp. 5 - 10, Kluwer, Boston, 1986.

Langley, Pat, "Machine Learning and Concept Formation", *Machine Learning*, Vol. 2, pp. 99 - 102, Kluwer, Boston, September 1987.

Langley, Pat, Gennari, J.H., and Iba, W., "Hill-Climbing Theories of Learning", Proc. *Fourth International Workshop on Machine Learning*, pp. 312 - 323, Irvine, CA, June 1987.

Lebowitz, Michael, "Experiments with Incremental Concept Formation: UNIMEM", *Machine Learning*, Vol. 2, pp. 103 - 138, Kluwer, Boston, September 1987.

Lenat, Douglas B., "AM: Discovery in Mathematics as Heuristic Search", in *Knowledge-Based Systems in Artificial Intelligence*, ed. R. Davis and D.B. Lenat, pp. 1 - 225, McGraw-Hill, New York, NY, 1982.

Michalski, Ryszard S., "A Theory and Methodology of Inductive Learning", in *Machine Learning I*, pp. 83 - 134, Morgan Kaufman, Los Altos, CA, 1983.

Michalski, Ryszard S. and Stepp, Robert E., "Learning from Observation: Conceptual Clustering", in *Machine Learning*, ed. R.S. Michalski, J.G. Carbonell, and T.M. Mitchell, Vol. I, pp. 331 - 363, Tioga, Palo Alto, CA, 1983.

Michalski, Ryszard S. and Winston, Patrick H., "Variable Precision Logic", *Artificial Intelligence*, Vol. 29, pp. 121-146, North-Holland, Amsterdam, 1986.

Morik, Katharina, "Sloppy Modeling", this volume.

Nordhausen, Bernd, "Conceptual Clustering Using Relational Information", Proc. *AAAI-86*, pp. 508 - 512, Morgan Kaufman, Los Altos, CA, USA, August 1986.

Quinlan, J. Ross, "Learning Efficient Classification Procedures and Their Application to Chess End Games", in *Machine Learning - An Artificial Intelligence Approach*, ed. R.S. Michalski, J.G. Carbonell, and T.M. Mitchell, pp. 463 - 482, Tioga, Palo Alto, CA, 1983.

Rendell, Larry, Seshu, Raj, and Tcheng, David, "More Robust Concept Learning Using Dynamically Variable Bias", Proc. *Fourth International Workshop on Machine Learning*, pp. 66 - 78, Irvine, CA, June 1987.

Rissland, Edwina L., "The Problem of Intelligent Example Selection", Proc. *2nd AAAI Workshop on Knowledge Acquisition for Knowledge-Based Systems*, pp. 16-0 - 16-24, Banff, Canada, October 1987 (also to appear in the Int. Journal of Man-Machine Studies).

Salzberg, Steven, "Heuristics for Inductive Learning", Proc. *IJCAI-85*, pp. 603 - 609, Los Angeles, CA, August 1985.

Schlimmer, Jeffrey C., "Incremental Adjustment of Representations for Learning", Proc. *Fourth International Workshop on Machine Learning*, pp. 79 - 90, Irvine, CA, June 1987.

Smith, Edward E. and Medin, Douglas L., "Categories and Concepts", Harvard University Press, London, England, 1981.

Stepp, Robert E. and Michalski, Ryszard S., "Conceptual Clustering of Structured Objects: A Goal-Oriented Approach", *Artificial Intelligence*, Vol. 28, pp. 43-69, Elsevier Science, Amsterdam, 1986.

Stepp, Robert E., "Concepts in Conceptual Clustering", Proc. *IJCAI-87*, pp. 211 - 213, Milan, Italy, August 1987.

Thieme, Sabine, "The Acquisition of Model Knowledge for a Model-Driven Machine Learning Approach", this volume.

Utgoff, Paul E., "Shift of Bias for Inductive Concept Learning", in *Machine Learning - An Artificial Intelligence Approach*, ed. R.S. Michalski, J.G. Carbonell, and T.M. Mitchell, Vol. II, pp. 107 - 148, Morgan Kaufman, Los Altos, CA, 1986.

Wrobel, Stefan, "Design Goals for Sloppy Modeling Systems", Proc. *2nd AAAI Workshop on Knowledge Acquisition for Knowledge-Based Systems*, pp. 25-0 - 25-17, Banff, Canada, October 1987 (also to appear in the Int. Journal of Man-Machine Studies).

Wrobel, Stefan, "Higher-Order Concepts in a Tractable Knowledge Representation", Proc. *GWAI-87 German Workshop on Artificial Intelligence*, pp. 129 - 138, Springer-Verlag, Berlin, West Germany, September 1987.

Lecture Notes in Computer Science

Vol. 296: R. Janßen (Ed.), Trends in Computer Algebra. Proceedings, 1987. V, 197 pages. 1988.

Vol. 297: E.N. Houstis, T.S. Papatheodorou, C.D. Polychronopoulos (Eds.), Supercomputing. Proceedings, 1987. X, 1093 pages. 1988.

Vol. 298: M. Main, A. Melton, M. Mislove, D. Schmidt (Eds.), Mathematical Foundations of Programming Language Semantics. Proceedings, 1987. VIII, 637 pages. 1988.

Vol. 299: M. Dauchet, M. Nivat (Eds.), CAAP '88. Proceedings, 1988. VI, 304 pages. 1988.

Vol. 300: H. Ganzinger (Ed.), ESOP '88. Proceedings, 1988. VI, 381 pages. 1988.

Vol. 301: J. Kittler (Ed.), Pattern Recognition. Proceedings, 1988. VII, 668 pages. 1988.

Vol. 302: D.M. Yellin, Attribute Grammar Inversion and Source-to-source Translation. VIII, 176 pages. 1988.

Vol. 303: J.W. Schmidt, S. Ceri, M. Missikoff (Eds.), Advances in Database Technology – EDBT '88. X, 620 pages. 1988.

Vol. 304: W.L. Price, D. Chaum (Eds.), Advances in Cryptology – EUROCRYPT '87. Proceedings, 1987. VII, 314 pages. 1988.

Vol. 305: J. Biskup, J. Demetrovics, J. Paredaens, B. Thalheim (Eds.), MFDBS 87. Proceedings, 1987. V, 247 pages. 1988.

Vol. 306: M. Boscarol, L. Carlucci Aiello, G. Levi (Eds.), Foundations of Logic and Functional Programming. Proceedings, 1986. V, 218 pages. 1988.

Vol. 307: Th. Beth, M. Clausen (Eds.), Applicable Algebra, Error-Correcting Codes, Combinatorics and Computer Algebra. Proceedings, 1986. VI, 215 pages. 1988.

Vol. 308: S. Kaplan, J.-P. Jouannaud (Eds.), Conditional Term Rewriting Systems. Proceedings, 1987. VI, 278 pages. 1988.

Vol. 309: J. Nehmer (Ed.), Experiences with Distributed Systems. Proceedings, 1987. VI, 292 pages. 1988.

Vol. 310: E. Lusk, R. Overbeek (Eds.), 9th International Conference on Automated Deduction. Proceedings, 1988. X, 775 pages. 1988.

Vol. 311: G. Cohen, P. Godlewski (Eds.), Coding Theory and Applications 1986. Proceedings, 1986. XIV, 196 pages. 1988.

Vol. 312: J. van Leeuwen (Ed.), Distributed Algorithms 1987. Proceedings, 1987. VII, 430 pages. 1988.

Vol. 313: B. Bouchon, L. Saitta, R.R. Yager (Eds.), Uncertainty and Intelligent Systems. IPMU '88. Proceedings, 1988. VIII, 408 pages. 1988.

Vol. 314: H. Göttler, H.J. Schneider (Eds.), Graph-Theoretic Concepts in Computer Science. Proceedings, 1987. VI, 254 pages. 1988.

Vol. 315: K. Furukawa, H. Tanaka, T. Fujisaki (Eds.), Logic Programming '87. Proceedings, 1987. VI, 327 pages. 1988.

Vol. 316: C. Choffrut (Ed.), Automata Networks. Proceedings, 1986. VII, 125 pages. 1988.

Vol. 317: T. Lepistö, A. Salomaa (Eds.), Automata, Languages and Programming. Proceedings, 1988. XI, 741 pages. 1988.

Vol. 318: R. Karlsson, A. Lingas (Eds.), SWAT 88. Proceedings, 1988. VI, 262 pages. 1988.

Vol. 319: J.H. Reif (Ed.), VLSI Algorithms and Architectures – AWOC 88. Proceedings, 1988. X, 476 pages. 1988.

Vol. 320: A. Blaser (Ed.), Natural Language at the Computer. Proceedings, 1988. III, 176 pages. 1988.

Vol. 322: S. Gjessing, K. Nygaard (Eds.), ECOOP '88. European Conference on Object-Oriented Programming. Proceedings, 1988. VI, 410 pages. 1988.

Vol. 323: P. Deransart, M. Jourdan, B. Lorho, Attribute Grammars. IX, 232 pages. 1988.

Vol. 324: M.P. Chytil, L. Janiga, V. Koubek (Eds.), Mathematical Foundations of Computer Science 1988. Proceedings. IX, 562 pages. 1988.

Vol. 325: G. Brassard, Modern Cryptology. VI, 107 pages. 1988.

Vol. 326: M. Gyssens, J. Paredaens, D. Van Gucht (Eds.), ICDT '88. 2nd International Conference on Database Theory. Proceedings, 1988. VI, 409 pages. 1988.

Vol. 327: G.A. Ford (Ed.), Software Engineering Education. Proceedings, 1988. V, 207 pages. 1988.

Vol. 328: R. Bloomfield, L. Marshall, R. Jones (Eds.), VDM '88. VDM – The Way Ahead. Proceedings, 1988. IX, 499 pages. 1988.

Vol. 329: E. Börger, H. Kleine Büning, M.M. Richter (Eds.), CSL '87. 1st Workshop on Computer Science Logic. Proceedings, 1987. VI, 346 pages. 1988.

Vol. 330: C.G. Günther (Ed.), Advances in Cryptology – EUROCRYPT '88. Proceedings, 1988. XI, 473 pages. 1988.

Vol. 331: M. Joseph (Ed.), Formal Techniques in Real-Time and Fault-Tolerant Systems. Proceedings, 1988. VI, 229 pages. 1988.

Vol. 332: D. Sannella, A. Tarlecki (Eds.), Recent Trends in Data Type Specification. V, 259 pages. 1988.

Vol. 333: H. Noltemeier (Ed.), Computational Geometry and its Applications. Proceedings, 1988. VI, 252 pages. 1988.

Vol. 334: K.R. Dittrich (Ed.), Advances in Object-Oriented Database Systems. Proceedings, 1988. VII, 373 pages. 1988.

Vol. 335: F.A. Vogt (Ed.), CONCURRENCY 88. Proceedings, 1988. VI, 401 pages. 1988.

Vol. 337: O. Günther, Efficient Structures for Geometric Data Management. XI, 135 pages. 1988.

Vol. 338: K.V. Nori, S. Kumar (Eds.), Foundations of Software Technology and Theoretical Computer Science. Proceedings, 1988. IX, 520 pages. 1988.

Vol. 339: M. Rafanelli, J.C. Klensin, P. Svensson (Eds.), Statistical and Scientific Database Management. Proceedings, 1988. IX, 454 pages. 1988.

Vol. 340: G. Rozenberg (Ed.), Advances in Petri Nets 1988. VI, 439 pages. 1988.

Vol. 341: S. Bittanti (Ed.), Software Reliability Modelling and Identification. VII, 209 pages. 1988.

Vol. 342: G. Wolf, T. Legendi, U. Schendel (Eds.), Parcella '88. Proceedings, 1988. 380 pages. 1989.

Vol. 343: J. Grabowski, P. Lescanne, W. Wechler (Eds.), Algebraic and Logic Programming. Proceedings, 1988. 278 pages. 1988.

Vol. 344: J. van Leeuwen, Graph-Theoretic Concepts in Computer Science. Proceedings, 1988. VII, 459 pages. 1989.

Vol. 345: see inside front cover (LNAI).

Vol. 346: see inside front cover (LNAI).

Vol. 347: see inside front cover (LNAI).